untuk mas Stefan

semoga bermanfaat

Ardjuna Hutagalung

Islamic Populism in Indonesia and the Middle East

In a novel approach to the field of Islamic politics, this provocative new study compares the evolution of Islamic populism in Indonesia, the country with the largest Muslim population in the world, to the Middle East. Utilising approaches from historical sociology and political economy, Vedi Hadiz argues that competing strands of Islamic politics can be understood as the product of contemporary struggles over power and material resources and the result of conflict across a variety of social and historical contexts. Drawing from detailed case studies across the Middle East and Southeast Asia, the book engages with broader theoretical questions about political change in the context of socio-economic transformations and presents an innovative, comparative framework to shed new light on the diverse trajectories of Islamic politics in the modern world.

VEDI R. HADIZ is Professor of Asian Studies at the University of Melbourne.

Islamic Populism in Indonesia and the Middle East

Vedi R. Hadiz

Asia Institute, University of Melbourne
Asia Research Centre, Murdoch University

CAMBRIDGE
UNIVERSITY PRESS

University Printing House, Cambridge CB2 8BS, United Kingdom

Cambridge University Press is part of the University of Cambridge.

It furthers the University's mission by disseminating knowledge in the pursuit of education, learning and research at the highest international levels of excellence.

www.cambridge.org
Information on this title: www.cambridge.org/9781107123601

© Vedi R. Hadiz 2016

This publication is in copyright. Subject to statutory exception and to the provisions of relevant collective licensing agreements, no reproduction of any part may take place without the written permission of Cambridge University Press.

First published 2016

A catalogue record for this publication is available from the British Library

Library of Congress Cataloguing in Publication data
Hadiz, Vedi R., 1964– author.
Islamic populism in Indonesia and the Middle East / Vedi R. Hadiz.
   pages   cm
ISBN 978-1-107-12360-1 (hardback)
1. Islam and politics – Indonesia. 2. Islam and politics – Middle East.
3. Populism – Indonesia. 4. Populism – Middle East. 5. Indonesia – Politics and government. 6. Middle East – Politics and government. I. Title.
BP173.7.H336   2016
320.55′70956–dc23
                                                                                 2015035042

ISBN 978-1-107-12360-1 Hardback

Cambridge University Press has no responsibility for the persistence or accuracy of URLs for external or third-party internet websites referred to in this publication, and does not guarantee that any content on such websites is, or will remain, accurate or appropriate.

For Adi Hadiz (1956–2010), who is greatly missed

Contents

Acknowledgements   *page* ix

1. Introduction   1
2. Islamic politics and the emergence of a new Islamic populism   20
3. The genesis of Islamic populism: historical legacies   48
4. Modernisation and the Cold War: paving the way   75
5. Pathways of political failure: dissent from the fringe   97
6. A study in political marginality: the Indonesian Darul Islam movement and its heirs   116
7. Navigating through democracy: a pathway to power?   137
8. Navigating through neoliberalism: a pathway to power?   159
9. Conclusion   184

Bibliography   190
Index   215

Acknowledgements

I owe a great debt to many individuals and institutions, in fact far too many to detail fully, in undertaking the research for and writing of this book. It is necessary to acknowledge, however, that the book would not have been possible without the Future Fellowship generously awarded to me by the Australian Research Council from 2010 to 2014 (FT0991885). It would not have been conceivable either without the incredibly supportive environment provided by the Asia Research Centre at Murdoch University and the many wonderful colleagues there – past and present – with whom I have had the great pleasure of working. A past director of the Centre, Garry Rodan, was the first to prod me towards seriously working on a topic that I had been only mulling over previously. He and Kanishka Jayasuriya, along with Craig McGarty, were instrumental in getting me to finally formulate the related ideas in a far more coherent manner than I had attempted before. Richard Robison, with whom I have collaborated previously on a number of writings, provided many reliably critical comments on an earlier draft of this book that have improved its organisation and structure considerably. Another past director of the Asia Research Centre, Caroline Hughes, also fully encouraged my research, as has its current director, Kevin Hewison. Tamara Dent assisted greatly in handling many of the administrative matters related to launching the project and its maintenance in the early period, while Sia Kozlowski and Ingebjoerg Scarpello have provided invaluable help towards its completion. I would also like to thank a number of postgraduate students at the Asia Research Centre for their able research assistance over the years, including Nicole Andres, Asep Iqbal, Yanti Muchtar, Diswandi, Airlangga Pribadi and Hikmawan Saefullah.

Andi Rahman Alamsyah has been an irreplaceable research assistant in Indonesia and someone who has adeptly accompanied my explorations of Islamic politics in a number of different locales in the country. I benefited greatly from his own expertise on the subject matter and his dazzling array of contacts. My investigations were also enriched by the knowledge and contacts provided by Usep Wiramiharja (without whom it would have been impossible to meet some key Darul Islam veterans) and by Beni Setiawan in Central Java and Yogyakarta (together with Khelmy Pribadi, Akhmad Ramdhon, Eko

Prasetyo and M. Fajar Shodiq), as well as Abdil Mughis, Farihin and my old friend in Medan, Elfenda Ananda.

In Turkey, my fieldwork benefited immeasurably from the research assistance and local know-how primarily provided by Harun Ercan. In Egypt, Abdulla Erfan and, subsequently, Mohamed Sulaiman provided the same kind of valuable assistance and knowledge. I thank all of them for helping me navigate through the intricacies of Turkish and Egyptian politics and societies, respectively, as well as for being the first people with whom I usually tested – in conversations over meals – ideas pertaining to their countries. In the course of conducting research, I also carried out more limited fieldwork in Tunisia and Morocco. The assistance and guidance provided respectively by Bouaicha Béchir and Amal Bakkali Hassani are greatly appreciated. Without the help and thoughtfulness of all of the named individuals in these countries, it would have been far more difficult to develop the comparative framework that I offer in this book.

Among the institutions to which I owe a great debt, Labsosio at the Department of Sociology, University of Indonesia, stands out for its assistance in managing my fieldwork facility. I also thank the Institute of Developing Economies in Tokyo – particularly Khoo Boo Teik, who was formerly based there and with whom I enjoyed collaboration on an edited book that partly came out of my Future Fellowship as well. An invitation from the School for Advanced Studies in the Social Sciences (EHESS) in Paris provided a lovely milieu where I was able to put together the first full draft of the book in early 2014. I am particularly grateful to my hosts there, Rémy Madinier and Andrée Feillard. I must also acknowledge the role of the National University of Singapore's Department of Sociology – the seeds of ideas to be developed much more fully at Murdoch originated during my last couple of years of teaching there; as well as the Institute of Social Studies in Holland, the Department of Sociology at the University of Indonesia and the Centre of Southeast Asian Studies at the University of Kyoto, where I spent several months each in 2009 – quite unintentionally preparing myself for what would soon become a multiyear project. Thank you as well to Cambridge University Press, particularly to Lucy Rhymer, for supporting the publication of this book and to the anonymous referees that provided insightful comments and much appreciated encouragement.

Last but not least, I thank my family for tolerating work habits that invariably involved long absences and too many hours in front of the laptop while at home. Thank you as always to Lina and Karla!

1 Introduction

9/11 and the Arab Spring

In recent times, two key events on the global stage have left an indelible imprint on popular perceptions of Islamic politics. These are, respectively, the 9/11 attacks on New York City (and the War on Terror it unleashed) and the tumultuous so-called Arab Spring. The first event seemed to lend credence to the well-rehearsed view of the world characterised by a 'clash of civilisations' and in which Islam would be a major source of threat to Western civilisation (Huntington 1993, 1996). But both 'Islam' and the 'West' are understood in highly, and implausibly, monochromatic terms in this viewpoint.[1] By contrast, the outbreak of the Arab Spring gave rise initially to the idea of a possibly triumphant Islamic politics that was not just democratising but also eager to engage with a global economic order by and large dominated by Western interests.

Some renowned experts, nevertheless, had brusquely dismissed the democratic prospects of the Arab Spring, but not because of predictions about the inevitable return of old elites via actions like military coups, as subsequently occurred in Egypt. Lewis, for example, warned that electoral democracy in the Arab world would only aggravate its existing problems and lead to the rise of radical Islamic movements but without much mention of what such movements would be in response. In somewhat overly cultural deterministic fashion, he proposed that Middle Eastern societies should look towards indigenous and historically rooted forms of governance to chart their future rather than to alien forms of democracy.[2]

---

[1] For highly critical assessments of this viewpoint, see Said (2001) and Halliday (2002).
[2] These comments are found in David Horowitz (2011), 'A Mass Expression of Outrage Against Injustice' (interview with Bernard Lewis), *Jerusalem Post*, 25 February 2011, www.jpost.com/Opinion/Columnists/Article.aspx?id=209770, accessed 15 April 2011. In the same interview, Lewis consigned the internally complex Muslim Brotherhood of Egypt to a category of organisation that is only 'relatively benign' when compared to Germany's Nazi Party of the last century. This view of the Muslim Brotherhood is also expressed by some of its domestic critics, however. Echoing Lewis, Mohamed M. Farid (businessman and member of the Supreme Council of the secular Free Egyptian Party) suggests that the Muslim Brotherhood would have committed atrocities of the same scale as the Nazis if given the opportunity. For him, the Muslim

To others (e.g. Berman 2013), by contrast, the sudden wave of dissent that swept the Arab world from late 2010/early 2011 offered exciting new democratic promises that had been previously unimaginable. These promises were especially prominent in Egypt, where the autocratic and formerly unassailable Hosni Mubarak was dramatically deposed in a popular uprising that took place before the eyes of a global audience. It was in this country that the Arab Spring truly caught the world's imagination through the stimuli provided by television cameras, YouTube videos and Internet chat rooms. Notably, the anti-Mubarak protesters scrutinised by the world were greatly inspired by the prior overthrow, by the Tunisian people, of their own corrupt Cold War-era dictator, Zine El-Abidine Ben Ali (Lynch 2012: 85–86). However, the toppling of the Muslim Brotherhood-led government in Egypt in yet another uprising in July 2013 put an end to much of that early optimism, as the supremacy of the armed forces over democratic processes came to be affirmed in that country.

It is maintained in this study that neither engagement with democratic politics (and/or embrace of global markets) nor continual attachment to a theocratic form of authoritarianism (and typically, hostility to a still Western-dominated international economic order) constitutes the inevitable terminus of modern Islamic politics. While the appeal of democratic politics is by no means certain to impact on the strategies undertaken by the social agents of Islamic politics, consignment to the political wilderness of violent activity is by no means inescapable. The study shows, by contrast, that the possible trajectories of Islamic politics are varied and that these are contingent on the broader constellations of power and interest encountered by social and political movements claiming to represent an *ummah* – the community of believers – that is increasingly defined in national rather than supranational terms. Furthermore, it is averred that while this community is notionally homogenous due to common faith, in actuality it has become more internally diverse due to decades of socio-economic change tied to capitalist development and neoliberal globalisation in much of the Muslim world. As such, it inevitably embodies a host of potential internal contradictions.

Before the hopes that were temporarily raised by the Arab Spring (Gerges 2013), Indonesia and Turkey were generally considered to be the rare exemplars of democratic Muslim-majority societies, notwithstanding the major faults in the way that their democracies have functioned. On the one hand, Indonesia's democracy, to put it succinctly, is rife with money politics and

---

Brotherhood-led Morsi government was rightly deposed in 2013 because it represented 'barbarians at the gate' who would have thrust Egypt into a divisive civil war. Interview, Cairo, 16 December 2014. In addition, see Lewis (1990, 1994) for his views on Islam, violence and democratic politics. In the latter article, he argues that Turkey has only democratised because of its close geographical proximity to Europe – an argument that would not hold much water for far away yet highly democratised Indonesia, of course.

corruption. On the other hand, the ruling Justice and Development Party (AKP) in Turkey has been accused of bullying the media, systematic brutality against the Kurdish movement and undertaking a malicious campaign of persecution against the country's once unassailable military.[3] More recently, it has been embroiled in a bitter struggle against erstwhile allies in the wealthy religious movement led by the long-exiled cleric Fethullah Gülen.

But it was the AKP's experience – emerging as it did from long established but often marginalised Islamic social and political networks – that had originally brought about the most serious reconsiderations of the relationship between Islamic politics and democratisation in the academic literature (e.g. Nasr 2005), even if the party prefers to portray itself as being 'conservative' rather than 'Islamic'. No doubt this is because Islamic parties in Indonesia had failed to fully capitalise on the openings offered by democratic politics after the fall of Soeharto in 1998, never attaining a position enabling possible ascendancy over the state.

In fact, major developments across the Muslim world in recent times have essentially raised a new fundamental question: what accounts for the different trajectories of Islamic politics in different contexts? Indonesia, Turkey and Egypt are all Muslim-majority countries that have undergone significant social, economic and political changes. But whereas the representatives of Islamic politics succeeded in gaining access to, and then dominating, the state in Turkey, their counterparts in Indonesia have continually failed to do the same. Moreover, the Egyptian case can be counterposed to both Indonesia and Turkey given the success of the Muslim Brotherhood in dominating civil society-based opposition in that country for decades but its inability to hold on to state power once it was presented with the opportunity to do so.

This book examines such divergent trajectories through the lens of a new Islamic populism, merging the interests, aspirations and grievances of a cross-section of social classes, particularly the urban poor, the new urban middle class and possibly peripheralised segments of the bourgeoisie, in potentially powerful ways. The development of these broad and varied social bases distinguishes the newer from the older form of Islamic populism that had been more fully rooted in the traditional urban and rural petty bourgeoisie, and significantly shapes Islamic politics in the contemporary era. It is noteworthy that the older form of Islamic populism was already in steep decline during the era of Western colonial domination over much of the Muslim world. Like all populisms, the Islamic variant involves the mobilisation and homogenisation of a range of disparate grievances of the 'masses' against identified 'elites'.

---

[3] See Tagma (2011) for a critical examination of the 'Turkish model', especially in relation to possible emulation in Arab countries.

It is therefore important to consider the social bases of populist politics (Ionescu and Gelner 1969). In this connection, it is critical that the transformation of the social bases of Islamic populism is connected to the social changes commonly associated with the advance of the capitalist economy, as always so uneven and contradiction-ridden, and to more recent pressures emanating from neoliberal globalisation processes. Another key factor in the shaping of the new Islamic populism is the legacy of the outcomes of Cold War-era social conflicts that entangled Islamic social and political movements, typically resulting in the eradication or domestication of leftist and even liberal political currents. In both the older and new forms, however, a central conception of Islamic populism is that of the *ummah* as proxy for 'the people' – the virtuous masses who are juxtaposed (in classic populist fashion) against an elite characterised as being immoral and rapacious.

In other words, the new Islamic populism is but a specific manifestation of populist politics. As discussed in the next chapter, contemporary populist politics, whether in the developing world or in the advanced industrialised countries, is very much connected to social contradictions intimately related to participation in the processes of neoliberal globalisation. This is the case even if the present manifestations borrow some of their ideological baggage from prior traditions of populist politics that had emerged under different sets of circumstances.

It is also suggested in this study that the main project of the new Islamic populism is defined in terms of the favourable repositioning of the marginalised *ummah* within the confines of the nation state through an array of possible strategies of contestation, which does not necessarily involve the overt call to establish a state based on Islamic law, the Sharia. At the same time, neither is there linear correspondence with an embrace of modern democratic politics; instead the relationship between the political agenda of the new Islamic populism and democratic procedures and rights is highly contingent, as it is with acceptance of the precepts of the neoliberal world order. The logic of this contingency is to be found in the specific contexts of political struggle within which the new Islamic populism has been forged.[4]

Thus, the conceptual foundations of this book differ markedly from that of Bayat's perceptive and highly influential work on 'post-Islamism', which is

---

[4] I refer to the idea of contingency as developed in the critical political economy literature. It features strongly in the work of Eva Bellin (e.g. 'Contingent Democrats', *World Politics* 52, 2000: 175–205), for example, in her discussion of the dispositions of capital and labour in relation to democracy in varying contexts. It should be pointed out that contingency is quite different from the idea of critical juncture, with which it may be confused. The latter is rooted in historical institutionalism and refers to a short period when structural conditions that impact on political choices are relaxed, therefore resulting in a greater range of political possibilities (Capoccia and Kelemen 2007: 342). By contrast, contingency in critical political economy is about how the direction of social change depends on the outcomes of social conflict within specific constellations of power and interests.

generally presented as political adaptation in a single direction: towards 'a more rights-centred and inclusive outlook that favors a civil/secular state operating within a pious society' (Bayat 2013b: 29). Not surprisingly, Bayat's original model was the case of Iran after it became increasingly clear that there was no viable or ready-made 'Islamic' template of economic and political governance to which the Islamic Republic could latch on.

Importantly, while the *ummah* is traditionally understood in supranational terms, it has come to develop an increasingly national outlook as Islamic movements evolved through a concrete struggle against national authoritarian states.[5] The latter is by no means a new observation. Writing specifically on the Middle East, Owen (2004: 15) notes how the *ummah* has come to be conceived more strongly in relation to the community of believers within a particular country. It is maintained here, additionally, that such a conception facilitates a process of homogenising political identities that can be useful in forging multi-class alliances in societies that are becoming increasingly complex. These need to primarily transcend the reality of diverse and mutually contradictory social interests emerging from the profound social changes that have been taking place over the last half-century.

It might also be added that even where the embrace of political and economic reforms has taken place, this has only resulted in the partial and hesitant shedding of the social conservatism that continues to serve as a major marker of Islamic political identity. Thus, there can remain considerable tentativeness about accepting women as equals to men in the public sphere,[6] and certainly, there continues to be almost uniformly strong rejection of homosexual rights even among Muslims who see themselves as 'modern' and 'liberal'. The impulse to place barriers on the role of religious minorities in the state and the economy can also remain strong. But rather than just the durable elements of a traditional 'Islamism' (Bayat 2013b: 29), all this can be viewed as part of

---

[5] As discussed further in this book, such is the case in spite of the Pan-Islamic outlook of the Hizbut Tahrir and the supranational ambitions of organisations like Al-Qaeda or Jemaah Islamiyah in Southeast Asia. The same might be said in relation to the subsequent rise of Islamic State in Iraq and Syria (ISIS), which clearly gained impetus during the protracted conflict in Syria against the Assad regime.

[6] On the patriarchal values that continue to imbue Egypt's Muslim Brotherhood, even as it took the democratic route to power, see Badran (2013). Also see Shehata (2012: 28–29) on its wavering position on equal rights for religious minorities. According to Marwa Adam, Egyptian political and feminist NGO activist, even the female activists of the Muslim Brotherhood, known as the 'Sisters', are only interested in penetrating society to spread fundamentalist ideas rather than to empower women. Interview, Alexandria, 20 December 2014. Buruma (2013) has observed that the economically liberalising and electorally successful AKP in Turkey can be simultaneously illiberal in the social values it promotes. Taşpinar (2012: 133) thus notes that AKP views on family and gender issues remain decidedly archaic and constitute a barrier to the progress of women in society. Their counterparts in Indonesia, as shown in this study, often hold similarly illiberal views on a host of social issues even if many will support democratic politics and, to some extent, the virtues of engagement with neoliberal globalisation.

the intricate mechanisms by which the new Islamic populism mobilises a kind of identity politics among an increasingly diverse *ummah* in order to forge social alliances that are, in effect, multi-class in nature for the purposes of contesting power and resources. It is in part the ability to claim authority over the symbols, terminology and imagery associated with religious identity that endows the new Islamic populism with the potential to bring together disparate members of society that have nevertheless commonly experienced modernity, though to different degrees, as socially, politically and economically marginalising.

In comparative perspective

Islamic politics have been most commonly studied in relation to the Middle East (and North Africa). However, new insights can be gained by positioning the case of Indonesia in a comparative study. Indonesia is host to the largest Muslim population in the world – around 88 per cent of its approximately 250 million people. Emphasis is placed here on Indonesia's evolving political economy and on the historical and sociological dynamics that have characterised that country's trajectory from the late colonial period to the present post-authoritarian phase, and the forging of the new Islamic populism within decades of social transformation. It is asserted that deeper understanding of the complexities of the Indonesian case can be achieved through a comparative exercise that will cast light not only on the specific features of Islamic politics in that country but also on the broader phenomenon of the new Islamic populism itself.

With this in mind, the book examines the Indonesian trajectory by drawing close comparisons with some Middle Eastern experiences, especially those of Egypt and Turkey. These are two other large Muslim-majority countries within which the evolution of Islamic populism has been clearly connected to contradictions emanating from Cold War-era social conflicts, integration into the world capitalist economy and democratisation struggles – however problematic or halting. All of these countries have problems, furthermore, rooted in development processes that have been skewed, leading to social disparities, including those expressed in the proliferation of the new urban poor as well as large cohorts of relatively highly educated youths who are either unemployed or have little prospect of meaningful employment, much less social and material advancement. References to other cases are also made, though to a lesser extent, including to Tunisia, Morocco and Iran.

It should be stated at the outset, therefore, that the book is focused on explaining the shaping of the new Islamic populism in conjunction with a number of key themes external to that of the doctrines of the Islamic religion itself and through a set of theoretical issues examined especially in Chapter 2. Most prominent among these themes are the historical legacies of the age of Western colonial domination, the reshaping of the socio-political landscape of most of the Muslim world during the Cold War, the concurrent evolution of mainly secular state power, and socio-economic change, principally but not exclusively in the present neoliberal and highly globalised phase. In the process, the book explores the evolution of Islamic politics in relation to social transformations that have altered the prevailing constellation of power and interest, providing the context for diverse trajectories. The approach adopted means that the new Islamic populism is understood as being deeply intertwined with distinctly modern kinds of politics and social conflict (Zubaida 2009: 63–64) that have come to the fore in conjunction with the entrenchment of particular modes of power and wealth distribution in many parts of the Muslim world. In this sense, it broadly follows a tradition in the scholarly analysis of Islamic politics associated with authors that range from Rodinson (1966 [2007]) to Halliday (1996), and more recently, Bayat (2007, 2013) and Zubaida (2011), who tend to emphasise social and historical context over the content of religious scripture or their interpretation.

Virtually all such authors, however, have focussed their writings on the Middle East or on Arab countries, the assumed 'core' of the Muslim world – and do not address cases outside of it – such as Indonesia and the broader Southeast Asian region. In helping to fill this gap, the interest in questions of historical sociology and political economy means that this study focusses on the development of Islamic populist politics within broader socio-economic and historical processes that have elicited political appeals often expressed in the terminology, imagery and the claimed social justice ideals of the Islamic religion.[7] The main implication of adopting such an approach is to direct scholarly attention away from a focus on interpretations of Islamic doctrine in shaping Islamic politics or the effects of varieties of religious traditions on the behaviour of social actors. Attempts to explain Islamic politics by way of interpretations of doctrine and cultural orientation have been a particularly strong characteristic of the literature relating to Indonesia and, by and large, to Southeast Asia more generally, especially since the advent of the War on Terror and the region's emergence as its presumptive 'second front' in the early 2000s (Gershman 2002). A major aim of the latter approach has been to understand the competing influences of intolerant and inflexible traditions of political behaviour among Muslims and those that are seen to be more inclusive and malleable.

---

[7] According to Tripp (2006: 69), there is little precedent for the idea of 'social justice' in classical Islamic thought but it came to the fore in the writings of modern thinkers like Qutb in Egypt, Mawdudi in South Asia and Bazargan and Syariati in Iran. While making reference to 'divine justice', their ideas of social justice were induced more directly by the encounter with the socially dislocating and marginalising effects of Western capitalism during the age of colonialism. See Qutb's (2000) work for texts that remain particularly influential among activists today.

However, this book takes a vastly different approach. Inspired by a stream within the study of Islamic politics in the Middle East that has been more strongly influenced by political economy and historical sociology considerations, it examines how the new Islamic populism has been made possible by the immensely altered social bases of Islamic politics over the last half-century.[8] It explores the implications of such changes for present-day – nationally defined – struggles over states and markets in the Muslim world. Thus, the main social agents of Islamic politics in the past were to be found among petty commodity producers, small urban traders – the so-called men of the bazaars – or among minor rural propertied interests. Nevertheless, as the social structures of Muslim-majority societies like Indonesia have become more complex, so too has the composition of the social agents of Islamic politics.

Though largely supplanted by subsequent developments, these petty commodity producers and traders did leave important historical legacies, not least the incorporation of social justice objectives within political agendas expressed in the idioms of Islam. While in seemingly perpetual decline since the apogee of global Western colonial domination, they had articulated their grievances and aspirations with reference to the ideals and morality they viewed to be inherent in the Islamic religion. But like today's representatives of Islamic politics, they were also inevitably projecting their own prosaic concerns onto their religious faith. Thus, the social justice concerns of the older form of Islamic populism were associated primarily with efforts to revive the fortunes or protect the social position of the traditional petty bourgeoisie in the face of continuing threats of marginalisation, as clearly seen in the much examined case of the Sarekat Islam (SI) in the colonial-era Dutch East Indies. In pursuing its agenda, the SI became the receptacle of struggle for social groups that were systematically marginalised under the colonial order in the 1910s and 1920s, not least small traders and producers increasingly besieged by Chinese

---

[8] The political economy aspects of this work also represent an application and extension of the theoretical concerns of what is often dubbed 'the Murdoch School of Political Economy', which emerged out of the Asia Research Centre at Murdoch University, Australia, in the 1990s. Influenced in particular by British, and to a lesser extent, Continental European traditions of scholarship in political economy, its researchers have mainly concentrated on Southeast Asia (see Rodan, Hewison and Robison 2006). From this point of view, the present study could be seen as an effort to extend the application of the work of the Murdoch School beyond the region and its environs and to a subject matter only rarely touched upon before (see Hadiz and Robison 2012). According to Robison (2014: 27), at the heart of this political economy of Islamic politics is the proposition that 'its various manifestations are part of larger processes of change as modern capitalism is entrenched and sweeps aside older forms of economic and social life based on land or rents or colonial authority. The new economic and social order, in this view, is shaped in conflicts over power between declining and emerging interests and alliances that change over time'. Thus, understanding 'Islamic politics means that we must examine how fundamental changes in capitalism itself creates new social forces and interests and consigns others to the margins.'

interlopers.[9] Given that their marginalisation was attributable to the workings of the existing state, one solution to the predicament appeared in the form of the establishment of a future state that was to be based on Islamic law, however it was to be imagined.

Today the SI is widely accepted as a major precursor of the Indonesian nationalist, anti-colonial movement, having progressed within a relatively short period as a formidable mass organisation before being sidelined in later developments by a combination of colonial state repression and, importantly, the appearance of new rivals, including the Indonesian Communist Party (PKI), to which it had ironically helped to give birth (McVey 1965 [2006]; Shiraishi 1990). In the process, the SI tried to establish footholds within the small Indonesian working class, based then in industries such as transportation and in the vital plantations sector. But the SI had to give way to the rising secular nationalist political tendencies as epitomised by the emergence of Soekarno, the future first president of the Republic of Indonesia. This was also the fate of the PKI, which would become the subject of intense colonial state repression and therefore reduced to a basically underground movement for two decades, before the outbreak of Indonesia's independence war following the end of the Japanese occupation in 1945.

Parallel experiences, in fact, can be found in many other Muslim-majority societies. Most strikingly, the inception of the Muslim Brotherhood in Egypt in the 1920s was as much a response to British colonial domination as it was facilitated by the demise of the Ottoman Caliphate after World War I. These gave rise to new yearnings for a supranational state belonging to the *ummah*. But this response 'drew much of its support from classes that feared change, namely the petty bourgeoisie and the trading and artisan classes' (Pargeter 2010: 10), for whom colonial domination meant marginalisation and an uncertain future. Like the SI, the Muslim Brotherhood came to develop strongholds within other sections of society; thus it initially had a significant following within the labour movement (Beinin and Lockman 1998).

Such then were the typical underpinnings of early Islamic-based social and political movements in a range of Muslim-majority societies in the first decades of the twentieth century. It should be noted that in societies where Islamic politics played only a small role in the rise of nationalist movements – such as in Tunisia – inspiration was nonetheless drawn subsequently from traditions associated with Islamic movements that had contributed to galvanising dissent

---

[9] Interestingly, leading SI activist Abdoel Moeis is noted to have described the organisation in strikingly populist terms. For him, the SI was 'a reaction to an already long digested backwardness, to a long felt oppression and withholding of all rights'. It was, moreover, 'a movement of protest amongst masses of the "little man" and their "scream for rights, for rights, for *rights*"'. This must have facilitated the fact that SI 'boasted a membership of over two million' at the height of its powers (Van Dijk 1981: 24).

against colonial rule. Thus, the stream within Tunisian politics that would eventually give rise to the En Nahda party, in power for more than two years following that country's Arab Spring, has drawn much from the experience of the Egyptian Muslim Brotherhood (Alexander 2010, 2012).

But as we see in Chapters 3 and 4, the representatives of Islamic political tendencies ultimately failed to dominate anti-colonial movements in much of the Muslim world where early post-colonial states tended to be secular nationalist and developmentalist in their outlook (Hadiz and Robison 2012). The most important tendencies within these anti-colonial movements, in fact, came to be dominated by secular elites drawn from the ranks of nationalist intellectuals and politicians who grew out of bureaucratic families, as well as small groups of professionals or military men that were cultivated within the colonial social order itself. These elites eventually gave rise to such nationalist parties as the National Liberation Front (FLN) in Algeria, the Ba'athists in Syria and Iraq, the Destour Party in Tunisia and the PNI (Indonesian National Party) in Indonesia. In the case of Egypt, the Muslim Brotherhood had to contend with the formidable pro-monarchist Wafd Party, although it was the Free Officers under Nasser who overthrew the monarchy and put an end to British domination, which gave rise to the dominant Arab Socialist Union.

All the post-colonial states dominated by such vehicles adopted economic nationalist agendas where domestic industry was to be protected and subsidised and thus the economy fell largely into the hands of state-owned corporations. This development continued the relative marginalisation of the traditional petty bourgeoisie (Hadiz and Robison 2012), this time by the new holders of state bureaucratic power. As Keyder (1987: 105) noted, such a statist model of economic development had already appeared in Turkey – the former centre of the last Caliphate – from the 1930s. Though Turkey never experienced direct colonial subjugation, the Kemalist revolution saw the emergence of a new secular nationalist state that was driven by reformers drawn from the military elite and the civilian bureaucracy and which, for decades, went on to suppress challenges that were ideologically framed through Islamic cultural references and which represented the interests of those sidelined since the triumph of the republic.[10]

In the early twenty-first century, however, those who articulate their grievances, aspirations and interests on the basis of references to Islamic ideals, especially of social justice and morality, represent a much greater cross-section of societal elements than ever before. These are now better ensconced in social classes emerging out of capitalist transformation and integration with the

---

[10] Kemalist ideology is formally made of up six principles introduced in 1931: 'republicanism, nationalism, populism, statism, secularism and something that can be translated as either permanent revolutionism or reformism' (Owen 2004: 20).

global economy, whether in the Middle East (Henry and Springborg 2001) or in Indonesia (Robison and Hadiz 2004). Many of those grievances have been directed against the presence of close-knit elites or even entrenched oligarchies that have sought to ensure their continued political ascendancy in the face of a host of social changes. From this point of view, there were many commonalities indeed between the position of the Soehartos in Indonesia within the New Order-forged oligarchy and that of the Mubaraks and their allies in Egypt. In Turkey, by contrast, the new Islamic populism developed largely as a response to a quite compact and culturally secular Kemalist establishment that was prone to authoritarian practices and which has long held sway over the commanding heights of the economy.

At the same time, there had been a narrowing of ideological options available for expressing dissent in the Muslim world due to the outcomes of the Cold War. Specifically, these had eradicated or severely weakened the Left and also made liberal and social democratic challenges against oligarchic and other elites, typically presiding over authoritarian states, less than viable (Halperin 2005; Pratt 2007). Political movements emerging out of pre-existing Islamic social networks thus filled the void and often developed contentious relationships with authoritarian states that were unable to decisively nullify challenges ostensibly based on religion in the way they could those having more secular ideological inspirations.

In truth, however, Islamic populism has always been directed at some very modern and profane issues – rather than the arcane concerns of a religion that emerged historically in a seventh-century desert society in the Arabian Peninsula. Such is the case whether the relevant social actors resort to electoral politics, mass organisations or violent methods undertaken by small shadowy groups, like suicide bombing, to further their objectives. It is well documented, for example, that the thinking of Sayyid Qutb (who, along with founder Hassan Al-Banna, is the most iconic of Muslim Brotherhood figures and a major source of inspiration for a range of Islamic movements today) was a direct response to the depredations of Egypt's Nasserist regime (see Qutb 2000) besides the earlier period of British domination. It was also no less shaped by the brutality personally experienced as a long-term occupant of British prison cells (Kepel 1984: 47–48). Nevertheless, this book addresses how the agenda of the new Islamic populism, especially pertaining to the embrace of democracy and of global markets, can fluctuate as it is shaped and reshaped by the need to respond to new external circumstances and challenges in varying contexts.

The book demonstrates also that there are significant overlaps that can be explored between populism, insofar as an appeal to the notion of a universally oppressed 'people' is involved more generically, and the new Islamic populism specifically, in that the latter resonates with the perception that members of the *ummah* have commonly experienced systemic marginalisation (see Chapter 2) in spite of their varied social positions. If traditional populisms conceive of a 'people' that are subordinated by avaricious elites, the new Islamic variant imagines an *ummah* that is dispossessed, in socio-economic as well as cultural terms, by powerful forces that preside over social orders that are perceived to be inherently exclusionary, unjust and therefore simultaneously immoral.

The matter that follows, however, is how the solutions to the problems of society are conceived – would they involve the adoption of, and immersion in, democratic electoral politics accompanied by confident participation in global capitalism? Would they rely on concerted if often semi-clandestine efforts to establish ideological and political hegemony over civil society as an eventual gateway to direct power? And would the latter type of solution necessarily include the adoption of violent political activity?

As we shall see in the course of analysis, the answers to such questions are not immutable but contingent on the specific circumstances that the social agents of the new Islamic populism encounter when waging their struggles as well as the nature of inherited historical legacies. They are also contingent on the internal composition of social alliances that underpin the new Islamic populist tendency itself. As such, this book is not about the inevitably unbridled development of violent terrorist tendencies within Islamic politics, posing a threat to global world order, much less to civilisation as we know it. But neither is it about the intractable forward march of Islamic politics into the world of democratic politics and unrestrained engagement with global capitalism (or with a self-consciously consumerist culture of everyday life). Instead, it is about how specific trajectories of Islamic politics are forged through actual political struggles, the outcomes of which – though not predetermined – cannot be extricated from specific social and historical contexts.

Interestingly, it was the presence of the Muslim Brotherhood as the most organised civil society-based force in Egypt that had raised many of the doubts about that country's democratic prospects, partly because of the underground violent strategies once associated with the organisation and its association with theocratic aspirations (see Hamzawi, Ottaway and Brown 2009). Nevertheless the Muslim Brotherhood quickly cemented its position as the dominant force in the post-Mubarak era by winning the first democratically held parliamentary as well as presidential elections convincingly. Moreover, the broad networks of the Muslim Brotherhood in Egypt had clearly dominated the political opposition against Mubarak, having engaged in clandestine activity as well as more overt civil society organising. They had even attained a measure of success within the heavily constrained electoral politics of the Mubarak era. In a nutshell, it was due to this sort of presence, experience and durability as well as organisational coherence that the Muslim Brotherhood was able to initially make effective use of the opportunities presented by the fall of Mubarak, even if it was not able to maintain its grip on power for long.

In the interim, though, sections of the Egyptian organisation had begun to show the sort of ambition demonstrated by key supporters of Turkey's AKP in exploring the opportunities potentially offered by more intensive participation in the global capitalist economy. Such ambition, and self-confidence, is crucially absent among their counterparts in Indonesia today, for reasons to be explained during the course of this study.

As alluded to earlier, Turkey's trajectory is prominently characterised by a political party emerging out of a long-existing but largely peripheralised Islamic movement gaining power gradually and democratically. Egypt, until the Arab Spring, showed a highly suppressed Islamic movement dominating the political opposition and civil society (Berman 2003) but still unable to seize control over the state. In Indonesia, this book's main case study, yet another distinct trajectory has been seen: that of continual failure of Islamic movements to win government or dominate the political opposition in the eras of both authoritarianism and democracy. Yet it is clear too that these movements could not be ignored, whether in the period of authoritarianism or after the advent of democratisation in 1998. Again, it is asserted that comparing the Indonesian trajectory to that of Egypt and Turkey is bound to yield new and important insights that analyses based on a straightforward single-case study are less likely to produce.

On a fundamental level, these different cases underscore that there is not just one 'Islamic' reply to the question of the possibility or desirability of democratic governance and their compatibility with doctrine (e.g. Lee 2010: 294). But what social conditions make acceptance or rejection of democracy, usually with corresponding attitudes towards neoliberal capitalism, a more prevalent ideological tendency within Islamic movements in any given social and historical context? Why are some Islamic movements more successful than others in making use of the opportunities offered by the democratic process and by closer integration with the world capitalist economy? Moreover, why do others remain intractably against these and highly critical of fellow members of the *ummah* they consider to have abandoned the cause of establishing an Islamic state in their pursuit of power and wealth?

Perhaps a clue is offered by the fact that those who are inclined to reject the principles of democracy and market capitalism are also apt to refer to its fragmenting effects on the *ummah*. These have recognised that struggles waged in the electoral arena by such vehicles as political parties can exacerbate social cleavages that have actually grown within the *ummah* due to socio-economic transformations, and that these may be overcome by accentuating the markers of Islamic identity. Another clue is provided by the fact that rejection of democracy and engagement with the global capitalist economy also tends to be stronger when the possibility of attaining victory through democratic means appears to be more remote, as does the prospect of thriving in notionally free-market competition. These issues are addressed in Chapters 5 and 6 of this book.

Indonesia and beyond

To summarise the foregoing discussion, this book elaborates on an understanding of the relationship between socio-economic change and democratising and globalising impulses in Muslim-majority societies that is based on insights from political economy and historical sociology. It does so through analysis of the cases of Egypt, Turkey but especially Indonesia. It should also be pointed out that the case of Indonesia is particularly instructive because, on the one hand, it can be celebrated as a successful case of 'transition to democracy' in a Muslim-majority society; on the other hand, Indonesia can be used to easily exemplify the dangers of the rise of religious violence and intolerance within a democracy, especially due to the activities of vigilante groups that employ religion to justify their presence.

There can be little doubt that significant insights on the different possible trajectories of Islamic politics can be gained by examining the case of Indonesia, the world's largest Muslim-majority country, and by drawing it more closely into the larger comparative and theoretical discussions that have mostly emerged from studies of North Africa and the Middle East. For example, there is the tradition of French scholarship led by Kepel (1984, 2003a, 2003b) and Roy (1994, 2004), which in spite of important internal differences effectively elaborate on the difficulties of sustaining populist coalitions behind Islamic banners. Their observations can be usefully, if critically, applied to the Indonesian case on the basis of an approach that integrates the study of Islamic politics with an analysis of broad socio-economic change as well as the outcomes of contests over power and tangible resources; in other words an approach that brings together the concerns of historical sociology and political economy.

It would be unfair to not recognise, however, that a number of authors writing on Indonesia have already identified issues of conflicts over power and wealth as well as changing socio-economic circumstances as significant in the analysis of Islam and politics (Liddle 1996; Hefner 2004). It should be mentioned too that Feillard and Madinier's work (2010) provides a commendable historical exposition of the broader political struggles within which Islamic political vehicles have been embroiled in Indonesia since the advent of national independence. Ricklefs's (2012) study is even more wide-ranging in time span though focussed on the most heavily populated island of Java. Nevertheless, such authors – as disparate as they are – remain mainly interested in ideational cleavages rather than in political economy imperatives that inevitably affect the agendas and priorities of Islamic politics. Thus Emmerson (2002), to take another example, laudably distinguishes between 'Islamist' aims that may include the establishment of an

Islamic state and those of jihadists who will use violence to pursue their desire for such a state. However, he does not provide very strong clues as to why these different tendencies have emerged and what sort of historical or sociological imperatives keep them alive in some contexts. Sidel's (2006) work in this regard is highly idiosyncratic and original in its situating of patterns of religious violence in Indonesia within changes in the structures of Islamic religious identity and authority. Yet his exploration tends to leave out the political economy underpinnings of the social conflicts he investigates.

In fact, much of the literature on Islamic politics in Indonesia is concerned with dichotomies regarding politically 'radical' and 'moderate' Islamic politics that have permeated through much of the security and foreign policy literature more generally (Rabasa 2005).[11] Moreover, the difference between the two remains predominantly understood in cultural and behavioural terms with only little connection to the profane struggles over power and resources that define politics in the modern world, except perhaps where Western geopolitical interests are more directly concerned.

At its core, this sort of literature has been directed to show how exclusivist forms of Islamic politics based on particular interpretations of doctrine or on their associated cultural dispositions are being countered by more tolerant tendencies that are amenable to democracy and able to accommodate secular society (Effendy 2003; Ota, Okamoto and Sueady 2010). In this vein, the so-called moderate Islamic tendency in Indonesia has received much attention from authors (e.g. Barton 2002). Such a tendency, moreover, is celebrated both for the clear hostility it displays towards 'radical' impulses and for its ostensible openness to cultural pluralism. It is not uncommon to view the favoured tendency as stemming from the 'eclectic' nature of 'peripheral' Southeast Asian Islam, as compared to its purer and more 'central' Middle Eastern counterpart.[12] In the Indonesian case, moderate forms of Islam are seen to be a natural corollary of the kind of syncretism most associated with religious practice as found on the heavily populated island of Java (Geertz 1960, 1971).

---

[11] See Hamilton-Hart (2005) for a trenchant critique of the works of security analysts on Islamic politics.

[12] Referring to the Middle East, a retired American military officer writing in an academic journal (published by the United States Army War College) declares unflinchingly that

> It is time to write off the Arab homelands of Islam as lost. They are as incapable of constructive change as they are unwilling even to consider liberal transformations. They have been left behind by history and their response has been to blame everyone but themselves – and to sponsor terror (sometimes casually, but often officially). Much of the Arab world has withdrawn into a fortress of intolerance and self-righteousness as psychologically comfortable as it is practically destructive. They are, through their own fault, as close to hopeless as any societies and cultures upon this earth (Peters 2002: 5–6).

Peters suggests that not all is lost outside of this 'homeland', however, including in Southeast Asia, where he urges more serious effort to influence the thinking and behaviour of Muslims.

It is the empirically rich and highly sophisticated work of Hefner (e.g. 2000) that has been most notable for its concern with identifying the culturally embedded potential for democratisation within Islam in Indonesia. His analysis partly hinges on the presence of a tradition of religious pluralism and tolerance that was once widely recognised as being dominant before it was challenged by more recent, sporadic, but bloody outbreaks of terrorist activity in that country. This and the emergence of an array of violent Islamic-oriented paramilitary groups after the fall of Soeharto subsequently caused Hefner to also examine the 'uncivil' manifestations of Indonesian Islamic politics. Informed by deep knowledge of different cultural, juridical and philosophical traditions within the Muslim world, he has relied on an approach that primarily explains the rise of 'uncivil Islam' in Indonesia on the basis of less dominant cultural dispositions that makes it possible for opportunistic political elites to exploit sectarian sentiments and which also allows for infiltration by Al-Qaeda militants into an otherwise religiously tolerant Indonesian society (Hefner 2005b: 275; also see Hefner 2009b). He has also contextualised the Indonesian case within more global developments in the Muslim world with regard to the presence or absence of democratising tendencies (Hefner 2005a). Nevertheless, Hefner remains generally keen to underline the importance of interpretations of Islamic law in Indonesia that are inclined towards democratic and human rights ideals (Hefner 2011).

The question that follows, however, is why sectarianism has become an effective weapon of choice by which to ferment unrest, whether or not in the hands of self-interested elites and their minions. Moreover, how can we explain the historical and sociological factors that have made such a weapon more readily available now than ever before, without resorting to overly simplistic narratives of elite manipulation of gullible masses in times of political flux or economic hardship? Why does such a weapon become discarded in a number of notable circumstances, in favour of democratic strategies of attaining power? It is put forward here that these sorts of questions can be most fruitfully examined through an understanding of Islamic politics based firmly on political economy and historical sociology-oriented traditions of scholarship.

But would political analysis based on a more institutional approach achieve this task just as well? Mirroring the tendency in Islamic political studies more generally (Dalacoura 2006; Haklai 2009), some recent works on Indonesia have addressed the importance of institutions in moulding the behaviour of social actors, though once more, the tendency remains relatively weaker in the literature on Indonesia and Southeast Asia than on the Middle East. Among the core issues in such studies is whether authoritarian rule curtails the inclination towards anti-liberal and anti-democratic Islamic political agendas and whether opposite ones are strengthened by the onset of democracy in the scramble for popular electoral support in Muslim-majority countries like Indonesia (Bubalo *et al.* 2008).

Ufen thus offers a 'moderation thesis' that suggests how Indonesian Islamic politics can remain predominantly moderate in the post-authoritarian era because of a political system that encourages the development of parties that are not rigidly ideological (Ufen 2011: 86–87). The thesis of 'moderation' and 'inclusion' is visited as well by Buehler (2012), who tweaks it to explain the political moderation of the PKS (Justice and Prosperity Party) in Indonesia (e.g. Permata 2008), which had emerged out of a semi-clandestine student movement inspired by the Egyptian Muslim Brotherhood. Such moderation is often attributed to a politically and doctrinally flexible central leadership that is able to organisationally instil discipline all the way to local party branches.[13] But why the party's central leadership developed such attributes in the first place surely requires more contextual explanation. Indeed, the lack of interest in historical and structural contexts means that the moderation thesis only partially explains the way that Islamic political vehicles have had to navigate their way through democratic institutions, in Indonesia and in the other cases addressed in this book, as well as to respond to ever-growing pressure to support greater integration with the global capitalist economy.

Given this discussion, one of the major intentions of this book is to help infuse the literature on Indonesian Islamic politics with the theoretical concerns that have characterised some of the most important contributions to the literature on North Africa and the Middle East especially. Thus far, most comparative analyses of Islamic politics in Indonesia have involved juxtapositions with other Southeast Asian cases – including Thailand and the Philippines – where issues of separatist politics provide an additional dimension (Sidel 2007; Means 2009; Saravanamuttu 2010).[14] However, distinctly political economy concerns have been mostly absent in such comparative efforts, even when they have taken into account the historical context within which Islamic politics has evolved (e.g. Hui 2013).

The infusion of concerns that have featured more prominently in the literature on the Middle East and North Africa, it is envisaged, would help to avoid

---

[13] The PKS had evolved from the Tarbiyah (a term denoting development through education) movement in Indonesian university campuses in the 1980s. This was a period of intense state repression against Islamic movements. After the fall of Soeharto, its activists formed the PK (Justice Party) and contested the 1999 elections, Indonesia's freest since 1955. Having done poorly, the party renamed itself the PKS and performed much better in parliamentary elections in 2004 and 2009, becoming the most successful of Islamic political parties in post-Soeharto Indonesia. However, its standing as a party of integrity and morality was severely compromised by the subsequent implication of party figures in cases of corruption. No less than the party president was handed a sixteen-year jail sentence in 2013 for his role in a high-profile case involving peddling in the beef import industry.

[14] On the separatist dimension of the conflict in Thailand, see ICG (2005a); McCargo (2008); Connors (2007); and Liow (2006). On the Philippines, see Abinales (2010), among others. On another oft-discussed Southeast Asian case, Malaysia, which is sometimes compared to Indonesia, see among others, Roff (1967); Kessler (1978); Nagata (1984); Mutalib (1990); Hamayotsu (2002); Stark (2004); Noor (2004); Khoo (2006); and Hadiz and Khoo (2011).

the pitfalls of a highly alarmist security-oriented narrative on the nature of Islamic politics that often reduces it to the global reach of violent jihadi movements (e.g. Brachman 2009). As is well known, this narrative tends to dichotomise 'good' and 'bad' Muslims largely according to Western geopolitical concerns (as was cogently observed by Mamdani 2004), in ways that run parallel to the 'moderate' and 'radical' juxtaposition. For quite some time after 9/11, the predominance of the security-oriented narrative allowed its conveyors to practically subsume the study of Islamic politics under the study of terrorism and violence (e.g. Frisch and Inbar 2008; Springer, Regens and Edger 2009), and, in the case of Indonesia, especially after the first Bali Bombing of 2002. Thus, the study of Islamic politics has been haunted by the spectre of Al-Qaeda (Vertigans 2009: 1) and, subsequently, of the so-called Islamic State emerging out of the chaos in Iraq and Syria.

Such analyses are exemplified, to different degrees, in the work of Abuza (2007); Gunaratna (2002, 2004); Singh (2007); Gunaratna, Acharya and Chua (2005); Ramakrishna and Tan (2003, 2004); and Ramakrishna (2009) as far as Indonesia and the broader Southeast Asian region are concerned. Significantly, otherwise historically and culturally well-informed analyses of Islamic politics (Barton 2004; Fealy and White 2008) have often fed into, somewhat unwittingly, the security-based narrative by providing the empirical knowledge to reinforce the 'good' versus 'bad' Muslim dichotomous worldview that is so central to it. Indeed, much of the security-oriented analysis would be confined to hyperbole without the sort of specialist knowledge provided by such country and area studies experts.

Outline of the book

The outline of the book is as follows: after this Introduction, Chapter 2 addresses the main theoretical issues of the evolution of the new Islamic populism in Indonesia and elsewhere, but especially in Egypt and Turkey. It also discusses how the literature on populism more generally can be usefully linked to some of the major theoretical concerns pertaining to the trajectories of contemporary Islamic politics in the context of neoliberal globalisation. Chapter 3 examines the genesis of Islamic populism in Indonesia, while delineating and explaining historical divergences and convergences with the Turkish and Egyptian cases. It explores, though in necessarily tentative fashion, the ramifications of different historical legacies for the present-day prospects of building alliances to sustain the new Islamic populist project.

Chapter 4 continues the analysis by scrutinising the relationship between the emergence of the new Islamic populism and social changes resulting from capitalist development. It also examines the impact of Cold War-era state authoritarianisms on the forging of the new Islamic populism in each of the cases, though the features of the Indonesian experience are particularly highlighted. Chapter 5 provides concrete examination of the different strategies and organisational vehicles through which the struggles of the new Islamic populism have been waged, including political parties, mass organisations, paramilitaries and, occasionally, entities involved in violent terrorist activity. The point is to explain when and how the democratic route to power is accepted by the social agents of the new Islamic populism, or conversely, rejected – and then to explore the broader ramifications in terms of the contending political agendas that may emerge. This is followed by Chapter 6, which provides a case study of the Darul Islam, a major movement in Indonesian political history that aimed to establish an Islamic state. Militarily defeated half a century ago, new manifestations of it have continually emerged along with new generations of the young, better educated and more alienated. However, the Darul Islam and its heirs have suffered constant state repression, isolation from the broader *ummah* and perpetual marginalisation.

Chapters 7 and 8 then explore the broad context within which the political project of the new Islamic populism is being further developed in the present day, namely in continuing contests over power and tangible resources in the post-authoritarian era and in an age of neoliberal globalisation. These are related to struggles to forge the agenda of Indonesian socio-economic and political change within a relatively new democracy, and one that is often chaotic and rife with money politics. The Indonesian experience is compared and contrasted with similar competition to define agendas of reform and change in Turkey and Egypt, within which the social agents of the new Islamic populism have been embroiled. The aim is to understand how similar social processes taking place in diverse socio-political and economic terrains have produced sometimes markedly different outcomes. Chapter 7 specifically addresses the ideological effects of successes and failures in new Islamic populist attempts to win state power through recourse to the mechanisms of electoral democracy. Chapter 8 is more focussed on the social conditions that may facilitate, or dissuade, the embrace of global markets by Islamic politics. The presence or absence of big business interests that identify with the *ummah* is shown to be a crucial factor. The final chapter of the book offers a conclusion that highlights its major findings. It also identifies their implications for research on Islamic politics in Indonesia specifically and for Muslim-majority societies in the modern world more generally.

2 Islamic politics and the emergence of a new Islamic populism

A central premise of this book is that theoretical debates on populism allow for the development of a distinctive understanding of Islamic politics and its trajectories in the modern world. But, of course, populism has been understood in different and contentious ways. This chapter examines the main approaches to populism but emphasises those that place the concerns of political economy and historical sociology at the forefront. This is in contrast to approaches that highlight populism's discursive, ideational or organisational aspects.

Additionally, the chapter outlines how class alliances providing the social base for the new Islamic populism have come to be forged by reference to the experiences of Indonesia, Turkey and Egypt, although far from equally successfully. Borrowing from the insights of the work of such authors as Oxhorn (1998) on populism and social mobilisation in Latin America, it argues that the new Islamic populism constitutes a specific form of 'social mobilisation based on asymmetrical multi-class coalitions'. As examined in more detail in subsequent chapters, these coalitions advance economic and political agendas that are much less rooted in, and driven by, interpretation of religious doctrine or cultural norms than concrete struggle over power and tangible resources within specific social and historical contexts. So rather than being rigidly predetermined by dominant values and ideals within the *ummah*, these agendas are continually and dynamically being reshaped by the imperatives of operating within particular constellations of social power and interests, as well as pressures emanating from participation in a contradiction-laden neoliberal global economy.

The politics of populism

Theoretical debates about political representation, mobilisation and ideology have prominently featured the theme of populism, primarily as a challenge to liberal notions of representative and democratic politics. That there has been resurgence in the discussion lately is due to the range of critical responses, made in the name of 'ordinary people', to the practice and discourse of globalisation. These have been typically linked to scepticism about the adequacy of liberal democratic mechanisms of governance and decision making. It is notable that such responses have emerged concurrently from the more (Albertazzi and McDonnell 2008a) as well as less economically developed parts of the world (Conniff 1999; Mizuno and Phongpaichit 2009).

In Europe, populist politics have been associated closely in recent years with anti-immigration tendencies represented by politicians like the Le Pens in France (Berezin 2009: 126–195), Fortuyn and Wilders in the Netherlands (Lucardie 2008: 164–165) and by the lately vigorous Far Right in Nordic countries like Norway, Sweden and Finland.[1] It has been analysed as a major challenge to liberal forms of politics throughout the Continent (Mudde and Kaltwasser 2012). In Australia, Pauline Hanson's bellicose One Nation Party once best represented a similarly xenophobic tendency (Johnson 1998), though there have been subsequent successors. There is no doubt that the xenophobia inherent in the anti-immigration position – as also expressed by many American politicians on the conservative side of the political spectrum – has been strengthened by deep-seated anxieties about the social and economic effects of globalisation (closely related to the decline of the welfare state), not least among the working and increasingly struggling middle classes of these societies.

But another major reason for the renewed scholarly attention given to populist politics has been the evident appeal of a number of controversial leaders in the developing world in recent times. Some of the most prominent among them have included Hugo Chavez (Hawkins 2003) in Venezuela before his death and Mahmud Ahmadinejad in Iran (Ansari 2008) before he stepped down from that country's presidency. As is well known, such leaders deployed the rhetoric of social justice and anti-Western-dominated global capitalism in equal measure, placing much blame on the latter for a host of problems in their respective countries. In some ways the rhetoric was reminiscent of the 'classical' populism portrayed in the literature on Latin America, especially pertaining to the regimes of Peron in Argentina and Vargas in Brazil (Jansen 2011), most obviously in its emphasis on national unity in the face of threats originating from powerful foreign countries.

A contentious issue

Much like 'nationalism', 'populism' is sometimes considered an elusive concept; thus it has been variously associated with Right as well as Left tendencies of politics. It has been linked in the twentieth century to rural-based movements in the United States typified by icons like Huey Long, the mostly urban labour-based movements of Peronism in Argentina and Vargas in Brazil, and even the belligerently anti-communist Fascist regimes of Europe. In East and Southeast Asia

---

[1] Also see the explication found in Mouffe (2005: 50–71).

after the 1997/1998 economic crisis, such disparate recent leaders as Thaksin Shinawatra in Thailand, Mahathir Mohammad in Malaysia, Joseph Estrada in the Philippines and Junichi Koizumi in Japan had been tagged – rather sweepingly – with the 'populist' label (Mizuno and Phongpaichit 2009). Authors like Conniff (1999: 5) thus suggest that populists tend to draw from 'existing sociopolitical models' and can even recombine them 'inconsistently'.

Nevertheless, it should not follow that populism is but a convenient term with which to associate crassly opportunistic politics designed to appeal to the ill-informed 'masses' or those premised on sheer demagoguery. Conniff, for example, has described populism as 'eclectic and flexible, designed to appeal to the largest number of voters at any given time' (1999: 5). Populist politics also should not become simply synonymous with 'political irrationality', whereby 'colourful and engaging politicians' attract the masses 'into their movements and hold their loyalty indefinitely, even after their deaths' (Conniff 1999: 4).

A potentially major problem emerges when this alleged political irrationality is then extended into the economic sphere, where populism becomes indistinguishable from irresponsible policies that cause 'inflation, indebtedness, and charges of malfeasance' (Conniff 1999: 6). If the point is to contrast the economic policies of populists with market economics, such a view is hard to reconcile, for example, with the rise in the 1990s of populist governments in Latin America that went together with purportedly 'rational' neoliberal economic policies (Weyland 2003). This sort of combination characterised the rule of Alberto Fujimori in Peru (Hawkins 2003) and Carlos Menem in Argentina (Barros 2005), during which market-oriented economic policies were instituted on the basis of political participation that frequently circumvented formal democratic institutions. It also cannot take into account the Turkish experience, where the democratically elected AKP (Justice and Development Party) government has strongly grafted an agenda of neoliberal reform onto many of the older social justice concerns of Islamic movements (Yavuz 2009; Tuğal 2009).[2]

The looseness with which populism has been customarily employed also does not mean that it should be abandoned in serious analytical discussion, as suggested by Marliere (2013), for example. Nor is it necessary to designate populist politics as 'empty signifier' – a mode of articulating 'social, political or ideological contents' that cannot be explained by way of historical context (Laclau 2005: 34; also see Laclau 2006).[3] Inspired by Laclau's sort of approach,

---

[2] Thus, Tayfun Görgün, secretary general of DISK (Confederation of Revolutionary Trade Unions of Turkey), a leftist trade union organisation, considers the ideology of the AKP to be neoliberal, but with a 'religious cloak'. Interview, Istanbul, 19 September 2011.

[3] Hawkins (2010: 43) 'personifies' the empty signifier by referring to the charismatic leader frequently at the helm of populist movements. But this only sustains the notion of the superficiality of populism, as he also suggests that this empty signifier-person is also bound to express 'a vague but appealing set of ideas and language'.

Dinçşahin's (2012) analysis of the populism of Turkey's AKP is thus based on a 'symptomatic reading' of its discourse, which he asserts to be superior to explorations of populist politics in specific historical circumstances. In spite of such assertions, there have been a number of noteworthy efforts to cast light on populist politics that have gradually advanced our understanding of its significance as a historically embedded phenomenon.

But many of the contributions to the literature have approached populism through noticeably different levels of analysis. At the ideational level, a recent work defines the major characteristic of populism as hinging on the notion of 'a virtuous and homogenous people' who are pitted 'against a set of elites and dangerous "others". The latter are depicted, in turn, as a collection of people who are 'depriving (or attempting to deprive) the sovereign people of their rights, values, prosperity, identity and voice' (Albertazzi and McDonnell 2008b: 3). This encapsulation, in many ways, revisits and elaborates on Canovan's (1981) well-known summary of populism as an anti-elitist form of politics that exalts 'the people' and mobilises them against an identified powerful political and economic establishment. Similarly, for Mudde (2004: 543), populism is 'an ideology' that conceives of society as being 'ultimately separated into two homogeneous and antagonistic groups, "the pure people" versus "the corrupt elite", and which argues that politics should be an expression of the volonté générale (general will) of the people'.

However, Mouzelis (1985: 342) had taken a different tack altogether back in the 1980s and argued that the specific feature of populist politics is to be found at the organisational level, where one finds a style of leadership 'that results in systematic attempts to by-pass intermediary groups' that operate within formal political institutions.[4] More recently, a study of Chavismo in Venezuela contrasted populist and pluralist politics by highlighting how the former pursues an 'agenda of direct democracy that questions the value of representative government, professional politicians, and bureaucrats' in order to 'better discover and honor the popular will' (Hawkins 2010: 45). At the organisational level, populist mobilisation of 'the masses' is thus typically aimed to broaden the scope of political participation allowed within the parameters of existing formal

---

[4] Mouzelis's intervention brought to mind an even earlier proposition, made by the American sociologist Edward Shils (1956), that populism envisages a more direct relationship between the population and its leaders than is afforded in representative forms of democratic politics. According to Kuzminski (2008), there is a long history of populist politics in the West based on such a yearning. Indeed the USA has a variety of traditions rooted in feelings of disenfranchisement caused by the remoteness of existing democratic political institutions from ordinary lives. Thus, such populist traditions have in common the longing for leadership that is more in touch with the needs of the 'common people' (see Taggart 2000: Chapter 3; Postel 2007). These sentiments still periodically resurface in present-day American politics – for example in the form of the billionaire Ross Perot's bids for the Presidency in the 1990s, and more recently, in the rise of the Tea Party within the most conservative and religious elements of the Republican Party.

institutional arrangements. Such a 'broadening' is in turn geared towards 'some reasonably permanent restructuring of the way that dominant and dominated groups are related to each other' (Mouzelis 1985: 342).

Mouzelis's meso-level observation is useful because the new Islamic populism has involved strategies for broadening participation that are both within the realms of formal electoral politics and beyond, through the merging of what might be considered social movement strategies involving mass organisations with those of conventional party politics. Thus, the PKS (Justice and Prosperity Party) in Indonesia is seen as both a social movement and a political party by some observers (Munandar 2011). Much the same can be said about the AKP (Justice and Development Party) in Turkey, not only due to its once close relationship with the influential and wealthy Fethulleh Gülen movement (e.g. Yavuz and Esposito 2003),[5] but also because of the way it is clearly descended from earlier and suppressed Islamic movements. In a similar vein, the Muslim Brotherhood of Egypt has operated both as a social movement and in parliamentary struggles (Hamid 2014: 8–16), though in a necessarily semi-clandestine manner for long periods. Mouzelis also points out, however, that the restructuring does not have to entail a 'concomitant radical transformation of the prevailing relations of production', an observation which is relevant to the new Islamic populism, the social agents of which are more likely than not to balk at the prospect of an outright overhaul of the existing social order as might be contemplated by radical leftists.[6]

Nonetheless, rather than just enumerating its ideational or organisational characteristics, theorists have also grappled, quite fruitfully, with the sociological and historical circumstances that may give rise to populism. An even earlier work compiled by Ionescu and Gellner (1969), for example, had shown that populism's class bases can be altogether very different and thus one task would be to analyse the specific historical conditions that gave rise to the varying sources of support for multiple forms of populism in the world.

The North American tradition of populism, for example, was shown to have been supported by both agrarian farmers and small and medium entrepreneurs at different times (Hofstadter 1969); whereas the Latin American cases have had distinct streams of 'old rural' populism supported by the peasantry and the more urban kinds that made Peronism possible (Hennessy 1969).[7] In cases where

---

[5] Fethulleh Gülen is a preacher and writer living in exile in the United States who is heavily influenced by Said Nursi, the revered Turkish theologian and leader of a Sufi religious order. The movement, which sponsors interfaith dialogue, has a pro-business outlook and runs charitable organisations as well as schools in Turkey and all over the world. Nursi himself, who died in 1960, was persecuted by the Kemalist state and was highly critical of materialist philosophies like communism.

[6] As a point of comparison, see Achchar's insightful interview with Rodinson in Achchar (2004) on the atavistic and simultaneously un-revolutionary aspects of projects that are associated with Islamic fundamentalisms.

[7] For a more recent and detailed analysis of the history of American populism, see Postel (2007).

'peasantism' was prominent, as identified in the Eastern European experiences discussed in that volume (Ionescu 1969), and similar to the African ones (Saul 1969), populism was seen to have strongly involved protecting 'traditional' modes of life against capitalist transformations and the veneration of the values and moral systems said to be associated with it. In the same vein, contemporary appeals to Islamic populism have resonance because of claims being made about establishing a morally resilient society against the threat of erosion posed by what are perceived to be the shallow materialist values and overly consumptive lifestyles associated with 'Western culture'. The twist, however, is that the new Islamic populism is more distinctly an urban socio-political phenomenon, or certainly one that continues to become increasingly urban, for reasons having to do with social transformations enveloping much of the Muslim world.

In the process, Ionescu and Gellner credibly paved the way for understandings of populist politics that emphasise its social foundations. Thus, Oxhorn (1998: 223) subsequently argued that populist movements in Latin America embodied a form of social mobilisation that embraced 'multi-class coalitions' and tapped into the frustrations of lower classes produced by the inequalities of development. At the same time, however, these movements have been typically led by members of the middle class who may be less marginalised than workers or peasants but have found their upward social mobility blocked by the preponderance of powerful sets of interests or cliques in the state and in the economy. In other words, these social movements were identified with the new poor produced by the capitalist modernisation process but were led by those ensconced in relatively more privileged positions within existing social hierarchies, much as is the case in the new Islamic populism.

Latin American cases, it should be mentioned, have given rise to an interesting tendency to tackle populism in ways that connect with the sociological literature on social movements and contentious politics. Taking the classical populist movements of Latin America as paradigmatic cases, Jansen (2011: 82), for example, argues that populism involves the political mobilisation of marginalised 'social sectors into visible and contentious political action', accompanied by a nationalist, anti-elite and pro-people rhetoric. He also argues that it must be understood primarily as a political practice that facilitates identity formation, organisational capacity, and therefore, collective action and indirectly reinforces Mouzelis's insights on the organisational and mobilisational aspects of populism.

Jansen's framework, however, does not address populisms that are infused by religious (or ethnic) rather than national symbols and imagery. In this, he follows indirectly Stewart's (1969: 183) proposition that populism is basically nationalistic in the sense that it heavily demonises a foreign 'other' in order to facilitate the forging of national unity. But this ignores the fact that nationalist traditions have not been the only source of populist rhetorical content, and why and how religion (or ethnicity) figures significantly in the forging of populist politics in some contexts requires investigation too. Some efforts towards this end have been made in relation to Islamic politics and social movement theory in such diverse works as those by Wickham (2002), Wictorowicz (2004) and Bayat (2007).

It should be underlined, nevertheless, that the appeal to Islamic populism does not necessarily entail displacement of the idea of the 'nation', even in the most romanticised forms, by religious identity. Commenting on the post-revolutionary Constitution of the Islamic Republic in Iran established by Khomeini, Matsunaga (2009: 141–142) observes that there was never a conception of a complete break with the long and continuing history of the Iranian people as imagined in that most vital of documents. Instead, what was being ushered in was supposedly a new phase in this history whereby the moral power of Islam would be the driving force of the 'Muslim nation of Iran'. Even in Turkey, nationhood can be conceived in terms of links to the Ottoman precursors of the contemporary Turkish state. Major AKP figure, Turkish foreign minister (and later prime minister from 2014) Ahmet Davutoğlu is thus regarded as a chief proponent of a so-called neo-Ottoman vision of modern Turkey (Goçek 2011: 1–2), within which a leading role in the affairs of the Balkans, Middle East as well as Central Asia is largely a matter of historical destiny.

But many activists of Islamic movements of an earlier age had also rejected the supposed inherent incompatibility between Islam and solidarity based on national identity. The Indonesian scholar Deliar Noer (1963: 122), for example, observes that the theme of 'Islam and nationalism' was a major part of debates about the future of an independent Indonesian political entity in the 1920s and 1930s. He points out that Abdoel Moeis – one of the most famous leaders of the Sarekat Islam – had argued against detractors who had accused it of being 'purely religious' by claiming that the organisation was instead 'nationalist Islamic' in nature (Noer 1963: 205). In his debates with Soekarno in the 1930s, a young Mohammad Natsir, future leader of the Masyumi Party and Dewan Dakwah Islamiyah Indonesia, argued too that Islam offered an existing bond among the Indonesian people that could be the basis for developing a sense of national solidarity. He also suggested that realising Islamic ideals would have the effect of improving the welfare of 'the people in general' (Noer 1963: 455–456). Even Kartosuwiryo, who rebelled against the nascent Indonesian republic with the Darul Islam movement, is legendary for his leadership of militia forces during the war of national independence against the Dutch army. He argued that the struggle by Indonesians to free themselves from the yoke of foreign imperialism was nothing less than religious duty (Formichi 2012: 90). Many who still idolise him today are thus able to claim to have inherited a major strand within

Indonesia's nationalist struggle. Because of all this, the social agents of the new Islamic populism in Indonesia can also claim to have simultaneously religious and nationalist credentials and are prone to depict the Islamic struggle as part of the struggle of the 'Indonesian people'.

This sort of argument dovetails nicely with the understanding employed in this book, which emphasises how the new Islamic populism involves a conception of the *ummah* that is based on evolution through social conflicts primarily taking place within the boundaries of nation states. This understanding, based on the social foundations of the new Islamic populism, has important points of intersection with the other approaches mentioned earlier. Even at the more purely ideational level, the way that the *ummah* is conceived in the present day can be seen as the product of particular kinds of responses to social circumstances arising from social marginalisation or exclusion. At the organisational level, it is explained (in Chapter 5) that the vehicles of the new Islamic populism can include political parties, but also an array of other possibilities like mass organisations, paramilitaries and terrorist cells; in other words those that are geared towards bypassing the mechanisms of representative democracy in favour of more direct forms of political participation. But which of these become predominant is largely contingent on the specific context, as we shall see. Therefore, primacy is given in the analysis to the make-up of new Islamic populist alliances and the way that these have to navigate through existing constellations of power and interest.

Internal contradictions

Populist alliances hinge on the idea of the homogeneity of interests of the 'people', which in the modern world will always belie the reality of mutually contradictory constituent elements (see Deiwiks 2009). There is thus a problem with notions of a populist 'heartland' wherein a 'virtuous and unified population' is to be found (Taggart 2000: 95). Such possible contradictions are rightly highlighted by Laclau (2005), however, who makes the point that in spite of the notion of representing a supposedly undifferentiated 'people', populism is simultaneously geared to uphold – first and foremost – the interests of those who are marginalised. This is achieved through a discursive process involving 'chains of equivalence' that allow the '*plebs* to see itself as the *populus*' (Laclau 2005: 86). It is through such a process, according to Laclau, that populist projects transcend inherent diversity within the masses, producing shared identities (2005: 117–124).

Diverging from Laclau, however, it is suggested here that it is fruitful to understand the social bases of populism and to explore the inherent internal contradictions that affect its evolution. Furthermore, it should not matter, for instance, that there is no social class that is abidingly populist in terms of its political project, as Laclau (2005: 15) has argued to dismiss the usefulness of historical analysis. The middle class, for example, has supported democratising political projects but also fascism in different contexts. But given this absence, what is entailed are close observations of the (shifting) social bases that give rise to populism and to locate these within key periods of social transformation – an undertaking that Laclau quite consistently opposed as a method of inquiry.

The divergence from Laclau represented here, however, is not necessarily absolute. It is surely correct, for example, that successful populist projects develop agendas that resonate with people of varying social positions who nonetheless commonly *experience* deprivation and who understand that their life chances are similarly being *systemically* defined and constrained within an existing social order. This implies that those who are only relatively deprived can find the 'equivalence' of their own hopes, anxieties and frustrations via experiences with the same social structures, institutions and processes that cause the oppression of those even more marginalised, as Laclau does suggest with considerable forcefulness. The social effect is to potentially develop a unity of cause across different segments of society against the alleged perpetrators of similar social injustices.

Such recognition, nonetheless, should not imply the implausibility of historically grounded analyses. In truth, the absence of a 'fixed' identifiable social base is not something that is wholly unique to populist politics, anyway. Bellin (2000), for instance, argues that the project of democratic politics has been historically opposed or backed by labour and capital, contingent on the specific circumstances that dictate where the material interests of these classes will tend to lie. In other words, providing support for democracy is not an abiding project of an assertive and politically organised proletariat (Rueschemeyer, Stephens and Stephens 1992), nor is it of an ascendant bourgeoisie (Moore 1966). However, few would argue for the dismissal of serious academic analyses of the roles of bourgeois or working-class social actors in democratisation projects simply because they have been inconsistent throughout history. Few would also dismiss the possibility of a serious analysis of democratic politics because these have emerged within vastly different historical circumstances.

It may be suggested that the same principle should apply to the new Islamic populism as a variant of populist politics that sustains a worldview whereby (notionally) upwardly mobile members of the middle class, excluded members of entrepreneurial groups and downtrodden members of the lumpenproletariat are able to find common cause against the 'status quo' that places obstacles on their path. They do so in many Muslim-majority societies due to social contradictions associated with capitalist development and greater integration with the world economy. The key divergence from traditional populist politics, as already pointed out, is that the concept of the *ummah* substitutes for the notion of 'the people' in the basic vernacular of the new Islamic populism (Hadiz 2014).

It is no coincidence, therefore, that the most ardent new Islamic populist today does not typically hail from the ranks of the most exploited of the 'people' or the 'masses'. Writing on the Middle East, Ayubi (1993) identifies the sociological origins of those who may be counted among them in a number of professions dominated by educated members of the urban middle class. Ayubi's observations are supported by the work of Gambetta and Hertog (2009) on the social backgrounds of those involved in 'militant' religious activities in the Middle East and North Africa. After identifying the prevalence of individuals who acquired tertiary education in the field of engineering, they suggested that the 'high ambitions' and 'high frustrations' of these engineers have seriously collided with their actual life experiences. But rather than rejecting the modern world, these engineers 'felt duped by the development rhetoric of their regimes', and in addition, believed that 'they deserved more than they could get' out of life (Gambetta and Hertog 2009: 224).

Interestingly, Gambetta and Hertog (2009: 224) also envisaged the appearance among these engineers of a collective sense of having let down society by a failure to carry out the 'vanguard' role as modernisers to which they had been cast in the very same rhetoric by which they had felt duped. Writing on Egypt in the 1980s, Gilsenan refers to pious individuals who have an 'attachment to a vigorous and simplistic view of the need for Islamic law to rule society.' These individuals are 'technocratic', in the sense of viewing themselves as free of ideology, and 'trained in the concept of the neutral quality of scientific knowledge', where 'there are problems to be solved and solutions available' (Gilsenan 1988: 183). In the case of Indonesia, Hasan (2006: p.219) has pointed to the fact that many young Islamic activists today come from newly urbanised middle-class families who remain relatively blocked from making rapid strides in social advancement in spite of making some headway in terms of occupation and educational attainment. They too did not necessarily experience formal religious training (Tan 2011); many were educated in 'secular' institutions instead – where command over knowledge and skill is revered as the key to meritocratic social advancement.

From this point of view, the development of mass education in modernising Muslim-majority countries, even where the curriculum is intended to foster a culture of allegiance to an existing regime, is clearly an important factor. Writing on Egypt in the 1990s, Strarrett (1998: 232) shows that one of its possible products is the well-educated, young Islamic militant who has freed himself of the necessity to rely on religious interpretation provided by the state-legitimising discourse of the state-funded *ulama*. In other words, while the role of the latter was intended to cultivate the kind of religiosity that is non-threatening to the existing social order, especially among the youthful beneficiaries of mass education, the unintended consequence was to enable the emergence of individuals for whom matters of religious discourse and interpretation were no longer quite so esoteric.

In spite of the differences with Laclau, it is maintained here that something akin to his notion of chains of 'equivalence' (2005: 77–83) can be useful if firmly placed within a more historical and structural explanation. Understanding the concrete conditions within which multi-class struggles waged under the banner of Islam emerge is crucial given Bayat's (2007: 6) fitting exhortation that 'discourse is *not* power unless it is given material force'. In fact, although he follows closely Laclau's emphasis on identifying the discursive logic of populism, Panizza shows the possibility of metamorphosis into more historical and structural analysis insofar as this logic intersects with key changes in people's material conditions of life. Among these changes, he points out, are typically 'urbanisation and modernisation, shifts in the demographic balance between social classes, and between regional and ethnic groups, as well as, more recently, globalisation' (Panizza 2005: 12–13).

The further task then is to understand how alliances bringing together disparate and potentially mutually antagonistic social forces – unified by diverse experiences of marginalisation – might come to underpin the project of the new Islamic populism. For the process is of course never automatic but relies on the exertions of practical politics. It is through this sort of analysis that one can comprehend how potential internal contradictions within new Islamic populist coalitions are resolved, or alternatively, continue to present a hindrance to the forging of an effective *ummah*-based political response to the new sets of social problems thrown up by capitalist transformations. It is through such analysis as well that different trajectories, such as found in the cases of Indonesia, Turkey and Egypt, can be understood.

Populism and Islam

Laclau (2005: x) is undoubtedly correct too when he suggests that the populist label is typically applied to social actors in denigrating fashion by those who are ideologically predisposed against mass-based politics in the name of some sort of 'modern' – usually meaning liberal democratic – political rationality.[8] In other words, few people refer to themselves as populist; instead it is their detractors who usually do so. Any number of analysts thus dismiss populism as 'pathology' (Taggart 2000); one that is sustained by charismatic leaders embodying the exact opposite of the notion of rule on the basis of legal–formal rationality. The latter is of course, in turn, regarded as one of the hallmarks of modernity, owing largely to the influence of the tradition of Weberian sociology.

---

[8] As Canovan points out, however, populists have a trump card over liberal democrats: their belief in popular sovereignty, after all, lies at the heart of democracy (2005: 5). This became significant in the Muslim world when Islamic-oriented parties in Egypt and Tunisia, in the initial period after the Arab Spring, demonstrated their traction with voters.

Weber himself famously thought that charismatic rule was largely exceptional and temporary, and therefore, that the ascendancy of legal–formal rationality would be the norm in modern societies (Weber 1978: 1111–1156). Panizza (2005: 9) underscores this point when he suggests that populism is a language of politics when 'politics as usual' becomes no longer possible. It is in fact by invoking Weber's concept of charismatic authority that critics like Ansari, for example, are able to portray the former Ahmadinejad government in Iran as being both irrational and 'inherently unstable' (2008: 696). In spite of the merits of Ansari's close and insightful analysis of political conflict in modern Iran, opposing populism to Weberian rationality remains a less-than-satisfactory theoretical response to an important socio-political phenomenon. It may help to sustain condescending or overly dismissive attitudes, even on the part of those who take populism seriously enough to write books about it.

This is why close examination of the social bases of populist politics, and outlining their relationships with specific political agendas, is necessary. Indonesia, for example, has had a strong secular tradition of nationalist populism – closely associated with the legacy of first president and independence struggle hero Soekarno. Such a tradition is quite distinguishable from those associated with the new Islamic populism in terms of the terminologies and imageries deployed to mobilise broad-based support. Moreover, they may conflict as a result of targeting significantly overlapping social constituencies. In fact concurrent efforts to establish footholds among the ever-growing urban poor have sometimes resulted in violent conflict between the representatives of 'nationalist' and 'Islamic' forms of populism in Indonesia (see Chapter 5), especially in contested urban slums. Moreover, the social bases of populist projects may be composed of different combinations of marginalised sections of society, as was already recognised by Ionescu and Gellner (1969). It is to be expected that differences in organisational form and the specific discursive content of different projects will be affected by the composition of any populist alliance and the relative strength of their elements.

But why should the response to social injustice take the form of populist politics that is idiomatically Islamic? The answer to this question is quite straightforward: populism is always 'culturally specific in that it must draw inevitably from references and symbolism that are meaningful' in a given context (Anderson 2009). It is in this sense that Wickham's (2002: 157) observation that the social agents of Islamic politics have been successful due to their ability to adapt 'a respected cultural repertoire to new purposes' is cogent. Moreover, as Halliday (2000: 133) suggested, Islam has 'a reserve of values, symbols and ideas from which it is possible to derive a contemporary politics and social code'. In other words, like other major systems of belief, Islam potentially provides a cultural resource for the expression of grievances against social conditions that might contrast with (what are, in historical reality, constantly reconstituted) notions of what is just and virtuous. As Bayat (2007: 5) points out, the process of reconstitution has less to do with Islamic doctrine as such than with the social position and concrete interests of its interpreters. For this reason, the latter argues that Islam can be *made* to be democratic, regardless of issues of strictly religious or scriptural content. There is nothing in this point of view that implies that engagement in material struggles signifies some sort of cynical attachment to religion only on the part of social agents. What it does mean, however, is that struggles waged under the banner of religion are inevitably entangled within material ones and that the close relationship between the two needs to be understood.[9]

Furthermore, even if profound social transformations have taken place due to the advance of market economies and of global economic integration, it is clear that identity-based politics have not been eradicated; it has been sometimes accentuated in many parts of the world today. This observation is quite in contrast to old-style modernisation theory as well as to strains of orthodox Marxism, both of which have contributed greatly to the 'secularisation thesis' that predicted an ever more irreligious and disenchanted world to go along with material and economic progress (Bellin 2008; Haynes and Ben-Porat 2010).[10] Though the complex reasons for divergence from the meta-narrative of secular modernism are beyond the scope of this book, the rise of xenophobic nationalisms and of ethnic and religious-based identity politics is well known, and this phenomenon is far from confined to Islam or to Muslim-majority societies only (Juergensmeyer 2008). For instance, the highly chauvinistic Hindutva movement in India, buttressed particularly by the high of caste and increasingly assertive upper and middle classes, has received attention of late (Desai 2004).

However, the analysis of the new Islamic populism does not have to culminate in identity politics alone. Aspirations and grievances may be symbolically conveyed, but ultimately, analyses of populist politics would need to account for the sets of interests that are served by them. It is from such a point of view that it is possible to appreciate the evolution of Islamic populism from a petty bourgeois-dominated form arising in the age of late colonialism and struggling for relevance in the early post-colonial period, to one that is far more distinctly cross-class in the present age of globalised capitalism. In other words – to invoke Halliday again (1995) – the 'sociology of religion' by itself cannot account for the character of Islamic populism. Analysis, therefore, surely cannot be undertaken with primary reference to Koranic passages, no matter how deeply or well understood by the scholar. This stance is substantially in

---

[9] See the discussion of these and related matters in Hirschkind (1997), in which the culturally Islamic response to the problems of socio-economic marginalisations is emphasised.

[10] As Bellin observes, much of this had to do with the conviction held by classical thinkers like Durkheim, Weber and Marx, about the inevitability of secularisation. Vertigans (2009: 95–96) writes about the failure of secularisation across much of the world.

accordance with the classic analysis of Islam and capitalism by Rodinson (1966 [2007]), in which economic underdevelopment in Muslim societies is explained without reifying Islam itself, but by referencing a host of historical and sociological factors that have affected economic behaviour and development trajectories.

The observations made by Tripp (2006) are also relevant to this sort of approach. Tripp shows that there has been a great deal of inventive capacity among intellectuals of the Muslim world in developing new ideas about the acceptable features of an economic system that would not deviate from the Islamic faith. As the present work also shows, this inventiveness is particularly induced when engagement with the world economy can prove beneficial materially to that faith's key interpreters or political exponents.

What is particularly entailed by such inventiveness is the enabling of a *kind* of capitalism, supported by an imagined benign state, which would operate in the interest of the *ummah* in facing the challenges of the globalised world, although how extensive this state role is supposed to be depends on such matters as the strength of a domestic bourgeoisie that self-identifies as Islamic. In one sense, this is reflective of deeply ingrained sentiments in much of the Muslim world about state protection of the interests of the marginalised *ummah* that had been prevalent in the early post-colonial period (Roy 1994: Chapter 8). The latter is in turn suggestive of continuities that may be present in the outlook of the newer and older – petty bourgeois-dominated – form of Islamic populism, as discussed further in Chapter 3. Nevertheless, there can be significant discontinuities too. Rudnyckyj (2010) thus tries to depict how new management practices in Indonesia that cultivate piety and instil the value of hard work and material progress serve to discipline workforces in the interest of neoliberal capitalism in ways that have few historical antecedents in the country.

The changing social bases of Islamic populism

It was earlier pointed out that many authors have made the link between populism and Islamic politics (see also White 2002 on Turkey; Abrahamian 1991 and Doraj 1990 on Iran). Writing on the Maghreb, Colas (2004: 233) argued that Islamic politics could be understood as a sort of populist response to the social contradictions generated by contemporary capitalist development. Moreover, he suggests that 'class-based political movements' in this part of the Muslim world have generally been less successful than those built around broader and more vague conceptions of 'the people'. What Colas does is to try to identify the structural underpinnings of the emergence of Islamic populism, especially in his main case study of Algeria, in the absence of viable leftist social and political movements as a Cold War-era legacy. From a somewhat different point of departure, Abrahamian argues that the political writings of Khomeini displayed many similarities with the concerns of classical Latin American populism, with their emphasis on the contradiction between the dispossessed and the wealthy, the oppressed and the powerful, replete with the petty bourgeois requirement of safeguarding private property against otherwise more revolutionary inclinations (Abrahamian 1991: 112–115). This is an important corrective to narratives of the Iranian Revolution that only emphasise its theocratic characteristics.

While the arguments made by Colas and Abrahamian are undoubtedly pertinent, it is useful to go a step further and specify the emergence, specifically, of a newer form of Islamic populism. As suggested in the Introduction, the newer type has been made possible by social transformations that are linked to the advance of the market economy and to the pressures of globalisation experienced in much of the Muslim world in recent decades but also the prior outcomes of Cold War-era social conflicts.

In the next chapter, an older type of Islamic populism is examined that was primarily concerned with safeguarding petty propertied urban and rural interests from encroachment by old and new competitors. For the adherents of the new Islamic populism, however, this older type is no longer adequate in light of the altered social bases of the *ummah* – understood in increasingly explicit terms as a mass of relatively disadvantaged but morally upright and virtuous 'ordinary people'. It is important too that today's Islamic populists are much less encumbered than their older counterparts by the presence of leftist rivals, who could have conceivably overtaken any impulse to seize state power or to reconfigure the distribution of wealth in the past in any meaningful manner.

Given the above considerations, it is useful to briefly outline the sorts of cross-class alliances concretely involved in underpinning the new Islamic populist project and some of their more prominent features especially in Indonesia, Egypt and Turkey. This outline serves as a point of reference for much of the empirical discussion that will follow.

The urban middle class

This is a social class that is commonly associated either with secular and liberal political agendas or with particular kinds of technocratic ideology. However, a major characteristic of the new Islamic populism is that it is often led by elements of the urban middle class, especially those that may be described as forming a kind of lumpen-intelligentsia (Roy 1994; Wickham 2002). The latter reference is to people with comparatively high levels of education but who find themselves stuck nonetheless in the lower tiers of the socio-economic and political hierarchy (Öniş 1997: 4; Roy 2004: 48; Dalacoura 2006: 511; Haklai 2009: 38). These sorts of individuals are often fixed to a social position that is typically only slightly better than that of the masses of the urban poor, a condition that has many possible deep implications relating to Laclau's notion of 'chains of equivalence'.

Roy, for instance, identifies culturally Muslim sections of the population who are the direct products of 'the modern education system' (rather than the result of traditional religious schools) and who hail from 'recently urbanized families or from the impoverished middle classes' (Roy 1994: 3). Again Roy portrays their social position as being very precarious, with downward social mobility always seemingly imminent. The lack of certainty is particularly acute where the short supply of viable employment opportunities appropriate to support middle-class lifestyles is a chronic condition. This is the case in Indonesia and much of the Middle East and North Africa, especially among young people, where unemployment and/or underemployment are usually at high levels. Official data on Indonesia, for example, suggests that a large portion of those classified as 'urban middle class' are only marginally better off than the poor. Their social position is precarious enough so that they can easily slip back into conditions of poverty (see data in Asian Development Bank 2010: 11).[11] Such is the case in spite of the acquisition of a host of credentials among many – made possible by the proliferation of mass education – that notionally promise ever-improving material life conditions as well as enhanced social prestige.

Despite this, Wickham has noted (2002: Chapter 3) that many of the individuals arising from the new urban middle class in Muslim-majority countries today cannot be expected to latch onto a liberal critique of despotism, unlike the prognostications of authors like Nasr (2009), or as might have been predicted in old-style modernisation theory. Instead, the reasons for this have been almost straightforwardly political, rather than cultural: they have to do with the outcomes of Cold War-era conflicts that resulted in a narrower spectrum of options with which to ideologically express dissent. It is no wonder that Bayat (2007: 6) observes how Islam 'has provided a means through which' some members of new middle class, in particular, 'can say "no" to what they considered their excluders – their national elites, secular governments ... and their Western allies'.

Such an observation is also relevant to Indonesia, where the new Islamic populism clearly is not confined to the bastions of rural tradition or those politically socialised via conventional religious educational institutions but through urban-based and largely informal structures, often found in the university or the high school. This is another reason why the advent of mass education that went along with economic development is particularly

---

[11] The precariousness of middle class-ness was seen quite dramatically during the Asian Economic Crisis of 1997–1998 when many professionals lost their jobs and had to pay inflated interest rates on their mortgages, leading many in large cities like Jakarta to try their luck as pedlars and hawkers in the informal sector.

important. Even today many lower middle-class youths in Indonesia are only newly urbanised because young villagers still have to move to increasingly urban environments to pursue education at progressively higher levels, given the absence of high schools, colleges and universities in many rural settings. The same observation can be transposed to Muslim-majority developing countries in the Middle East and North Africa.

The political socialisation of members of the middle class via experiences in the institutions of learning, including secular ones, is therefore of particular significance. It may be useful to illustrate this point by making a quick reference to the workings of the so-called *usroh* system that was put in place during the authoritarian New Order period in Indonesia,[12] within which 'senior' students in universities and high schools acted to discipline 'juniors' through the inculcation of Islamic precepts. It was the means through which a culture of obedience and loyalty to different Islamic movement leaders was nurtured. The system eventually served as the basis for the development of an important source of support for the PKS in the post-Soeharto democratic period (Hilmy 2010: 208). It also provided the recruiting ground for the student organisation KAMMI, or Joint Action of Indonesian Muslim Students (Machmudi 2006), closely linked to the PKS, which was a component of the student movement that was active in the anti-Soeharto demonstrations of 1998.

Moreover, it is notable that the *usroh* system adopted displayed the direct influence of the Egyptian Muslim Brotherhood, from where it was consciously borrowed by some of its purveyors in Indonesia. Not surprisingly, in Egypt too a similar system was in operation as a means of evading the long arm of state surveillance that began with the Nasser-era crackdowns on Islamic activists. In Indonesia, such a system became a necessity after the New Order began to turn from communist suppression to containing Islamic social organisations and movements in the 1970s and 1980s, therefore encouraging semi-clandestine forms of associational life among its activists.

The importance of such semi-clandestine forms of organisation is amplified when they take place in the midst of deep social changes. Thus we find internal transformations within organisations like the Muslim Brotherhood in Egypt mainly resulting from the changing composition of its membership. Rather than religious teachers and preachers coming from rural or semi-rural backgrounds – as in the cases of Hassan Al-Banna and Sayyid Qutb – many of its activists today are the product of the pervasive secular system of national education that was put in place during the time of Nasser. This education system has by now contributed significantly to the formation of a new educated and more ambitious urban middle class, some members of which came to find a

---

[12] The term *usroh* used in Indonesia – denoting a family – is usually transliterated into English from the Arabic as *usra*.

home in the Muslim Brotherhood to develop ideas and strategies of challenging an authoritarian state that stifled meritocratic advancement. Such developments partly explain how the Muslim Brotherhood was able to gain control of numerous professional 'syndicates' made up of engineers, doctors, lawyers and the like, before the Egyptian state clamped down forcefully on them in the 1990s.

In the same vein, it is evident that the leadership of the AKP in Turkey – a party which came to serve as a model for the Muslim Brotherhood-spawned Freedom and Justice Party in Egypt and a range of others following the Arab uprisings of 2011 – derives in great part from among professional sections of the middle class for whom traditional religious education was not an option due to official prohibitions. This is the case even if some may have gone through the so-called Imam Hatip secondary schools that were originally set up by the early Republican state to train new generations of imam (individuals who deliver religious sermons) and to replace formerly privately run and mosque-based institutions of learning.[13] In spite of their special function, the Imam Hatip schools teach a curriculum not so radically dissimilar to that of secular educational institutions.[14] Thus, the deeply secular nature of education in Turkey since the advent of the Republic ensures that many of the social agents of the new Islamic populism would have had comparatively little formal religious education, certainly less so than in the cases of their counterparts in Indonesia and Egypt.

The major point to be made, however, is that that new middle classes, educated but whose material conditions of life can be quite precarious, have emerged out of an economic modernisation process that has taken place throughout many parts of the Muslim world, even if in ways that can be both halting and highly contradictory. For such middle-class individuals some interpretations of Islam can provide a useful lens through which to understand the social world that they encounter and their place within it. They might also provide ways of imagining an alternative one that could be forged and which would be more accommodating to their interests and aspirations.

The bourgeoisie

Another important potential component of alliances that underpin the new Islamic populist project is the bourgeoisie. This may be surprising at first glance, given the social justice concerns that colour the rhetoric of populism

---

[13] See 'Turkey's Religious Schools Being Used as Model to Fight Islamic Extremism' (2010).
[14] No less than AKP founder and Turkish prime minister (and later president) Recep Tayyip Erdogan is proudly a graduate of the Imam Hatip system. Interview with Omer Faric Kalayci, deputy chair of Foreign Affairs, AKP, Istanbul, 13 October 2010, who happened to have attended the same Imam Hatip as Erdogan.

(though it might be useful to recall that many American multi-billionaires, like the brothers Koch, have been keen supporters of the Tea Party and other populist tendencies). But there is little doubt that new Islamic populism has grown to be more viable where it has successfully drawn on the support of sections of the capital-owning class. This has been the case, most clearly, in Turkey, where there has been a resurgent (and previously marginalised) Anatolian bourgeoisie, eager to forge the sort of links to state power that might enable them to overcome the dominance of the 'Kemalist' big businesses traditionally based in Istanbul (Yavuz 2006). Such is also the case to a large extent in Egypt, where a major pillar of the new Islamic populism has been businesses connected to the Muslim Brotherhood that had been facing increased state repression during the latter part of the Mubarak period. This was especially true after the movement's startling electoral successes in 2005 in spite of its illegal status.[15]

Compared to these cases, the Indonesian one is far more problematic in this respect for reasons having to do with a largely absent culturally Islamic big bourgeoisie and the long-held dominance of an ethnically Chinese one excluded from definitions of the *ummah*. It is no coincidence, from this vantage point, that it is also in the Indonesian case that the new Islamic populism has found more limited success than in Turkey or Egypt, in spite of the challenges or setbacks experienced in the latter countries.

In spite of the Indonesian experience, the stronger involvement of sections of the bourgeoisie in Turkey and Egypt in new Islamic populist alliances prominently displays how a major part of their objective is thoroughly modern and profane – to struggle for a system of power that would favour those roughly imagined as being synonymous with the long marginalised *ummah*. It is significant that the objective may be more realistically achieved without rejecting the capitalist economy or integration with globalisation processes, but through favourable repositioning within the existing state and the market. This idea will of course appeal to entrepreneurs and members of the middle class who would be fearful of large-scale social revolutions that might be driven especially by the interests and grievances of the poorest sections of society. So while there is typically intense criticism – much of it couched in moral terms – directed against Western capitalism and economic domination, whether in Indonesia, Turkey or Egypt – it is crucial that the new Islamic populism does not necessarily preclude capitalist accumulation as such. Instead, the concern is really about the exclusion of the *ummah* from taking part in the process on a larger scale.

It is therefore notable that in the case of Turkey, where the new Islamic populism has been most politically successful so far, the objective of the project

---

[15] See 'Muslim Inc: How Rich is Khairat El-Shater?' (2012) for a brief discussion of the matter.

has been defined strongly to exclude the aim of establishing an overtly Islamic state. This most overtly distinguishes the AKP government from the old Welfare Party (Refah)-led one of the mid-1990s which was under the control of the 'grand old man' of Turkish Islamic political struggles, the late Necmettin Erbakan. Heavily influenced by the Muslim Brotherhood's Qutb (Uslu 2011), Erbakan was much less favourably inclined towards global capitalism and possessed an economic vision that was more directed towards protecting petty commodity traders and producers from being trampled by big business, domestic or foreign.[16] The new Islamic populist alliance in Turkey today, however, as represented by the AKP, is in fact strongly wedded to neoliberal economic policies that intensify the engagement of the Turkish economy with global capitalism (see Tuğal 2009). This is so even as the rhetoric against Western economic domination is sometimes retained, partly as reply to the European Union's (EU) reluctance to embrace Turkey as one of its own. Thus leaders of the pro-AKP business association, MUSIAD (Independent Industrialists' and Businessmen's Association), can defiantly state that Turkey is economically in better shape now than the EU given the latest European economic crisis. Such is the case even if they realise that the advance of a culturally Muslim bourgeoisie in Turkey has been made possible by pro-globalisation and European-friendly economic policies.[17]

From this vantage point, the economic sensibilities associated with the Turkish new Islamic populism bring to mind the so-called Latin American neo-populism that was also aligned to neoliberal economic policy (e.g. Weyland 2003). Nevertheless, the merging of populism with neoliberalism (Öniş 2012) in the Turkish case is very much tied to specific kinds of social conflict that are rooted in the particular trajectory of its modernisation process. It is important to remember, for instance, that the struggles of the AKP inevitably involve sustained attacks on the bulwarks of Kemalism, especially within the state, something which sits well with the material interests of the Anatolian and more culturally Muslim bourgeoisie[18]

---

[16] Keddie (1994) notes, for example, the importance of the role of traders in modern Islamic 'revolts' from the eighteenth century throughout much of the Muslim world.
[17] Interview with Eyup Vural Aydin (MUSIAD secretary general) and Dr Hatice Karahan Pişkin (MUSIAD deputy secretary general), Istanbul, 20 September 2011.
[18] While the appearance of the Anatolian bourgeoisie obviously predates the political dominance of the party starting from 2002, it is to be expected that ties to the AKP have been a boon. MUSIAD is the business association established to represent the collective interests of this section of the bourgeoisie. It is the main rival of the business association linked closely to the old Istanbul-based bourgeoisie, TUSIAD (Turkish Industrialists' and Businessmen's Association). In addition, there is another business association, TUSKON (Turkish Confederation of Businessmen and Industrialists), connected to the enterprises of the so-called Fethulah Gülen movement, a *tariqa* that was known to be closely related to the AKP and which has grown substantially in wealth over the years (Yavuz and Esposito 2003). More recently, however, movement leaders have been in conflict with the AKP leadership under Erdogan, causing a major split in the alliance that had put the AKP into power.

It is also instructive that, in well-worn populist parlance, members of the rising Turkish bourgeoisie often suggest that their newfound influence can help to advance the 'common good' (Demir, Acar and Toprak 2004: 173). The obvious inference is that this common good was all but ignored by the secular Kemalist establishment due to an inherent rapacity and to a certain cultural aloofness from the generally devoutly religious population. Thus, the influential Turkish public commentator and social scientist Ihsan Dagi suggests precisely this sort of interpretation for the rise in popularity of the AKP.[19] It is significant, that while relegating to the background any serious public talk about an Islamic state based on Sharia, the proponents of the new Islamic populism in Turkey continue to espouse the virtues of conservative Islamic morality, as these remain important markers of an *ummah*-based political identity. Of course, this propensity has been partly induced by specifically Turkish political exigencies, namely constitutional constraints on religious parties as well as still vividly held social memories of the impact of Ataturk's state-imposed agenda of secularisation on organised religion. Nevertheless, it is clear that the exaltation of religious morality by the AKP, and therefore integrity (Öniş 2003), presents no hindrance to the joining together of more traditional concerns of Islamic populism (for issues of social justice and social solidarity) with a self-consciously more modern and cosmopolitan outlook that enthusiastically embraces, rather than disdains, engagement with global capitalism.

There have been new attempts to replicate the recent Turkish experience, especially in the initial aftermath of the Arab Spring, but these would call for a strong, disciplined and grassroots-based party that upholds Islamic values and empowers the *ummah* without resorting to a call for the establishment of an overtly Islamic state. Some of the most obvious attempts took place in Tunisia through the En Nahda Party and in Egypt through the Muslim Brotherhood, although their critics have always insisted that such an ultimate aim remains, even if it is left unstated.[20] In the latter case, it is apparent that businesses associated with the Muslim Brotherhood were developing a greater interest to embrace the economic opportunities presented by deeper integration into the

---

[19] Interview, Ankara, 22 October 2010. Besides teaching at the Middle East Technology Institute in Ankara, he is also a columnist for *Today's Zaman*, a newspaper widely considered to be sympathetic to Islamic political networks. At the same time, he repeats the AKP's claim, required to protect itself from a fate similar to that of Erbakan's Welfare (Refah) Party, that Erdogan's vehicle is not 'Islamic' but merely 'conservative'.

[20] Indeed, it might be said that at the grassroots level, the activists of organisations like the Muslim Brotherhood are less reticent than their leaders about a longing for an Islamic state. Two such activists, coalescing with an 'alliance of anti-coup students' following the fall of Morsi, suggest that their ideal remains the establishment of a state based on Sharia, 'though this will not be imposed' and only undertaken when people become aware of the virtues of such a state. Interview with University of Cairo engineering students (names withheld for their own safety), Cairo, 13 December 2014. Also see Hamid (2014: 55–56).

world economy, in spite of lingering concerns about their potential morally detrimental effects. In the Egyptian context, it was clear that these opportunities would be best realised if the business conglomerates associated with the old Mubarak regime and its NDP (National Democratic Party) could be dislodged from the overwhelmingly dominant position they have occupied for decades.

Thus, it was widely reported that the Freedom and Justice Party was in favour of 'free-market capitalism, but without manipulation or monopoly'.[21] While such a formulation of what the party stood for, before its fall from power in 2013, signalled strong opposition to Mubarak-era cronyism and corruption, it said nothing about resistance to private accumulation or to integration with global markets in principle. Thus, businessman and key Muslim Brotherhood financier Hassan Malek argued that 'manufacturing, a trained labour force and enabling the private sector' are the keys to reviving the Egyptian economy. Suggesting that Mubarak's market policies were already 'on the right track', he once declared that Muslim Brotherhood businesses aimed to grow bigger given the removal of the political obstacles that had once hindered them.[22] Quite instructively, Khairat El-Shater – a major businessman in his own right – was number two in the organisation and considered its major driving force. Still, the euphoria expressed by the likes of Malek has naturally subsided following the subsequent overthrow of the Muslim Brotherhood-led government under President Morsi just a year after it won the right to govern. A key issue, therefore, is how the sudden fall from power will affect the economic vision and ambitions of the business community that had been nurtured under the auspices of the Muslim Brotherhood.

In Indonesia, however, Islamic-oriented parties and movements can only dream of the sort of capitalist social order that might actually side with the interests of members of the *ummah*. Although a newer so-called *pribumi* (indigenous), and therefore, culturally more Muslim section of the bourgeoisie had emerged in the latter part of the Soeharto dictatorship (Sidel 2006: 53–54), it was neither deeply-rooted in existing Islamic social and political networks nor in any position to challenge the dominant and ethnically Chinese business conglomerates. In fact, the leading lights of the New Order-era *pribumi* bourgeoisie were Soeharto's own children, close relatives and various assorted cronies. This was so in spite of the much heralded rise of a section of state elites connected with an entity called the Indonesian Association of Muslim Intellectuals (ICMI) in the 1990s, under Soeharto's sponsorship (Hefner 1993) and which was supposed to advance the socio-economic and political position of the *ummah*.

---

[21] See El-Wardani (2011), for a brief discussion of the party's position.
[22] See the discussion of his views in Awad (2011).

Notwithstanding the absence of a big Muslim bourgeoisie in Indonesia, members of the PKS continue to be inspired by the AKP route to power.[23] As discussed later in this book, PKS members also do not display innate hostility towards private capital accumulation although they invariably reiterate the necessity of eradicating the practice of *riba* or usury as a matter of religious faith – and the injunction to pay *zakat* (alms).[24] In fact, the rather formalistic obsession with usury is not just found strongly in Indonesia but also in places like Egypt, Tunisia and Morocco, where Islamic business and political figures are prone to speak of the virtues of notionally *riba*-free Islamic banking.[25] The implications of this matter for the reconceptualisation of the interests of the *ummah* in relation to processes of neoliberal globalisation are considered further in Chapter 8.

The urban poor

Finally, we should now turn our attention to the role of that other important constituent of potentially successful new Islamic populist cross-class alliances: the urban poor. Their ranks have typically swelled in a number of Muslim-majority societies, as the same capitalist modernisation process that produces larger and more diversified middle classes and bourgeoisie transforms the socio-economic landscape. In Egypt, for example, it was recently estimated that no less than 16 million people inhabit vast urban sprawls, especially in ever-expanding Greater Cairo, living under enormously appalling conditions.[26] Significantly, where peripheralised sections of the urban middle class and bourgeoisie have managed to combine with large sections of the disorganised urban poor, the result can be a kind of populism that powerfully harnesses cross-class anxieties and frustrations to a politics of Islamic identity (Hadiz and Robison 2012).

After all, it is in relation to the hard-pressed urban poor of the sprawling cities and towns of the Muslim world that the new Islamic populism is most visibly a response to the contradictions of modernisation and to neoliberal globalisation. Given the harsh circumstances of everyday life in these urban

---

[23] For example, see Bubalo, Fealy and Mason (2008: 71–72). Influential PKS secretary general and future president Anis Matta is described here as expressing great interest in studying the success of the AKP, which he attributes to adeptness in combining Islam with political and economic competence or credibility.

[24] Interview with Rama Pratama, PKS Economic Section, 14 July 2010.

[25] Interview with Emad Hamdi, stockbrocker and civil society activist and Ahmed Salah, researcher and civil society activist, Cairo, 20 March 2011; Ihab El Fouly, Muslim Brotherhood-linked businessman and adviser to Khairat El-Shater, Heliopolis, 4 April 2012; Interview with Amine Makkaoui and Slim Hajji, League of Young Engineers, Tunis, 17 April 2013; Interview with Abdeslam Ballaji, PJD (Justice and Development Party) member of Moroccan parliament, Rabat, 24 April 2013.

[26] See the discussion in Khalifa (2013).

social formations, it is easy to envisage how a social milieu can emerge that is conducive to the forging of solidarities and self-identities based on religion, particularly among young and poor urbanites with commonly bleak futures (Berman and Rose 2006). This is the case especially given the earlier elimination of the Left as a viable force in most Muslim-majority societies. It is because of this historical legacy, no doubt, that Sidel (2006: 52) suggests that advancing industrialisation under the New Order had created an 'urban and suburban underclass' available for mobilisation – not as a class-conscious proletariat – but as members of a broader *ummah*. A new Islamic populist alliance channels the aspirations and grievances of this section of society in directions defined by solidarity based on being part of a nationally composed *ummah* – whose members are all notionally victimised by predatory elites who have long presided over the secular nationalist state.

In fact similar experiences are found in many other parts of the Muslim world today. In Colas's work on the Maghreb, for example, it is put forward that social contradictions sharpened particularly after the phase of state-led, resource-based industrialisation was superseded by compliance to the dictates of neoliberal economic globalisation in the 1980s. In this case, hostility quickly emerged among the urban poor towards austerity measures undertaken in line with such dictates, as they typically involved acquiescence to structural adjustment policies promoted by international development organisations. Thus, Colas (2004: 237–238) evocatively suggests that 'a highly alienated generation of Algerians epitomised in the figure of the *hittiste*' – a term describing 'young urban men who prop up walls' while 'listlessly watching life passing them by' – became increasingly prevalent amidst declining general living conditions and worsening unemployment. At the same time, the economically liberalising governments such as that of Chedli Benjedid in Algeria (1979–1992) had given rise to a 'political-financial mafia' and 'a new capitalist *nomenklatura*' (Colas 2004: 237) widely detested by these same young people.

This finding is supported by the work of Lubeck (1998), who suggests that an environment was created in many Muslim-majority societies in the 1970s and 1980s for Islamic-oriented organisations to make inroads with the poor because many governments had retreated from providing key social services to reduce state expenditure. As he describes for a variety of cases, Islamist movements gained ground through civil society organisations that took over the delivery of these much-needed social services. As the poor became more and more reliant on the provision of basic goods and services by religious charities and organisations (Lubeck 1998: 299), they came to form a major constituency for the new Islamic populism, given the narrowing of possible ideologies of dissent as a result of Cold War-related social conflicts both in the Middle East and in Indonesia. In Iran, where the fall of Mossadegh in the 1950s had signalled the beginning of a round of concerted attacks on the Left, labour did regroup following the expansion of the working class resulting from the subsequent spread of capitalist relations under the Shah's modernisation policies (Halliday 1988). It even contributed to the broad-based movement that coalesced under Khomeini and which toppled the Shah. However, leftists within the movement were to be 'disarmed' by the Islamic populism of the new regime which succeeded in gather considerable support among workers (Moghadam 1987: 153) who found enough that was appealing in the espoused social justice aims of the Islamic Republic.

Significantly, it is not that easy to separate the proletariat-proper and the so-called lumpenproletariat in the contexts in question, in spite of the battle lines drawn up in the debate between Zizek and Laclau (Butler, Laclau and Zizek 2000) about their respective and distinctive 'historical' roles. Of course, traditional Marxist theory regards the lumpenproletariat as being most vulnerable to political manipulation by enemies of the working class, as Zizek continues to argue. But because rural–urban migration is a continuing process in developing societies, much of today's urban poor will have in common the fact they are not too far removed from those that had arrived from the villages, regardless of mode of employment. As one can easily slide back and forth between the proletariat and lumpenproletariat in labour surplus and neoliberalised economies, it may not be promising to invest either with rigidly opposing political attitudes. On the most heavily populated and economically developed Indonesian island of Java, for example, these migrations take place in relation to the associated process of 'urbanisation of the rural' (Young 1994) – a feature of social and economic change which assures diminishing cultural differences attached to urban and rural life experiences due to changes in the material conditions of existence in the village itself. For much of the recently urbanised poor, changing rural circumstances had facilitated their transition to urban life in the first place (Hadiz 1997).

But it is in Turkey again where the absorption of the urban poor into the populist alliance has been achieved with a relatively high degree of success. The social and political networks that are intertwined with the AKP are well known to have made inroads with the urban poor through concerted activities involving the provision of a range of social services and the fulfilment of some of their more immediate economic needs.[27] These efforts have been even internationalised, with humanitarian relief organisations in operation that are widely considered to be closely associated with the AKP[28] and with the Gülen movement, servicing Turkey as well as many other parts of the world.[29] In Egypt, notable successes on

---

[27] Interview with Sadi Yazici, Mayor of Tuzla Municipality, in Istanbul, 12 October 2010.
[28] Interview with Husein Oruc, vice president of the Board of Trustees of IHH (Humanitarian Relief Foundation), in Istanbul, 15 October 2010. This organisation famously organised the flotilla that had intended to breach Israel's blockade of Gaza by bringing in food and medicine.
[29] Interview with Metin Çetiner, director of Protocol Relations, Kimse Yok Mu, Istanbul, 15 September 2011.

this front were achieved under conditions of harsh authoritarianism. After all, it was the initial experience of the Muslim Brotherhood that had provided the blueprint for strategies around the world to mobilise political support for the Islamic cause through grassroots activities directed at the poor, including in such area as health care. Here, for example, there is an established tradition of middle-class doctors working part time for hospitals and clinics established by the organisation, usually in low-income urban neighbourhoods.[30]

In the Indonesian case, Sidel (2006) has also reiterated the consequence of colonial policies that had privileged minority Christians and ethnic Chinese in terms of educational attainment and material conditions of life. It is therefore important that, to many, the impressive levels of economic growth generated under Soeharto seemed to accentuate existing social cleavages based on class and ethnicity due to the overt rise of very wealthy Chinese business conglomerates (Robison 1986). Thus the desperation of the poorest, especially in the cities and towns, gelled to some degree with the still frustrated aspirations of Indonesia's new upwardly mobile educated and professionals. Moreover, traditional antipathy found in the broader public towards the role of the Chinese in the Indonesian economy became easily combined with hostility towards members of top politico-bureaucratic families who had also effectively utilised state connections to transform themselves into successful capitalists, the most prominent being the children of President Soeharto himself. The situation has not been rectified given the continually ascendant position of the ethnic Chinese bourgeoisie and their ability to reposition themselves within newly forged alliances in the post-authoritarian period (Chua 2008).

It is in the Indonesian case too that the urban poor have been drawn into the new Islamic populist coalition in the least convincing manner. Like the North African and Middle East cases, the violent destruction of the Left (taking place in Indonesia in the 1960s) has surely meant a dearth of leftist vehicles available to the new urban poor, in spite of vehicles associated with the originally student-based Democratic People's Party (PRD) and its affiliates (Lane 2008). However, the Indonesian case also displays the factor of Soekarnoist populism – as preserved in milder forms by successor organisations to the old PNI (Indonesian National Party), especially the PDI-P (Indonesian Democratic Party for Struggle) led by Soekarno's own daughter, former president Megawati Soekarnoputri. These have often challenged Islamic incursions into the urban poor constituency, even during the late Soeharto era, when the PDI-P was a major platform for broad-based opposition to the New Order.

Importantly, the equivalent of Indonesian Soekarnoism – Egyptian Nasserism – had been so compromised by Mubarak that its major vehicles

---

[30] See Clarke (2004) for an exposition of how these activities have also benefited the middle-class actors involved in them.

failed to become a focal point of opposition to authoritarian rule all the way to the outbreak of mass protests most visible in Cairo's iconic Tahrir Square. In the period after Morsi was deposed, Nasserists continue to struggle to re-establish their political relevance and regain long-lost bases of support within society, especially among the poor.[31] In Turkey, the problem is that the dominant forms of nationalist and secular populism have been distinctly statist and closely linked to the Kemalist establishment, although the dramatic escalation of public opposition to AKP rule during the Gezi Park demonstrations of mid-2013 clearly showed a level of discontent that has been largely politically dormant until then. It might be added that in the Indonesian case, Golkar – the old electoral vehicle of the New Order – had also helped to hinder new Islamic populist incursions into the urban poor. In spite of its own highly statist character, Golkar did develop affiliated organisations and grassroots networks that tended to limit the space within civil society where Islamic social agents could freely operate.

Conclusion

This chapter has explored the utility of understanding modern struggles waged under the banner of Islam from the vantage point of the emergence of a new Islamic populism in many Muslim-majority societies in recent decades. Such a development is related to the resurgence of broader populist responses emanating from around the world that have been critical of the socio-political and economic consequence of neoliberal globalisation. In the process, the chapter also explored the relevance of more fundamental debates about the nature of populist politics to an understanding of the forging of the new Islamic populism in Indonesia and elsewhere.

The discussion has suggested that the new Islamic populism has achieved only varying levels of success. This means that the potential for the cross-class alliances that underpin the new Islamic populism is not always fully realised. But even when a strong basis for such alliances is established, does the new Islamic populism pose a direct threat to existing secular orders? Certainly, many of the social agents of the new Islamic populism have put forward the idea of establishing some sort of ideal society guided by Sharia. It should be noted too, however, that there has been a significant degree of malleability in the pursuit of this aim. Therefore, there is a strong possibility that the 'relations of domination' (Mouzelis 1985) that characterise secular social orders in the Muslim world can be reorganised– to include advancing the social, economic

---

[31] Interview with Ahmed Kamel Elbahery, Cairo, 15 December 2014. He was the spokesman for the Nasserist candidate, Hamdeen Sabahy, during his presidential campaigns in 2012 and 2014 as well as a co-founder of the new Nasserist vehicle, the Popular Current Party.

Conclusion

and political position of the *ummah* –without necessarily instituting radical changes on state–society relationships or between the national and global economies.

A key argument put forward is that understanding the new Islamic populism requires analysis of the historical and sociological circumstances that made its emergence and development possible. This necessitates scrutiny of the way in which multi- or cross-class alliances are concretely built, or attempted, and the struggles that forge them, a task which cannot be achieved exclusively through discursive analysis *à la* Laclau. For this reason, the next chapter addresses the historical genesis of Islamic populism in Indonesia, highlighting points of convergence and divergence especially with the cases of Turkey and Egypt. In the process, the confluence of factors involved in the emergence and evolution of Islamic populism in these countries is underscored.

3 The genesis of Islamic populism
Historical legacies

The new Islamic populism owes much to its direct precursor: the more traditional form that was predominantly petty bourgeois in its social base and leadership. This older Islamic populism must also be placed in historical and sociological context; in most societies it was mainly a response to pressures on petty urban traders and commodity producers and rural elites imposed by a Western-dominated colonial order that had characterised much of the world outside of Europe and North America by the turn of the twentieth century. As Western colonialism brought in new forms of production, trade networks and even political authority, the social position of the traditional urban and rural petty bourgeoisie had become increasingly precarious across much of the Muslim world.

The political agenda of the older form of Islamic populism was therefore largely defensive, to forestall the rapid disappearance of the social world of its main constituency. From this point of view, the assertion of the aim of establishing an Islamic state was mainly a defensive measure rather than one that reflected growing self-confidence. Significantly, the anxieties of the traditional petty bourgeoisie found equivalence, to borrow the term from Laclau (2005), with the trials and tribulations of ordinary workers and rural folk who could be conceived as being part of a broader *ummah* that was being just as systematically marginalised by Western incursions. This perceived condition of systemic social marginalisation, it is suggested here, accounts for the highly egalitarian rhetoric of colonial-era Islamist organisations and their focus on social justice issues. Such marginalisation of the *ummah* was juxtaposed, in populist mode, against those regarded as benefiting from an unfair, and therefore immoral, social order, including the perceived local agents of Western colonialism. In Indonesia, this prominently included the ethnic Chinese minority. It is notable that this sort of rhetorical content has continued to feature in the political discourse of the newer form of Islamic populism even if the latter has developed in an age shaped by the more complex imperatives of globalisation than by the naked ambitions of colonialism.

Not surprisingly, Islamic politics in the early twentieth century would intermingle closely with concurrently growing nationalist sentiments in many parts of the Muslim world, which was also a response to the growing sense of colonial injustices. As heirs to this legacy, it is not surprising that Islamic populists today see no necessary contradiction between their allegiance to the *ummah* and to the nation[1], as pointed out in the previous chapter.[2]

In spite of concerns that were already becoming more 'nationally' directed with the rise of anti-colonial movements, the older Islamic populism initially developed out of the Pan-Islamist tendency that had arisen across the Muslim world from North Africa through South Asia to the Dutch East Indies, which offered the vision of an alternative world order based on Islamic unity across the globe. By promising to empower the global *ummah*, the Pan-Islamic vision was ultimately about returning Muslims to an almost mythical age of glory. It was no surprise then that the promise emerged most strongly when the internally decrepit Ottoman Caliphate was already standing on its last legs (Formichi 2010). But this close relationship did not hinder the involvement of Islamic movements in nationally focussed independence struggles.

It is also significant that such a vision co-existed, and was disseminated almost concurrently, with another internationalist alternative that was being offered to the oppressed peoples of the colonial world by socialist and communist insurgents, especially following the success of the Bolshevik Revolution of 1917. Indeed socialist or socialist-like ideas permeated through a host of fledgling anti-colonial movements, including those arising within Muslim-majority societies, in spite of their common association with irreligious and even atheistic worldviews. Such a global environment arguably contributed as well to the highly egalitarian and pro-social justice dispositions that permeated through the political rhetoric of the older Islamic populism and which have been inherited by many of their counterparts today. In Indonesia, Sarekat Islam leader Haji Agus Salim, for example, wished for a political order that would bring about 'happiness and equality' and exhorted the powerful to help 'the weak' and 'the less capable' (Noer 1963: 197). Similar sentiments featured strongly too within the Egyptian Muslim Brotherhood during the era of British domination, including in its mobilisations of the working class.

In fact, Muslim political thinkers have long drawn from a repertoire of idioms originating from other political traditions when these help to address

---

[1] Interestingly, even some individuals regarded to have links with regional or global movements to establish a new caliphate uniting Muslims see value in national allegiances. For example, interview with Abdul Rohim, spokesman for the Jamaah Anshorut Tauhid (JAT), Ngruki, Sukoharjo, Solo, 12 July 2011. He is the son and widely regarded heir apparent to Abubakar Ba'asyir, alleged one-time spiritual leader of the Jemaah Islamiyah (ICG 2002) in Indonesia/Southeast Asia.

[2] Interview with Jusuf Supendi, a leading figure of the Tarbiyah movement that led to the establishment of the PK and then the PKS, Jakarta, 6 July 2011. He argues in no uncertain terms that 'nationalism is part of Islam' and that 'nationalism is neither contradictory nor superior to Islam'.

the challenges being faced by the *ummah*. As Tripp (2006: 7) cogently observed, such thinkers have been concerned '...like the early Christian socialists, utopian socialists, anarchists and Marxists, to identify not simply the injustice underpinning capitalist practice' but also the processes through which capitalism derives its power. Some have been interested too in '...contributing to its undoing'. Because of this, a range of Muslim intellectuals over time have been influenced by critiques of capitalism that originate from different political traditions.

In turn, the egalitarian and anti-colonial outlook adopted made it possible for some of the older manifestations of Islamic populism to gain inroads into nascent working-class movements, as the Muslim Brotherhood in Egypt notably did, as well as the Sarekat Islam in Indonesia in the early decades of the twentieth century. Such was the case in spite of the basically petty bourgeois origins of the leadership of Islamic populist movements at the time. As a consequence, however, they intersected and sometimes clashed with left-wing tendencies well after the end of the era of Western colonial domination, battling them over the allegiance of overlapping social constituencies. Such battles would reach their peak as they met with the imperatives of the Cold War that spread across the globe.

While the above description summarises the early experiences of Islamic populism in the cases of Indonesia and Egypt, the case of Turkey, never colonised by a Western power, displays some divergent features. Here a new culturally Muslim petty bourgeoisie, spread across the towns and countryside of the Anatolian hinterland, were emerging in the early twentieth century but had to consolidate their position in society before being able to assert themselves politically and economically. It was at this time that Muslim merchants took over the vacant positions in the economic field left by displaced Greeks, Armenians and Jews, along with their physical property, in the midst of the tumultuous population swaps of the period, instigated by the state (see Keyder 1987: especially Chapters 4 and 5; and Mardin 2006: 75–77).[3] In this sense, the petty bourgeoisie owed much of its existence to the state, not just of the Republican era but also of the Young Turks period. Significantly, however, they were to find themselves largely marginal to the requirements of the economically and politically centralising new nation-building project of the Turkish Republic, especially in the way it was implemented from the 1930s.

In spite of such caveats, Islamic populism was, in large part, the ideological expression of the interests of petty bourgeoisie clinging to a precarious social position, struggling under commonly inhospitable circumstances, both during

---

[3] This generation of petty bourgeoisie was therefore rather distinctive from the stratum of merchants and craftsmen that had emerged by the late nineteenth century in some localities, culturally Muslim but linked closely with provincial notables – and whose trajectory, in general terms – constituted a virtual sociological dead end (Mardin 2006: 66–67).

and immediately after the age of global Western colonial domination. In all of these cases too, there are continuities – as well as breaks owing largely to changing social bases of support – between the form of populism born of the old colonial world order and the more recent one, still being shaped in an age of neoliberal globalisation. It is true that the newer form of Islamic populism is in large part a response to the challenges posed by further capitalist advance and closer integration with the global economy to different Muslim-majority societies, as well as the social contradictions that have ensued in the process. Nevertheless, this chapter shows that it has inherited the concern for protecting the socio-economic position of the *ummah*, expressed in references to social justice issues, which had been the main characteristic of the predecessor form of Islamic populism.

Historical antecedents: Indonesia and Egypt

Authors as varied as Rodinson (1966 [2007]) and Nasr (2009) have explored the claim of incompatibility of Islam and capitalism (also see Introvigne 2006: 23–48, specifically on Turkey) from different theoretical standpoints. In doing so, they have basically tackled issues that were first raised by Max Weber's (1978) classic exposition on the relationship between religion and economic behaviour. But it is useful to eschew over-generalisation and understand the responses of those adhering to the Islamic religion to the advance of capitalism in their specific historical contexts. It is not surprising that such responses have logically vacillated over time along with the particular tensions and contradictions accompanying social change and issues of political exigency. This can be seen clearly when comparing the genesis of Islamic populism in Indonesia and Egypt.

It is significant, for example, that the propagandists of the Sarekat Islam in the Dutch East Indies – the precursor to modern Indonesia – spoke out strongly against 'sinful capitalism' (McVey 1965 [2006]: 24), not just on the basis of religious injunctions against usury and the like, but because of the widely held perception of its exploitative and socially marginalising character. One of the most highly respected leaders of the Sarekat Islam, future Indonesian foreign minister Haji Agus Salim, went so far as to state, quite remarkably, that everything that was in Karl Marx's thinking was already contained in the Koran, even the idea of dialectical materialism (McVey 1965 [2006]: 104). But of course Haji Agus Salim, born to a family of West Sumatran local elites and the son of a colonial-era official of the judiciary, was no rabid revolutionary. Interestingly, his comments seem to have been made to thwart growing competition from leftists for leadership of the nascent anti-colonial movement as much as they were directed against the colonial state.

As a matter of fact, it is evident that the class base of petty bourgeois-dominated Islamic populism, in the Dutch East Indies and elsewhere in the

Muslim world, virtually guaranteed that its social agents would be averse to the sort of revolutionary changes that could have wiped out their own claims to private property, in spite of moral admonitions typically expressed about the excessive drive to collect worldly possessions associated with capitalism. The social agents of Islamic populism, old and new, have therefore stopped short of the kind of project that would call for the radical redistribution of wealth and power, certainly one based on common claims to property. Rather than by a classless society, social justice would be guaranteed by the promulgation of a state based on Sharia that would raise the social position of a deprived *ummah*. In the Indonesian case, such sentiments infused a number of vehicles, including the Muhammadiyah, a reformist organisation run by urban traders and petty commodity producers that advocated the inculcation of personal piety through modern educational methods (Lapidus 2002: 663).[4]

However, anti-colonial struggles in the Dutch East Indies were hardly dominated for long by the social agents of Islam populism, except for a small window of history before the rise of Indonesian communism and of subsequently more powerful secular-nationalist tendencies. In 1921, the Sarekat Islam broke up on the basis of the two 'wings' that had been developing their own distinctive characteristics. Thus, the Indonesian Communist Party (PKI) was partially born out of the so-called red wing of the SI, which was opposed to the white wing associated with people like Agus Salim and the propagandist and novelist Abdoel Moeis (McVey 1965 [2006]: 115).

Out of the red wing emerged such idiosyncratic historical luminaries as Haji Misbach. The son of a batik merchant in Solo, Central Java, he once declared that it was impossible to be a true Muslim without being a communist simultaneously and vice-versa (1925). But the red wing's main leader was the youthful Semaoen – initially an employee of the tram service in Surabaya, East Java – and a direct political protégé of the Dutch revolutionary Henk Sneevliet (Shiraishi 1990). The latter was actively agitating against the colonialism practised by his home country in the Indies in the 1910s. After being expelled from the Sarekat Islam, Semaoen became chairman of the PKI.

Given subsequent conflict between the social agents of Islamic and communist movements, it is worth pointing out that the 'Muslim-as-communist' or leftist was not yet a sociological oddity at this historical juncture. While it might be hard to envisage today, Muslim communists and assorted leftists were

---

[4] See Deliar Noer's (1963) classic exposition on the rise of Islamic reformism and modernism in the Dutch East Indies in the early twentieth century. He notes the schism between Sarekat Islam and Muhammadiyah in the later 1920s, whose membership had earlier intersected significantly – notably in the person of Agus Salim (also see Feillard and Madinier 2010: 20). The main source of schism was apparently Muhammadiyah's rapid expansion in the latter half of that decade, seen to be due to its acceptance of subsidies and assistance from the colonial government, which the Sarekat Islam leadership considered to be an 'a-nationalist' or 'anti-nationalist' act (Noer 1963: 387).

historically important in the Dutch East Indies where anti-colonial stirrings inspired to different degrees by Pan-Islamism, and socialist or communist ideas, were simultaneously appearing as responses to the social injustices of the colonial order. Thus, the celebrated Indonesian communist leader Tan Malaka,[5] who eventually broke ranks with the communist mainstream, famously supported the position that the international communist movement should align itself with Pan-Islamism (Malaka 1922). The point to be made here is that the historical and sociological roots of Islamic politics in Indonesia are extremely rich and complex, and it even included significant intermingling with leftist political currents at its inception. The result was to reinforce the pro-social justice and egalitarian tendencies in the Islamic populist vocabulary, and induce the petty bourgeoisie to move out of its relatively confined shell, if only out of the continual necessity to compete with the Left in establishing grass-roots support.

So in Indonesia, the red wing of the Sarekat Islam particularly embraced the necessity of organising elements of society that lay outside of traditional local elites, whether in petty bourgeois or minor aristocratic circles. These included transport sector and dockworkers and the rural proletariat who toiled in the plantations that were so crucial to the sustainability of the colonial-era economy. In fact, some individuals who clearly lay outside of the red wing of the Sarekat Islam were also active in organising colonial-era workers; an eminent example is Soerjopranoto, the Javanese aristocrat who painstakingly helped to organise strike action among sugar plantation workers in the 1920s (Shiraishi 1990).

It makes sense then that Java's Haji Misbach and West Sumatra's Haji Datuk Batuah (Anwar 2004) – both advocates of 'Islamic Communism' (McVey 2009) – were a sociological possibility and historical reality in the Dutch East Indies. Like Misbach, the less well-known Batuah was ardently opposed to Dutch rule, and furthermore, is credited with introducing communism to the region's historically important Thawalib community (Noer 1963: 73).[6] When rebellions broke out against the Dutch in West Sumatra as well as in Banten (on the Western end of Java island) in 1926–1927, led by religious leaders who announced their communist aspirations (Williams 2009; Zed 2004), that community was significantly involved. Given such a background, it is perhaps understandable that, inspite of the tense rivalries between Islamic populist

---

[5] See his political journey as masterfully depicted by Poeze (1999).
[6] Still active today, the Thawalib community promoted a 'reformist' brand of Islam in West Sumatra in the early twentieth century, influence by developments in the Middle East. A luminary of the community's school system was the father of the highly respected religious scholar Haji Abdul Karim Amarullah (known later as Buya Hamka) (see '*Perguruan Thawalib Padang Panjang*', http://thawalibppanjang1911.blogspot.com/). Indonesian political scientist Deliar Noer (1963: 72–73) qualified the 'communist' label, however, by suggesting that it tended to be applied to people who were the most radically opposed to Dutch colonialism rather than who necessarily adhered to 'historical materialism'.

forces and radical leftists subsequently, some members of later generations of the PKI were still able to conceive of themselves as being simultaneously Muslim and communist (see, for example, Raid 2001).[7] Nevertheless, the emergence of individuals such as these is not exactly unique to Indonesia or even necessarily to that tumultuous period of world history when all sorts of new political crossbreeds may have appeared possible, even if temporarily.

It is often forgotten, for example, because of the obsession with all things racial in Malaysia (and Singapore) today, that Muslims-as-communists also existed in the Malayan Peninsula when Malay Muslims contributed to the armed anti-colonial struggles of a Chinese-dominated Malayan Communist Party during the so-called Emergency.[8] Roff (2009: 125) also notes the existence of a radical Left Malay National Party (MNP) in the 1940s whose following included many *ulama*. This Emergency notably spanned the late period of British colonialism as well as several years of the early history of post-colonial Malaysia, which were dominated politically by the traditional aristocracy. Later, in another part of the world, the leftist Mujahideen Khalq – an Islamic organisation in Iran greatly influenced by communist ideals – played a major role in ensuring the success of the Islamic Revolution in Iran of 1979. This was before more overtly pro-Khomeini forces violently turned against the group once they had achieved a common victory over the Western-backed and highly unpopular regime of the last Shah, Reza Pahlevi. For years, these Islamic 'quasi-Marxists' constituted a major oppositional group against the Islamic Republic.[9]

The attempt by Islamic social and political movements to make incursions into labour-organising during the colonial period was also not unique to Indonesia. The Muslim Brotherhood in Egypt, as mentioned, had similarly developed support among the country's peri-urban and rural workers, eventually forming a section dedicated especially to workers by 1944 (Beinin and Lockman 1998: 367). This is in spite of an Egyptian colonial-era economic profile that was, like that of the Dutch East Indies, only characterised by a very limited degree of industrialisation and in which small-scale employers predominated in the manufacturing sector (Hadiz 1997: Chapter 3; Beinin and Lockman 1998: 37–40).

In gathering such support, the Muslim Brotherhood may have been motivated by sympathy for the plight of workers and the intention to improve their

---

[7] This work is the autobiography of a long time PKI member who considers himself a Muslim as well as a communist. In his PhD thesis, written in a time of great tension between some Islamic and communist-affiliated organisations, Noer (1963: 1–2) was still able to remind his readers that Muslims were found among radical leftists in the early twentieth century and that many members of the PKI continued to be Muslims.

[8] See, for example, the memoirs of Maidin (2005) and Abdullah (2005).

[9] See Abrahamian (2009) and Hooglund (1992) for relevant analyses.

material as well as spiritual lives (Beinin and Lockman 1998: 364), even if the organisation's leadership was predominantly petty bourgeois in social origin. Its founder, for example, the still highly revered Hassan Al-Banna, was born in the town of Mahmuddiya to a family headed by a religious teacher who was also proprietor of a watch repair shop (Mitchell 1993: 1). The other most well-known Muslim Brotherhood figure, the ideologue Sayyid Qutb, was a member of a family of medium-scale landowners – originally from the village of Musha, in the Upper Egypt province of Asyut – whose economic fortunes had been steadily in decline since the turn of the twentieth century (Calvert 2010: 25–27). Thus, much like the white wing of the SI in Indonesia, the Muslim Brotherhood was against communist ideas because of their penchant for creating discord *within* the *ummah,* by pitting Muslims against one another in class conflict (Beinin and Lockman 1998: 365). In response, the organisation projected itself as the defender of the interests of the *ummah* as a whole, even if it was actually driven in the main by the interests of the declining colonial-era petty bourgeoisie.

Nevertheless, the account that the Muslim Brotherhood began with Al-Banna's activities with a small group of workers at the Suez Canal town of Ismailia, helping them to gain religious knowledge (Soage and Franganillo 2010: 39), and thereby free themselves from corrupting Western influences, is highly celebrated. Al-Banna was no doubt thoroughly disgusted by the presence of British soldiers, the Suez Company and the blatant inequalities in the conditions of life between the Westerner and the Egyptians who toiled there (Mitchell 1993: 9). He came to believe that the social order dominated by British interests and that of their domestic allies, such as within the monarchy, was perpetuating the sad state of the *ummah* in Egypt (Rutherford 2008: 79).

Driven by such convictions, the Muslim Brotherhood gradually became a serious presence in the nascent Egyptian labour movement. At the same time, the organisation challenged the dominant position of assorted leftists, communists and more liberal Wafd sympathisers within the early labour struggles of Egypt (Beinin and Lockman 1998: 368–374). In basic terms, however, the Muslim Brotherhood substituted solidarity premised on the concept of the *ummah* for any inclination towards class conflict. In fact, for Al-Banna and his early followers, foreign corporations operating on Egyptian soil were exploitative and generally malevolent because they were operating in un-Islamic fashion (Beinin and Lockman 1998: 388), rather than because they were capitalist and therefore inherently exploitative. Not surprisingly, many of his present-day political heirs, as we shall see more clearly, have no fundamental problems with capitalism as such but strive to ensure that members of the *ummah* have more control over Egyptian capitalism in particular.

In both Indonesia and Egypt, however, Islamic movements came to lose their pre-eminence during further struggles leading to the formation of independent national states. In Indonesia, those who came out of Islamic social and political associations were notably unsuccessful in imposing a more discernibly Islamic stamp on the post-Independence Constitution (Boland 1971: Chapters 1 and 2), even after prolonged wrangling that famously lasted well into the 1950s (Nasution 1995). They also failed to exert pressure to push the state in the direction of cultivating a strong 'indigenous' and Muslim bourgeoisie, in order to challenge ethnic Chinese businessmen who had prospered as 'middlemen' in the colonial economy. The high point of this effort was represented in the ultimately unfruitful Benteng programme, whereby the state allocated import licences to *pribumi*, and hence theoretically Muslim, entrepreneurs. In practice, the programme was captured by powerful interests already ensconced in the developing post-colonial state that utilised it to develop patronage networks within the business community rather than to produce a stronger Muslim bourgeoisie. The effort was also represented by the rise of a movement inspired by the politician Asaat Datuk Mudo, which paved the way for a 1959 presidential regulation that was aimed to restrict Chinese control over retail in rural areas (see Robison 1986: Chapters 2 and 3).

It is notable that Muslim entrepreneurs by this time had most often come to support the 'modernist' Masyumi party, though some were associated too with the 'traditionalist' and more syncretic Nahdlatul Ulama. Both of these had long surpassed the SI as the primary political vehicles of the *ummah* by then, reduced as it was to a minor political party. The two did very well in the 1955 general elections in Indonesia – the first held in the post-colonial period – but so did the Indonesian National Party, ideologically linked to Soekarno, and the PKI.[10] Importantly, however, a big blow was dealt to these entrepreneurs when some Masyumi figures were implicated in 'half-hearted' separatist rebellions (Harvey 1977) in the late 1950s, spurred by the grievances of commodity exporters in the 'outer islands' of Indonesia who were economically undermined by the taxation and inflationary economic policies of the central government. In response, Soekarno had the Masyumi Party banned in 1960. Nevertheless, some of the party's political and ideological descendants continued to articulate the interests of an eclipsed old petty bourgeoisie based in small trade and manufacturing for decades to come.

Unlike the Sarekat Islam in Indonesia, the Muslim Brotherhood continued to be the primary vehicle of the struggles of the *ummah* well after the departure of the colonialists. Established in 1928 – or six years after semi-independence from Britain was achieved – the Muslim Brotherhood quickly developed a mass following. Between 1930 and 1949 it is said to have grown dramatically

---

[10] The Indonesian National Party (PNI) won 22.3 per cent of the vote, while the Masyumi (with constituencies that tended to lie in urban formations and in the outer islands) won 20.9 per cent, the more rural and Java-based Nahdlatul Ulama won 18.4 per cent, and the Indonesian Communist Party won 16.4 per cent (Noer 1963: 4).

from five to two thousand branches and a membership of up to 300,000 people. The Muslim Brotherhood reached out to the poor in the villages and in the cities, rallying people around the concept of a state based on Sharia, social equality and poverty alleviation through the mechanisms of *zakat* (Farah 2009: 107). It undertook such an expansion by a combination of activities centred on *dakwah* (preaching) and the provision of social services, utilising venues as varied as mosques, coffee shops and clinics in order to spread its message of personal piety and of social reform.

By the late 1930s, however, the Muslim Brotherhood had supplemented this mode of struggle by forming the infamous Secret Apparatus (Nizam al-Khass) (Pargeter 2010: 27). The latter effectively served as the armed militia wing of the organisation, and is alleged to have been behind a number of violent incidents during its history. The foray into this kind of activity eventually led to a course of events resulting in the assassination of Hassan Al-Banna himself in 1949, following the murder of the Egyptian prime minister by a member of the Muslim Brotherhood (Sullivan and Abed-Kotob 1999: 42).

Still, the Muslim Brotherhood continued to vie with the Wafd Party for leadership of Egypt's nationalist movement. Nevertheless, it was not the Wafd but the corps of military personnel under the leadership of Gamal Abdel Nasser – the so-called Free Officers – that ultimately took the immediate future of a new Egypt, free of the British, out of the hands of the Muslim Brotherhood. It was this group that instigated the 1952 Revolution, deposing the long moribund monarchy descended from the Ottoman-era viceroy and challenger, Mohamed Ali.[11]

Although the Muslim Brotherhood initially supported the military overthrow of the monarchy, it came to be the subject of ever increasing repression by the new military-dominated state. The brutality experienced by the Muslim Brotherhood under Nasser clearly helped to radicalise it significantly, as reflected in the personal trajectory of Sayyid Qutb, executed by the state in 1966 after periods of imprisonment and torture, and in the growing popularity and influence of his writings subsequently (Martin and Barzegar 2010: 1–2; Calvert 2010).[12]

There were a number of reasons for the state repression against the Muslim Brotherhood. First, essentially accompanying the Nasserist vision of a socialist Egyptian economy in which the state would play a major role was a vast

---

[11] The Free Officers proclaimed that their aim was to pursue economic development, build up the military, develop democracy and fight against feudalism and imperialism. They underlined their anti-imperialist credentials when the last of the British troops in Egypt left in mid-1954, thereby also putting an end to the behind-the-scenes power and influence of the British High Commission (Farah 2009: 31–32).

[12] His writings became influential well beyond his homeland. They had been disseminated, as is well known, in original form or in translation in various countries, including in Indonesia, by the 1970s (Solahudin 2011: 151–152).

apparatus of state bureaucracy that became increasingly centralised and authoritarian. The rise of an economy directed by a centralised authoritarian state basically meant that the Muslim petty bourgeoisie would remain as effectively on the sidelines as they had been during the days of British domination. Furthermore, the significant organisational capabilities and support enjoyed by the Muslim Brotherhood at the grassroots level meant that it posed as an alternative centre of authority that potentially competed with the Nasserist regime that was then consolidating its grip on society. For even then the organisation was already showing the potential to develop an 'Islamic sector' existing in 'parallel' fashion to the modern state that was in formation, and to its nascent institutions (Wickham 2002: Chapter 5). Such was the self-confidence of the Muslim Brotherhood that it had rather brazenly demanded veto power over legislative matters (Farah 2009: 109).

Additionally, even though the Muslim Brotherhood also advocated land reform and protection of labour rights (Mitchell 1993: 273), Nasser's tendency to mobilise support from the working class and the peasantry against landowners and entrepreneurs threatened to divide the *ummah* through the propagation of class conflict. Such was the case even if Nasserist class mobilisations were part of a kind of radical nationalism that remained highly vigilant about the danger of their appropriation by the communist stream of politics (Beinin and Lockman 1998: 429).

It should be noted that the political relationship between the Islamic petty bourgeoisie and the modern Egyptian nation state had features that were different from the relationship between its counterparts and the state in Indonesia. This was partly reflected in the institutional ties between religion and the state that have long been stronger and more institutionalised in Egypt than in the Indonesian case. The model set in Egypt since the time of Mohamed Ali – who had managed to win a large degree of autonomy from the Ottoman Caliph – was one of co-optation if not complete domestication of religious authority by the state (Farah 2009: 98–99). This model of relationship between the *ulama* and the state was more or less intact throughout the periods of colonial rule and monarchy, and from Nasser (who further exerted state control over the *ulama*), all the way to Sadat – who portrayed himself as the pious 'Believer-President' (Wickham 2002: 95) – and then finally to Mubarak. In fact, this relationship was formalised through a 1961 law that 'nationalised' the globally respected Al-Azhar.[13]

In Indonesia, by contrast, the model set by the colonial government was one of loose connection at best; in fact Hefner (2001: 24) observed that Dutch colonialism never had the effect of concentrating religious authority on the state, thus providing no precedent to facilitate the smooth incorporation of

---

[13] See El-Hodaiby's (2013) brief discussion in 'Egypt: In the Shadow of the State'.

Islamic politics into the post-colonial state. The close association between the state and *ulama* in Egypt meant that it took a new generation of religious teachers and preachers, of the likes of Al-Banna, to spur a new popular commitment to Islam (Lapidus 2002: 521) and to a reformist political project premised on Islamic ideals. However, neither the regimes of Soekarno nor of Soeharto ever exercised authority over the highly diverse Indonesian *ulama*, even if the latter did initiate the establishment of the Majelis Ulama Indonesia (MUI) to facilitate his increasingly authoritarian rule and to domesticate Islamic dissenters.

It might have been expected that the rule of the Ottoman Caliphate over Egypt would have hindered a link between Islam and budding aspirations for a modern national state. But direct Ottoman authority over Egypt had been weakened since the rule of Mohamed Ali. The latter had even instigated an ambitious and independent modernisation and industrialisation programme during the first half of the nineteenth century, but which was effectively stalled by the imposition of 'free trade' by the British. Still, the gradual severing of the country from the yoke of (Muslim) Ottoman suzerainty, by the British, allowed the cultural resources of Islam to play a role in Egypt resembling that in Indonesia in the fledgling development of nationalist sentiment and anti-colonial activity. Soon after the end of World War I, the greater overlap between nationalist stirrings and Islamic populist tendencies was ensured as British domination came to be increasingly perceived to cause economic hardship, growing inequalities and foreign exploitation of Egyptian resources by a range of elements within society (Farah 2009: 105).

Significantly, however, those opposed to British rule could already, by that time, reference a set of ideas that had been outlined, as early as the late nineteenth century, by Muslim thinkers like Muhammad Abduh (a disciple of another influential reformist, Al-Afghani)[14] as well as the Syrian thinker, Rashid Ridha. Abduh had already expounded anti-British views during his lifetime and voiced support for rebellions spearheaded by an Egyptian military whose members were poorly paid by a state whose budget was increasingly burdened by debt to its European creditors. Hassan Al-Banna's strongly held idea that British rule had been injurious to Egypt's dignity and honour (Sullivan and Abed-Kotob 1999: 9) could be seen as a direct continuation of Abduh's thoughts.[15]

Abduh had in fact become a major reference point too for Islamic movements in the far away Dutch East Indies, whose activists were influenced by the

---

[14] According to Keddie (1994: 484–485), Al-Afghani too was militantly anti-imperialist throughout his life and joined the Pan-Islamist movement after large-scale Western incursions into Muslim lands in the nineteenth century.

[15] Indeed, Al-Banna's father was a student at Al-Azhar University when Abduh was teaching there. See Mitchell (1993: 1, 322).

reformist impulse that was emanating from the Middle East and South Asia in the late nineteenth and early twentieth centuries. This was no doubt facilitated by the vast trade networks and connections between Muslim merchants which stretched from the Middle East to Southeast Asia, the expansion of the *haj* due to advances in seafaring transportation (Formichi 2010: 127) and to ties established through religious educational institutions, which saw many children of the Indonesian petty bourgeoisie studying in Mecca or Cairo. Thus, the ideas of Abduh and others like him would become widely known among many Southeast Asian Muslims from the Malay Peninsula to Java (Lapidus 2002: 661–665). Deliar Noer (1963: 48–49; 88) notes that Abduh's writings, including those that appeared in the journal *Al Urwat al-Wutsqa* (which he edited with his mentor, Al-Afghani), were read widely by students of Islamic religious institutions in the Dutch East Indies, even if they had to be covertly smuggled in.[16] Among their readers was Kyai Haji Ahmad Dahlan, the founder of the venerable Muhammadiyah movement.

But why did the ideas of Abduh resonate with his successors in Egypt as well as Muslim social and political activists in faraway lands like the Dutch East Indies? In a nutshell, such resonance was made possible by common need to make sense of – and respond to – the backwardness to which the *ummah* was consigned in the age of Western colonialism. In some manifestations, this response included the desire to emulate Western successes in technological and institutional development; in other words the desire to be 'modern'. Nevertheless, accompanying this was always an equally strong intent to 'purify' Islam from the corrupting influences seen to have been responsible for Islamic decline. The overall result was that the anti-colonial Islamic activists of Indonesia and Egypt did not see any necessary contradiction in being simultaneously Muslim and the aspiration to be modern, though how the latter was to be defined could be contentious.

Nevertheless, in the case of Egypt, the state itself can take much of the credit for the strong link between Islamic and national identity. All governments since the toppling of the monarchy in 1952 have attempted to deploy Islam as an instrument of their rule, a task made easier by the pliancy of the religious establishment represented by the Al-Azhar *ulama*.[17] In fact, the authoritarian-era Egyptian constitution had already stated that Sharia was the source of all laws in the country in spite of the state's systematic attempts, certainly under Mubarak, to stem the influence of the Muslim Brotherhood. This was attributable to the period during which Anwar Sadat, eager to display his credentials as a pious Muslim, tried to accommodate the forces of Islam in the 1970s as a

---

[16] On this point, also see Formichi (2010: 129).
[17] The young Al-Banna was reportedly disappointed with the reception from the Al-Azhar *ulama* to his nascent anti-British ideas, leading him to seek spiritual guidance from the leaders of then preponderant Sufi Orders. See Mitchell (1993).

means of curtailing the challenge then posed by assorted leftists (Farah 2009: 113–114).[18] Nonetheless, the partial absorption of the symbols and idioms of Islam by the state did not address the main social and economic grievances of the *ummah* and, therefore, failed to undercut the outlawed Muslim Brotherhood, whose appeal came to be partly sustained by growing public hostility against predatory elites within or closely linked to the state.

In Indonesia, by contrast, the social agents of Islamic populism never even won this kind of symbolic victory. The idioms of Islam were not so easily absorbed into the post-colonial body politic of Indonesia, partly because there was no recognised central religious authority such as Al-Azhar at the end of the colonial period to facilitate the process. In fact, the early post-colonial state had many problems in dealing with Islamic movements that operated outside of the nascent formal institutions of politics.

The most important of these was the Darul Islam movement, which was active as an armed insurgency from 1949 to 1962, as to be discussed further. Led by the independence fighter Kartosuwiryo, its aim was ostensibly the establishment of an Islamic state. However, the background to the outbreak of the Darul Islam rebellion was complex and had much to do with disagreement about the role of irregular forces in the Indonesian military. Kartosuwiryo himself was a commander of a militia force in West Java during the 1940s Indonesian war of independence. It also had to do with disenchantment among some of these irregulars about the way that the Indonesian fledgling nationalist government was negotiating an end to hostilities with the Dutch (Solahudin 2011).

Interestingly, the Imam of Indonesia's Darul Islam movement was a nephew of Marco Kertodikromo, the respected Indonesian Communist Party and Sarekat Islam activist and journalist, showing again the intersections between Islam and leftist political currents in the early twentieth century. It should be noted too that Kartosuwiryo's brand of Islam had actually synthesised local folk beliefs and was therefore far from puritanical (KPG and Tempo 2011), being largely free of Middle Eastern Wahhabi influences, unlike some of the present-day activists that consider themselves heirs to his legacy. Even if Kartosuwiryo's mastery of the classical Arabic language needed to read the Koran in its original text was reportedly limited, some of his closest associates continue to regard his religious expertise as virtually unimpeachable, one of them even proclaiming him to have been the greatest *ulama* that had ever lived.[19]

---

[18] It is widely believed Sadat was secretly a member of the Muslim Brotherhood in the 1940s, as were Nasser and many others of the Free Officers who had deposed the last monarch, King Faruk, or that they were at least closely associated with the organisation at the time.

[19] Interview with Munir Fatah, former DI fighter and a former Kartosuwiryo bodyguard, Cibiru, Bandung, 22 January 2012.

In spite of its military defeat in 1962, the Darul Islam movement continued to have longer-term historical significance for a number of reasons. First, the movement has become an almost mythic example of 'heroic' struggles to establish an Islamic state – effectively merging nationalist and religious aspirations in modern Indonesia in the figure of the enigmatic Kartosuwiryo himself. Hence, the movement still serves as a model for contemporary activists who seek to establish an Islamic state to replace the secular one based on the amorphous state ideology of Pancasila.[20] That model still has appeal today because of the relative failure of Islamic parties in Indonesia to attain and exert control over the state through electoral means. Second, various manifestations of Darul Islam would serve as underground vehicles through which opposition to the Soeharto regime was sustained under highly authoritarian conditions, particularly in the 1970s and 1980s. Thirdly, these vehicles have had an important role in politically socialising many of the current generation of Islamic political activists too, especially those that remain on the margins of state and society.

Even so, the role of religion in Indonesia's developing national consciousness was affected by Dutch colonialism because of the particular character of rule in relation to the division of labour that it left behind. Deliar Noer (1963: 8–9) reminds us of how the Dutch administration and law was premised on identity politics, with Christians enjoying formal or informal privileges, and claims that they were better placed in terms of employment, promotion prospects and access to government schools. Moreover, because of the strong presence of the ethnic Chinese (who were more likely to be Christian than Muslim) in the petty commodity production and trade sectors of the East Indies colonial economy, and their strategic position as 'middlemen', nascent Islamic populism in Indonesia would be partly defined by the merging of class and religious as well as ethnic politics, in ways it could not in Egypt. This was in spite of the presence of a minority Coptic Christian community that was already well established in business and commerce during the Ottoman era but was nevertheless not viewed as an alien population.

Widespread anti-Chinese sentiments stemming from the colonial period have continually resurfaced in post-colonial times in Indonesia, and frequently fed into support for Islamic-oriented groups (Sidel 2006). As discussed further, such sentiments were arguably heightened during the New Order, when the cosy ties between the families of President Soeharto and top ethnic Chinese tycoon Liem Sioe Liong best exemplified the corrupt and cronyistic relationship between state and business (Chua 2008).

---

[20] This is usually translated as the Five Principles, encompassing Belief in God, Humanitarianism, National Unity, Consultative Democracy and Social Justice. Framed originally by Soekarno, it was imposed on all spheres of life by the New Order regime of Soeharto partly to undermine the mobilisational capacities of Islamic oppositional groups in the 1980s (See Bourchier and Hadiz 2003: Chapter 6).

It is not a coincidence, therefore, that state suppression of Islamic organisations and activism took place most strongly in the 1970s and 1980s, precisely at the time that these business alliances were becoming dominant within the Indonesian political economy. What such alliances did was to revive and to powerfully reinforce the painful social memory of a colonial order that was, by its very logic, stacked against the interests of the *ummah*. In other words, they served to resuscitate the worldview of the early members of the Islamic petty bourgeoisie that had formed the Sarekat Islam in the early twentieth century albeit within an already significantly altered social environment. Among other things, the state and business alliances that pervaded through the New Order provided renewed sustenance to the idea that the social, economic and political advancement of the *ummah* required the establishment of an Islamic state, however it was to be defined.

Historical antecedents: Indonesia and Turkey

The Turkish case diverges from Indonesia and Egypt in terms of the genesis of Islamic populism. This owes much to the fact that Turkey was never directly colonised by the Western powers. Thus, when Ataturk was 'saving' Turkey from the West by effectively westernising it himself, Islam in Indonesia was becoming a cultural resource for populist opposition to a Western subjugation seen to be both economically exploitative and culturally humiliating. Such divergence would have major implications for the evolving relationship between Islamic populism and the state in subsequent periods.

Turkey was never colonised largely because the Ottoman Empire had served as a buffer between the European powers engaged in increasingly intense competition in the Middle East and Central Asia since the mid-nineteenth century (Lapidus 2002: 489). In this regard, the Turkish experience with the West has some commonalities with that of Iran (and Thailand in Southeast Asia) and is starkly different from that of Indonesia/the Dutch East Indies. Indeed, the first Pahlevi Shah was inspired by the Kemalist model of centralising powers within the institutions of a modern bureaucracy, which would wield authority over politics, the economy and the cultural sphere (Gheissari and Nasr 2006: 39).

Nevertheless, the early twentieth century was a period of tumultuous change in Turkey too, which would provide the setting for a more slowly developing older form of Islamic populism based on the interests of a petty bourgeoisie occupying traditional sectors of economic activity. However, there was little that resembled the early Sarekat Islam in Indonesia with regard to aligning the interests of the traditional petty bourgeoisie with larger anti-colonial and nationalist struggles. Rather than the experience of subordination to foreign colonial capital, the populist inclinations of Turkish Islamic politics were spurred directly out of the experience of marginalisation within a national state building project being presided over and dominated by Westernising domestic state elites.

But Keyder argued that the absence of direct colonial subjugation actually provided a set of conditions that made it possible for Turkey to have a head start in moving onto an economic development pathway that was not so significantly different from those pursued by many post-colonial countries. This is the pathway that was characterised by centralised state capitalism and which went hand in hand with the process of formation of a modern nation state (Keyder 1987: 105), replete with its regularised bureaucratic apparatus. In the Turkish case, the model had begun to gain prominence as early as in the 1930s, when the Republican government moved to purchase or nationalise many foreign-owned enterprises, especially in railways and public services. As the state came to be the major development actor, it propagated European-derived ideas emphasising a kind of social solidarity averse to notions of class conflict and a state that was above all class interests. These sorts of ideas were to be eventually developed in Indonesia too by the ideologues of the secular nationalist state (Bourchier 1996).

The key factor in the early emergence of this model in Turkey was of course the rise of a new republic in the 1920s from the ashes of the Ottoman Empire, where a social order based on loyalty and obedience to the sultan and caliph had little use for nationalism or modern conceptions of citizenship. In this society it was Islam that provided the most important cultural resource for perpetuating the legitimacy of Ottoman rule, for the sultan was not just the ruler of the empire, but also the caliph or leader of the global *ummah* (Eligur 2010: 37). It was in such a context that a complicated division of labour based on ethnicity and religion, regulated by the state, would develop, in which Christians consolidated dominance over trade due to their importance *vis-à-vis* economic ties with Europe (Mardin 2006: 69–70). However, the emergence of national identity among the many peoples under the jurisdiction of the Ottomans was considered a threat (Eligur 2010: 38), as it would have further whittled away the dynasty's long declining authority over diverse populations in the Middle East and North Africa.

In other words, it was only Ottoman defeat in World War I that provided an opportunity for the emergence of an entirely new polity – within which Islam's role in state and society would be necessarily repositioned.[21] Such a situation

---

[21] Having said this, the ideas that characterised Turkish Republicanism did not come out of thin air. It would be incorrect not to recognise that many of the seeds of the modernising reforms undertaken in the early Turkish Republic had already been planted by the later sultans (Sunar and Toprak 1983: 424–425) and by the Young Turk movement. For example, the need for a more regularised bureaucratic apparatus had already become increasingly apparent through encounters from the late nineteenth century with the resurgent Western European powers (Eligur 2010: 38).

did not allow much room for Islamic cultural resources to be influential in the ways that the modern nation-state was to be imagined, unlike in the Dutch East Indies at precisely the same time.

There were nevertheless important similarities in the experiences of Indonesia and Turkey. Like in Indonesia, the expansion of Western colonialism had a huge impact on Ottoman society in the late nineteenth and early twentieth centuries. While intra-European rivalry had allowed the Ottoman Empire to survive until after World War I, it was nevertheless constantly subject to British and Russian demands and came to be dependent on military advisers and investors from Germany (Lapidus 2002: 457). Thus, the Ottoman Empire had been reduced from its former glories to the unwanted status of 'sick man' of Europe for a long time before the War. Furthermore, growing European trade interests had affected the economy throughout different parts of the Ottoman Empire in ways that were experienced in many other parts of the colonial world. As Lapidus aptly summarised (2002: 457), European powers 'extracted raw materials, and introduced European manufactures in competition with indigenous merchants and artisans'. Thus, in Anatolia, the Europeans encouraged specialisation in 'the production of cash crops such as grain, dried fruit and cotton', while they 'generally depressed the handicraft and manufacturing industries' throughout the Empire.

It might have been expected, therefore, that Christian and Jewish middlemen that occupied petty trade and agricultural production in the territory which now constitutes modern Turkey could have served the same role as the ethnic Chinese did in the Dutch East Indies in terms of being the target of social animosities. Indeed, Mardin suggests that Muslim Turks were disenchanted about their economic lot when compared to that of their Christian and Jewish contemporaries – giving rise to notions about the need to wrest away control over sections of the economy from these communities (Mardin 2006: 70). Indeed, Christian Armenians and Greeks, as well as Jews – communities that played a dominant role in commerce in the Ottoman era – were ultimately eliminated en masse soon after World War I in a state-directed process, in the context of continuing threats from the European powers on Turkish lands and sovereignty. To replace them, a hotchpotch of Muslims from surrounding areas (the Balkans, Russia) had become 'Turkish' during the late period of the sultanate and the early Republican years. Many of these took over the property of those who had been forced to leave their positions in rural commercial agriculture and in urban petty trade (Mardin 2006: 76).[22] It is clear that this process of replacement involved mass migration, deportation and even genocide that impacted the lives of millions of people, regardless of their religion.

Moreover, even the principles of the secular state that underpinned the Turkish Republic had their antecedents: a Young Ottoman movement had previously called for synthesis between modernity and Islamic tradition – and argued for a constitutional basis for the Islamic state (Turam 2007: 39).

[22] On the Armenian genocide, see Akçam (2004).

Therefore, when the Indonesian Muslim petty bourgeoisie was already firmly embroiled in anti-colonial political activity, their Turkish counterparts were essentially busy consolidating a relatively new social position; they were certainly in no condition to respond immediately to the unfolding of a new national state building project that would be characterised by centralised state capitalism, political authoritarianism and secularisation. These relative newcomers instead became obedient subjects of the modern nation-state-in-formation for quite some time (Keyder 1987: 80–83). In a nutshell, the Turkish Muslim petty bourgeoisie of the 1920s and 1930s were too precariously placed to be expected to behave assertively in the economic or political fields (Keyder 1987: Chapter 4) so as to spur a strong Islamic populist impulse in the early years of the Turkish Republic.

Moreover, there may have been little to indicate, initially, that nation-state building in Turkey would go hand in hand necessarily with statist developmentalism. There could have been enough to suggest that an Islamic petty bourgeoisie might yet have thrived within that project. Such was the case even if the early Republican government had begun to pursue policies that relied on foreign investment especially in newly important areas like banking and infrastructural development (Keyder 1987: 94), and which did not include the nascent culturally Muslim petty bourgeoisie.

Significantly, the cultural policies that came to be pursued by Mustafa Kemal Ataturk, the military hero and founder of the Republic, were to foster resentment, particularly among provincial and religious elements of Turkish society.[23] These policies involved such matters as the banning of clothing and headgear associated with Ottoman-era traditions and encouragement of Western-style clothes and hats instead. But the objective of such a policy was by no means petty: it was part of a broader effort to suppress the influence of religious norms on Turkish society because they had been 'the legitimizing principle of the old Empire' and infused the 'vocabulary most commonly available to the opponents of the new legitimating principle' of Turkish nationalism (Keyder 1987: 89). The ultimate aim was no less than to substitute long-entrenched notions of 'loyalty of subject to Sultan' with a modern idea of citizenship in the European vein.

The broader point to be made is that Islamic populism, when it did arise, had a more problematic and contradictory relationship with early imaginings of a modern Turkish nation-state than it did in Indonesia and in Egypt. Such imaginings were based more firmly upon the Republican government's radical steps to

---

[23] The most famous of the religious scholars and *tariqa* leaders, Said Nursi, for example, appeared to support the nation-building project of the Republican revolution until it was clear that it intended to shunt Islam away from public life. Challenging the state by advocating a 'return to Islam', he was to die while still in prolonged exile in 1960 (e.g. Turam 2007: 42). Nevertheless, he would leave a long-standing legacy for Turkish politics, not least as the main ideological inspiration for the powerful Gülen movement.

'Europeanise' or 'Westernise' Turkey, geared to put it on equal footing with the Western powers (Casier and Jongerden 2011: 2), while eliminating religion from matters of state. Therefore, even as Islam helped to shape the aspirations for a post-colonial, modern Indonesia-to-come, it was something to be subdued in a post-Ottoman Turkish state. This was so even if religion had, paradoxically, served as signifier of Turkish nationhood in the face of Western allied invasion following World War I (Zubaida 2000: 71). In fact, the early Turkish Republic relied to a considerable extent on Islamic identity to demarcate its *national* territorial boundaries following the demise of the far-flung Ottoman Empire. But even at this point, there appeared to be a strong element of pragmatism in Ataturk's mobilisation of religious identity against the threat posed by invading armies bringing threatening territorial claims with them (Ebaugh 2010: 15).

Such is the complex historical legacy that exponents of the newer form of Islamic populism in Turkey have inherited. Claiming nationalist as well as religious credentials, they now make positive references to the nation-building project begun in the early Republican period, in spite of the well-known cost born by devout Muslims (Turam 2007: 26–30; interview MUSIAD 20 October 2011). At the same time the exalted position of Islam in the Ottoman era is looked upon with quite a degree of nostalgia.

This assertion of nationalist credentials by the social agents of the Islamic populist tendency in modern Turkey does have historical basis, however: clearly the founders of the Turkish Republic had wanted the geographical area to which it claimed sovereignty to be immune to the sort of disintegration experienced by the Ottoman Empire. To this end they tried to ensure that, at least notionally, the new Turkey would not be composed of a multi-ethnic or multi-religious population (Karakas 2008: 12). Such a history gives some explanation as to why minorities like the Kurds have been long ruthlessly pressed to accept a Turkish identity and to erase their own (Yegen 2011: 69–71).[24] It should be recalled, moreover, that such suppression has taken place both under Kemalist governments as well as under AKP rule.[25]

On balance, nevertheless, the guardians of the early Turkish Republic went to great lengths to undermine the existing institutional underpinnings of Islamic organisational life and to create new ones that it could control.[26] A major result was that religion had to find refuge in the private sphere of life, the boundaries of

---

[24] Thus the Kurds would be dubbed, with a strong hint of racism, 'Mountain Turks'. Such a history explains the great pain and anxiety today amongst Kemalists and supporters of the AKP alike caused by the resilient Kurdish separatist movement.

[25] According to Reyhan Yalçındağ, a prominent human rights activist, violence against Kurds has not declined under AKP rule, with extrajudiciary killings still taking place regularly. The perpetrators, she suggests, have been police as well as gendarmes and regularly military forces. Interview, Diyarbakir, 27 August 2014.

[26] From the abolishment of the Caliphate in 1924, the Directorate of Religious of Affairs – directly under the jurisdiction of the prime minister (Eligur 2010: 37) – was established to take care of

which then expanded to accommodate clandestinely organised Islamic groupings. For even as the collective practice of religion became stigmatised and established religious orders and their leaders found themselves attacked by the state, Islamic secret societies emerged in response (Turam 2007: 42). Crystallising out of the old Sufi *tariqa*, these served the important function of keeping Islam alive as a cultural resource for the future development of political vehicles premised on the interests of the *ummah* and for Islamic political dissent.

In some respects, their experience points to semi-clandestine religious and political activities undertaken by some Indonesian Islamic groups, at a much later stage of history, during the heyday of Soeharto-era repression. Though the format of such activities in Indonesia was quite different, they too served the function of maintaining Islam as a cultural resource from which political dissent against an authoritarian secular state could emerge.

In the Turkish case, such dissent had become evident in the 1950s, when the predominantly provincial and culturally Muslim petty bourgeoisie threw its support behind an upstart Democratic Party. Keyder shows (1987: 124–125), in particular, that the victory of the Democratic Party in the 1950 general elections over the CHP (Republican People's Party) – the heretofore all-powerful Kemalist electoral vehicle – was indicative of the growing resentment of a petty bourgeoisie, based in trade, small commodity production and commercial farming, towards the increasingly privileged state and bureaucratic elites. In many ways, the victory of the Democratic Party was a watershed moment. First, it broke the monopoly on state power that was enjoyed by Kemalist political institutions. Second, it provided the first opportunities for the political representatives of the Turkish Muslim petty bourgeoisie to exert influence over the state after years of being on the receiving end of state policy that suppressed Islamic groups, including attacks on a number of important Sufi *tariqa*. It might be said that they had 'caught up' with the Indonesian Muslim petty bourgeoisie, who in the 1950s were agitating for government policy that would support the development of *pribumi* and predominantly Muslim-owned businesses (Robison 1986: Chapter 2).

However, the period ended abruptly with the launching of a military coup in 1960 against the Democratic Party-led government of Adnan Menderes, who was then executed by hanging. Significantly, Menderes's government had been notable for its willingness to accommodate the Muslim petty bourgeoisie, which had grown steadily alienated from the authoritarian statism that had become the hallmark of Kemalist rule.[27] Nevertheless the floodgates had been opened and it was no longer possible to exclude Islamic populists from further contests over power.

---

matters having to do with Islam. Control over education was handed over completely to the Ministry of Education (Ebaugh 2010: 14).

[27] See Sunar and Toprak (1983: 428–431) for a discussion of the relationship between the Democratic Party and the social agents of Islamic politics.

By the late 1960s, the most iconic figure in the history of modern Turkish Islamic politics was to have emerged: Necmettin Erbakan. Educated as an engineer, he was to lead several Islamic parties (forced to close down at one time or another), one of which was even in a coalition government with the CHP in the 1970s. Furthermore, for a short time in the mid-1990s, he was prime minister of Turkey as head of the Refah (Welfare) Party – the first Islamic party to lead a Turkish Republic government – until it was deposed in the so-called post-modern coup of 1997.[28]

As is well known, the Refah party was banned by the Turkish courts, which accused it of contravening the secular Constitution, while Erbakan was himself temporarily expelled from politics. In contrast to the AKP, the influence of traditional petty bourgeois tendencies on Refah was displayed in its noticeable aversion to free markets and in its reluctance to look to the West for a model of development.[29] Instead Erbakan preferred a more state paternalistic system of protection of domestic industry against foreign competition, but one that favoured the interests of Muslim businesses.

One observer summarised the position of Erbakan's Refah Party in this way (Leezenberg 2001: 6):

> In their populist appeal to the masses, Refah leaders criticized the ostentatious display of wealth characteristic of the *nouveau riche*, but its social and political programs placed more emphasis on the improvement of morals and good manners than on the redistribution of wealth and property. Thus, Refah leader Erbakan, with his rhetoric of *adil ekonomik düzen* or 'just economic order', blamed the plight of the poor in Turkey on the international economic constellation, in particular Turkey's heavy dependence on, and indebtedness to, the World Bank and the IMF; but given his ultimately conservative outlook, he did not call for radical economic reform or redistribution.

From this point of view, Erbakan's sensibilities were quite similar to the leadership of the Indonesian Masyumi Party of the 1950s. The vision of development espoused by both included social justice concerns prompted by the desire to promote the interests of marginalised smaller businesses associated with the *ummah*.[30] Another similarity with Masyumi was that the Welfare Party, like Erbakan's other political vehicles, was vehemently

---

[28] Interview with Ihsan Dagi, Middle East Technical Institute, Ankara, 22 October, 2010. The commonly used term 'post-modern' coup is widely held to be a reference to the unusual fact that the military ousted a government without having to dissolve parliament or suspend the constitution.

[29] Interview with Mehmet Bekaroğlu, former Welfare Party Member of Parliament, Istanbul, 14 October 2010.

[30] But Erbakan rather blatantly invited danger by tying such aims with overtly Islamic themes and even with the promise of rolling back the Kemalist revolution (Nasr 2009: 240). There can be little doubt that the AKP's preference to present itself as a 'conservative' rather than Islamist party has much to do with the process of learning from the mistakes committed by Erbakan when in power.

anti-communist in its orientation. In the Turkish case, this was a result of competition as the major source of opposition to the Kemalist establishment.

But an important divergence in the Turkish case from that of Indonesia is that Islamic populist incursions into the working class and the urban poor would come considerably later, even if they would be ultimately more successful. There is not much of a history of older Islamic populist movements in Turkey that involved working class organisations or the broader urban poor.[31] Indonesia in the 1950s, by contrast, had many Islamic-oriented labour unions and federations, though most of these tended to be based among workers who were less blue collar than those who were associated with SOBSI, the union federation linked to the Indonesian Communist Party (Tedjasukmana 1957; Hawkins 1963; Hadiz 1997).

In Egypt too, as already mentioned, the Muslim Brotherhood battled leftists and liberals for support among workers, although it tended to be favoured as well by the white-collar elements of the working class (Beinin and Lockman 1998: 383). The Brotherhood even set up its own small textile firm in 1946–1947, the purpose of which was ostensibly to help provide jobs for the poor, but also to showcase how worker–employer relations under Islam would be inherently non-confrontational (Beinan and Lockman 1998: 374–375). No such developments took place in Turkey.

In fact what links that the older traditions of Islamic populism had with the poor in Turkey were mostly restricted to the smallholding rural peasantry – which increased in numbers quite considerably in the 1950s and 1960s – as the proportion of landless peasants correspondingly fell (Keyder 1987: 131). This was partly the result of state policies to formalise the transfer of newly opened state land in the Anatolian hinterland to peasants, including more prosperous ones who were able to purchase modern instruments of agricultural production. The overall outcome of land distribution policy in Turkey, however, was an agrarian social structure that was overwhelmingly small holder based, quite entrepreneurial in orientation, and which was fairly integrated with the world market (Keyder 1987: 131–132). It was such a social structure that helped to give rise, in turn, to a class of rural smallholders that became an important support base for Adnan Menderes's ultimately ill-fated Democratic Party-led government.

Of course, similar to Indonesia and Egypt, urbanisation and certainly proletarianisation didn't occur at significant levels in Turkey until closer to the 1970s when industrialisation really took off. By the next decade, as Keyder noted, few major manufacturing concerns in Turkey could trace their origins to a period

---

[31] It is notable that Özgür Gökmen's rare and valuable review of the Turkish labour movement between the world wars makes no mention of the existence of pro-Islamic unions in the country during this period. See Gökmen (2004).

before the 1950s, suggesting the failure of that generation of petty bourgeoisie to seize the commanding heights of the modern economy. Besides, once industrialisation did proceed, organised labour came to be a major constituency of the Turkish Left with little or no competition from Islamic populist forces. It was only in the 1980s that a labour union – Hak-is – had emerged in Turkey with an ideological orientation that was clearly Islamic in nature to counter leftist influences.

Although established initially in 1976, it is significant that Hak-is only began to operate effectively after another military coup took place in 1980, but more specifically following the promulgation of the technocratic and economically liberalising government of Turgut Özal.[32] Backed by the military, this government was known to have gone as far as to recruit members of the *tariqa* into government positions as part of broader efforts to repel what remained of the Left.[33] The overall result, as we shall see, was to pave the way for a set of processes that would eventually make possible the rise of the AKP at the beginning of the next millennium and to provide the social and political space for the most successful implementation of a new Islamic populist project thus far in the Muslim world, and which provides an attractive model for contemporaries in Indonesia as well as in Egypt. Today, both Hak-is and Memur-sen, its counterpart in the public sector, are widely perceived as allies of the AKP government.[34]

In any case, the fact that the older form of Islamic populism in Indonesia was first and foremost a reaction against colonial-era economic encroachment by ethnic Chinese and non-Muslim business interests represents an important historical legacy that finds no parallel in Turkish modern history. This is of course attributable to the colonial division of labour that was exercised in the Dutch East Indies, on the one hand, and the displacement of the predominantly Christian petty bourgeoisie by a culturally Muslim one during the late Ottoman period, on the other hand, facilitated by some particularly ruthless state

---

[32] Interview with Osman Yidiz, assistant to the president of Hak-Is, Ankara, 25 October 2010.
[33] What was in fact taking place was a so-called Turkish-Islamic Synthesis (Karakas 2007: 16–19) or an alliance, effectively, of the Kemalist establishment with heretofore marginalised Muslim groups, instigated by the need to rid Turkey of its vibrant though chaotic Left. The requirement had come to the fore because the Left had come to dominate, not just organised labour, but also the Kurdish separatist movement that threatened Turkish national integrity. Moreover, Turkey was also about to embark on a series of economic adjustment policies that required insulation from disruptive leftist influences. The significance of this synthesis will be revisited in later sections of this book.
[34] The identification of Hak-is with the policies of the AKP government is hotly rejected by Osman Yidiz in an interview in Ankara, 25 October 2010. As assistant to the president of the organisation, he insists that the union is independent and often clashes with the minister of labour, in particular, due to the latter's penchant for instituting neoliberal policies in the labour area that derail workers' rights. He also insists that the union has always tried to look out for the interest of workers when state companies have been privatised by the AKP government. This view is regularly ridiculed by Hak-is's opponents within the broader labour movement.

policies. The way in which Islamic populism converged with nationalist anti-colonial sentiment in Indonesia and in Egypt also finds little to compare with in Turkish history. The demands of the Muslim petty bourgeoisie in Turkey, once it had consolidated its social position, were directed instead against a Westernising and autocratic Kemalist state.

In other words, in the Indonesian case the prevalent understanding of the *ummah* was partly reinforced by the historical inducement to exclude the ethnic Chinese from the 'people' at the outset because they were regarded to have been beneficiaries of the colonial social order. Indeed, the *ummah* was juxtaposed against them as much as it was against the colonialists, whom authors like Noer thought of as also privileging Christians more generally as a means of securing their hold on the colony (1963: 31–32).

To underscore a theme that shall be revisited, therefore, it is important that the big bourgeoisie in Indonesia remains dominated by ethnic Chinese businesses – partly due to the sorts of state and business alliances that were pervasive during the New Order – and therefore cannot be expected to constitute a natural ally to any new Islamic populist alliance. As proposed in the previous chapter, the absence of a 'foreign' or 'alien' big bourgeoisie *within* Turkish society today, as in Egypt, means greater possibilities for developing bridges between culturally Muslim owners of capital and society at large, including the middle class and the urban poor, once this had become possible. The product would be stronger new Islamic populist alliances than in Indonesia. In a nutshell, the varying historical legacies would prove important for the levels of success in building newer Islamic populist alliances in the different countries whose experiences are compared in this book.

Conclusion

This chapter has argued that the new Islamic populism owes a great deal to the legacy of the older form that emerged out of a global order characterised by Western colonial domination over the Muslim world. It is true that the older form of Islamic populism is closely associated with the traditional urban and rural petty bourgeoisie whose social position was quite precarious at the early decades of the twentieth century, whether in Indonesia, Egypt or Turkey. Even so, the struggles of this petty bourgeoisie were conceived as being synonymous with the struggles of a broader *ummah* marginalised within a world order characterised by Western colonial domination.

It was shown that in Indonesia and Egypt, the older form of Islamic populism had made inroads into the working class and converged with broader anti-colonial and nationalist movements.

Such developments underscored the pro-social justice and egalitarian elements of the older Islamic populism and highlighted its contributions to imaginings of future modern national states. Another commonality between Indonesia and Egypt is that Islamic organisations would be either eclipsed or surpassed by other social actors in later stages of the anti-colonial struggle and who would dominate the post-colonial political terrain in ways that would continue to confine the space within which the Islamic populist project could be pursued. Nevertheless, there were important differences between the Indonesian and Egyptian experiences. One major divergence was that Indonesian Islamic populism, at its inception, involved defining the *ummah* in opposition to ethnic Chinese whose businesses had encroached upon areas traditionally occupied by the Muslim petty bourgeoisie in view of their privileged position in relation to the Dutch. Another involves the relative ease with which Islamic symbolism and idioms were absorbed into the Egyptian state compared to Indonesia.

Turkey, however, was never colonised and the older Islamic populism stayed more firmly within the confines of an insecurely positioned and largely 'imported' Muslim petty bourgeoisie. Unlike in Indonesia (and Egypt), the relationship between Islamic populism and the modern nation state was contradictory here because of the absence of an experience of direct colonial subjugation. On the one hand, Turkey was carved out of Ottoman territory as a nation within which Turkish Muslims predominated and in reaction to military invasion from European powers and their Greek allies. On the other hand, the political project of the Turkish Republic was characterised by radical secularisation aimed at undermining and eliminating the cultural resource that had provided ideological justification for rule by the sultan and caliph. This project also involved a state-led capitalist development model within which new strata of state bureaucrats and managers would develop ascendancy. Thus the Turkish Muslim petty bourgeoisie found itself doubly marginalised – on the economic front by state enterprises and on the cultural front by the enforced confinement of religious activity to the private sphere.

The experience of Turkey contrasted more with Egypt than Indonesia in terms of historical legacies that impeded the absorption of Islam into the state. Nevertheless, it also differed from the Indonesian experience where some of the representatives of Islamic populism had a place within formal political party life, but were nevertheless unsuccessful in stamping their authority on the Constitution and in enforcing an agenda that would promote the social and economic position of the *ummah* within the post-colonial state. In the Turkish case, although the social agents of the struggles of this *ummah* did politically emerge by the 1950s, the exigencies of Turkish politics disallowed the expression of socio-political aspirations through the idioms of Islam for years to come. In other words, if Islam was only problematically absorbed into the Indonesian state, it was virtually barred from it in Turkey during the first decades of the Republic.

A major point of convergence between Turkey and Egypt, however, is that Islamic populism would be mainly directed against the state and associated elites, whereas in Indonesia hostility towards the state was combined with animosity that continued to be directed against the ethnic Chinese due to the legacy of the colonial-era division of labour. While some elements of the petty bourgeoisie in Egypt and Turkey subsequently graduated into the ranks of the bigger bourgeoisie, their counterparts in Indonesia have largely failed to challenge the dominance of Chinese big business, in spite of the emergence of businesses owned by the Soeharto clan and its cronies during the New Order era. But these were never conceived as being representatives of the struggles of the *ummah*, notwithstanding efforts by Soeharto and his family to identify with Islam in the late New Order, especially through support of a state-sponsored organisation known as ICMI (Association of Indonesian Muslim Intellectuals) (Hefner 1993; Liddle 1996). As we shall see, these differences in historical legacies would have significant ramifications for the future.

4 Modernisation and the Cold War
Paving the way

No political project can be understood without accounting for the social and historical context that made it possible, and the new Islamic populism is no exception. It has been argued so far that socio-economic changes in a number of Muslim-majority societies have provided the setting for the emergence of a new Islamic populism; premised on the interests of a new set of social classes, a much-transformed *ummah*-based identity has now been cultivated. This is the case notwithstanding the debt owed to the earlier petty bourgeois-dominated form of Islamic populism discussed previously.

The main concern of the present chapter is with the closely related outcomes of social conflict arising from the Cold War era. It addresses the question of how the outcomes of the Cold War and closely related domestic conflicts about distribution of the fruits of modernisation helped to set the stage for the new Islamic populism. This is discussed especially in relation to the case of Indonesia, though again comparisons are made with experiences in North Africa and the Middle East, especially that of Egypt and Turkey. It is shown that the outcomes of Cold War-era conflicts, both domestically and internationally rooted, made it possible for religion to become a major cultural reference point for expressions of dissent against corrupt and abusive governments in much of the Muslim world. It is argued, more specifically, that these outcomes facilitated the intersection of ideals linked to past experiences of social marginalisation with new aspirations for the development of more just societies as modernisation projects proceeded (Hadiz 2011).

A key factor, it is suggested, was the weakening or eradication of leftist social forces during those Cold War-era struggles, which created new spaces for Islamic expressions of dissent. The result was that the identity between the *ummah* and the 'people' came to be reinforced, in much the same way that the *plebs* had become the *populus* in Laclau's conceptual framework.

Such processes were most dramatically highlighted in the case of the mass killings and displacement in Indonesia that accompanied the destruction of the PKI. Here, as already noted, Islamic paramilitaries were closely involved on the side of the military during the obliteration of Indonesian communism in the 1960s. Moreover, it is generally accepted that some former Darul Islamist rebels of the 1950s and early 1960s were reactivated and mobilised by the military in order to partake in a number of anti-communist actions.[1] At the same time, the HMI (Islamic Students Association), a national organisation that was to spawn countless New Order-era apparatchiks, was at the forefront of anti-Soekarno street protests in the cities while also striking up an alliance with the military.

It will be recalled that Anwar Sadat – who brought Egypt into the orbit of the West in the 1970s while simultaneously suppressing the legacy of Nasserism – had also drawn on Islamic support to destroy leftist forces, though the process here was certainly not as bloody as it was in Indonesia. This was before the Egyptian state turned against Islamic movements once more – thus precipitating Sadat's assassination in 1981. In Turkey, meanwhile, it was the 1980s that saw a temporary alliance come into being between the officials of the Kemalist state and Islamist forces – leading to what was then dubbed a 'new synthesis', aimed at stemming a resuscitated leftist current. Significantly, the latter had been making strong inroads into the new proletariat, youthful members of the middle class and perhaps most worryingly, the resilient Kurdish movement (Jongerden and Akkaya 2011: 126–130). Nevertheless, the tables were eventually turned here too, as seen when its adversaries deposed the Refah (or Welfare) Party-led government in 1997, the rise of which owed much to the earlier so-called synthesis.

It is further suggested, therefore, that there were two core developments that all these three countries had in common. First, there was the emergence of temporary alliances between secular nationalist holders of state power – including its coercive apparatus – and Islamic forces that were primarily directed against the Left but which would have broader political repercussions. This took place in Indonesia largely and most dramatically in the 1960s, in Egypt in the 1970s and in Turkey in the 1980s. Second, in all of these cases the relationship between the state and Islam also vacillated to such a degree that the same Islamic political movements would suffer from state repression soon after the leftist challenge about the nature of the modernisation and its beneficiaries had been dealt with.

Modernisation and authoritarianism in the Muslim world

The outcomes of Cold War-era social conflicts essentially helped to create the environment allowing 'Islamist organisations' to present 'themselves as the principal alternative to traditional nationalist, socialist and liberal organisations'.

---

[1] Interview with Mursalin Dahlan, West Java Muhammadiyah official and former DI activist, Bandung, 23 January 2012; and Maman Abdurrahman, DI activist, Cikarang, Bekasi, 25 January 2012.

This was so especially once the social contradictions associated with capitalist development had intensified (Colas 2004: 238) in the era of neoliberal globalisation. In other words, much of the ground for contemporary Islamic populist politics was made available by the diminution of ideological alternatives to convey dissent during harsh periods of political repression that coincided with the Cold War.[2]

Still, Soekarno-style populist nationalism in Indonesia – largely excised from the state apparatus by the New Order – managed to regain its mass appeal at times and was notably a focal point for dissent against Soeharto in his last years in power. Tunisia provides another interesting case: here trade unions, though partly cultivated by and organically linked to the state, were influential in organising opposition to the Ben Ali government in the years preceding 2010, which finally saw the end of his rule. But the Tunisian case was rather exceptional, certainly in the Arab world, where trade unionism had by this time lost much of its former vigour. Zubaida (2000: 61) notes for the case of Egypt, for example, that 'many of the leftists and Nasserists turned to Islam as the authentic vehicle of popular contestation and national liberation', something that signalled how the Left had been made largely redundant by the practices of authoritarian rule.

However, in addition to the cases mentioned above, there is another – that of Iran – which eminently displays the interplay between the development of Islamic social and political movements, state-led modernisation programmes and Cold War-era exigencies. Iran, of course, stands out as the only country where an Islamic Revolution has been successful. In spite of such uniqueness, insights from the Iranian case remain helpful in developing an understanding of the trajectories of Indonesia – as well as Egypt and Turkey – where such a revolution never took place. The relevant main outlines of the Iranian experiences are therefore explored below to develop such insights.

Halliday's (1988; also see Halliday 2004) work is particularly useful in highlighting the context within which the Islamic Revolution in Iran occurred, defined as it was by the broad socio-economic transformations associated with the ambitious but contradiction-ridden modernisation process undertaken by the government of Shah Reza Pahlevi. This modernisation project was accompanied by growing societal tensions, best illustrated by the widening material and cultural gap between Westernised elites and newly urbanised sections of the population composed of recent migrants from the countryside. These migrants had flocked into the cities in search of employment opportunities and were enticed by the promises of social advancement (Halliday 1988: 53).

---

[2] Shadid (1997) even speaks of former Marxists in Egypt, Turkey and other countries in the Middle East who had, by the 1990s, transformed themselves into 'Islamists', considering this the only viable route left for politically progressive agendas.

At the same time, Moghadam (1987: 10–11) has rightly characterised the Shah's modernisation push as being 'very rapid' and 'heavy-handed' as well as being more concerned with growth than with social needs.

Skocpol (1982), among others, has noted how members of the *bazaari* were key supporters of the Iranian Revolution. This is because they had developed animosity towards the state as new and more politically connected businesses achieved ascendance over the expanding modern sectors of the economy. Furthermore, Gabriel (2001) pointed out that the Shah's land-reform policies – which provided the trigger for widespread urban migration, effectively releasing large numbers of people from the land and making them available for wage work – had hit squarely at the material base of a landowning class with traditionally strong family links to Islamic clerics. For such reasons, the Islamic Revolution provided an early example of a successful cross-class challenge to the modernising secular state and the posing of an alternative, more just, society through the language, idioms and symbolism of Islam. Importantly, the purveyors of the challenge were actually a range of societal elements that had developed a concrete material interest to oppose the Shah's authoritarian state. Zubaida thus recalled (2000: 64) that the 'thousands or millions brought out on the street were discontented, marginalised recent rural migrants who could identify with the combination of religious and liberationist slogans raised by the revolutionaries, though the rural poor were not distinguished by their piety'. For similar reasons, Keshavarzian sees the 1979 revolution in Iran as 'more than Islamic' (2010: 234) in spite of its ultimate outcome and the prominent role subsequently taken up by a highly institutionalised Shia clergy within the state.

It is also significant that the Iranian Revolution would have been less likely if during an earlier struggle – so intricately related to Cold War exigencies – there had not been the overthrow of Mossadegh's government in 1953 (Matin-Asgari 2004; Mirsepassi 2004). Indeed, it was the CIA and MI5 that instigated the coup against him in close cooperation with the supporters of the Shah, including within the military. The most obvious reasons for such superpower intervention in Iranian politics were Mossadegh's nationalisation of Western oil firms and his tolerance of the communist Tudeh Party. Not surprisingly, the overthrow of Mossadegh instigated a clampdown on the Left more generally, although his own relationship with the pro-Soviet Tudeh, in reality, was only ever less than cordial.

The consequences of the fall of Mossadegh on the specific Iranian trajectory became abundantly clear two-and-a-half decades later when forces rallying behind the charismatic Ayatollah Khomeini had emerged as the major source of opposition to the Shah. At this time, a much reduced and more fragmented Left played the role of junior allies within these forces when the big confrontation with the Pahlevi regime finally ensued in 1978–1979. Afterwards, however, the leftist component of the Iranian revolution was virtually eradicated during a further round of violent struggles over state power and the direction of the revolution (Gheissari and Nasr 2006: 89–97) – what Moghadam calls the period of 'mini-civil war' in 1981–1983 (1987: 6).

Not surprisingly, the strata of ruling clerics have been among the greatest beneficiaries of the Iranian Revolution since then; they provided the ideological glue for Khomeini's Islamic Republic and have prospered along with newer sets of political and business clients. They have done so largely by means of control over state institutions and resources, even if the broader economy has often floundered at the expense of large sections of the population, including workers, the urban salaried and middle-class intelligentsia (Zubaida 2000: 62). No doubt such developments helped to fuel more recently expressed discontent with the ruling regime, as witnessed in the emergence of the so-called Green Movement in 2009 (Hashemi and Postel 2010). As should be expected, Iran's Islamic Revolution had important consequences on such profane matters as the way that economic and political power would be organised and the kinds of social interests that would benefit most greatly from it.

Though the political outcomes have been different, the post-colonial states of Indonesia and Egypt as well as the Republic set up following Ataturk's revolution in post-World War I Turkey embarked upon modernisation projects constituted primarily by the objectives of nation building, state expansion and economic development. From this point view, elements of the Pahlevi vision can be found in the way in which modernisation has been conceived and implemented in all of these societies. Though no Islamic revolution would occur, the Islamic religion became a major reference point for the development of popular dissent as modernisation invariably came hand in hand with new forms of social marginalisation and inequities.

In Indonesia, Egypt and Turkey, the modernisation project would continue to be led for many more decades by states under the control of secular nationalist elites that sometimes made room for but at other times resolutely peripheralised social interests claiming to represent the *ummah*. Although representatives of leftist (and liberal) politics can still be found with varying levels of efficacy in Indonesia, Egypt and Turkey, the Islamic populist tendency became a major force in promoting social justice issues and voicing opposition to state corruption and abuse of power. But there were differences with the Iranian case in at least two important respects.

First was the absence of a powerful clergy in all three countries equipped to provide leadership and ideological coherence to class interests more or less peripheralised within the modernisation project. This is the case in Egypt too in spite of the presence of Al-Azhar, which had been domesticated as far back as the reforms of the Ottoman Khedive, Mohamed Ali. Second, in all these cases, the state was able to manipulate conflict between leftist and Islamic forces to the extent that effective alliances between their vehicles against the modernising state became virtually impossible. As we have seen, the development of such alliances, no matter how temporary and internally problematic, was a central feature in the overthrow of the Shah.

State authoritarianism against Islam

Whether in Iran, Indonesia, Turkey or Egypt, major political actors have never disputed the desirability of modernisation and industrialisation though their outcomes were inevitably imagined on the basis of existing templates derived from the experience of the West or the socialist bloc countries. The main bone of contention, not surprisingly, has been about the kinds of social interests that would become their primary beneficiaries and the kinds that would be sidelined. The social agents of Islamic politics too shared in the forward-looking imaginings of a modern society. For quite some time, the almost inescapable conclusion was that the state itself would act as the main agent of modernisation and economic development – particularly given the relative absence of a big domestic bourgeoisie and the historical dominance of the formal sector of the economy by foreign interests. It is notable too that many variants of Islamic political thinking posit an important role for the state in maintaining social cohesion and social solidarity on the basis of Islamic morality and precepts of justice (Tripp 2006).

In actuality, however, the state hardly ever was neutral, much less benign, but primarily became an arena of contestation among competing interests within and outside of its apparatus. What typically transpired as a result of such competition was the concentration of power and authority on the upper echelons of state officialdom, including those ensconced in the military/security forces. Challenges from outside of the state, including those emanating from social agents espousing Islamic populist aspirations, were largely put in check or otherwise staved off harshly, especially when they were not so useful in crushing other sources of threat to the ascendancy of officialdom, such as those that had emerged from the Left.

Such a materialist-oriented reading does not suggest that arguments about the virtues of a pious lifestyle and about the threat of moral decay posed by modern society were a mere façade for the ambitions of those who have put them forward. What it does suggest is that these pronouncements were never independent from vigorous contests over the control and shaping of the institutions of power, which might be expected to be a highly contentious process in any context. Thus, as the Darul Islam movement was waging guerrilla warfare against the newly independent Republic of Indonesia, for example, it had become increasingly clear that a new social order would *not* come into being that would uphold some sort of privileged position for the *ummah* (including in the normative and formal senses, as reflected in the constitution). It had become evident too that the economic structure inherited from the colonial period – in which *pribumi*/Muslim entrepreneurs were on the sidelines of economic activity – was not going to be substantively modified on the basis of parliamentary struggles, in spite of such initiatives as the Benteng programme of 1950–1957. This was the case even if there were two large parties – the Nahdlatul Ulama and Masyumi – emerging from (competing) Islamic social and political networks among the major players in the Indonesian parliament.[3]

But why did Islamic political parties take the parliamentary route and reject the Darul Islam movement's espoused project of militarily struggling for an Islamic state?[4] The reasons were not due to doctrinal relaxation that allowed for a link to be made between Islam and the practices of parliamentary democracy. In truth, these parties had come to develop their own stake in the longevity of the system and were among the big losers when Soekarno eventually pulled the plug on it. Also important was the Cold War context. It was fear of the PKI's agenda of private property expropriation that led the Masyumi, in particular, to turn to the West as an ally (Feillard and Madinier 2010: 19–20), and also the military. The influence of Cold War exigencies on the strategies undertaken by organisations claiming to represent the *ummah* is therefore clearly shown in the Indonesian case even if the alliances forged in the process would not prove enduring. As we shall see, the 1970s and 1980s were characterised by harsh repression against Islamic movements, including those that saw themselves as heirs to the Darul Islam struggle.

The meta-narrative that highlights the marginalisation of the pious Muslim majority in the building of a modern national state and economy is certainly not unique to the case of Indonesia. There is no doubt, for instance, that the Egyptian Muslim Brotherhood's leaders in the 1950s and 1960s sincerely disdained what they saw as the corrupting effects of Western cultural influences and of the secular modernising project as pursued by Nasser and his Free Officers. Qutb's trenchant critique of the moral decadence of the West provides some of the strongest evidence of this (Qutb 2007: 3–4). But members of the organisation could not have but bristled too at their continuing political and

---

[3] Masyumi emerged after 1945 as a federation of several Islamic political vehicles, but lost the important NU component when the latter set up its own party in 1952. Before the break-up it could be considered to have been the largest party in Indonesia, and according to Feillard and Madinier (2010: 17), 'also the largest Muslim party in the world'.

[4] This is the case even though Masyumi leader Natsir was widely regarded by DI activists as having let down Kartosuwiryo during the conflict with the young republican government by not providing protection and support in spite of presumably common ideals based on the Islamic religion and due to Kartosuwiryo's past membership in the Masyumi. It is often said that Natsir had sent a letter to Kartosuwiryo, urging him to cancel his plan to declare an Indonesian Islamic State (NII) as rival to the Republic, but that it arrived several days too late. Interview with Ustad Syuhada Bahri, chairman, Dewan Dakwah Islamiyah Indonesia (DDII) and former personal secretary to Mohammad Natsir, Jakarta, 3 January 2011.

economic exclusion following the end of British rule and the ouster of the ineffective and widely disliked monarchy. This is because the Muslim Brotherhood was also let down by the false promise of greater access to state power that had seemed to accompany the demise of the monarchy and colonial domination, which it had virulently opposed at great cost.

It will be recalled that a similar promise emerged in Turkey to the social agents of a nascent but increasingly discontented tradition of Islamic populism in the 1950s. That decade saw the rise of the Democratic Party, supported largely by sections of the state elite that had developed ties with the economically and politically peripheral petty bourgeoisie of the Anatolian hinterland. The latter were largely alienated from the Western-oriented Kemalist bureaucratic, military and business establishment, which they viewed as being culturally aloof as well as unfairly dominant in the economic and political spheres. In fact, it is arguable that the secular-nationalist Kemalist modernising agenda only ever made limited inroads into the Anatolian smaller cities and towns (Zubaida 2000: 71),[5] where demands were nurtured instead for a less state-dominated social order within which the Islamic petty bourgeoisie, by now more well-entrenched than after the post-World War I population swaps, could potentially benefit.

It is plausible as well that the growing discontent of this petty bourgeoisie contributed to the abrupt move by Ismet Inonu – Mustafa Kemal Ataturk's immediate successor – to promote political liberalisation following the end of World War II (Vanderlippe 2005). This is especially so because the opposition Democratic Party appeared to be led by former members of the CHP who had only split from the party due to petty internal factionalism and who did not seem to pose a serious threat (Tursan 2004: 46). But here too the promise of political change turned out to be false once the forces of Islamic populism had achieved concrete advances into state power on the back of that Democratic Party. The military coup against the government of Adnan Menderes therefore acted as a check on the direct progress of such forces on the state, one that would only be incrementally overcome during the following decades amidst more profound social transformations.[6]

Thus, we see the central development across a significant part of the Muslim world alluded to earlier: the rise of secular nationalist elites with authoritarian tendencies that would at times embrace, and at other times suppress, Islamic

---

[5] Also, observations by Umit Kardas, retired senior military judge in an interview, Istanbul, 14 September 2011.

[6] The party then led by Necmettin Erbakan was briefly part of a coalition government in the mid-1970s; in the following decade, the Motherland Party-led government of the technocrat Turgut Özal would be receptive to individuals whose political socialisation had taken place from within Islamic networks, many of whom had necessarily operated outside the sphere of formal politics. Özal's personal background was also within one of the major Sufi religious orders (Zubaida 2000: 72).

movements. The fluctuations in their relationship with these movements had to do with the exigencies of domestic political conflicts that frequently intersected with international ones that permeated through the globe during the Cold War.

In fact, the coercive powers of the authoritarian 'Arab state' have been much touted by many analysts. Ayubi (1995: 3) points out that such a state has typically relied heavily on its monopoly on coercion, although by the same token, it has been frequently more 'fierce' than institutionally 'strong'. For Ayubi, the fact that the Arab state characteristically resorted to coercion to ensure the compliance of the population at large was indicative of its limited 'infrastructural power' (Mann 1984, 1986), making the cultivation of an atmosphere of fear and intimidation more important than ideological hegemony to the maintenance of power. Bellin (2004) basically concurs with this observation, arguing that the longevity of authoritarianism in the Middle East was ultimately attributable to the workings of the coercive apparatus of the state, which insulated entrenched elites from significant societal pressure and freed them from any impulse to undertake significant economic and political reforms.

Nevertheless, such observations should not detract from the ability of Arab ruling elites to develop networks of patronage through more sophisticated clientelist practices and methods of co-optation (Stacher 2012), such as those constructed by Soeharto in Indonesia. In Egypt, the penchant for co-optation was demonstrated in the cases of the longstanding symbol of Egyptian political liberalism, the Wafd Party (Hinnebusch 1984), as well as the major party of the Left, the Tagammu, both of which were largely discredited during the Mubarak era for their frequently close cooperation with the regime. It is argued by some that even the Muslim Brotherhood had become increasingly integrated into the workings of the regime,[7] although the relationship between the two was always turbulent. Besides, as Bellin recognised (2004), the loyalty of those who manned the state's coercive apparatus was usually guaranteed by their own inclusion within powerful and enduring patronage networks – hence the economic might wielded by not only the militaries of Egypt, but also those of Indonesia and Turkey.

In other words, Arab authoritarianism has been wont to combine the carrot and the stick in perpetuating itself (Ottaway and Choucair-Vizoso 2008), as is the case with many other authoritarian experiences, including in Indonesia. Of course, the reign of Soeharto in Indonesia became largely synonymous too with harsh authoritarianism, although it was in fact highly successful in establishing a vast and highly centralised network of patronage based not only on co-optation but also an extensive apparatus of regulation (Robison and Hadiz

---

[7] Interview with Hanna Grace, Coptic Member of Egyptian National Assembly and Nabil Morcos, development consultant and Coptic community leader, Cairo, 31 March 2012.

2004), which functioned alongside the apparatus of state violence. It was through the interplay of these that the fruits of development were distributed in selective fashion throughout Soeharto's long rule.

Significantly, compared to the case of Egypt, the New Order's authoritarianism was more successful in the economic field for longer periods. Economic growth in Indonesia during much of the New Order was notably high for significant stretches of time – ranging between over 7 per cent to over 9 per cent annually between 1989 and 1996 (the year before the unfolding of the Asian Economic Crisis) – leading to accolades and predictions about being an Asian 'miracle' economy. Egyptian growth within the same time frame had occasion to dip to just 1.1 per cent in 1991 after achieving the relatively modest heights of 5.7 per cent in the previous year.[8] Moreover, while Egyptian economic growth reportedly stood at around 7 per cent between 2005 and 2008 following the implementation of a series of neoliberal structural adjustment policies, this did little to avert the prevailing sense in the country that it was suffering from a continual process of economic stagnation. Such a sense was reinforced by the general deterioration of infrastructure and public services and in the perceptible decline in people's standard of living (Stacher 2012: 6–7; Soliman 2011), including among the urban educated that struggled to live the middle-class lifestyle to which they felt entitled.

Of course, Indonesia too had carried out a series of 'economic deregulation' policies for the purpose of enhancing global economic competitiveness in the 1980s (Robison and Hadiz 2004: Chapter 3). In fact, as examined more deeply later in this book, developments in Indonesia mirrored those that were occurring in much of the Muslim world, where structural adjustment policies in line with the neoliberal economic orthodoxy prevailing within international development organisations were taking hold at about the same time.

Another point to make is that that Ayubi's 'fierce' Arab regimes were *not* in fact completely insulated by way of their repressive policies. For example, even if Mubarak's highly securitised rule was effective against a range of domestic challenges, like Soeharto's, it was certainly not free from pressure deriving from external demands for greater integration within the global economy. Besides structural adjustment policies, Arab rulers also introduced modifications to the political systems they presided over, which included introducing forms of electoral competition (Sadiki 2009) – Egypt again being the most notable case in point – though similar developments were seen at somewhat different junctures in countries like Tunisia and Morocco.

In Egypt, the coupling of economic liberalisation and limited political liberalisation was best seen during the later Mubarak years, which had even partially accommodated the Muslim Brotherhood within the official institutions

---

[8] See the World Bank-furnished data in 'GDP Growth (annual%)'.

of the political system. Though still illegal, it was allowed to take part within the heavily regulated elections by fielding candidates under the banner of recognised political parties or as independents. That system suffered a great jolt, however, when eighty-eight Muslim Brotherhood candidates victoriously entered parliament following the 2005 parliamentary elections (Sadiki 2009: 75). The reaction of the government was to unleash a new wave of repression against the Muslim Brotherhood, which, given the experience of nearby Algeria in the 1990s, would have conceivably dampened optimism about the electoral path to power among many of the organisation's supporters.

Such a reaction made it obvious that the political changes undertaken, like most in the Arab world, were basically ornamental (Sivan 2003). Furthermore, the especially tightly controlled elections of late 2010, in which not a single candidate representing the Muslim Brotherhood won a seat, clearly contributed to the rebellious mood of the populace a few months later. Indeed, equally cosmetic political 'reforms' throughout the Arab world did not stop the emergence of the Arab Spring in 2011.

The similarities between Egypt and Indonesia in this regard are actually quite striking. Here economic liberalisation had gone together for a short while with a period of so-called political openness, characterised by freer public discussion of issues like economic as well as political democracy. That all of this was quite superficial too, nevertheless, was underlined by the abruptness with which 'political openness' ended when the press began to take too many liberties and was thus brusquely muzzled in the mid-1990s (Bourchier and Hadiz 2003: Chapter 8). It was the coming of the Asian Crisis in 1997–1998 that finally set the stage for a remarkable process of democratisation in Indonesia, as tensions within the regime, mass mobilisations outside of it and economic hardship due to sudden economic crisis combined to de-legitimise and topple Soeharto.

In Turkey, a succession of governments had also embarked on economic liberalisation policies starting from the technocratically inclined Özal government, which was installed in 1983 or three years after the military coup at the start of that decade. While economic growth levels tended to fluctuate greatly here as well,[9] political liberalisation appeared to accompany economic reforms in Turkey quite strongly, as seen in the accommodation of some Islamists within the Özal government. Here Turkey's own economic crisis of 2001 played a big part in assuring the electoral victory of the AKP the following year (Öniş 2003: 97), by allowing it to paint the Kemalist forces that had dominated the previous government as being incompetent and corrupt. But the Turkish case was different in one way from that of Indonesia and Egypt: authoritarian tendencies had for

---

[9] Reaching 9.5 per cent and 9.3 per cent in 1987 and 1990, for example, but registering negative figures twice in the 1990s, and again of course in 2001. Indonesia's low points, as to be expected, occurred during the Asian Economic Crisis, when negative growth of 13.1 per cent was registered in 1998. See 'GDP Growth (annual%)' 2012.

a longer time existed in a contradictory relationship with democratising ones that emerged from the specific way that the country came to be entangled in the Cold War.

One key distinguishing factor was Turkey's membership of the very core of the Western alliance that emerged after the end of World War II, ostensibly championing capitalism *and* democracy, in the context of an emerging Cold War-based international system of rivalry between the United States and the Soviet Union and their respective allies (e.g. Tursan 2004: 50). The choice to side unreservedly with the West was an easy one for Turkish elites to make given that the Soviet Union was then staking a claim on Turkish territory. Such siding with the West coincided with the emergence of fledgling commercial elites outside of the establishment that, as already mentioned, took advantage of political liberalisation to strengthen their own social position. By contrast, Soekarno in Indonesia and Nasser in Egypt were leading figures in the emerging Third World Movement of the 1950s, to the chagrin of the West, and were under no external pressure to adopt the latter's political models for any immediate purposes.

Nevertheless, Turkish democratisation was interrupted by coups that took place without fail during every decade from the 1960s to the 1990s against democratically elected governments. Each of these served to periodically strengthen the authoritarian elements of the state, especially its coercive apparatus, against civil society-based political movements – not just of the Islamic petty bourgeoisie but also of the leftist and ultra-nationalist streams of Turkish politics. Leftist politics, moreover, had become increasingly merged with the Kurdish struggle by this time, rather than just being ensconced in traditional vehicles like trade unions, and thus was considered a threat to the territorial integrity of the nation-state itself.

Therefore, the evolution of Indonesian state authoritarianism appears to more closely resemble that of Egypt in terms of its distinctive phases. In many ways, the virulent nationalism and Third Worldism of the Soekarno years was comparable to that which was espoused by Nasser during a period of rule that largely overlapped. The long Soeharto period too, in which the transforming effects of economic development and, later, neoliberal globalisation, were most visible, could be seen to have interesting parallels with the reign of Sadat and then Mubarak's own three decades of rule in Egypt. Both of these leaders opened up Egypt increasingly to the forces of the global capitalist economy after the Nasserist period had come to an end, although without similarly rapid growth rates associated with most of New Order rule in Indonesia. In both the cases of Indonesia and Egypt, political and economic power would mainly come to be the domain of a close-knit capitalist oligarchy – at the head of which was the Presidential family – and that fused bureaucratic and growing business interests within a centralised system of patronage in ways that never transpired in Turkey.

The key point to make, however, is that all three cases show that the relationship between the state and political vehicles of the *ummah* were determined by domestic struggles over power that often intersected with broader international conflicts relating to the Cold War. This is important in terms of understanding how these political vehicles have come to evolve into the present time and the way that they have navigated their way through new sets of social, economic and political circumstances. To highlight this point, analysis of the Indonesian case is now to be delved into more deeply.

Forging the authoritarian state in Indonesia: setting the stage

The remainder of this chapter zooms in on the relationship between the evolution of state authoritarianism and the development of Islamic populist politics in the book's main case study, that of Indonesia. What should be underlined at this juncture is how the chaotic authoritarianism of Soekarno contributed to the rise of the modernising state authoritarianism of Soeharto, which in turn, paved the way for the eventual domination of state and market by a predatory politico-business oligarchy (Robison and Hadiz 2004). In basic terms, the new Islamic populism as it came to emerge in Indonesia was intextricably linked to reactions by the social agents of Islamic politics to the rapacity of Soeharto-era oligarchic power, which was deemed to have continued the social, economic and political marginalisation of the *ummah*.

It is especially significant, therefore, that with the destruction of the Left in Cold War-era struggles, it was the prospect of political mobilisation in the name of the *ummah* that was considered the single biggest potential source of threat to the institutional arrangement of power that was insulating the emergence of that oligarchy in the 1970s and 1980s. We have already seen how domestic conflicts about the distribution of the fruits of the modernising project in Indonesia closely intersected with those rooted in the Cold War international context, just as they had in Egypt and Turkey, though the specific manifestations of such intersections were different from case to case. In all of these cases, it is notable that the destruction of the Left involved cooperation from Islamic political forces.

What stands out about Indonesia, however, is the especially deep and lasting impact of this process of destruction, the bloody nature of which was unparalleled elsewhere. While this left a void that could be partially filled by calls for social justice that referred to a tradition of Islamic politics that goes back to the colonial period, it also meant that those making such calls would be the primary objects of state repression for long periods when there were few other sources of credible threats to rule by the New Order oligarchy. Thus, while Islamic forces were being accommodated, albeit cautiously and only to a limited extent, in Egypt and Turkey by the 1980s, in Indonesia they were to experience their most difficult decade.

Consolidating the state

It was the late colonial state, albeit in utter decay following World War II and national revolution, that was the direct precursor to the rise of the authoritarian post-colonial state in Indonesia, even if there was some interruption during the brief period of parliamentary democracy in the 1950s. Though damaged and tattered, the apparatus of the colonial state did in fact survive the struggle for national independence. Indeed, it was to be appropriated, revived and manned by an emergent corps of officials and their families that straddled the state bureaucracy, the world of nascent middle-class professionals and military officers as well as that of small propertied interests. It was this corps of officials that would drive the project of economic development as well as the building of a modern national state in Indonesia (see Robison and Hadiz 2004: Chapter 3; also Hadiz and Robison 2012). As mentioned earlier, post-colonial Indonesia's state-led modernising project was envisioned in ways that had much in common with those launched, albeit at different points in time, in Turkey and Egypt. Nevertheless, while the late colonial state had presided over a social order in which no large landowning or capitalist class could appropriate the state apparatus, the ascendancy of the state and its corps of officials over civil society-based interests actually took place over a prolonged process in Indonesia (Anderson 1983; Robison 1986).

That there was a lag between independence and the consolidation of the state is understandable. First of all, achieving state cohesion took time because of the ravages of the Japanese occupation of 1942–1945 and the tumult of the 1945–1949 national war of independence. In truth, it was only following the chaotic and fragmented authoritarianism of Soekarno's Guided Democracy that succeeded the period of parliamentary democracy that a rigidly centralised form of state authoritarianism was finally to be achieved. This was marked by the establishment of the New Order in 1966, itself an outcome of Cold War-era struggles as they were manifest and intersected with social conflicts within Indonesia.

Such was the context within which the organisational vehicles of the petty bourgeoisie of the immediate post-colonial era had to operate. Their agenda, as put forward through a range of political parties (the Masyumi and the NU being the most prominent), was primarily to arrest the decline in fortunes that had become increasingly marked since the heyday of the Sarekat Islam. The idea of an Islamic state, which would be logically dominated by the *ummah*, continued to be attractive, as it was to Islamic movements elsewhere in the Muslim world at the time.

In the Indonesian case, a rival had re-emerged in the form of the PKI and its much more radical redistributive agenda. The PKI had quickly developed in the early post-colonial era into the most organised vehicle in Indonesian politics, developing grassroots support among the peasantry and Indonesia's still relatively small urban working class.

It was the two currents of Islam and communism that would compete and become embroiled in tense conflict with each other in Indonesia's early post-colonial period, bringing Islamic political vehicles into the orbit of the military, which was also involved in its own conflict with the PKI. This could be seen plainly in rivalries that developed among a number of associations representing different components of society that were linked, respectively, to Islamic or communist political vehicles, although such affiliations were by no means confined to these sorts of parties only. For example, organisations called Sarbumusi (linked to the NU) and Gasbiindo (linked to the Masyumi)[10] would compete for labour support with SOBSI, the dominant labour federation associated with the PKI. But the there was also the KBSI,[11] which was linked to the small Indonesian Socialist Party that was anti-PKI, intelligentsia-based and which worked closely with both the military and some Muslim organisations as well. No less importantly, there was also the Soekarnoist PNI, which held sway over a number of large mass organisations, including those that presided over workers and youths.

Violence, however, was to eventually emerge most evidently on the rural front, when peasant groups affiliated with the PKI – under the umbrella of the BTI (Indonesian Peasants' Front) – undertook 'unilateral' action in the early 1960s in the most heavily populated island of Java in the name of implementing land reform policy. Nonetheless, because of the structure of land-ownership, these actions were in fact aimed to seize control over parcels of land that often belonged to only slightly better-off peasants. Many such peasants might have been linked to Islamic organisations, especially the highly rural and Java-based NU (Lyon 1970), at the apex of which were families from which the strata of traditionalist religious teachers derived.

This was no simple conflict between the ardently religious and the nominally atheistic, however. Propertied petty bourgeois interests that underpinned Muslim organisational life were, as to be expected, profoundly averse to the agenda of expropriating private property represented by a self-confident Indonesian communism. Viewed from a comparative perspective, such a development was not surprising – we have also noted the same aversion to communism on the part of the Muslim Brotherhood in Egypt given the nature of the social origins of its

---

[10] Respectively, Sarbumusi was the Sarekat Buruh Muslimin Indonesia, or Indonesian Muslim Trade Unions Federation, while Gasbiindo was the Gabungan Serikat Buruh Islam Indonesia, or Conglomeration of Indonesian Islamic Trade Unions.

[11] Kongres Buruh Seluruh Indonesia, or the All Indonesia Labour Congress.

leadership. Later, Islamic populists in Turkey were also to compete for bases of mass support with that country's variety of leftist organisations.

In Indonesia, the conflict between Islamic and communist political vehicles was already prominent in the period of parliamentary democracy, but escalated during the so-called period of Guided Democracy (1959–1965). This was in spite of Soekarno's concept of 'Nasakom' – which was supposed to have combined nationalists, 'religionists' and communists in a common united front against the forces of 'Nekolim' (basically those representing Western neo-colonialism and imperialism) (see Mortimer 1974).

It was at this point that domestic social conflicts and the Cold War intersected in important ways in Indonesia. It is well known that the United States government was actively courting sections of the Indonesian army at this time. Indeed it was training key members of the Indonesian army's officer corps – including individuals who would come to play a prominent role in military and government during the New Order. American military aid to Indonesia thus rose by a considerable amount from the late 1950s, as documented by Simpson (2008: 47). The United States would also assist the Indonesian police force through the provision of training and educational programmes and even consultations on structural reorganisation. The latter was undertaken under a broad policy that also extended assistance to the police forces of countries like Thailand and Turkey (Simpson 2008: 80–81), at the front lines as they were, so to speak, of the Cold War.

In effect, American aid helped directly in the consolidation of the position of the coercive apparatus of the state as a self-interested actor within Indonesian politics. Such aid was aimed at not just improving martial prowess, but to instruct officers in taking up civilian, administrative and economic roles (Simpson 2008: 70–71). Given the military's growing strength and stature, it is no wonder that Islamic organisational vehicles turned to it for support in their rivalry with the PKI to develop mass bases of support within civil society.

When the carnage did come in 1965–1966, it has been revealed that the British and US governments actively supplied lists of communists to the army-led groups vigorously exterminating the PKI from the Indonesian polity (Roosa 2006). It is not surprising, therefore, that the response within American government and diplomatic circles to the slaughter to which they had contributed has been described as 'enthusiastic' and 'effusive' (Simpson 2008: 189).

Islamic politics, Soekarno and Soeharto

In many ways the bloody events of these years had served to overcome a long-standing stalemate in Indonesian politics, which Soekarno had unsuccessfully tried to address through the instalment of Guided Democracy. It is well documented, for example, that the parliamentary system of the 1950s was characterised by the swift rise and fall of fragile coalition governments. This meant that the system did not serve as an effective avenue through which authority over the state and its institutions could be firmly established by any single party or even coalition of parties (Feith 1962). It was within this system that Islamic political parties continued to fail in efforts to enshrine a constitutional framework that would privilege the *ummah*, and as a consequence, notionally provide them with advantage under the fluid conditions of political competition that then existed. Such was the case in spite of the fact that the major Islamic parties, the Masyumi and NU, did very well in the 1955 general elections, widely considered to be the country's most democratic until 1999.

Soekarno's grab for power took the form of dissolving parliament and instituting so-called Guided Democracy, within which authority would be more centralised on the Presidency and corporatist-style representation would become more important. His move was notably supported by the military – an institution that had been as equally marginalised as the presidency from the formal mechanisms of parliamentary democracy. By providing such support, the military gained representation as a 'functional group', thus affirming its status as one of the most powerful political institutions in post-colonial Indonesia. That this was achieved was indicated by two other related developments.

First, against the protestations of the communists and many trade unions, the military had gained managerial control over foreign enterprises nationalised by the state in 1957, something that gave it considerable economic power and ensured that it quickly developed a strong material interest to repel militant unionism. Second, the military was effectively already running the machineries of local government when martial law was declared, also in the late 1950s, against secessionist rebellions in outlying, mainly export-oriented regions, which had suffered the most from the central state's inflationary economic policies (Harvey 1977). It was in this way that the Indonesian military developed not just as a major political actor, but also a major economic one with a great stake in the way that domestic conflicts over the distribution of wealth would take place, just as their counterparts in Egypt and Turkey have done so as well.

It is significant that the PKI, which had benefited too from parliamentary democracy, threw its considerable weight behind Soekarno. Indeed, the first President of Indonesia had become more and more staunchly anti-imperialist and anti-Western in his rhetoric and inclinations as the 1960s approached, and therefore appeared to draw ideologically closer to the communists. It is true that that the demise of parliamentary democracy closed the door once and for all to the possibility of attaining power through the ballot box by the PKI. But the party's strategy was quickly revised with the advent of Guided Democracy

(Mortimer 1974). In simple terms, the route to power that came to be preferred by the PKI – then under the leadership of a relatively youthful generation under Dipa Nusantara Aidit – lay in an alliance with Soekarno rather than in parliament or revolutionary action.[12]

By contrast, the Islamic political parties were among the biggest losers in the demise of parliamentary democracy and the shift to authoritarian rule in Indonesia. From this point of view, they were as much a victim of a renewed state authoritarian impulse as the Democratic Party in Turkey was soon to become following the 1960 military coup in that country. It is worth pointing out that, given that parties like the Masyumi and NU had performed well in the 1955 elections *and* played key roles in many cabinets, they were in no way at all anti-democratic in their disposition and outlook. In fact, the experience of the 1950s no doubt provided a strong precedent for Islamic political party participation in electoral democracy in Indonesia after the fall of Soeharto. The largely unsuccessful PBB (Crescent and Star Party), for example, sees itself as the continuation of the much-fabled Masyumi. Such is the case even if the older parties' presence in parliament and in government ministries had turned out to be insufficient to advance an agenda that would ensure the advancement of the *ummah*. In much the same way, though not an Islamic party, the Democratic Party in Turkey has served as a reference point for Islamic activists that have pursued the electoral route to power in that country. Interestingly, those who have recently attempted to advance the position of the social alliance constituting the *ummah* in Egypt through democratic means are bereft of any similarly powerful historical reference points.

In the Indonesian case, the shift to authoritarianism under Soekarno thus confirmed that the section of society that formed one of the main social bases of support for these parties – the petty bourgeoisie ensconced in small trading and manufacturing activity – had failed to wield enough state power to transform their fortunes, which were already well in decline from the late colonial period. Their failure was most clearly demonstrated by the travesty that was the Benteng programme, through which *pribumi*/Muslim businesses were supposed to have been supported by preferential allocation

---

[12] This generation had taken over within a few years of the great debacle at the East Javanese town of Madiun in 1948. Here the PKI, under the leadership of an older generation beholden to the veteran revolutionary and agitator, Musso, was defeated by Republican troops and accused of stabbing the nation in the back by making a grab for power during the fight against the Dutch. The events surrounding the Madiun rebellion and its quashing remain somewhat controversial in the Indonesian historiography (Swift 2010). Hizbullah forces that had been created as an Islamic militia during the Japanese occupation, and had become based in the famed Batallion 426, are known to have taken part in defeating the PKI at Madiun. Interview with Adabi Darban, historian, Gadjah Mada University, 23 July 2010. The armed conflict at Madiun, taking place during the independence struggle and in the early years of the Cold War, can be seen as a key event in furthering animosity between the representatives of Islamic and communist politics in Indonesia.

of trading licences. Instead, the programme merely benefited political powerbrokers and intermediaries linked to powerful political parties, as Robison has noted (1986: 44–45).

To add insult to injury, the Islamic petty bourgeoisie was virtually ignored in the period of Guided Democracy (Feith 1962: 481–487). In fact, the petty bourgeoisie would suffer further setbacks at this time due to the outcomes of the aforementioned regional rebellions – supported by the West because of growing concerns about Soekarno's growing belligerence (Harvey 1977; Kahin and Kahin 1995). These setbacks were exacerbated because the Masyumi, the major party of urban traders and petty commodity producers, was implicated in the defeated rebellions focussed on the export-oriented Outer Islands. As a result, the party was banned by Soekarno in 1960, as was the much smaller Indonesian Socialist Party, supported by sections of the tiny middle class intelligentsia. Even if the heirs of the Masyumi tradition were to continue to be politically active through a range of organisational vehicles, some of which were more or less underground in nature, they would forever lament the passing of their greatest political vehicle. The Masyumi's major competitor, the more flexible NU, however, was to continue to exist and find new ways to ride the winds of political change throughout subsequent decades of harsh authoritarian rule.

Besides opening the door to long-lasting authoritarianism, the consequences of Guided Democracy for Indonesia's future were evident in the sphere of ideology. What was ideologically on offer under Soekarno was the notion that the state transcended vested interests and embodied the 'common good' due to the inherent unity of state and society. Hence the preference for corporatist forms of representation in Guided Democracy's revamped parliament. The New Order took this notion to greater lengths by fancifully referring to an indigenous culture that was naturally inclined towards mutual cooperation rather than egotistical individualism associated with political liberalism or polarising Marxist-style class conflict.

It was under Soeharto that the state became the undisputed arbiter of the common good even if, in reality, a range of predatory social interests had expropriated it. Moreover, the New Order would continue to uphold the restrictions of a political system purportedly based on Pancasila as being culturally authentic even as ever greater integration with globalisation processes were pursued, the benefits of which accrued to the politico-business oligarchy that had become entrenched in both state and market at this time. The implication of this ideological stance was that dissent was basically deemed socially dysfunctional as well as culturally alien, which would of course have great ramifications for any attempt at launching oppositional movements against the New Order (Bourchier 1996), including under the banner of Islam.

But there were major differences: while Soeharto's New Order presided over a mostly sustained and widely admired economic growth process, Soekarno's

Guided Economy produced a disastrous situation that would contribute to the events leading to his own downfall. Inflation had hit 600 per cent in 1965 – creating discontent, notably from the urban salaried – and spurred student protests that would eventually generate alliances between some student leaders and the military, notably those linked to the PMKI (Catholic Students Association) and the HMI (Islamic Students Association). Student activists linked with vestiges of the old Socialist Party were also instrumental in organising the anti-Soekarno protests. Ultimately, it was the army, with support from student groups, representatives of Islamic forces and the West, which toppled Soekarno.

The other big difference of course was that the authoritarian state under Soeharto reconnected with the West politically and economically and became the driving force of a more market-driven capitalist modernising project, but within which state intervention in the service of state-linked predatory interests became the norm. The Cold War context was pivotal again in this regard. Welcoming the sudden elimination of the world's third largest communist party along with the increasingly Third Worldist and anti-Western Soekarno, Western governments happily extended economic aid to Indonesia, which was henceforth considered as an ally in the struggle against the encroachment of communism across the Southeast Asian region. Foreign aid, which was followed by new inflows of private foreign investment (Simpson 2008: 229–236), thus served to reboot and revive the floundering national economy (Winters 1995). In many ways, what would happen in Egypt in Sadat just a few years later mirrored the Indonesian experience. In his attempt to revive an economy inherited from Nasser that was encumbered by bureaucratic inertia and mismanagement, Sadat – like Soeharto – was to turn to the once demonised West in order to gain access to foreign aid and investment.

In the Indonesian case, Robison and Hadiz (2004) have shown how a politico-business oligarchy evolved over different economic phases during New Order rule, firstly the oil boom of the 1970s and early 1980s and then the period of 'economic deregulation' afterwards. It was during this extended time as well that a powerful big bourgeoisie came to emerge and consolidate in Indonesia. Nevertheless, it has been pointed out that the big bourgeoisie was mainly made up of ethnic Chinese businesspeople, not the culturally Muslim entrepreneurs that had been claiming a greater stake in the economy since the early post-colonial period. This is the case even if a few notable *pribumi* enterprises also made it to the top ranks of the business league, primarily but not exclusively those originating from within the Soeharto family itself. The continued overwhelming dominance of the ethnic Chinese within the Indonesian big bourgeoisie has made it virtually impossible to incorporate large businesses into a multi-class alliance operating under the banner of the *ummah*, unlike in Egypt, and considerably more successfully in Turkey.

The alliance between big business and the officials of the state in Indonesia was partly protected by a political system characterised by three-party competition dominated by the state electoral vehicle, Golkar, corporatist 'representation', and the so-called floating mass, under which society was to be depoliticised to the furthest extent possible for the sake of stability and economic development. The two other political parties, the 'Islamic' United Development Party (PPP) and the 'nationalist' Indonesian Democratic Party (PDI) were in fact mere appendages to the system. Their ineffectuality as rivals to Golkar was already ascertained by the fact that they, respectively, hosted mutually antagonistic streams of political Islam (e.g. 'modernist' and 'traditionalist', represented by the heirs to the Masyumi and by the Javanese-dominated NU), and a hotchpotch of nationalist, pseudo-socialist, Protestant and Catholic political vehicles with very little to bind them together. So rather than a concession to the *ummah*, the PPP was an instrument to pre-empt its political mobilisation, although even within the highly regimented political framework that existed, extra efforts were sometimes exerted to ensure that the appeal of the party to religious sentiment was well contained.

In the mid-1980s the blatantly authoritarian tendencies of the New Order had been brought to their logical culmination by legislation that enshrined Pancasila as *azas tunggal* (sole principle), and which forced all political and societal groups to espouse their allegiance to it. Not surprisingly, among the biggest opponents of *azas tunggal* were to be found among the Islamic organisations at which it was mostly directed (Bourchier and Hadiz 2003: Chapter 6).[13] In effect, while the *ummah* was partly being placated in Egypt by the official privileging of Islam within the Egyptian Constitutions, and as the 'Turkish synthesis' was gathering momentum in Turkey, their counterparts in Indonesia were finding themselves more marginalised and oppressed than they had ever been since the period of Dutch colonial rule.

Conclusion

The relationship between the secular state and the forces of Islamic politics has fluctuated over time, in the context of state-led modernisation projects initiated in a Cold War-dominated global environment. This chapter has shown that the general patterns of the relationship in Indonesia have followed those that can be found in other societies in the Muslim world, although their specific manifestations have been different in each individual case.

In Indonesia, but also in Egypt and Turkey, the experience of societal marginalisation by state-dominated modernisation projects and entanglement

---

[13] See especially the excerpts by Syafruddin Prawiranegara, a former Masyumi leader and cabinet minister, and by the Islamic Students' Association (HMI).

in broader Cold War-era conflicts has left an indelible mark on Islamic movements. Thus, the demise of the Left during the Cold War – with the help of Islamic forces – has been an important factor in all these cases. But as was elaborated for the Indonesian case in particular, the holders of secular state power then turned against their erstwhile Muslim allies, so much so that the 1970s and 1980s constituted a period of intense repression against Islamic political vehicles. Though the timing of similar developments in Turkey and Egypt, respectively, have been different, the holders of secular state power there also turned against their Muslim allies following the vanquishing of the Left. Given further contradictions emanating from the economic development process, including the widening of the gap between rich and poor, the result was to reinforce the notion that being a member of the *ummah* was virtually identical to being part of the oppressed masses. All this clearly helped pave the way for the development of a new Islamic populism, based on the aspirations and frustrations of an *ummah* that increasingly came to reflect a multi-class alliance of those systematically marginalised within existing social orders. It is in such ways that the idioms of the *ummah* have substituted for those of the 'people', which have more commonly featured in populist rhetoric around the globe. Even as the *ummah* itself has become more complex in its sociological profile, a process of imagined homogenisation of its components took place, mirroring the way the *plebs* became the *populus*, to borrow from Laclau's lexicon.

The next several chapters address the concrete means through which the struggles of the *ummah* have been waged under continually evolving socio-economic circumstances and the challenges that these have presented. Such means involve the adoption of organisational vehicles that range from those that enmesh themselves in the process of democratic politics to those that are prone to resort to violence and intimidation or even terrorist activity.

5 Pathways of political failure
Dissent from the fringe

The new Islamic populism has encountered varying levels of success and failure largely depending on the broader social context within which it has evolved. The pathway to success has been premised on the development of cohesive multi-class alliances and organisational vehicles. By and large, these have then been able to contest power through democratic politics and repositioning within domestic and global markets. In this chapter, however, it is the pathway of failure and to the fringes of state and society that is the focus of attention. This sort of pathway is characterised by the comparative lack of development of cohesive multi-class alliances as well as excessive organisational fragmentation. This easily leads to a trajectory characterised by the activity of a host of vehicles, sometimes mutually competing, that can resort to acts of intimidation and violence, including to the extent of engaging in terrorist activity. Such an observation may become more relevant over time to Egypt, where the apparent triumph of the Muslim Brotherhood after the fall of Mubarak was quickly followed by dramatic defeat, sudden organisational chaos and plausible long-term political exclusion and repression.[1]

This chapter delves most deeply into the case of Indonesia, however, where a range of vehicles have long continued to operate outside of the sphere of formal democratic politics while competing for the support of, particularly, elements of the urban poor and the young educated members of the middle class. Together with new generations of petty bourgeoisie, these are the same sources of support for Islamist political parties that have failed to present the democratic route as a viable one through which control over the institutions of state power can be attained on behalf of the *ummah*. In Turkey, by contrast, the new Islamic populism's consistent successes within formal institutions of power, and plausible claims of having promoted social interests previously ignored by Kemalist elites, have eroded the appeal of those working outside them, especially vehicles that are intent

---

[1] Such chaos was to lead to the arrest and imprisonment of virtually all the top leadership of the Muslim Brotherhood, including the highly influential Khairat El-Shater and, startlingly, the Supreme Guide Mohamed Badia.

on mobilising support from the *ummah* for strategies of intimidation and violence. This chapter shows that there are strong links between the inability to compete in the democratic arena and the impulse within organisational vehicles of the new Islamic populism to retreat to conservative interpretations of religious dogma as they further entrench – and largely isolate – themselves on the fringes of state and society.

Genealogies of repression and violence

Outside of the Indonesian case, those of Egypt and Turkey have also displayed the existence of organisations deploying violent strategies in the recent past in advancing the struggles of a nationally conceived *ummah*. Nevertheless, particularly in the case of Turkey, violent strategies came to be more definitively supplanted by efforts to advance the *ummah* through more conventionally democratic ones, accompanied by engagement in global markets. In Egypt, violent strategies had been increasingly abandoned in favour of immersion in electoral politics even under the highly restrictive atmosphere of the Mubarak era. Quite instructively, however, the overthrow of the Morsi government in 2013 seemed to quickly trigger an upsurge of violent activity against the institutions of the state by unidentified groups, although these events were at first largely confined to peripheral regions. While it should be noted that attacks on Egyptian security forces had taken place in the Sinai by obscure militant Islamic groups as early as 2012, the genealogies of such groups were more rooted in local Bedouin tribes and in the Palestinian struggle on the Gaza Strip rather than in broader contests over the Egyptian state and the social interests it predominantly serves (El-Rashidi 2012).

In the Turkish experience, small Islamic groupings utilising violence had gained some measure of prominence by the 1960s. Karmon (1997) thus refers to a document compiled by the Turkish intelligence agency and police force in 1991 that mentioned the existence of no less than ten violent organisations. These were the Turkish Islamic Liberation Army (IKO), the Turkish Islamic Liberation Front (TIK-C), the Fighters of the Islamic Revolution (IDAM), the Turkish Islamic Liberation Union (TIKB), the World Sharia Liberation Army (DSKO), the Universal Brotherhood Front-Sharia Revenge Squad (EKC-SIM), Islamic Liberation Party Front (IKP-C), Turkish Fighters of the Universal Islamic War of Liberation (EIK-TM), Turkish Islamic Fighters Army (IMO) and Turkish Sharia Revenge Commandos (TSIK). Karmon mentions additional organisations, such as the Islami Harekat and Islamic Jihad and the particularly mysterious Great Eastern Islamic Fighters Front. Nevertheless, many such organisations had suffered greatly after the military coup of 1980, which was ostensibly aimed to restore order by striking at violent groups emanating from the entire political spectrum.

Subsequently, violent political activities in the name of the Islamic religion sharply declined. By the 2010s, actions labelled as 'terrorist' in Turkey were usually connected to the activities of the Kurdistan Workers' Party (PKK), the main armed group fighting for the establishment of an independent, or at least semi-autonomous, Kurdish homeland. But the promoters of Kurdish nationalism have been generally associated with leftist rather than Islamic political tendencies. This is not surprising given that the Islamic religion could not be expected to be particularly effective in ideologically mobilising an overwhelmingly Muslim Kurdish populace against their co-religionists, in spite of the variety of localised forms of Islam among the Kurds (Leezenberg 2001). Still, religion was not completely excluded from the long-simmering conflict: among the most virulent opponents of Kurdish nationalism has been the Hizbullah militia (not to be confused with its namesake in Lebanon). This murky Islamic militia was often engaged in violent conflict with Kurdish separatist groups in the 1990s and early 2000s, with the alleged backing of the Turkish state. According to Karmon (1997), the militia, which was linked to the Islami Harekat, particularly despised the PKK as a belligerent leftist and atheist movement. More importantly, however, its utilisation by the state is an extension of the longer history of deployment of Islamic forces in campaigns against the Left when required by political expediency.[2]

It would be erroneous, nevertheless, to relate the decline of violent forms of 'Islamic' political activity to the operations of the Turkish state's security apparatus only. Such decline should be explained as well in relation to the greater success that alliances struggling for the *ummah* have experienced in the sphere of Turkish electoral politics since the 1990s. As already pointed out, the AKP itself is basically a product of long-standing formal and informal social and political networks that had been marginalised within the Kemalist social order – having a lineage that is traceable to the various vehicles that helped sustain Islam as a potential force during the height of the radically secular nationalist project associated with the establishment of the Turkish Republic. But the successes attained by the AKP have arguably made promoting the interests of the *ummah* through the electoral route more appealing than ever before, especially when combined with previous, though interrupted, achievements attained through Refah and, before that, association with the *tariqa*-friendly Özal government of the 1980s.

In Egypt too, where the Muslim Brotherhood had earned a reputation as the most coherent and disciplined of civil society organisations, the appeal of

---

[2] According to leading Kurdish movement activists, the AKP has more recently attempted to use religious piety among Kurds to weaken the resilience of the Kurdish movement. It has attempted to encourage an 'Islamic' alternative to the existing movements, going as far as to free anti-PKK former Hizbullah fighters from prison. Interview with senior officials of the DTK (Democratic Society Congress), Diyarbakir, 26 August 2013.

terrorist acts undertaken in the name of the *ummah* had also been steadily eroded well before the movement briefly attained power following the Arab Spring. This general recoil from violence in fact goes back at least to the 1980s, when the Muslim Brotherhood began to engage, albeit semi-clandestinely, with the formal institutions of power under the authoritarian regime, which allowed it both to participate in official politics and to continue to run its social and charitable activities. The extent to which a stable accommodation with the regime was ever accomplished is a contentious matter, though domestic critics have gone so far as to depict the organisation as a peripheral part of Mubarak's authoritarian regime, as noted before. Nevertheless, the dismantling of the Brotherhood's militia wing by the 1970s represented perhaps the most concrete manifestation of the abandonment of violent strategies – although not necessarily by splinter groups that were then opposed to such a development. Set up in the 1930s as the notorious Nizam al-Khass (Secret Apparatus) (Pargeter 2010: 27), it had been accused of a number of violent activities in the past, including high-profile political assassinations.[3]

Since then the Muslim Brotherhood had made steady inroads into formal politics in the authoritarian era, culminating initially in their success in the 2005 parliamentary elections, while continuing to maintain a rich tradition of civil society activism. Though the organisation remained illegal, Muslim Brotherhood candidates ran under the banner of other parties in the 1980s and then as independents in ensuing elections. This valuable experience no doubt made the organisation better equipped to operate in the electoral politics of the immediate post-Mubarak era, in spite of the entrenched position of a powerful Egyptian military.

Even the Gama'a al-Islamiyya,[4] an organisation that had once merged and then broken ranks with the Muslim Brotherhood – over the latter's perceived greater propensity to make compromises with the regime – had long renounced violence (Meijer 2011), although not before perpetrating the infamous massacre at Luxor in 1997.[5] Just prior to Morsi's fall, quite curiously, a leading member of the organisation had been appointed governor of the very same region. There is no question that the campaign against violent groups undertaken by the Egyptian state – resulting in a bloated, brutal and increasingly

---

[3] Nevertheless, some of its opponents still consider it to be a violent organisation because of its history, and oppose cooperation on this basis. Interview with the El Khalwatiyah *tariqa*, Cairo, 20 March 2011. The sheik of this Sufi Order accuses the Muslim Brotherhood of decades-long persecution of the followers of Egyptian Sufism.
[4] The organisation's name would be transliterated in Indonesian as Jemaah Islamiyah, but there is no direct connection between these two vehicles.
[5] Interestingly, Temby (2010: 35) points out that would-be members of Indonesia's Jemaah Islamiyah had a close relationship to members of its Egyptian namesake while both were fighting in Afghanistan, with both perceiving themselves to be the victims of persecution by illegitimate tyrannical regimes.

expensive internal security force (Stacher 2012; Soliman 2011) – contributed to this sort of dramatic change of direction. The organisation did attempt to 'justify' the change by citing the 'fact' that Egypt was already an Islamic state because of its recognition of Islamic sources of law. Nevertheless, 'a fundamental reason for Gama'a's revised strategy was the failure of armed struggle to achieve its objective. In effect Gama'a came to the conclusion: when you see that you cannot win, then stop fighting' (Bayat 2013a: 217).

It is notable then that the Gama'a al-Islamiyya subsequently joined forces with the broader Salafist push to stamp a greater Islamic character on the 'Egyptian Revolution' of 2011, through an electoral vehicle rather blandly called the Building and Development Party. It did so by joining a Salafist-led electoral bloc in 2011–2012, which thus merged two tendencies – the Salafist Call (Al-Da'wa Al Salafiyaa) and the Gama'a al-Islamiyya – both of which had only recently opposed engagement in secular electoral politics. This basically left an organisation called Islamic Jihad as the main purveyor of violent activity – a former ally of the Gama'a al-Islamiyya, it had come to develop links to Al-Qaeda.

An important development in the Egyptian case was in fact the decision of the Salafist Call – as an umbrella organisation for a range of smaller groupings – to launch itself into electoral politics. This was in contradiction to a previously held rejection of this manner of politics that had been presented as a matter of religious doctrine. The Salafist movement was even widely accused, not least by rank-and-file followers of the Muslim Brotherhood, of being opportunistic: that it had avoided involvement in secular politics in the past to distance itself from oppositional activities against the Mubarak regime, while later seeking to reap the rewards from its fall. Such criticism no doubt gained credibility when the Salafist stream of Egyptian politics found that it was somehow able to accommodate the military-led ouster of the Muslim Brotherhood-dominated government led by President Morsi and provide support for the subsequent government of military strongman, General Abdel Fattah Al-Sisi.

The previous ostensibly apolitical stance of the Salafists, in fact, had served them quite well, for they were not perceived as posing a serious threat to the Mubarak regime. Even if Salafists were sometimes harassed and jailed by a security apparatus obsessed with keeping order and control (much like Indonesia's under Soeharto), their networks enjoyed room to develop and expand through highly dispersed preaching and charity activity that largely failed to catch the eye of analysts.[6] The Salafist movement as a whole also benefited from being allowed to broadcast their message through television stations they operated – a privilege that would have never been extended to the more directly threatening Muslim Brotherhood.

---

[6] Interview with Mohamed Nour, spokesman for Al-Nour Party (a Salafi electoral vehicle), Cairo, 1 April 2012.

It is clear that the Salafist movement's involvement in electoral politics in Egypt had little to do with any theological reconsideration of the merits of liberal or secular ideas. Its participation was triggered more obviously by a realisation that to remain withdrawn from the sphere of official politics would not fulfil any purpose when opportunities abounded to make direct inroads into power due to the unravelling of the old regime. Thus, in spite of significant internal fissures – characterised by the existence of numerous competing leaders, even in a single city like the Salafi stronghold of Alexandria – the movement still managed to produce a formidable party called Al-Nour. It was Al-Nour that led the so-called Alliance of Egypt during the 2011–2012 parliamentary elections, which included the Building and Development Party. With constituencies in rural and urban poor communities, petty traders and the lower middle class, Al-Nour and its allies represented the second biggest winner of the first post-Mubarak elections – attaining more than 25 per cent of the popular vote in an exceedingly complex electoral system.

In the Indonesian case, New Order brutality had clearly induced various kinds of underground activity carried out by a range of vehicles, as had been induced in different phases of Turkish and Egyptian history. What they had in common was that they became ensconced only at the outer fringes of politics even when elite rivalries brought Soeharto to embrace certain individuals and groups that claimed to represent the *ummah* as a whole, particularly through ICMI. Nothing illustrates this better than the fact that such underground groups were largely spectators to events when the end of the New Order finally came. Though some of these were later activated in various guises by sections of the New Order elite in order to save the doomed Habibie presidency, they were generally not in any position to be involved in the hurly-burly of establishing and developing political parties once the new institutions of democratic politics were in place. Not surprisingly, therefore, this led to a propensity to continue to reject electoral politics altogether, which had developed a tarnished reputation during the Soeharto era anyway, due to alleged manipulation of results and their rigidly controlled nature. It is useful to keep in mind Sidel's (2006) basic idea, in this connection, that the prominence of violent *jihadi* groups in the initial post-Soeharto period was actually indicative of weakness and desperation after decades of suppression, rather than vigour and strength.

In addition, the New Order was never able to ideologically address social discontent that was being expressed in the form of Islamic dissent through underground political vehicles. Even the establishment of ICMI in the early 1990s did not achieve this, although it is arguable that it was never designed specifically to do so. If ICMI helped to neutralise some Islamic-based opposition to the New Order, it did not absorb the varied elements of Islamic political dissent into its formidable network of patronage, no matter how well oiled its machinery was. This is because it was particularly concerned with co-opting upwardly mobile members of the middle class and providing conduits to bureaucratic power, including to middle-class activists and critics of the regime. It did little to produce a bourgeoisie organically connected to the *ummah* and neither did it make inroads into the masses of Indonesian rural and urban poor so long separated from political activity due to the New Order's enduring 'floating mass' policy.

Suppressing Islam in the New Order

Thus, the social agents of Islamic politics who remained left out in the cold would continue to be hostile to the New Order's brand of highly centralised state authoritarianism and consigned to the margins of state and society. Significantly, some of these considered themselves the heirs of the old Darul Islam (DI) movement and rebellion. After the fall of the New Order, such individuals would be found operating within militia groups, religious associations advocating an Islamic state and, in more rare cases, Islamic terror networks, as well. They recruited followers from both within the masses of the lumpenproletariat and among sections of the educated middle class that found no AKP or Muslim Brotherhood to follow. As shut out from the corridors of power in the democratic era as they had been under New Order authoritarianism, they held on to the idea that only an Islamic state would release the *ummah* from a position of continual socio-economic marginalisation. Though some would forge murky alliances with sections of the state security apparatus that had found themselves in retreat due to the advent of democratisation, this too proved to be no real avenue to socio-economic or political advancement.

Interestingly, there had been much optimism among the leaders of the social and political organisations claiming to represent the interests of the *ummah* at the start of the New Order. These had naturally hoped to be rewarded by the military for their role in establishing the New Order on top of the destruction of the PKI. It certainly should have worked in their favour that the alliance with the army leadership was ostensibly premised on a joint military and societal effort to save the nation and the state from the clutches of communism. In fact, they had achieved together the common aim of thwarting the communist project that seemed to threaten the interests of petty commodity producers and traders and the military alike. It should be recalled that the latter had taken over managerial control of a range of state enterprises and was, therefore, often pitted against radical communist-linked unions (Hadiz 1997: Chapter 3).

However, the expectations of these Muslim leaders were to be quickly dashed for obvious reasons. With the elimination of the communists from the social and political landscape, and the concomitant crippling of the more radical of the Soekarnoist mass organisations, political Islam was the only force in Indonesia to have the potential to mobilise at the grassroots level against the New Order. The mere presence of Islamic forces with a strong grassroots base simply went against a founding logic of the New Order – which was to undertake development on the basis of the political demobilisation and disorganisation of society at large. The potential capacity for political mobilisation on the basis of a common identity founded on membership of a socially and economically marginalised *ummah* was perhaps the only major threat to the institutional arrangements of power that were being cultivated in the early New Order.

That Islamic organisations would be the main target of this evolving system of stringent control was already evident in the strong interference by state officials in the formation of a potentially strong Muslim electoral vehicle – the Parmusi – in the late 1960s. The concern among these officials was that the party might have competed seriously with Golkar, the state electoral vehicle. The New Order instead artificially created the aforementioned PPP – within which many Parmusi advocates were eventually absorbed – to function ostensibly as the electoral vehicle of the *ummah* in Indonesia.[7]

Indeed, wariness of Islamic political mobilisation had ensured from the beginning that the alliance against the Left led by the military could not fully absorb all Islamist elements in Indonesian society. Among those only embraced with difficulty were former participants in the armed Darul Islam rebellion, even if some had been reactivated by the military temporarily in the fight against the communists. While it is widely accepted that some members of the movement had been domesticated through the provision of small business opportunities by their former military foes – and that several worked subsequently as agents for the intelligence apparatus – most would nurse genuinely great antipathy towards the New Order. Operating continually on the fringes of the formal institutions of political and social life, and being economically marginal, they would be among the most frequent victims of state repression. Not surprisingly, some widely read International Crisis Group (ICG) reports (e.g. 2002) identify the genealogies of many perpetrators of terrorist activity in post-Soeharto Indonesia within the old DI.

For Darul Islamists and their sympathisers, the New Order's 'abandonment' of the *ummah* was seen in the apparently growing influence of bureaucrats and

---

[7] It is instructive, however, that there was nothing in the PPP's name that outwardly suggested an Islamic orientation; it was in fact rather anachronistically technocratic in nature. The very establishment of the party was surely a move calculated to ensure the absence of a naturally appealing vehicle to Muslim voters from the electoral scene while simultaneously appearing to accommodate the aspirations of the more pious among them. In later developments, the PPP was even prevented from using the *ka'bah* (the most holy of Muslim shrines in Mecca) as its symbol. Indeed, in spite of being generally compliant, the PPP did cause several stirs during its history. First, it opposed New Order-era legislation on marriage and on religion, the latter of which bestowed official recognition to *aliran kepercayaan* – generally seen to refer to traditional Javanist beliefs (Feillard and Madinier 2010: 33–34). Second, the PPP also caused embarrassment for the New Order by performing better than was apparently tolerated in general elections that took place in the late 1970s and early 1980s.

military figures with an *abangan* (or Javanese syncretic) outlook, or who were Christians, but also in the rapid rise of ethnic Chinese business groups. Thus, helping to encourage a sense of Muslim marginalisation were such developments as the rise of CSIS (Centre for Strategic and International Studies) in the 1970s, a think tank that was under the direct protection of Ali Moertopo, and which enjoyed the support of prominent ethnic Chinese business leaders. CSIS was in fact a major architect of the system of highly regulated elections, state-created corporatist organisations and 'floating mass politics' that effectively curtailed the possibility of the *ummah*'s mass mobilisation.[8] Within CSIS, Moertopo had collected a coterie of associates and protégés from minority religious or ethnic backgrounds. It is no wonder the system was viewed by some as a means of safeguarding the interest of minority elites against the much larger *ummah*.

Notably, a key advocate of Moertopo's political demobilisation project was the elusive but influential figure of the Jesuit priest Father Josephus Gerardus Beek. A stringent Dutch anti-communist, he had long presided over now-fabled training courses designed to produce skilled and mentally disciplined Catholic political cadres (see Bourchier 1996). Strongly associated with sections of the military and intelligence forces under the influence of Moertopo, he was part of the inner circle of the CSIS clique. Though Beek's political role was always behind the scenes, he was well known for having been concerned with the possibility of Islamic dominance over Indonesian politics and remains a legend among many Catholic intellectuals today.[9]

While the clique linked to Beek was growing in influence, state interference with the establishment of the aforementioned Parmusi had effectively terminated the already-stalled political careers of numerous Islamist leaders. Among the most prominent of these was the highly respected Mohammad Natsir – a former leader of the Masyumi and a former prime minister of Indonesia during the period of parliamentary democracy. Once a strong detractor of Soekarno's 'Old Order', he became a strident critic of the New Order as well. His political career blocked, Natsir was to play a key role instead in the growth and development of an organisation called the Dewan Dakwah Islamiyah Indonesia (DDII), which was devoted to preaching and proselytising activities. It would come to be regarded as a consistent, if not always vocal, source of opposition to the New Order at least till the early 1990s, as well as a mainstay of socially conservative Islamic thinking. During its development, the DDII would benefit from Natsir's high standing among the governments and Islamic scholars of the Middle East, from which the organisation garnered the financial resources to carry out its activities, including a programme of sending Indonesians to study the Islamic religion in the Middle East.[10]

---

[8] See Moertopo (1973) for the major outlines of this political system.
[9] See Soedarmanta (2008), for a reverential treatment of Beek's life.
[10] Interview with Ustad Syuhada Bahri, chairman, Dewan Dakwah Islamiyah Indonesia (DDII) and former personal secretary to Mohammad Natsir, Jakarta, 3 January 2011.

It was stated in the previous chapter that the New Order imposed the eclectic state ideology of Pancasila on all political parties and social organisations in the mid-1980s. It is obvious that Islamic groups were the main targets of the *azas tunggal* legislation. That the New Order had to resort to such legislation reflected the reality that such Islamic groups were difficult to dismiss as an expression of 'alien' influences like Marxism or political liberalism. It was certainly not possible to eliminate them in the same bloody fashion experienced by the PKI. The chosen solution to the problem was thus to especially curtail independent organising by Islamic groups by placing more obstacles to their activity in civil society. One way was to legalistically reduce their capability to mobilise support on the basis of common identity founded on a marginalised *ummah*. It is useful to note that even before the advent of *azas tunggal*, state propaganda –produced with significant contribution by Moertopo and his cohorts – had already gone to great lengths to portray the challenge posed by Islamists as being associated with terrorist activity that induced chaos and disrupted economic development.

But of course suppression did not just rely on legal codes or propaganda but involved a heavy dose of old-fashioned physical violence and intimidation against Islamic activists. As such, New Order brutality had clearly induced various kinds of underground activity carried out by a range of vehicles. These had been already so ensconced in the outer fringes of politics and society that they were not able to take much advantage when elite rivalries brought Soeharto to provide support for ICMI, and notionally, to the *ummah* as a whole. This also explains why there was almost nothing in their previous experiences that would have placed them in a position to compete successfully in the business of developing political parties once it was possible to do so freely, except for communists, after the fall of Soeharto.

In spite of intense state repression, political opposition throughout the New Order nevertheless frequently took the form of criticism against the government expressed during what were ostensibly religious lectures and sermons, including those given by DDII-linked individuals. For a short time in the early New Order, such sermons could even be broadcast on the local radio in some areas, such as in Solo, Central Java, which would become an important site for political socialisation into underground political activity in later years. However, criticism of the government via radio broadcasting had been blocked by the early 1970s, by which time the New Order had become more confident in exercising its authoritarian rule over Islamic groups.[11]

Much of the politically infused preaching and proselytising took place in many rural areas that had been strongholds of the PKI – for the peasantry that lived there had good reason to acquire stronger religious credentials and cooperate with proselytisers who would 'convert' them to Islam (or Christianity). This was

---

[11] Interview with Ustad Taufik Usman, Ngruki, Solo, 18 July 2007.

to avoid being targeted as communists and thereby prevent being imprisoned without trial or summarily executed. But gradually such activity was also being undertaken through mosques situated in the congested, lower-class urban neighbourhoods of Jakarta and other urban centres. As Raillon (1994: 211) noted, 'many mosque complexes include facilities for supporting not only religious activity, but also cultural promotion and daily politics: clinics, dormitories, canteens, shops, printing workshops, libraries, sports equipment, etc'.

It was in this kind of environment that some individuals would gain a kind of underground celebrity status, and by the early 1980s, many even had their sermons taped and distributed from hand to hand, especially among an especially targeted urban-lower and lower-middle-class audience. Such social groups were of course a product of the process of rapid capitalist development during the New Order, which had the effect of stimulating migration from the villages to the ever more congested cities, especially on the main island of Java. The members of what developed into a lumpenproletariat would have found much that resonated with them in sermons railing against social injustices or political corruption given their encounters with the harsh realities of urban life.

This was not the only form of expression of Islamic-oriented discontent, however, for more overtly violent reactions were also to come to the fore from groups that had heretofore remained mostly in the political underground (Solahudin 2011 Chapters 3–6). The most well known of these was the shadowy entity known as the Komando Jihad, which is discussed in more detail in the next chapter. Suffice to say that it was one of a number of violent groups that appeared in official statements and press reports of the period, and which tended to share the common theme of continuing the Darul Islam struggle to establish an Islamic state that was supposed to have been terminated in the early 1960s. Indeed, the relationship between Komando Jihad and the Darul Islam has been examined extensively (e.g. Temby 2010). It received worldwide attention in 1981, when several alleged members hijacked an Indonesian commercial aircraft which they forced to land at the airport in Bangkok, where they were thwarted by a successful operation by Indonesian elite military commandos working in tandem with Thai forces (see Jenkins 2002).[12]

---

[12] This is known as the 'Woyla' incident, after the moniker of the DC-9 aeroplane that was scheduled to fly from Medan to Palembang, both cities on the island of Sumatra, before it was hijacked and then diverted to Bangkok. The alleged mastermind of the plot was a man who would be popularly known as 'Imran'. Some of the initiators of the *usroh* system of caderisation and recruitment in Bandung and who knew him recall how he had mysteriously arrived on the scene in West Java, claiming to be an Imam and actively recruited followers to his cause. They hold the belief that Imran was an imposter who was planted within the Komando Jihad and the broader Darul Islam network by the Indonesian intelligence services, using well-tested tactics. Interview with Bambang Pranggono and Syarif Hidayat, Istiqomah Mosque activists, Bandung, 14 July 2012. The veracity of this claim is hard to establish but it is one that is often heard within present-day Darul Islamist circles.

No matter how sceptically one might approach interpretations that are derived from Indonesian military or intelligence sources of that period, it was quite clear that the military defeat of Kartosuwiryo in 1962 and his death by execution did not mean the end of the entire Darul Islam saga. Beyond Komando Jihad, reports (e.g. ICG 2002) suggest that two individuals associated with the broad DI movement subsequently founded the notorious Jemaah Islamiyah in the 1990s: the late Abdullah Sungkar and his colleague, Abubakar Ba'asyir. Importantly, both clerics, who in their younger days were part of the Masyumi's youth organisation (Feillard and Madinier 2010: 108), had founded the Al-Mukmin *pesantren* in Ngruki, near Solo, Central Java, in the 1970s, as part of proselytising activity that followed the destruction of the PKI in its former strongholds. In this effort, they were supported by Mohammad Natsir's Dewan Dakwah Islamiyah Indonesia, for which Sungkar had acted as representative in Central Java.

As critics of the Soeharto regime, both had been forced to flee into exile in Malaysia in the mid-1980s to avoid potentially lengthy prison terms in Indonesia. It was during their Malaysian sojourn that they were reportedly active in recruiting Indonesians and other Southeast Asians to fight with the Taliban against the Soviet-supported government in Afghanistan. These efforts essentially constituted the beginnings of Jemaah Islamiyah (JI), the structures of which are said to have developed from 1993 to 1995 after a process of slow evolution (Solahudin 2011: 227–236). Interestingly, according to Hastings (2010: 50–51), Indonesian and Southeast Asian recruits were instructed that they were to utilise their experience of fighting in Afghanistan for a later struggle to form a Southeast Asian transnational Islamic state, but one that actually focussed on Indonesia as the largest country in the region. It would be too simplistic, therefore, to suggest that JI has been merely an Al Qaeda arm in Southeast Asia, even if some of their fighters had fought alongside each other in Afghanistan.

In the meantime, tensions between state authorities and Islamic activists in Indonesia had reached a breaking point at about the same time that Sungkar and Ba'asyir had been captured and then went on self-imposed exile. This was indicated, among others, by the occurrence of a particularly bloody event in the Northern Jakarta working-class enclave around the historic port of Tanjung Priok. The event involved an infamous massacre that was ostensibly sparked by the defilement of a local mosque by a low-level security officer, the protests against which resulted in the arrest of four members of its congregation. After several days of heightened unrest in the vicinity of the mosque, government troops shot and killed a disputed number of Muslim street demonstrators who were demanding the release of these individuals on the evening of 12 September 1984.

Among those slain was the leader of the protesters, a businessman and political activist named Amir Biki. Previously a Muslim student leader who had supported the military-led toppling of Soekarno, Biki became an entrepreneur who did business with the state oil company Pertamina (see Raillon 1994). By the late 1970s, however, he had apparently become disenchanted with what he viewed as the New Order's favourable treatment of Chinese businesses and his own relative lack of advancement. In this way, Biki was quite typical of members of the Islamic petty bourgeoisie whose high hopes were quickly dashed in the early years of the New Order.[13]

The Tanjung Priok massacre has been usually blamed on the heavy-handedness of the late general Benny Moerdani, a Catholic who had been regarded as a protégé of Ali Moertopo earlier in his career and also of Father Beek. As commander-in-chief of the Armed Forces (1983–1988) and minister of defence (1988–1993), the widely feared Moerdani was yet another key Soeharto aide for a number of years. Also implicated in the incident was General Try Sutrisno, then commander of the Jakarta military command and subsequently vice president of Indonesia (1993–1998).

But they were not the only New Order generals to have been implicated in atrocities committed against Islamic political activists. Another was General Hendropriyono, later also a military commander of Jakarta, then chief of the national intelligence body and a post-Soeharto cabinet minister. He was a key figure in a bloody incident that took place in 1989, far from the gaze of the pre-Internet world, in the small village of Talangsari in the province of Lampung, on the southern tip of Sumatra. It was here that security forces under his command (then as a colonel) brutally attacked scores of migrant villagers believed to have been clandestinely involved in a project to resuscitate the Darul Islam movement and to establish an Islamic state (Van Bruinessen 1996).[14] The number of people killed in the attack remains unknown, though it could have been easily in the hundreds.

It was already mentioned that tensions between sections of political Islam and the state in the 1980s were also reflected in the vehement rejection by a number of Muslim organisations of the aforementioned legislation that installed Pancasila as *azas tunggal*. They correctly saw that the legislation on Pancasila was aimed at further constraining the possible appeal of Islam as political ideology that could mobilise the masses, sections of which had grown disenchanted with Soeharto. Many mainstream Islamic organisations – like the HMI (Himpunan Mahasiswa Islam; Islamic Students Association) – eventually relented, however, and formally accepted Pancasila. Perhaps this was not all too surprising: continued opposition entailed risking personal well-being given

---

[13] Prior to the massacre, Biki had given a fiery anti-government speech to his supporters. Key parts of this speech are presented in Biki (2003).

[14] Also, interview with Nurhidayat, Jakarta, 2 July 2012. A Darul Islam activist of the 1970s and 1980s generation, Nurhidayat was instrumental in the planning and implementation of the plan to settle Darul Islamist activists and their families in Talangsari, Lampung.

the brutality of the security apparatus under Soeharto. Even if this were to be evaded, there would have been costs in terms of personal careers, as being locked out from the New Order's system of patronage meant consigning oneself to political and even economic oblivion.

Significantly, those who had had little part anyway in these networks, and had little chance of being recruited into them, continued to resent the legislation as a coercive attempt to place man's law above that of God's. As discussed further in the next chapter, these included activists in Darul Islam networks that had been long working through underground cells by this time, typically with a great degree of autonomy from each other. In any case, a continuing atmosphere of mutual mistrust would be a feature of the relationship between the state and Islamic social and political organisations for many years to come.

In short, for Islamic political activists in Indonesia operating in such a context, the ideal of an Islamic state – even if established through violence – grew more in its appeal as it became clearer that the authoritarianism of the secular state was a major impediment to the advancement of the *ummah*. In Turkey and Egypt, by contrast, there were nascent developments that began to suggest the possibility of other pathways. Thus, when repression against the social agents of Islamic politics reached its height in the 1980s, the Muslim Brotherhood in Egypt was starting to immerse itself in the Mubarak-era system of electoral politics. At the same time, some of the political precursors of the AKP in Turkey were starting to benefit from the 'highly controlled opening to religious groups' that was then being initiated by a state controlled by military Kemalists and some of their technocratic allies (Tuğal 2013: 116).

To Be or Not to Be an Islamic state

A key proposition being offered in this chapter is that the strategies and vehicles of the new Islamic populism are basically contingent in nature, and they can therefore vary greatly from case to case. This is so even if all populisms juxtapose 'the people' against 'the elite' and the objective of the new Islamic populism in particular remains a reconfiguration of existing relations of domination that would advance the position of the *ummah*. Thus, the AKP has prominently relegated the struggle for an Islamic state to one aimed at safeguarding a morally upright community as well as good governance reforms, with the social effect of broadening the party's reach to those who may find greater appeal in its economic management record.

But the AKP experience cannot simply be emulated without regard to the historical and structural factors that made it possible. As explained, the party has arrived at a winning electoral formula by merging moral concerns – based on Islamic precepts – with a neoliberal good governance agenda that enthusiastically embraces the market and globalisation. Finding much support from a predominantly export-oriented so-called 'Anatolian bourgeoisie' – traditionally subordinate to the 'Istanbul bourgeoisie' associated closely with the 'Kemalist' establishment (Gumuscu 2010) – the AKP has also relied on well-educated members of the new middle class now found across the professions. These are attracted to, on the one hand, ideas of Islamic morality that imply the eradication of cronyistic practices and the promotion of a culture of advancement through skills and education. On the other hand, the social justice ideals that had been pervasive within the networks that sustained Islam as a social force during the Kemalist onslaught continue to be cultivated through engagement with charitable activities and the provision of social services to the poor. Although the electoral vehicle spawned by the Muslim Brotherhood in Egypt, the Freedom and Justice Party, evidently looked at the AKP for inspiration, somewhat ironically, it was the Muslim Brotherhood's extensive involvement in welfare activities that had provided the original model for politics through social and charitable engagement in Turkey.

The Freedom and Justice Party, too, indicated that it would relegate the struggle for an Islamic state in favour of broader governance reform issues. But it did so in an atmosphere of growing schism between religious and secular liberal and leftist elements in Egyptian political activists and sporadic violence between Muslims and Coptic Christians – whether or not instigated by a Machiavellian security apparatus. Though to a lesser degree than ethnic Chinese Indonesians, the Coptic Christian community in Egypt has been open as well to the accusation that it is overly represented among wealthy sections of society (Bayat 2010: 203), thus providing added credence for movements that conceive of the oppressed 'people' as being more or less synonymous with the *ummah*. Of course, Turkey had 'dealt' with a similar issue, historically, through the massive population swaps of the early twentieth century, which no doubt involved incalculable human suffering. All of this is suggestive of the fact that the Turkish 'model' cannot be so easily adopted in other contexts, including that of Egypt, where the Muslim Brotherhood/FJP appeared to be overly driven to emulate the successes of the AKP in establishing dominance over state institutions within a much shorter time.

In Indonesia, non-parliamentary vehicles and strategies of various kinds have retained a significant measure of attractiveness whether during the era of harsh state authoritarianism or the period of democratic reforms. Thus, the post-Soeharto era has seen the proliferation of Islamic paramilitary groups and the appearance of secretive terror cells – initially under the umbrella of the notorious Jemaah Islamiyah but more recently in a number of more atomised groupings – which have proven their capacity for deadly, albeit sporadic, violence. Not surprisingly, compared to those who do battle in the electoral arena, these groups are much more prone to espouse the virtues of the Islamic state and the imposition of religious morality. Among the paramilitary groups that self-identify with such virtues are the Islamic Defenders' Front (FPI),[15] Forkabi (Forum Komunikasi Anak Betawi) and FBR (Forum Betawi Rempug), all of which either originate from or are exclusively based in the urban harshness that is the Greater Jakarta area (e.g. Wilson 2008). In addition, there is also the Hizbut Tahrir Indonesia (HTI), a self-proclaimed political party (and 'branch' of the global Hizbut Tahrir founded in Palestine) that opposes participation in Western-style electoral politics. Notoriously secretive about its structure and leadership, it has made inroads, especially among urbanising middle-class students and youths.

Significantly, many of these vehicles are also highly localised, so that in the Yogyakarta, for instance, we find branches of FPI, but also the paramilitary wing of the Majelis Mujahidin Indonesia, the Gerakan Pemuda Ka'bah (which is linked to the old Soeharto-era political party, the PPP), and the now-defunct Lasykar Jihad. Others, such as Hizbullah, Jundullah, FPIS and JAT, are based in Solo, Central Java. In this city there is also an 'Islamic' street criminal organisation that came to form its own militia, known as Hisbah. Operating in the city's slum areas in and around the Semanggi area, it has often come up against organised gangs linked to the PDI-P, the major descendant of Soekarnoist secular nationalism, but also other 'Islamic' militia and gangs.[16]

Indeed, some Islamic militia groups – most notably the FPI – are widely believed to be involved in criminal activity, including racketeering, even as they ardently oppose the presence of 'dens of vice' such as nightclubs, pubs and massage parlours. Anachronistically, the FBR has deployed its members to work as security guards in major nightclubs in the section of the capital city that is known for a wide range of illicit trades. This provides some evidence of the great flexibility that can be employed even by self-consciously hard-line organisations in terms of actions that can be justified by their espoused beliefs.[17] Perhaps it is due to this kind of pragmatism, as well, that the FBR has become involved in a range of battles with organisations like the Pemuda Pancasila – the main Golkar and army-related youth/gangster organisation of the Soeharto era – for control of particular corners of the Jakarta underworld.

[15] The FPI is arguably the most infamous of these groups. See Jahroni (2008) for a discussion.
[16] Interview with Abdul Rauf, former second in command of Hisbah, Solo, 9 July 2011. In 2011, Hisbah came to lose its leader, one Sigit Qurdowi, who was killed by police officers from Densus 88, the elite anti-terrorist unit of the national police force. Densus 88 had apparently regarded him as having veered from thuggery and racketeering towards terrorist-related activity. According to Rauf, Qurdowi had close links with the local military command, which had developed an intense rivalry with Densus 88 units in Solo. Rauf was among the fighters imported from Java in the communal conflict in Maluku in the early 2000s.
[17] Interview with Luthfi Hakim, leader of the Forum Betawi Rempug, Cakung, Jakarta, 29 December 2010. The 'Betawi' people, actually an admixture of numerous ethnicities that converged in what is now Jakarta during the colonial era, see themselves as the indigenous inhabitants of the capital city. They also commonly perceive themselves as marginalised in their 'own' city, poor and devoutly Islamic.

In spite of this apparently high level of activity, it is arguable that an impasse of sorts has been reached by virtually all of these organisational vehicles in spite of the continuing alarmism with which security-oriented analysts greet the purveyors of Islamic politics. Leaders of mass organisations, such as the Majelis Mujahidin Indonesia (MMI), and numerous paramilitaries that agitate for an Islamic state, also admit that they have no idea when their efforts might bear any fruit.[18] The same goes for the JAT, formed by the Ngruki-based cleric Abubakar Ba'asyir, once regarded as the spiritual leader of Jemaah Islamiyah. It is significant though that some of the JAT's current crop of leaders seem to suggest that *dakwah* should be the primary activity of those desiring the implementation of Sharia. They also consider the acts of those who continue on the path of violence as being 'too hurried' or impatient.[19]

The return to emphasis on relatively unspectacular *dakwah* activity – to enhance religious consciousness in society – by so-called 'hard-liners', including by the Jemaah Islamiyah itself according to Ward (2008), is striking to say the least. It appears to signal the clear limitations of the waging of 'radical' Islamic politics at the margins (see Fealy 2004), including that which employs outright violence. Of course, there is an interest among social actors associated with violent activity to downplay such tendencies, given the operations of the Indonesian security apparatus that are designed to curb them. However, such statements probably also indicate some realisation that violent action has produced little that is tangible besides virtual isolation from much of the *ummah* itself (ICG 2010) as well as inviting state repression. Even convicted Bali bomber Ali Imron, for example, laments the lack of consideration of political repercussions and of possible public backlash that went into the bombing operation in which he was involved.[20] In important ways, this condition resonates with Roy's observations about the 'failure of political Islam' (1994) to mobilise and consolidate support for traditional targets such as the establishment of a state based on Sharia.

Conclusion

This chapter has focussed on pathways to the fringes of politics, discussing particularly one derived from the Indonesian experience. Such pathways have been presented as the product of situations where cohesive multi-class alliances

---

[18] Interview with Sobarin Syakur, secretary general of the MMI, Solo, 17 July 2007.
[19] Interview with Abdul Rohim, spokesman for Jamaah Anshorut Tauhid, Ngruki, Sukoharjo, Solo, 12 July 2011. He is the son of Abubakar Ba'asyir, the alleged spiritual leader of the Jemaah Islamiyah.
[20] Interview, Jakarta, 7 July 2012. He also states that the operation was not particularly planned in detail, certainly not to the extent of providing the instigators with a viable way of escaping the authorities.

and organisational vehicles battling for power under the banner of the *ummah* have not been fully realised. In Indonesia, therefore, an array of organisational vehicles are able to claim status as representatives of the interests of the *ummah* while espousing political strategies that are most appropriate for struggle waged from the margins of state and society. These include various mass organisations, militia groups and even terrorist organisations. Clearly their influence on the workings of Indonesian politics cannot be compared to that of organisations such as the Muhammadiyah or NU and the various political parties these organisations have directly or indirectly spawned, nor the once widely admired PKS. But as a consequence, political salvation for those situated on the fringes of politics is basically contingent on the successful establishment of an Islamic state, rather than a democratic one. It is only through a state based on Sharia that they would notionally gain access to the sorts of privileges afforded by access to power and resources from which they have been barred due to the outcomes of prior political struggles.

It is also suggested, however, that such organisations have not met with much success. It is no wonder that there has been a call among them for a return to more straightforward *dakwah* types of activity. Perhaps underpinning this call is the newer conviction that it is necessary to have a strong cultural impact on society – to 'Islamise' it more profoundly – before a frontal assault on the secular state could be possible. Such an idea unwittingly recalls the Gramscian notion of a counter-hegemonic 'war of position' (Kandil 2011: 42) that was once influential among leftists in the West. A war of position essentially entails hidden and gradual activities to change the values that are prevalent in society – thus essentially creating a backdoor to power when an overt grab for it would clearly fail. This was the path that appeared to be taken most obviously in Egypt by the Muslim Brotherhood before 2011 (see Bayat 2007; Kandil 2011). In the Indonesian case, though, how such a 'war of position' would be waged does not seem to be theorised. The return to *dakwah*, therefore, seems more like a course of action necessitated by diminished options following continual setbacks and persistent organisational as well as leadership disarray (Witular and Widhiarto 2010).

It has been noted though that fringe vehicles prone to violent activity have existed in the experiences of Egypt and Turkey, too. In Turkey they were supplanted, not just by the responses of the state security apparatus, but because the sheer success of the AKP made them seemingly redundant. Egypt provides a tantalising case where the appeal of violent strategies was replaced by the promise of advancement through the electoral route, but which now seems to have starkly led to yet another political dead end. Will the banning of the Muslim Brotherhood after the ouster of the Morsi government, and the stunning levels of repression that its followers have suffered since then, bring back extra-electoral – and violent – political strategies to prominence? Will a sense of betrayal by democracy encourage more and more social agents of Islamic politics to adopt such strategies long after their appeal and influence had been on the wane (Kingsley 2013)? Given the insights attained from the comparative aspects of the foregoing discussion, this possibility is difficult to dismiss out of hand, certainly in the short to medium term.

6 A study in political marginality
The Indonesian Darul Islam movement and its heirs

Past forms of political struggles can provide important reference points for subsequent ones even if they can hardly be emulated in full because of inevitably changed social circumstances. A specific model bequeathed by Indonesian history is that of open and protracted armed rebellion based on guerrilla warfare against the national state, geared to carve out slivers of territory for a competing Islamic state to govern. Such guerrilla warfare was taken up by the Darul Islam movement in the environment of an early post-colonial period in which the state was weak and fragmented, due to the disarray caused by the war for national independence and the slow formation of a coherent post-colonial bureaucratic apparatus. These circumstances were not salient in the cases of Egypt and Turkey.

There is no doubt that the legacy of the Darul Islam continues to influence and inspire new generations of Islamic political activists (Pringle 2010: 75) in Indonesia even if the strategy it originally adopted is now largely irrelevant. But it is in an altogether different sense that the tradition of the Darul Islam is important to the present analysis. The Darul Islam and its assorted political heirs are addressed in this chapter as providing an example of the pathway leading to continual marginalisation, the manifestations of which are found in perpetual inability to make use of the formal institutions of politics and the market as effective arenas of contestation. Indeed, it is suggested here that the Darul Islam movement provides a concrete study in political marginality itself, one that finds no real parallels in either Egypt or Turkey, where a gradual but certainly non-linear process of political incorporation of Islamic sources of resistance was already taking place in spite of the political repression simultaneously meted out to them.

Thus, it is shown in this chapter that, in spite of the numerous internal transformations experienced by the Darul Islam movement and its various offshoots, these did not result in the forging of broader social alliances that counteracted perennial confinement to the margins of politics and society. They have been nothing like the Muslim Brotherhood in Egypt, which had been deeply ingrained within the mainstream of civil society during the Mubarak era, through charities, social work and strong presence within professional syndicates. Instead, floating mass politics in Indonesia during the authoritarian rule of the New Order had ensured that Darul Islamists would never be able to organise at the grassroots level even if new recruits were continually made available from the increasingly large pool of lumpenproletariat ensconced in vast urban and peri-urban sprawls. From this point of view, the maintenance of tendencies within Islamic politics that are radically anti-democratic in Indonesia can be explained again outside of issues of doctrinal interpretation or fixed cultural propensities, and by virtue of the broader sociological and political-economy milieu within which they have emerged.

All of the foregoing is related to the previous point made that, as the *ummah* has become increasingly diversified in Indonesia due to social transformations, so, too, have its organisational vehicles become more varied rather than consolidated. But this variety is also partly attributable to the social effects of New Order suppression – leading to the requirement that its activists develop strategies, sometimes highly localised, to cope with a harshly authoritarian regime in semi- or outright clandestine fashion to avoid arrest and imprisonment. Significantly, these were not the sorts of strategies that would be most useful in preparing for involvement in competition over resources and power when the democratic period eventually arrived and the institutions of New Order centralised authoritarianism unravelled.

Resilience and change

It has been pointed out that many, though certainly not all, of the organisations that reject Indonesian democracy as being contrary to Islamic teachings and that favour an outright Islamic state based on Sharia have genealogies that can be traced back to the storied Darul Islam movement (Van Bruinessen 2002). The existence of JI itself owes much to the prior experience and networks of DI – from which it split in 1993 – even though cooperation between elements of both surely continued (Temby 2010: 34–35). Indeed, Darul Islamists had been at the heart of Islamic-inspired political dissent during the heyday of New Order authoritarianism. Though some top members might have flirted with state officialdom in the early Soeharto years, in particular through connections with the intelligence services, they were soon to be comprehensively betrayed and hence were never truly incorporated into the institutions of New Order rule.

There are at least two factors accounting for the maintenance of the Darul Islamist tradition in spite of the movement's military defeat more than half a century ago. First, Darul Islamists benefited from the anti-communist campaign of the early New Order, the aftermath of which opened up new fertile ground for proselytising and recruitment in areas that used to be bastions of communism or radical nationalism, such as the densely populated hinterland of Central Java. Second, they indirectly benefited, too, from the social transformations presided over by the New Order, which had produced new generations of potential recruits to the movement, each quite different in terms of sociological outlook than their predecessors. Thus, the internal make-up of the organisational vehicles of Darul Islamism, in the process, has also been transformed. At the same time, the strategies undertaken and kinds of vehicles adopted by those who see themselves as heirs to the struggle of the Darul Islam have necessarily changed greatly. And yet, throughout all these changes, the condition of almost absolute marginality within a social order presided over by the secular state has been maintained.

Much has been written about the Darul Islam movement led by Sekarmaji Marijan Kartosuwiryo (e.g. Van Dijk 1981; Jackson 1980; Soebardi 1983; Formichi 2010; Temby 2010; and Solahudin 2011), who was the revered Imam and president of the Indonesian Islamic State (NII) proclaimed in Tasikmalaya, West Java, in 1949. He also commanded an Indonesian Islamic Army (TII) until its surrender to the Republic's Siliwangi Division in June 1962.[1] Controlling swathes

---

[1] Born in Cepu, Central Java, either in 1905 or 1907, Kartosuwiryo was a member of that great movement of the colonial-era petty bourgeoisie, the Sarekat Islam – and the political party it eventually spawned, the Party of the Sarekat Islam of Indonesia (PSII). His father worked at the lower tiers of the colonial government, with responsibility, rather ironically, for overseeing the government-regulated opium trade. Indeed, Kartosuwiryo came from a family of colonial-era petty officials (KPG and Tempo 2011: 8), the kind that were relatively well-off but never would have had much prospect for substantial advancement within the prevailing system of rule.

It was not until his early teens (when he moved to nearby Bojonegero in East Java for school) that Kartosuwiryo studied the Islamic religion closely and learnt to recite the Koran. However, the Imam's mastery of Arabic apparently never reached a high level because of his basically secular process of education (Van Dijk 1981: 21). When he did informally study religion, it was to be under the tutelage of PSII activist Notodihardjo, who is said to have dressed in garb associated with adherence to the folk traditions of Islam in rural Java. This sort of background perhaps accounts for Kartosuwiryo's ability to develop support bases among Sundanese rural peasants in West Java, who were syncretic in many respects too (Newland 2000: 199–222). Such was the case in spite of the Darul Islam rebellion's reputation for Puritanism and its stated objective of establishing an Islamic state. This is less of an oddity, however, if it is accepted that rebellion represented a particular response to the unnerving changes being experienced within sections of society as a result of Indonesia's newly acquired independence rather than one that was inspired by religious precepts only.

In fact, Kartosuwiryo's life trajectory amply showed the strong intersections between an early form of Islamic populism and nationalism in colonial-era Indonesia discussed in Chapter 3 (also see Formichi 2010). He was ultimately a product of the colonial social order and of the nationalist struggle against the Dutch, to which he gave his allegiance. Like Soekarno he was a disciple of the charismatic Javanese nobleman Raden Mas Haji Omar Said Tjokroaminoto (Soebardi 1983: 109), a highly respected leader of the SI. Interestingly, Kartosuwiryo had explored communism too – through his uncle Mas Marco Kertodikromo – the celebrated journalist and early Indonesian Communist Party figure (KPG and Tempo 2011: 25).

Active within the SI, PSII and Masyumi, Kartosuwiryo was clearly aware of the purifying tendencies resulting from close contact between the Dutch East Indies and the Middle East via the haj and religious education as well as persisting trade networks (Formichi 2010). Nevertheless, he did not obviously experience the strong pull of the ideas of reformists like Abduh, Ridha or Al-Afghani, unlike some of his contemporaries. Indeed, one of his surviving sons, Sarjono Kartosuwiryo, claims that his father was heir to a Sufi rather than any orthodox form of Islam, and certainly not one that is brandished in contemporary times by the likes of the

of rural West Java during its long campaign against the Indonesian state, it also made incursions into the northern parts of Central Java (Tegal, Brebes, Pekalongan) and in Kebumen in the south. Kartosuwiryo's army forged alliances, as well, with other rebellions (Van Dijk 1981: Chapter 3),[2] particularly in Aceh (led by Daud Bereuh) and South Sulawesi (led by Kahar Muzakkar). A 'branch' of the Darul Islam movement was also to operate in South Kalimantan, led by the former army officer Ibnu Hadjar, until it was militarily crushed in 1963. The South Sulawesi rebellion was only defeated in 1965, while the one in Aceh would resurface later as a more fully fledged independence movement (Aspinall 2009).

In many ways the Darul Islam movement remains stubbornly enigmatic, however. First of all, what kind of Islamic movement was it and what was it a direct response to? It was already mentioned in Chapter 3 that spurring Kartosuwiryo's rebellion was a dispute over the status of his irregulars within the Indonesian armed forces as well as prior opposition to the stipulations of the Renville Peace Treaty of 1948 between the Dutch and Indonesian nationalists that greatly diminished the territory under control of the latter. Under the terms of the agreement, the Siliwangi Division of the fledgling Republican government was forced to 'vacate' West Java and undertake a long march to Central Java. Kartosuwiryo prominently rejected such terms and remained in his strongholds to fight the colonial forces.

A not dissimilar situation had developed in South Sulawesi, where local militia leader Kahar Muzakkar became disdainful of the intent of national political elites to disband his troops, which had also fought the Dutch under arduous circumstances. Insultingly, his fighters – like Kartosuwiryo's – were not going to be absorbed into the regular Indonesian armed forces, leaving them in limbo (Van Dijk 1981: 170; 194). The rebellion in Aceh was also related to new issues of local politics brought about by the emergence of the new Indonesian national state. It was mainly an expression of local elite intent to secure a high level of autonomy from Jakarta, especially with regard to control over the region's wealth of natural resources.

Jemaah Islamiyah. Interview, Bandung, 27 January 2012.
  Furthermore, though Kartosuwiryo originally showed some enthusiasm for an international effort to create a just world according to the precepts of God, involvement in a national struggle led him to emphasise liberation from the shackles of colonialism in Indonesia itself. As he subsequently confronted the Indonesian national state, his thinking became even more confined to struggles taking place mainly in his base of West Java (Formichi 2010: 146). Thus, Kartosuwiryo's experience was relevant to the evolution of Islamic populism in Indonesia more generally, within which the conception of the *ummah* and its battles became more focussed on the existing nation state.

[2] Sarjono Kartosuwiryo, the Imam's youngest son, who spent his early childhood in the midst of guerrilla warfare, believes that the drawn-out nature of the military struggle in West Java was partly due to the fact that many of the foot soldiers of the Siliwangi Division had relatives in the villages from which the Darul Islam derived most of its supporters. Interview, Bandung, 27 January 2012.

According to Van Dijk's detailed study, the Darul Islam was able to combine appeals to Islamic ideals of social justice in response to these kinds of prosaic developments. In West Java, such appeals intersected closely with local elite resistance against early attempts by the national state to expand its authority and thereby possibly dislodge them (in ways that partly mimicked Aceh) in addition to the policy of demobilising irregular troops enacted by the central Republican leadership. Added to this was the process of agrarian change begun in the colonial period that had created pressure on traditional forms of social ties because of the resultant process of social differentiation within the rural population (Van Dijk 1981: Chapter 7). In class terms, it may be said that a more traditional form of Islamic populism had come to gel the interests of local rural elites with that of the peasantry with the DI in a turbulent period of social change, bringing together their fears and insecurities in a particular political response against the emergent post-colonial state.

By contrast, the resuscitation of the DI after its military defeat was intricately connected to the interests of the wielders of state power in the early New Order. Many of the first generation DI would meet at the house of movement veteran Danu Muhammad Hasan in Bandung in 1971, in a 'reunion' reputedly sponsored by the State Intelligence Coordinating Agency (BAKIN), and in which army officers were present. Chief among them was Colonel Pitut Soeharto (Solahudin 2011: 87), who was then considered the main specialist on Islamic politics within the Indonesian intelligence services. The immediate mission of such officers was only to enlist the DI in garnering Islamic support for the state electoral vehicle, Golkar, in view of an upcoming parliamentary poll. These kinds of developments provide some clear indications that the longevity of the Darul Islam has had much to do with the policies pursued by those who established the New Order and then developed the institutional framework within which state and society relations would be governed for decades.

But the DI old guard was already partially giving way to a new generation that had emerged in the 1970s and whose sociological backgrounds were quite different from theirs. These were largely campus-based activists and reflected the beginnings of a more urbanised Muslim middle class emerging out of the professions and the civil service as the New Order became more entrenched. In many ways these individuals were typical of the lumpen-intellegentsia identified by Roy and others. More educated than their forbears, they were also the first among the Darul Islamists to have read widely beyond standard Indonesian texts, for example, the works of Hassan Al-Banna and Sayyid Qutb, and to learn from the experiences of the Muslim Brotherhood. They also read Mawdudi and the Iranian thinker Ali Shariati. Still this generation would not be most noted for its intellectual prowess. Its members formed the majority of the foot soldiers of Komando Jihad and similar expressions of Islamic-oriented violent dissent against the New Order in the 1970s and 1980s.

Yet another generation of Darul Islamists came to the fore over the next decade with characteristics that were also distinctive. Many exhibited the influence of Islamic political thinking that had developed out of social conflict taking place in other Muslim-majority societies. The most notable of these was the result of the encounter between the Muslim Brotherhood, outside of its native Egyptian habitat, and the doctrinally rigid Wahhabi influences originating from Saudi Arabia. Eventually, some members were to be politically socialised in completely new ways in Afghanistan, where actual experience in warfare must have gone some way towards solidifying claims of political descent from the fighters of the Kartosuwiryo era.

In spite of such external influences, however, the internal shifts within the Darul Islam movement were ultimately tied up more closely to the profound social changes taking place in Indonesia itself. Perhaps the most important among these was the steady production of cohorts of young, urbanised and relatively well-educated individuals who nevertheless remained alienated from the social order that Soeharto was building. Due to their own marginality, they easily developed a sense of solidarity with the poorest and the most dispossessed, even if they were unable to organise them in any cohesive fashion in the context of floating mass politics. They were angered by the perceived social injustices that were being perpetuated by ever-stronger alliances between state and capital. For such individuals, moreover, the growing prosperity of large Chinese businesses could not but invoke memories of colonial-era circumstances that had led to such developments as the rise of the Sarekat Islam (see Chapter 3), an organisation that had been uniformly accorded heroic status within Indonesia.

Generations

Following their military defeat and the death of their leader and Imam by execution in 1962, Darul Islam activists became more widely dispersed throughout Indonesia because of a policy enacted by their military vanquishers: after their surrender, most of Kartosuwiryo's troops were returned to their villages of origin, but others, significantly, took up the offer of transmigrating to other regions in the sprawling Indonesian archipelago.[3] The movement thus became more decentralised, as members would come to profess allegiance to a number of competing leaders who were each usually referred to as the Imam of the movement as a whole, well and truly operating underground by the 1970s.

While geographical spread over a sprawling archipelago may have helped the movement to survive, a very significant lifeline was soon provided by the

---

[3] For example, Interview with Darma Syuhada ('Mang Ede') – a former Darul Islam soldier – Kampung Jawa, Limbangan, Garut, 24 January 2012.

campaign against communism in the 1960s, to which many Darul Islamists were recruited by the military (Solahudin 2011: 84). Equally important was the subsequent Islamisation of areas that had been communist or radical nationalist strongholds. In this regard, the activities of the Dewan Dakwah Islamiyah Indonesia (DDII), which was heavily involved in 'converting' communists and followers of Javanese folk religion to Islam, were helpful in the gradual revival of Darul Islamist networks. Thus, one Darul Islamist recalled how his fellow activists were easily to be found in DDII branch offices at least all the way up to the 1980s.[4]

While the new generation of Darul Islamists that emerged by the mid-1970s were more urbanised and educated than their predecessors, they were also the indirect product of DDII efforts to develop support in university campuses and in surrounding areas through control over local mosques – as urged by its founder, Mohammad Natsir. The members of this generation owed a huge debt also to the engineer Imaduddin Abdulrachim, who established a focal point for the political socialisation of students into Islamic politics at the well-known Salman Mosque of the respected Bandung Institute of Technology (ITB) (Bertrand 2004: 85). Serving as a lecturer there, he founded the fabled Lembaga Mujahid Dakwah (LMD),[5] where many young Islamic activists passed through, and introduced ideas associated with the Muslim Brotherhood.[6] He also found many comrades during a stint as a lecturer in Malaysia, where he became closely involved with ABIM (The Malaysian Islamic Youth Movement), which had become enamoured, too, with the ideas of the Muslim Brotherhood (Hamid 2009: 145–147).

In further developments, some members of this generation of DI, however, would fall much further into the manipulative hands of the Indonesian intelligence apparatus. They became embroiled in the aforementioned Komando Jihad, for example, or closely related groups. Forced by the exigencies of floating mass politics to organise underground, many found the strategy of violent resistance to be appealing. Nevertheless, the origins of Komando Jihad remain contentious. It has been more than credibly argued that Komando Jihad was all but invented by intelligence czar General Ali Moertopo and his operatives.

---

[4] Interview with Maman Abdurrahman, Darul Islamist and New Order-era political prisoner, Cikarang, Bekasi, 25 January 2012.
[5] The name is very difficult to translate into English but roughly denotes an institution within which struggle takes place through predication.
[6] According to Darul Islamist Maman Abdurrahman (interview, 25 January 2012 in Cikarang, Bekasi), Imaduddin Abdulrachim was himself a member of the Darul Islam movement. He claims intimate knowledge because his own involvement with DI was due to Imaduddin and other like-minded Islamic intellectuals in Bandung. However, most discussions of Imaduddin's role in the development of campus-based Islamic politics do not mention that he was actually a movement member.

This accusation was supported by Ustad Wahyuddin, who was imprisoned in the 1980s for his alleged involvement in the related Teror Warman group, which had resorted to armed robbery to fund its struggle.[7] He claims that Komando Jihad was artificially created by Ali Moertopo to flush out Islamic 'hard-liners' who could have potentially mobilised against the regime.[8] The devious scheme supposedly involved the 'invitation' to known Muslim activists to join 'a new coalition' against the communists, whom they were told were in the process of reorganising in order to seek retribution for the bloody events of the mid-1960s.[9] It should be recalled that any possible return of communism as a political force would have been cause for concern not least because of the role played by Darul Islamists in the PKI's physical annihilation, in an alliance with the military (Temby 2010: 6).

Similar to the initial Darul Islam rebellion, the legacy of the Komando Jihad has endured beyond its own relatively short lifespan. For example, a key figure, Haji Ismail Pranoto (known by the acronym 'Hispran'), is believed to have inducted Abdullah Sungkar and Abubakar Ba'asyir – the alleged founders of Jemaah Islamiyah terrorist network– into the Darul Islam underground movement in the 1970s (Feillard and Madinier 2010: 109). From this point of view, it could be reasonably said that JI would not have been possible if not for Komando Jihad, which, in turn, would not have been possible if not for the political schemes hatched by the architects of the early New Order. Significantly, Hispran (who like Danu Muhammad Hasan was a direct associate of Kartosuwiryo) is widely considered to have been a government informant by those who still identify with the Darul Islam movement and community. Such a background suggests that the emergence of terrorist activity in Indonesia in the late 1990s and early 2000s was not necessarily attributable to the breakdown of authority due to a sudden shift from harsh authoritarian rule to democratisation, as some have suggested (Abuza 2007). Another factor was the social effects of New Order policy towards the social agents of Islamic politics, which had included everything from outright suppression to murky arrangements involving tutelage and cultivation for apparently cynical political purposes.

---

[7] Interview with Ustad Wahyuddin, Director of the Al-Mukmin *pesantren* at Ngruki, 16 July 2007.
[8] There is ample supply of anecdotal, as well as written, evidence to support Haji Wahyuddin's view. In 1982, for example, two sons of Kartosuwiryo were tried for being involved in underground activities geared towards the establishment of an Islamic state. Their defence was that they had acted on behalf of the state intelligence agency to recruit Muslims in a new fight against resurgent communism (Raillon 1994: 215). Muhammad Danu Hasan, who was instrumental in forging links between the vestiges of the movement and Ali Moertopo, also accused the latter of manipulating his comrades during his trial in 1983 (Feillard and Madinier 2010: 41).
[9] Interview with Ustad Wahyuddin, director of the Al-Mukmin *pesantren* at Ngruki, Solo, 16 July 2007.

But such arrangements were so murky that even today there is sufficient room for intelligence officials to deny allegations regarding Moertopo's close dealings with Komando Jihad[10] or for suggestions that he simply came to lose control of the Darul Islam he had unleashed (Temby 2010: 23) for narrow purposes like discrediting the PPP. Whatever the truth of the matter, New Order repression of Islamic political groupings, which had intensified by the mid-1980s, was justified by the violent activities attributed to the offshoots of Darul Islamism, including the bombing of the ninth-century Borobudur Temple in Central Java and two branches of Bank Central Asia in Jakarta, a large private bank owned by the ethnic Chinese tycoon Liem Sioe Liong. It was represented by a number of shocking and violent incidents, such as the massacres at Tanjung Priok (Jakarta) and in the village of Talangsari in Lampung referred to earlier.

The next generation of Darul Islamists that would surface more distinctly by the middle of the 1980s and throughout the 1990s was partly a product of this kind of political environment. Its sociological profile was more varied as some of its members had come from long-urbanised families and were quite self-consciously middle class. But many also hailed from families that had more recently moved to the cities from largely rural surroundings and who were just starting to precariously climb up the ladder to middle-class status. The intersections between DI and JI would largely arise from this generation of activists, especially those that came to fight in Afghanistan due to a recruitment and deployment campaign undertaken by various Islamic groups during the struggle in that country with the Soviet army.[11] Though some of these new foot soldiers would have had some formal religious training in the many *pesantren* that continued to proliferate in rural and peri-urban areas throughout the 1980s and 1990s, experience of modern secular education was still largely the norm among them.

In other words, this later generation reflected a more pronounced hybrid of experiences of political socialisation within typically urban environments and secular educational institutions and within more rural or peri-urban settings involving *pesantren* training. Obviously, the experience of Afghanistan among some of them was also crucial because it contributed to close acquaintance with strategies based on violence as well as the skills and expertise required to use them. A biography of Utomo Pamungkas (alias Fadlullah Hasan alias Mubarak alias Amin), one of the Bali Bombers, displayed a life trajectory that involved growing up in peri-urbanised parts of Java, receiving formal religious training

---

[10] Such a denial was issued by the deputy chief of Indonesian national intelligence Asad Ali, who also serves in the national leadership of the NU. Interview, Jakarta, 7 July 2010. Asad Ali was then the most senior civilian official of BIN – the National Intelligence Body.

[11] Abdullah Sungkar was a major recruiter. But others, such as the GPI (Islamic Youth Movement), were also active in this endeavour. Interview with Iqbal Siregar (GPI), Jakarta, 8 July 2010.

in the Al-Mukmin *pesantren* in Ngruki and combat experience in Afghanistan (Ismail 2010).

Not surprisingly, some of this generation of Darul Islam activists would emerge from within the ever-growing masses of informally employed in the urban centres of Java and other islands. Such a fact reflected the extended reach of urban DI networks, initially based on campuses, but eventually operating through neighbourhood mosques away from universities and student rental houses and into the urban slums. One 1990s Darul Islamist in Bandung, West Java, for example, admits to having been a street thug and drug addict before being recruited into a DI grouping when he started frequenting such a mosque. Having had almost an exclusively secular education, he is still an ardent reader of Kartosuwiryo's works and claims to have studied the major Muslim Brotherhood thinkers in Indonesian translations of their works. Though never apprehended by authorities for terrorism, he cites peripheral involvement in one of the church bombings that rocked the country in 2000.[12]

The appearance of such individuals notwithstanding, another key development was the proliferation of Ngruki graduates in a number of newly established *pesantren* around Central Java in the 1990s. A good example is Darusy Syahadah, established by an Al-Mukmin graduate called Mustaqim near the town of Boyolali, reportedly with financial assistance from the DDII. This particular *pesantren* has been rumoured by Central Java locals to be a site where students undergo military training as part of the curriculum, although the school's administrators deny this charge vehemently.[13]

Still other newer *pesantren* of the rigidly Salafi type were directly established by graduates of study programmes in the Middle East. Though a large number of such graduates had gone on scholarships organised through the DDII, they eventually came to develop their own connections and funding sources in the Middle East.[14] Moreover, on the outskirts of neighbouring Yogyakarta, one finds the *pesantren* called Ihya As-Sunnah, led by the well-known Salafist preacher Jafar Umar Thalib. The latter was responsible for the establishment of the militia known as Lasykar Jihad – which in its heyday had enjoyed close links to sections of the Indonesian security forces – and sent

---

[12] Interview with anonymous, Bandung, 25 January 2012.
[13] Interview with Ustad Qosdi Ridwanullah, Darusy Syahadah, Simo, Boyolali, 21 January 2011. However, Abdul Rauf, who attended Darusy Syahadah as a youth, gives a different testimony. He claims that students were trained in the martial arts and shooting by members of elite Indonesian military forces. Rauf, who fought in the communal conflict in Maluku, went on to be second in command of the Hisbah militia in Solo. Interview, Solo, 9 July 2011.
[14] Thus, one Saudi Arabia graduate who had been supported by a DDII scholarship subsequently obtained funding from Kuwaiti donors to establish the Imam Buchori *pesantren* in Karanganyar, Central Java. Interview with Ustad Muhammad Mukti Rofi'i, Imam Bukhori *pesantren*, Karanganyar, Selokatan, 20 January 2011. For a brief overview of the development of these sorts of educational institutions, see Hefner (2009a: 87–91).

fighters to such hotbeds of communal conflict in the early 2000s as Ambon and Poso (Aragon 2001; Hasan 2006; Van Klinken 2007). Jafar Umar Thalib's personal history involves connections with the DDII as well, though more relevant links appear to lie in Yemen, where he claims to have studied Salafi teachings following a stint as a fighter in Afghanistan.[15]

More doctrinally rigid and Salafi-oriented *pesantren* would come to be established even on the island of Sumbawa, where a bomb-making group was uncovered in 2011, allegedly tied to JAT activists. Importantly, Sumbawa was not within the sphere of influence of the original DI movement, and thus, the establishment of such schools by people who consider themselves heir to Kartosuwiryo's legacy attests to the geographical spread of Darul Islam in spite of its military defeat. In this case, the process may have been facilitated by historical links between the West Nusa Tenggara islands and South Sulawesi, where the Kahar Muzakkar branch of the original Darul Islam movement and rebellion against the Indonesian Republic had operated. By the 1970s and 1980s, in any case, DI leading figure Abdul Qadir Baraja had emerged from Sumbawa and was implicated in the operations of the Komando Jihad (ICG 2005b). In spite of his origins, however, Baraja was politically active mainly in Lampung and Java rather than on his home island. Hence, the more recent appearance of JAT in Sumbawa is likely to represent the rise of newer Darul Islamist recruits via networks established by, or in the name of, Abubakar Ba'asyir – following the crackdown on JI by Indonesian security forces in response to such events as the bombings in Bali.

Central Java: An odd Darul Islamist stronghold?

Understanding the evolution of movements that were inspired by the Darul Islam in the context of capitalist transformation during the New Order is helpful to explain the broader evolution of Islamic dissent against the secular state in Indonesia up to the present day. In this respect, it is intriguing that it was the heartland of Central Java that became known in the 2000s as the most fertile ground for the growth of such radicalism. This is so because the area has long been the site of *kejawen* traditions – of a kind of Islam that is deeply imbued with an older Javanese syncretism. Hence there is the paradox of the simultaneous coexistence of *kejawen* traditions and those of puritanical forms of Islam in this relatively small, though densely populated, geographical area.[16]

A way of understanding the nature of this paradox is suggested in the concerted religious activity and conversions to Islam – but also to Christianity – that

---

[15] Interview with Ustad Jafar Umar Thalib, Ihya As-Sunnah *pesantren*, Sleman, Yogyakarta, 19 July 2010.
[16] Interview with Hari Mulyadi, NGO activist and researcher, 17 July 2007; the late Soedarmono, historian, 26 July 2007 and 20 June 2011.

took place in Solo and its environs following the events of 1965. This was a time when a multitude of people practising Javanese syncretism sought to escape being branded as godless atheists and therefore communists (Ricklefs 2012: 133), due to the very real danger of imprisonment, exile or even execution by military-led mobs. In fact, the establishment of Al-Mukmin was intricately connected to a perceived need for proselytising and moral education in the area, which one leading Islamic figure describes as having been 'hedonistic'.[17] Again, a key player initially was the DDII, which was keen to 'upgrade the moral quality' of the formerly 'heathen' population of the region.[18]

Of course Solo and its environs could always claim to have had strong Islamic influences – after all, Muslim traders hailing from there were instrumental in the formation of the Sarekat Islam. Solo also gave rise to Haji Misbach, the militantly anti-colonial Islamic communist of the early twentieth century. While the influence of the activities initiated in the area by the DDII at the beginning of the rule of Soeharto appears to persist, it is also evident that Islamic vehicles have never been able to shake off the competing influences of syncretic Javanese traditions. The latter remains influential with the poor, for example, and this has helped the secular nationalist PDI-P to continue to dominate the formal arena of politics. To the vexation of those based in Solo, 'secular nationalist' mayoral candidates have consistently won elections after *reformasi*, in spite of the very visible presence of a number of Islamic organisations that overtly favour the enforcement of a state based on Sharia.[19] This includes Joko Widodo (Jokowi), the one-time mayor backed by the PDI-P who emerged as the victor in the Indonesian presidential election of 2014.

This background should be recalled when viewing the activities of Densus 88, the special anti-terrorism unit of the Indonesian police force that has hunted down 'Islamic terrorists' in places considered solid support bases for the Indonesian Communist Party or of Soekarnoist radical nationalism a half-century ago. More so, given that the alleged terrorists are frequently linked to groupings that can be genealogically traced to the Darul Islam movement. The irony is that Darul Islam did not have more than a negligible presence in this part of Central Java, having been largely stalled in portions of Northern and Southern Central Java during Kartosuwiryo's guerrilla struggle. This is so even if the famed Batalion 426 of the Indonesian army, which originated from Central Java with close links to Hizbullah (again not to be confused with namesakes in Turkey and Lebanon), provided fighters who would become a key element of Kartosuwiryo's anti-Dutch forces in West Java.

---

[17] Interview with Ustad Taufik Usman, Ngruki, Solo, 18 July 2007.
[18] Interview Sudirman Marsudi, first secretary, Dewan Dakwah Islamiyah in Central Java, Solo, 19 July 2007.
[19] This was noted, with satisfaction, by local PDI-P leaders Y.F. Sukisno (chair of the Solo City Council), Putut Gunawan and Teguh Prakosa in an interview in Solo on 25 July 2010.

But of course the Darul Islam itself was in no position to take the lead in efforts to capitalise on the demise of the PKI. In fact that role fell to the DDII, the vehicle to which Mohammad Natsir devoted himself after his return to politics was pre-empted in the early New Order. Organised and supported by DDII, religious teachers and preachers were deployed to the towns and villages that were known to have been PKI strongholds. The opening of Al-Mukmin in Ngruki was notably officiated by Natsir himself, and it ushered in a period of significant change within the village. Long-time residents of Ngruki – located in Sukahordjo, on the outskirts of Solo city – recall how it used to be a culturally *abangan* and politically leftist-inclined community. H.M. Amir, co-founder of Al-Mukmin together with Abdullah Sungkar and Abubakar Ba'asyir, still remembers how prayer meetings he had organised as a young cleric used to be attended by only a handful of people.[20] A long-time resident of the area surrounding the *pesantren* suggests that by the 1980s it was already filled with more self-consciously Muslim residents whose extended families had been largely radical nationalist and even communist two decades earlier, supplemented by many newcomers arriving from nearby communities where processes of 'Islamisation' had occurred.[21] In fact, any visitor today would not fail to notice the signs of religious piety displayed by the inhabitants in their dress and behaviour and the significance of the *pesantren* in a community located in what used to be a bastion of leftist Indonesian politics.

It is against such a background that the existence of organisations like the Forum Komunikasi Keluarga Darul (FKKD; Communications Forum of Darul Families) can be understood, as well. This is an organisation that emerged in Central Java localities like Tawangmangu and Jatiyoso, other examples of former mainstays of communist support in which actors espousing Islamic-oriented political ideologies have gained prominence. Composed of Islamic puritans claiming to be present in no less than fifteen villages, the FKKD's activities include everything from conducting prayer meetings to organising protests against corrupt officials. With membership dominated by relatively young people in their twenties and thirties, most of whom lack formal religious training, the puzzle is how their puritanical tendencies came to emerge in the first place – when they tend to hail from families traditionally practising *kejawen* and which had supported the PKI[22]

Significantly, many of these young FKKD members adopted their puritanical outlook through life journeys that took them to the towns and cities for

---

[20] Interview, Solo, 12 July 2011. Interestingly, Amir seemed to have had much less of a problem with the New Order and its espoused ideology – to the extent of having taught Pancasila at university level in Yogyakarta. But such was his personal trajectory – in the early 1960s he had been involved in military-coordinated training in preparation for conflict with the PKI.

[21] Interview with Sujoko, Ngruki, Cemani, Sukoharjo, 20 January 2011.

[22] Interview with FKKD members, Tawangmangu, Karanganyar, Central Java, 25 July 2010.

education and work where Islam had become a major cultural resource to develop ideological opposition to the state. A leader of an FKKD grouping thus summarised his life story as involving discovery of 'true' Islam as a teenager in Solo due to contacts with activists there. This would notably create lasting distance with most of his family and neighbours – even if the latter have become more pious than they were in the 1960s.[23] What this shows is that such groups remain isolated from mainstream rural Javanese society, much like the more puritanically inclined newer generations of Darul Islamists, notwithstanding the religious transformation of Central Java that roughly took place after the demise of the PKI.

Such developments, it should be noted, have been greatly linked to profound changes in the conditions of material life in the locality. For instance, FKKD members express their disdain for what goes on when the more well-to-do of surrounding cities come to Tawangmangu, a hilly and cool area now full of villas and small resort hotels catering to local tourists– citing tales of drunkenness and debauchery. They claim that wealthy Chinese own most of these establishments and that employees come from outside Tawangmangu, leaving locals either to work in factories around Solo or to venture overseas to live the harsh life of migrant workers.[24] A human rights activist and close associate of FKKD suggests that some of its members had fought in Ambon, Poso and other hotspots, an experience that would have hardened their views. He also suggests the existence of close links with nearby *pesantren* run by Salafists.[25] Their presence in the villages – the most remote of which are now fairly approachable from any Central Javanese city, thus allowing for constant cross-fertilisation of influences between the urban and the rural – would have assisted the cultural and religious transformation of communities that had been mainstays of Javanese folk beliefs and of Left-wing political ideologies.

Significantly, as the social backgrounds of those involved in the political struggles of the *ummah* became more varied, so did their geographical origins. For example, 1980s Darul Islamist and subsequent Majelis Mujahidin Indonesia (MMI) leader Irfan S. Awwas came from the island of Lombok, also in West Nusatenggara province, where the movement had no meaningful presence during the time of guerrilla warfare against the nationalist state. However, he came into contact with Darul Islamist networks when he migrated to Java for his education. The aforementioned Imran, or Imran Muhammad Zein, was West Sumatran-born and North Sumatran-raised, having lived the life of a street tough in the city of Medan before he appeared to find religion. The son of a small-scale textile merchant, Imran was to be active in organising

---

[23] Interview with 'Abu Hanifah', Tawangmangu, Karanganyar, Central Java, 25 July 2010.
[24] Interview with FKKD members, Tawangmangu, Karanganyar, Central Java, 25 July 2010.
[25] Interview with Eko Prasetyo, Yogyakarta-based researcher and human rights activist, Yogyakarta, 20 July 2010.

underground activity against the New Order and came to be identified within the New Order narrative as being the man most responsible for the Woyla hijacking in 1981.[26]

But the geographical origins of some present-day DI activists are not completely unrelated to those of their predecessors: in South Sulawesi, for example, the offspring of Kahar Muzakkar have been influential within a group called the Preparatory Committee for the Upholding of Islamic Law (KPPSI) (Roth 2007: 142). This group, however, has not been deterred from entering the fray of local electoral politics. Moreover, from a small village in Garut, West Java, one of the sons of a former Darul Islam official has declared himself to be the president of an Islamic Republic of Indonesia, running a 'government' replete with cabinet ministers.[27] Also in West Java, a DI veteran known as Panji Gumilang has made claims to being the entire movement's present-day Imam, founding the financially well-endowed but controversial Az Zaytun *pesantren* in Indramayu. Both lie within the territory formerly controlled by the old Darul Islam rebellion. Az Zaytun, a sprawling and highly prosperous Islamic boarding school, was once well connected to highly placed New Order elites and continues to have strong ties with officialdom.[28]

Interestingly, in spite of Panji Gumilang's considerable personal pedigree, Az Zaytun's operations have been dismissed as an embarrassing, long-running financial scam, not least by the vast majority of other Darul Islamists. They point out that these operations have become virtually sect-like and allegedly involve the initiation of troubled youths who are then pressured to steadily donate sums of money, which they do by recourse to petty criminal activity.[29] To its critics, Az Zaytun's activities have deviated too much from the ideals of the original Darul Islam movement to be considered a continuation or successor.

In a nutshell, the emergence of numerous self-proclaimed heirs to Kartosuwiryo's legacy, including such opportunistic ones as Panji Gumilang, underscores how the Darul Islam movement is organisationally fragmented and ideologically inchoate (Al Chaidar 2006). Stuck on the margins of state and

---

[26] See 'Sebuah pengadilan untuk imam IM' 1982; 'Dituntut hukuman mati sang imam pun menangis' 1982; and 'Imran, Imran Sampai di Sini' 1983. Executed for his troubles, it has been mentioned that some of his contemporaries insist that Imran had no real links to Darul Islam or Komando Jihad, but was instead planted by state security forces as part of a broader plot to smash Islamic resistance to the New Order. Interview with Bambang Pranggono and Syarif Hidayat, Istiqomah Mosque activists, Bandung, 14 July 2012.

[27] Interview with Deden Rahayu, brother of Sensen Komara, the 'president' of this government, Babakan Cipari, Garut, West Java, 24 January 2012. The younger brother serves as 'minister of the state secretariat'.

[28] Interview with Imam Supriyanto, Panji Gumilang's former 'minister of production intensification', Jakarta, 24 January 2013.

[29] This is confirmed in an interview with Seno Andriansyah and Dewi Triana, former initiates, Depok, 11 July 2010.

society, those who have taken up the mantle of Kartosuwiryo's struggle could not participate as an effective and coherent force within today's electoral democracy, with credible claims of representing an inherently heterogeneous *ummah*, well after a decade and a half after Soeharto's fall. Nor are Kartosuwiryo's political heirs well situated to develop vehicles that could plausibly wage a substantive underground, civil society-focussed 'war of position' in a way that the Muslim Brotherhood had done in Egypt before 2011, virtually creating a parallel state with institutions of social organisation and which provided social services. In this sense, they have collectively amounted to a study in political marginality.

Islam and social conflict in Solo

The city of Solo in Central Java, and its surroundings, provides a useful picture of the inroads made by Islamic politics in Indonesia after the Cold War but also good indicators of the barriers continually confronted by its purveyors. While the destruction of the communist stream of politics provided fertile new ground for a range of organisations that claim to represent the interests of the *ummah*, in fact these have perpetually failed to establish their dominance over local politics.

This is the case even if analysts have referred to the Central Javanese city of Solo as a bastion of Islamic 'radicalism' (e.g. Wildan 2013). However, it is perhaps more accurate to see the city as a melting pot of different and mutually competing social and political traditions. Steeped in Javanese culture and history, it is where the palaces of no less than two Javanese royal families can be found. At the same time, Solo and its environs also provided bases of support for Indonesian communism and radical nationalism since at least the 1920s, partly thanks to the export-oriented sugar plantations established there by the Dutch during the colonial period (Mulyadi and Soedarmono 1999: 25–27). Added to the rich cultural mix, today Solo has a significant Christian minority population (Ricklefs 2012: 143–144).

Historically, though, Solo was a major location for economic activity centred on the textile industry and particularly *batik* production. It is therefore not surprising that Solo witnessed some of the strongest early stirrings of colonial-era petty bourgeois Islamic politics leading to the founding of Sarekat Islam there in 1912 (Mulyadi and Soedarmono 1999), although the legendary Javanese aristocrat, journalist and activist Raden Mas Tirtoadisoeryo surely played a major role in establishing a precursor in Bogor.[30] The predominantly

---

[30] The novels of the late, great, Pramoedya Ananta Toer (especially his famous 'Buru Quartet' of works, written while imprisoned for about a dozen years without trial by the New Order for his leftist sympathies) provide a fascinating, if fictionalised, account of the life, times and struggles of Tirtoadisoeryo.

Muslim petty bourgeoisie of Solo was already facing competition from Chinese merchants for control of local trade at that time.

During the period of rapid industrialisation under the New Order, Solo and its surroundings again became a significant site of light-manufacturing production, triggering the growth of a new, urban working class. The rise of this industry was to be dominated, however, by Chinese business interests (Mulyadi and Soedarmono 1999: 258–259) and New Order state officials. In May 1998, when anti-Chinese riots rocked Jakarta, they also hit Solo. The frenzy in Solo spilled over into the destruction of property known to belong to Harmoko, the widely derided long-time Soeharto-era minister of information and later speaker of parliament, who owned a major share in PT Sritex, a prominent textile manufacturer in the city.

In the interim Solo had also become an important base of operations for those who see themselves as heirs to the Darul Islam movement. Key associated figures, as already mentioned, became ensconced in the so-called Ngruki network based nearby and were allegedly involved in the development of the Jemaah Islamiyah (ICG 2002).

But also based in Solo and lying on the fringes of political life are such organisations as the FKAM (Forum Komunikasi Aktivis Masjid; Communications Forum for Mosque Activists), which initiated a militia group, the Lasykar Jundullah.[31] The FPIS (Front Pemuda Islam Surakarta; Surakarta Islamic Youth Front) gave rise to the militant FPIS Brigade,[32] which is closely connected to another controversial *pesantren*, Al-Islam, located in the city's lower-class Gumuk neighbourhood and led by veteran cleric Haji Mudzakir (Ul Haq 2008). The Korps Hizbullah, though named after the pro-Darul Islam military of the 1940s, is indirectly linked to the unsuccessful post-New Order Islamic Party, the Partai Bulan Bintang (Crescent and Star Party).

While such organisational vehicles are rightly considered to be among those that take the most intransigent positions on such issues as establishing an Islamic state, they should not be conflated with those that undertake terrorist activity. Many have gained a degree of prominence due to their contentious activities in promoting public morality. Rather than suicide bombing, their most prominent techniques include that of 'sweeping': actions designed to force the closure of entertainment venues such as pubs, cafes and massage parlours.[33]

It is useful to consider the social backgrounds of the leading figures of these organisations. First of all, what stands out is that few are able to claim much of a role in politics prior to the fall of Soeharto. They were neither prominent in the opposition nor key actors in vehicles like ICMI, through which Soeharto

---

[31] Interview with Kalono (FKAM), Solo, 16 July, 2007.
[32] Interview with Warsito Adnan (FPIS), Solo, 18 July 2007.
[33] Although this strategy was later eschewed by the FPIS, perhaps because of the bad publicity it generated; interview with Warsito Adnan, Solo, 18 July 2007.

attempted to project an image more friendly to Islam in the latter period of his rule. A partial exception would be the leadership of an organisation called MTA (Majelis Tafsir Al Quran), which from its inception in the early 1970s had developed a non-confrontational relationship with the New Order, to the extent of having close ties with Golkar. The policy of maintaining cordial relations with the holders of state power has been maintained in the present. Thus, it was no less than then President Susilo Bambang Yudhoyono, who officiated at the opening of the organisation's plush new headquarters in central Solo back in 2009. Such was the case even if the MTA is known for operating a radio station that airs aggressively sectarian views that the president was notionally against, given his penchant for championing cultural pluralism on the international stage.

More typical for Solo, however, is the leader of the FPIS, who is a schoolteacher with civil servant status and who was not politically active before 1998. He was nevertheless closely linked to the so-called Gumuk community, which was always religiously conservative and linked to ideas about setting up an Islamic state but hardly a major local political player in the Soeharto years. The leader of the FKAM, also a former schoolteacher, had moved into a range of small businesses involving textiles, contracting and printing, but had not been involved in any serious political or organisational activities by the time the New Order ended.[34] The leader of the Korps Hizbullah – who essentially heads a breakaway unit from the similarly named militia force of the PBB – is a one-time head of the PPP's security force in the Surakarta region, and activist of the HMI in the 1980s. However, he had had little involvement in politics between his student days and just a year or so before the fall of Soeharto.[35]

It is also of interest that none of the aforementioned actors were recipients of formal religious training, although they all claim to have grown up in devoutly Muslim, and anti-communist, families. The main point to make, nevertheless, is that practically no one among them was important enough to be co-opted by the state before 1998, nor had they taken a leading role in the growingly boisterous anti-Soeharto movement. Until relatively recently, therefore, only a few of such individuals would have had the credentials to represent themselves as believable political leaders of the Islamic community. Not surprisingly, 'many of the rank-and-file of these new militia-type groups' had not 'been active in Muslim organisations before' but tended to belong to the large reservoir of irregularly employed 'street toughs' (Van Bruinessen 2002: 140) in many major Indonesian towns and cities. Brown and Wilson (2007) thus characterise the paramilitaries to which they belong as vehicles where 'criminals meet fanatics'.[36]

---

[34] Interviews with Warsito Adnan (FPIS), Solo, 18 July, 2007; Kalono (FKAM), Solo, 16 July, 2007. Warsito Adnan has been employed as a school teacher and headmaster.
[35] Interview with Yanni Rusmanto (Korps Hizbullah), Solo, 18 July 2007.
[36] Also see Wilson (2008).

There are exceptions to this general observation. Moedrick Sangidoe, for example, who projects authority over various Islamic militias in the city, had begun to challenge the New Order around 1997,[37] although for many years prior he was merely a leading member of the local branch of the artificially created PPP. More significantly, also prominent among those organising in the name of the *ummah* from the fringes are individuals who formed the Majelis Mujahidin Indonesia (MMI) in 2000 – which spawned yet another militia group, the Lasykar Mujahidin. Though its organisational headquarters was in nearby Yogyakarta rather than in Solo, the MMI was once closely linked to Abubakar Ba'asyir.[38] According to Van Bruinessen (2002: 146), the organisation 'appears to be a front of various groups that all have some relation with the Darul Islam underground'. In fact, the MMI includes a range of people, like Irwan S. Awwas, who had been imprisoned during the Soeharto era for their underground activities. Its Lasykar Mujahidin is led by a Darul Islamist of the 1970s generation, Gustam Effendi (known as 'Kang Oni'), who was reportedly part of the so-called Warman Terror Group and imprisoned for killing a police officer during its period of activity.[39] MMI's secretary general, Sobarin Syakur, who is resident in Solo, had served seven and a half years in prison for alleged subversive activities in the 1980s.[40]

Still, the initiators of the MMI were very much on the margins of political activity when the Soeharto period came to an end. Like most of the individuals mentioned earlier, not one of them appeared to have had any role, for example, in the turmoil surrounding the fall of Soeharto in 1998. Before this, none were important enough to receive significant state patronage even when Soeharto was trying to gain the political support of pious sections of the urban middle class through ICMI.

Interestingly, the various Islamic militia groups regularly compete for control over the city with rivals that prominently include the PDI-P's militia and closely related street gangs.[41] In one particularly infamous event in 2008, a battle erupted between 'Islamic' and 'nationalist' gangs in the lower-class Joyosuran area of Solo, lying adjacent to the especially gang-infested slums of Semanggi, resulting in the gory death of a key local underworld figure with ties to the PDI-P.[42] More

---

[37] Interview with Moedrick Sangidoe, Solo, 20 July 2007.
[38] Interview with Sobarin Syakur, secretary general of Majelis Mujahidin Indonesia (MMI), Solo, 17 July 2007.
[39] Interview with Gustam Effendi, Tasikmalaya, West Java, 26 January 2012; and with Ridwan Al-Anwari, former member of DI Special Forces, Cisarua, Bogor, 29 January 2012.
[40] Interview with Sobarin Syakur, Solo, 17 July 2007.
[41] Interview with Bimo Putranto, PDI-P youth leader in Solo and founder of the DMC street gang, Solo, 19 January 2011. Another prominent PDI-P related gang is known as 'Gondes'.
[42] Interviews with Bimo Putranto, PDI-P youth leader in Solo and founder of the DMC street gang, Solo, 19 January 2011; and Abdul Rauf, former second in command of Hisbah, Solo, 9 July 2011.

mass fighting over turf would break out periodically between various gangs in the city's poorer neighbourhoods over the years, as both types continued to vie for control over the city's growing lumpenproletariat and protection rackets.[43] What this shows is that many of the Islamic paramilitary groups, while not equipped to undertake serious contestation over state power, even at the local level, are quite well entrenched on the murkier side of street politics. Such is the case even if they seemingly do not have the capacity to translate this position into one of greater ideological influence over civil society in general.

Conclusion

This chapter examined the nature of Islamic political vehicles in Indonesia operating on the fringes of state and society, especially those that can be linked to the old Darul Islam rebellion, whether in terms of their own claims or due to political genealogy. It showed how historical circumstances had dictated that they were not able to make use of the democratic openings available since 1998 beyond the freedom to organise. Darul Islamists were so marginalised that they never attained any kind of foothold in the official realm of politics during the authoritarian era. Moreover, while social transformations in Indonesia ensured that the internal make-up of the Darul Islam movement and its offshoots would become increasingly diverse, they are still unable to develop the sort of coherently organised, broad-based social alliances important to successful new Islamic populism. Neither have they been successful in establishing substantial bases of support within civil society, as they were more involved in criminality than in the provision of social services, for example. By the end of the Soeharto period they were so isolated, even from the increasingly complex *ummah* whose interest they claimed to represent, that they carried little political weight beyond the ability to sporadically utilise violence.

Nevertheless, Darul Islamists have largely retained their traditional animosity towards the secular nationalist state that had left Kartosuwiryo and his original followers out in the cold at the attainment of independence from Dutch colonial rule. This stance may have even hardened in the democratic period, given the persisting inability to make use of the institutions of democratic contestation. The incapacity to exploit openings provided by democratic politics has ensured their insistence on the incompatibility between democratic politics and Islamic precepts. But with no clear route to state power, and also isolated from the broader *ummah* that they make claims of representing, many have stagnated in activities involving intimidation that regularly make

---

[43] Interview with Y.F. Sukisno (chair of the Solo City Council); Putut Gunawan (PDI-P leadership in Solo) and Teguh Prakosa (PDI-P leadership in Solo), Solo, 25 July 2010.

newspaper headlines but hardly overcome the barriers that halt their political progression. This situation contrasts with their contemporaries in other parts of the Muslim world – the Egyptian Muslim Brotherhood comes to mind, for example – that still managed such inroads in spite of state repression, including during the Mubarak dictatorship.

7 Navigating through democracy
A pathway to power?

The new Islamic populism is being continually reshaped by contests over economic and political power that have been frequently chaotic, turbulent and non-linear, not least where the outcomes of democratisation are at stake. This chapter further elaborates on an issue that has been examined only partially in this book: in what ways have ideological positions shifted among those self-identifying with the advancement of the *ummah* in matters of engagement with democracy? In the process, it investigates the consequences of 'ruling democratically' for Islamic-oriented political vehicles, as shown in the cases of Turkey, and, more recently, Egypt, albeit only temporarily. It also delves more deeply into consequences of democratic engagement for the trajectories of political vehicles that fail 'to rule', as in the case of Indonesia.[1] At the heart of all these matters lies a basic theoretical question: how much weight should be given to the much-discussed institutional thesis that incorporation into democracy 'moderates' the politics of 'radical' Islamic movements (Buehler 2012)? Hamid, for example, puts forward the counter-assertion that state repression has sometimes induced a degree of political moderation. He suggests that this was witnessed in Egypt and Jordan prior to 2010, as Muslim Brotherhood movements there strategically used democracy as a rallying call against authoritarian regimes and to portray themselves as politically responsible actors willing to forge broader alliances with liberal forces (Hamid 2014: 38–52).

Undoubtedly, the scramble to win votes may induce ideological moderation on the part of Islamic political parties involved in electoral contests. It could conceivably encourage them to occupy some sort of political middle ground rather than intractable positions on matters such as the status of Sharia within the state. However, it is shown in this chapter that such moderation should not

---

[1] Tomsa (2012: 491–493) suggests that one effect has been growing factionalism within the Islamic party, the PKS, spurred by changes designed to make it more appealing to non-Muslims. Significantly, rather than simply a bid to gain a wider potential voter base, the move appears to be aimed at courting the support of elements of the wealthy Chinese big bourgeoisie, obviously lying outside of the *ummah*. Interview with Anis Matta, who was soon to be appointed president of the PKS, 28 January 2013.

be taken for granted – but neither should the diametrically opposed view that democracy simply opens up space for religious turmoil. Bukay (2009: 25), a follower of the clash of civilisations thesis, obviously subscribes to the latter when he asserts that Arab countries have 'long histories of authoritarianism influenced by both culture and religion' and that military authoritarianism has been the sole factor preventing religious violence from surfacing more regularly to disrupt regional security.

These mutually contradictory assertions return us to the theme of contingency introduced at the beginning of this book regarding the political agenda of the new Islamic populism. Such a political agenda is not innate but will be shaped by the specific kinds of social interests that have converged, albeit with inevitably varying levels of internal coherence, within the multi-class alliances that sociologically enable the new Islamic populism. It is also shaped, however, by the broader constellation of power through which the new Islamic populism has had to navigate in order to attain more favourable positions to compete for access to state institutions and to tangible economic resources.

It should be kept in mind, therefore, that struggles over the forging of institutions of political and economic governance after authoritarianism are more likely than not to involve previously dominant interests. These have proven resilient within the contentious processes of political change in Indonesia, as well as in Egypt and Turkey. In Indonesia, Robison and Hadiz (2004) have analysed the continuing salience of the Soeharto-era oligarchy within democratic institutions like parties and parliaments including via pervasive money politics. Similarly, Stacher (2012) is clearly correct that the social interests that had underpinned authoritarianism in Egypt in the Mubarak era will retain considerable power into the future due to their entrenched position within the state and historically proven adaptability.[2] Such a scenario is strongly suggested by the overthrow of the Morsi government in 2013, which involved mass protests and intervention by a military apparatus that had been closely associated with the protection of the *felool*, the old regimists, with whom the Muslim Brotherhood had failed to reach a strong-enough accommodation to save its rule.

Thus, the release of the deposed dictator, Mubarak, from prison soon after the coup, while scores of Muslim Brotherhood leaders took his place,[3] was naturally accompanied by commentary that the old regime had been virtually

---

[2] Trager (2013) quotes Mohammed Al-Beltagy, a senior Muslim Brotherhood leader, thus: 'There is a part of the system that, until now, is still connected with the old regime ... This is found in many of the [state] apparatuses, like the police, media, and judiciary.'

[3] Quite incredibly, among these leaders was Supreme Guide Mohamed Badia, who was untouched even during the Mubarak regime. Besides Morsi, also detained was Badia's powerful deputy, the businessman Khairat El-Shater, as mentioned earlier. By contrast, Mubarak was placed under house arrest in an army hospital.

resuscitated.[4] This point of view gained credibility when such a major business crony of the Mubarak regime as the controversial steel tycoon Ahmed Ezz was also released from detention.[5] Given the subsequent banning and persecution of the Muslim Brotherhood,[6] it has become evident that democratic victory only provided a short-lived pathway to power for the Egyptian new Islamic populism in spite of decades-long successes in organising at the level of civil society.

In Turkey too the AKP has battled a Turkish military, bureaucratic and business establishment that had been complicit in suppressing the party's precursors (Taşpınar 2012). These conflicts have clearly influenced the way the AKP has navigated through the democratic process and how religious idiom and symbolism have been deployed to mobilise cross-class support for its rule. In Indonesia, in contrast to the other cases, a particularly rapacious and chaotic democratic system based on money politics has come to shape the agenda of a distinctly fractious new Islamic populism rather than any confrontation with a 'deep state' dominated by the military.

Ideological permutations and political contingency

It has been pointed out that the political agendas of Islamic movements today have been predominantly moulded in conflicts with domestic rulers within the Muslim world itself rather than in reaction to Western interests; as we have seen, these have profoundly affected the ideological permutations of Islamic politics over the last half century. Further permutations, however, can be expected where Islamic movements have had the opportunity to rule through democratic institutions. Their outcomes may not always lead to distinctly liberal directions, being almost inevitably entangled in multifaceted struggles over control of these very institutions and their associated resources.

At the same time, the perception that Islamic political parties are inevitably bound to a 'hidden agenda' to impose an Islamic state are founded on rather simplistic notions of how religious doctrine trumps the changing imperatives of conflict over power and tangible resources in Muslim-majority societies. While some of these notions are clearly influenced by the declarations of many Islamic political actors and thinkers themselves, these need to be always situated within specific social and historical contexts.

Thus, for quite some time the most internally well-organised Indonesian Islamic party, the PKS (Hamoyatsu 2011), has been continually facing questions about whether it has been secretly plotting the establishment of an Islamic

---

[4] See, for example, Hauslohner (2013).
[5] See 'Court Postpones Retrial of Egypt Steel Tycoon Ezz' 2013.
[6] See 'Egypt Court Bans All Brotherhood Activities' 2013.

state. That one of the PKS's most influential leaders, Hilmy Aminuddin, is the son of the noted Darul Islam veteran Danu Muhammad Hasan has only added weight to these suspicions. However, while the PKS can be traced to semi-clandestine student organisations that operated in university campuses during the New Order, it is evident now that party leaders and activists have developed a stake in the survival of Indonesia's democracy. It is easily observable that this has resulted in important ideological shifts stemming from the need to survive within Indonesia's money-politics-driven and often-chaotic democratic process rather than from the imperatives of religious doctrine.

In the same vein, fears had also grown in the West around the initial political advances made by Islamic political parties in Tunisia and even Morocco immediately following the Arab Spring.[7] The concern expressed was typically that these advances signalled the advent of Islamic theocracies, which would be anti-Western and anti-liberal at the core. Domestic secular critics have also directed a constant stream of allegations about the hidden intentions of such vehicles as Tunisia's En Nahda party and the Muslim Brotherhood's Freedom and Justice Party (FJP).[8] Interestingly, some of these critics hail from the once more robust leftist political traditions that are simultaneously opposed to the hold of Western interests on the region.[9]

Hence there was a strong reaction in the West and among Egyptian critics when the Mohamed Morsi presidency attempted to take up sweeping powers by decree in late 2012 (Hamid 2014: 156–157). This act was but a miscalculated bid to extend its authority over the institutions of the state, where Mubarak-era

---

[7] Morocco did not really have an Arab Spring save for some relatively muted protests. Nevertheless the PJD – Justice and Development Party (with links to both the Muslim Brotherhood and the AKP) – has benefited most from the limited political liberalisation undertaken by the King since then and actively collaborates with the monarchy. Interviews with Hami El Din and with Abdeslam Ballaji, both PJD members of the Moroccan parliament, Rabat, respectively 23 and 24 April 2013.

[8] In Egypt, for example, interview with George Ishak, Egyptian Coptic politician and former Kifaya co-founder, Cairo, 31 March 2012. For him, the Muslim Brotherhood had an Islamist agenda that constituted no less than a counter-revolution (to the one that deposed Mubarak). Also, interview with Abdelmonaem Emam, secretary general of the politically liberal El Adl Party, Cairo, 13 December 2014. For him, the choice available to Egypt in mid-2013, when Morsi was deposed, was either a military-dominated state under General Abdel Fattah Al-Sisi or a theocratic one, which he believed the Muslim Brotherhood was plotting to bring to the country.

[9] Interview with Samir Cheffi, deputy secretary general of UGTT, Tunis, 16 April 2013. For him, it was the Left and the trade unions that had fought the anti-colonial struggle in Tunisia and built the modern state, even as they entered into conflicts with Habib Bourguiba, the country's first president and strongman. According to Cheffi, En Nahda is descended from Islamists who only emerged in the 1970s, cultivated by the holders of state power at the time to fight the Left. Interview with Ahmed Naguib, self-described leftist and former spokesman of the Egyptian Current Party, Cairo, 13 December 2014. Commenting on the military-dominated politics of Egypt after the fall of Mohamed Morsi, he was resigned to the fact that political liberals and leftists had no weight but received solace from the idea that the values of the 'revolution' of 2011 – which he says was a response to neoliberalism – would be transmitted to newer generations.

stalwarts remained entrenched. It was such a move – taken in a context of continuing economic malaise – that triggered the massive anti-Muslim Brotherhood street protests in 2013, this time with military backing, which finally overthrew the Morsi government.

In spite of successive convincing electoral victories, there remain reservations too about the AKP's commitment to the democratic path in Turkey. This kind of scepticism has been reinforced by such acts as the persecution of journalists working for the news portal OdaTV in 2012, for providing 'moral support' for a coup purportedly being planned at the highest levels of the military establishment.[10] The government's heavy-handed response to a wave of public protests in June 2013 against a plan to demolish Gezi Park, at the very heart of Istanbul, did little to embellish its democratic credentials (Buruma 2013).[11] These credentials suffered even more greatly when the Erdogan government, already ruffled by the Gezi Park protests, acted to circumvent the use of social media like Twitter in response to the proliferation of rumours about corruption within the AKP in the following year.

Interestingly, the same kinds of concerns continue to surround Indonesian Islamic parties collectively in spite of their relatively modest electoral performances since the fall of Soeharto. This is partly because democratisation has been accompanied by the production of a slew of local government by-laws colloquially known as *perda* Sharia.[12] The majority of such *perda* pertain to regulating women's dress and behaviour, while others address matters like alcohol consumption and prostitution (Robison 2009: 171–172; Sahid 2012). The legality of many of them, however, has been widely questioned because they so obviously contravene existing national legislation (Silaen 2007).[13] Notably, the Sharia-oriented *perda* were made possible in the first place because Indonesian democratisation was followed by substantial decentralisation, which transferred a range of powers to the local level of government (Hadiz 2010). At this level, officials are keen to stake a claim on more authority, in spite of the fact that religious matters, by law, continue to be the domain of the central government (Ricklefs 2012: 282).

---

[10] See 'The Odatv and Ergenekon Cases' 2012 and 'One Suspect Released in Oda TV Case' 2012.
[11] Among the protesters were supporters of the CHP, the ultra-nationalist MHP, as well as the Kurdish movement. However, the main driving force of the Gezi protests were the more than one hundred organisations that were organised under the umbrella of a loose association called Taksim Solidarity. Interview with Cihan Uzunçarşılı Baysal, Taksim Solidarity activist, Istanbul, 21 August 2013.

The Kurdish movement hesitated to be fully involved because of the presence of such actors as the CHP and MHP and the possibility that the protests would be abused by the military. Interview with Mehdi Perincek, Diyarbakir, 26 August 2013, senior official of the BDP (Peace and Democracy Party) – the Kurdish movement's political party represented in parliament.
[12] '*Perda*' is short for *peraturan daerah*, or local by-law.
[13] Some of these have even been revoked by the central government. See Gatra (2012) for some elaboration.

However, many local governments seem to have produced these by-laws rather opportunistically (Bush 2008), including as a means to pre-empt challenges that could be mounted against them by vehicles like the FPI.[14] Indeed, their adoption by local governments run by secular nationalist parties can provide these vehicles with a pretext to enter informal cooperative arrangements even with organisations that otherwise remain outside of the formal arena of politics, ostensibly for reasons of principle. Moreover, attending to religious morality is possibly calculated to be helpful in producing a veneer of respectability when vast numbers of local government or party figures in Indonesia are regularly embroiled in corruption cases and therefore deemed to lack integrity.[15] From this point of view, it is not surprising that some local governments have been unwilling to confront acts of intimidation against religious minorities.[16] Rather than some sort of political 'middle ground', the dynamics of Indonesian local democratic politics have, therefore, sometimes produced hard-line positions on the part of local governments, even if not inspired by religious zealousness.[17] Such situations cast doubt on the thesis that democratic inclusion necessarily induces political 'moderation', though for reasons that have little to do with matters like lack of ability to absorb liberal democratic principles.

It remains tempting for some to conclude, therefore, that Islamic 'radicals' will inevitably 'hijack' any process of democratisation in Muslim-majority societies (e.g. Bradley 2012; Bukay 2009). Perhaps for this reason there is a well-known adage that Islamic political parties adhere to the principle of 'one man, one vote', but for 'one time' only (Akbarzadeh 2011a: 6). It is only recently, after all, that Posusney and Angrist (2005: 5) reminded us that the 'prevailing cultural theory for authoritarianism in the Middle East' still 'links it to the Islamic religion'. The problem with this theory, however, is that it is premised on the notion that the political behaviour of Muslims is basically dictated by their religion (Al-Azmeh 2003), in spite of other more tangible matters obviously at stake in contests over power in the modern world. It is no less than a theory of Muslim exceptionalism.

Of course there is no shortage of Islamic leaders and thinkers who maintain the essential contradiction between religion and democratic politics. Qutb, for

---

[14] Interview with Wasidi Swastomo, regent of Cianjur in 2001–2006, 7 July 2012, in Bogor, West Java.
[15] See 'Ribuan Pejabat Daerah Terlibat Kasus Korupsi' 2013.
[16] An infamous case is that of the Yasmin Church in Bogor, which remained shut down due to the activities of groups that claim to represent the interests of Muslims in the neighbourhood surrounding it. The mayor of the city has supported their actions. Interview with Ari Prabowo, Forkami (Forum Komunikasi Muslim) and Hizbut Tahrir Indonesia activist, Cimanggu, Bogor, 21 January 2013.
[17] Nevertheless, the tendency to produce the so-called *perda* Sharia seems to have peaked by about 2007 (see Bush 2008), indicating that they have not been unambiguously successful in mobilising support for local governments that enact them.

example, was belligerently anti-Western and believed in the supremacy of God's law over democratic systems invented by Europeans (Moussalli 2010: 12). Today, Egyptian Salafi leader Mohamed El-Zawahiri suggests that to reject the ultimate sovereignty of an omnipotent God would constitute nothing less than heresy.[18] Meanwhile, Abubakar Ba'asyir of Indonesia tirelessly reiterates that Islam is a comprehensive religion that proscribes any form of state besides the caliphate.[19] For such individuals adherence to modern democratic systems violates religious doctrine (Tan 2011: 51) because it leads to the fragmentation of the *ummah* along party lines, besides national ones.

It is in this connection that the Hizbut Tahrir – a particularly strong presence in opposition movements in Central Asia – is worthy of scrutiny, for its insistence that democracy, and the system of nation states to which it is attached, contradicts the precepts of Islam (Akbarzadeh 2011b; Osman 2012). The organisation is, nevertheless, atypical in a number of ways because it is a vehicle for a transnational movement that advocates a global caliphate and, therefore, ostensibly does not focus on national-based struggles. Also peculiarly, the various branches of the Hizbut Tahrir regard themselves as being subordinate to a central structure and leadership (Munabari 2010: 175) that remains highly secretive. In the Indonesian context, the HTI (Hizbut Tahrir Indonesia) began as an underground movement in the 1980s,[20] with support initially among students of the elite Bogor Institute of Agriculture (IPB) (Rahmat 2008: 100–101).

But the more pertinent point is that the HTI, like similarly anti-democratic organisations in Indonesia, has never been well positioned to make use of the mechanisms of electoral democracy. Remaining an underground movement with limited reach outside of a student base, it was placed distinctly outside the highly developed New Order-era system of patronage and was thus poorly geared to reposition itself when the era of free electoral competition dawned in Indonesia. In other words, the rejection of democracy by HTI and other organisations is as much due to unfavourable social position as reasons of doctrine.

In this regard, the contrast with the much larger and entrenched Nahdlatul Ulama (NU) is striking. Under the leadership of Abdurrahman Wahid ('Gus Dur'), democratisation in the early post-Soeharto period promised to be highly useful to the largest Islamic association in Indonesia, which, for so long, had been

---

[18] See 'Elections Violate Islamic Law: Egypt's Mohamed El-Zawahiri' 2013.
[19] Discussion with Abubakar Ba'asyir, founder of Jemaah Anshorut Tauhid (JAT), Jakarta Police Headquarters cell blocks, Jakarta, 6 July 2012.
[20] Munabari (2010: 177) cites a Lebanese-Australian Hizbut Tahrir figure, Abdurrahman Al-Baghdadi, as the most instrumental person in the early process of establishing an Indonesian branch of the organisation. This process began with the recruitment of students at the highly respected Bogor Institute of Agriculture (IPB) into this fledgling branch.

well integrated into the mechanics of New Order rule. Democratisation therefore provided the NU with a clear opportunity to enhance its bargaining position *vis-à-vis* those major pillars of the Soeharto regime, Golkar and the military.

It is no wonder then that the NU plunged itself into electoral politics with glee, forming the National Awakening Party (PKB) in 1998. Of course there were pressing matters at stake in the jostling for power that shaped the post-Soeharto democratic institutional framework, to which the NU, through the PKB, devoted much attention and energy. This was indicated in the fact that Wahid's brief presidency in 1999–2001 was utilised, among other things, to place key allies within the NU community in the top positions of a number of politically and economically important institutions, including the ministry that presided over lucrative state-owned enterprises (Robison and Hadiz 2004: 214).

For the HTI, however, even further afield than the PKS from the New Order elites that came to dominate Indonesia's democracy, there appeared little to be gained from democratic engagement and much more to lose in terms of claims to ideological purity. The contrast between these organisations reinforces the point made that the battle over modes of economic and political governance in Muslim-majority societies is less about ideas and values, including those based on religious doctrine, than about the social position and interests of their bearers.

Embracing democracy

Counting on the democratic advantage

Although many organisations in different countries have borrowed from the model offered by Egypt's Muslim Brotherhood, it is significant there was never a central structure, akin to the old Comintern, for example, that exerted control over them (Rubin 2010: 1–2; Halliday 2012: 211). The reason is simple: these organisations developed in relation to nationally defined battles and thus had veered significantly away from the Pan-Islamism of another era. The consequence was that the struggles of Islamic political vehicles are far less directed towards the establishment of a vaguely organised modern-day caliphate than towards concrete issues related to attaining social justice and freedoms within the nation states with which they identified. The way that these struggles would be waged – whether or not through democratic institutions, for instance – would be largely determined by domestic circumstances.

So even if the Muslim Brotherhood model has been adopted as a template within individual countries (rather than an overarching Pan-Islamic one), different vehicles have developed their own distinctive features in accordance with the requirements of specific contexts. The Syrian Muslim Brotherhood, for example, because of the nature of the Assad regime (Stacher 2012: 163–165), is not readily geared for participation in electoral contests. It appears more equipped for protracted warfare and therefore unlikely to quickly embrace the democratic route. Others, however, such as the En Nahda Party in Tunisia, which grew out of a local adaptation of the Muslim Brotherhood, proved capable of exploiting the openings offered by democratic politics after the fall of Ben Ali. For such vehicles as En Nahda, bolstering democratic credentials alongside Islamic ones has been advantageous in its long battle against an authoritarian state that was often radically secular. Ben Ali's predecessor, Habib Bourguiba, for example, was well known for his contempt for the cultural backwardness he associated with Islam (Alexander 2012: 41).

But it is the Turkish experience that is highly informative because the rewards that have accrued to the AKP from its navigation through democratic politics are particularly plain. Though the party is regularly accused of wanting to impose socially conservative religious values on the Turkish Republic, its leaders know success at democratic competition has in fact provided a powerful shield against threats emanating from the self-appointed guardians of the country's secular Constitution, especially within the judiciary and the military.

The way that such matters external to mere religious precepts have reshaped attitudes towards democratic competition has also been seen, quite dramatically, in Egypt. Here the Salafi current jumped on to the democratic bandwagon shortly after the fall of Mubarak even if its leadership struggled to theologically validate the decision.[21] At this time it was apparent that democracy would provide it with useful instruments to compete in steering the direction of social, economic and political change in Egypt, including with the Muslim Brotherhood itself, with which it was in competition especially in the more impoverished communities around the country.[22]

Given the significant Salafi presence in contemporary Egyptian politics (Al-Anani 2012: 31), it is useful to consider the malleability of its agenda in the face of social change. In fact Salafi politics in Egypt has been pliable enough to allow not only for the movement's adaptation to electoral competition but also its considerable acceptance of global capitalism – though predictably, one that is laced with declarations about religious ethics and morality.[23] The reason for such shifts is arguably the changing make-up of the Salafi movement itself, which no longer only includes old-style preachers and firebrands, but secularly educated young students and professionals as well as smatterings of small- and

---

[21] One leading member of the party even dismisses debate about how democratic participation may be philosophically contradictory to Islam by saying that it could be the subject of 'endless discussion in universities'. Interview with Mohamed Nour, Al-Nour Party spokesman and International Relations Coordinator, Cairo, 1 April 2012.

[22] Interview with Mohamed Afan, Egyptian Current Party co-founder, Cairo, 28 March 2012.

[23] Interview with Mohamed Nour, Al-Nour Party spokesman and owner of Nourayn multimedia company, Cairo, 1 April 2012.

medium-scale business owners in the modern sector of the economy.[24] Providing more illustration of their political malleability, Salafi vehicles quickly repositioned themselves to ally with the military after the fall of the Morsi government, clearly in the hope of filling a vacuum that would be left by the Muslim Brotherhood once it had been driven further underground by a sudden and vigorous new round of political repression. It is therefore evident that the Salafi movement is far more complex, due to engagement in modern competition over power and resources, than one that stereotypically aims to turn the Egyptian clock back to medieval times as a result of the imperatives of religious doctrine.

In this we see an important distinction with Turkey that is also relevant when considering the Indonesian case. Unlike the AKP – which clearly towers over any rival even after the subsequent break with the Gülen movement – the Muslim Brotherhood has faced competition from a resurgent Salafi movement that encroaches on its claim to represent a community of the powerless and dispossessed that is homogenised by a common faith. Such competition might further induce elements within the Muslim Brotherhood to adopt more overtly conservative Islamic rhetoric along with violent strategies – not just to hold their Salafi rivals at bay[25] but also to make up for its abject failure to hold on to power through appeals to democratic legitimacy. Intriguingly, further fragmentation within the Muslim Brotherhood, which is quite possible given the crippling of its central leadership by the Egyptian military, would result in a situation closer to Indonesia than Turkey in terms of the varied expressions of the new Islamic populism.

But, of course, the point for both the Muslim Brotherhood and the Salafi was to utilise democratic mechanisms to enable access to, and control over, the state and its institutions to further the interests of the multi-class coalition identifying with the *ummah*. It was against such a backdrop that protracted conflict had earlier taken place about a new Egyptian Constitution and its possible 'Islamisation', involving criticism – by an assortment of liberal, leftist and Nasserist groups, as well as Coptic Christians – of a document that was eventually ratified in 2012 through a controversial national referendum. Much of the criticism focussed on the Constitution's vague language, particularly with regard to the rights of women and minorities. The conflict was not just a matter of ideology, however, even though this may have been suggested by the fact that the Brotherhood and the Salafis temporarily combined against liberals and leftists.[26] Equally at stake was how an Islamic stamp on the

---

[24] Interview with Mohamed Nour, Al-Nour Party spokesman and owner of Nourayn multimedia company, Cairo, 1 April 2012.

[25] A similar situation is faced by Tunisia's En Nahda, which is sometimes pressured by small local Salafi groupings to prove it has not lost its Islamic credentials (Alexander 2012).

[26] See 'Egypt Opposition Says Islamists Trying to Stifle Dissent' 2012.

Constitution would by default privilege Islamic political vehicles, which then meant the Muslim Brotherhood, and facilitate its aggressive attempt to exert hegemonic control over the state's material resources and coercive capacities.

That such pragmatic considerations were important in the struggle over the Constitution is indicated in the way the powerful military was then being placated. The document stated, for instance, that the minister of defence could not be a civilian and that the military budget was to remain free of civilian oversight (El-Kouedi 2013), exactly as was demanded by the top military hierarchy. All this suggests an attempt – though ultimately unsuccessful – at an accommodation between the Muslim Brotherhood and the military that recognised the latter's vast interests, including in the economy. It also indicated that a broader process of negotiation was continuously going on behind the scenes between the Muslim Brotherhood and interests linked to the *felool* in the context of struggles with other claimants to power in post-Mubarak Egypt. This provides some verification for the earlier assertion that the objectives of the new Islamic populism have been far less than revolutionary (Chapter 2).

Interestingly, however, the question of putting an Islamic stamp on Indonesia's Constitution has hardly figured in the dynamics of electoral competition since the fall of Soeharto. The only real exceptions were some unproductive and half-hearted calls to return to the so-called Jakarta Charter version of Pancasila, which enjoins Muslims to practise the requirements of their religion. These calls were made during the 2001 and 2002 sessions of the People's Consultative Assembly (Van Bruinessen 2002). Notwithstanding such events, the most important constitutional debates in Indonesia about the place of Islam within the state took place, in fact, all the way back in the 1950s (Nasution 1995), when the post-colonial state was still in its protracted process of consolidation.[27]

A major issue in Indonesia is the absence of vehicles that can credibly claim the role of leader of such a community of the pious and marginalised. In the electoral arena, the PKS – which remains the best expression of the new Islamic populist tendency – faces regular competition from a range of other Islamic parties, including the New Order-era vehicle, the PPP. Outside of it, competitors include formidable organisations, with entrenched patronage networks,

---

[27] More recent debates in Turkey have also been related, though more obliquely, to the question of how an amended Constitution would accommodate ostensibly Islamic ideals. Initially, the focus was rather predictably on whether the AKP would try to place a stronger Islamic imprint on the Constitution, particularly after the party overwhelmingly won a referendum in 2010 that allowed for new amendments. See Kalaycıoğlu (2010).

Interestingly, however, the main issue eventually shifted to the desirability of altering the existing parliamentary system to a presidential one, which would potentially allow AKP leader Recep Tayyip Erdogan to continue to wield real power from that position once he was no longer prime minister. See 'Parliament to Make Last-Ditch Charter Bid' 2012.

like the NU and the Muhammadiyah. Because of its traditionally more urban following, the latter has particularly looked at the PKS as a direct threat to its grassroots bases of support,[28] especially given that traditional families of petty traders and commodity producers have produced many offspring who tend to be the kind of educated middle-class professionals attracted to the PKS. Rivals are also found among those operating at the margins of politics and society, discussed in the previous two chapters, which see the PKS as traitors to the Islamic cause for its willingness to engage in electoral democracy.

A further problem is that the PKS remains decidedly young and urban middle class in much of its social base compared to its counterparts in Egypt and Turkey. Tentative attempts to expand its social base have largely failed. For example, party efforts to forge links with the labour movement during the 2009 Indonesian general elections were botched, with some labour activists left believing that the PKS did not have more than superficial concern for working-class issues.[29] While the party has moved into charity and educational work to develop followings among the urban poor, including by effectively taking control of existing charitable organisations,[30] it has not done so with the aplomb of its counterparts in Egypt and Turkey given limited resources.[31] Moreover, attempts to forge links with the big bourgeoisie, dominated by ethnic Chinese Indonesians[32] – by declaring the party open to non-Muslims – have yet to bear fruit.

Nevertheless, PKS leaders have come to develop the argument that it is not compulsory to rigidly and literally implement the Sharia. Instead, they tend to suggest that Muslims can obey modern laws, including those that govern democratic life, as long as these do not go against the spirit of God's injunctions.[33] In other words, the party has espoused a non-literalist understanding of scripture, notwithstanding its origins as a semi-underground

---

[28] Interview with Marpuji Ali, head of the Central Java Muhammadiyah, Solo, 28 July 2010; and Haedar Nashir, head of the Muhammadiyah's-cadre forming activities, Yogyakarta, 22 July 2010.

[29] Interview with M. Iqbal, chair of the Federation of Metalworkers' Unions (FSPMI), Jakarta, 30 December 2010; Siti Arifah, National Workers' Union (SPN), Tangerang, 4 January 2011. Also interview with Bambang Wiroyoso, chairman of the SPN, Jakarta, 5 January 2011.

[30] Interview with Ahmad Juwaini, executive director of Dompet Dhuafa, Jakarta, 28 December 2011. On schools initiated by PKS activists see Hefner (2009a: 73–78). Catering mostly to the middle class and lower middle class, Hefner notes that the curriculum of these schools cannot differ so much from that of the Ministry of Education. This is not only due to government pressure but also because their students generally have aspirations of going to state universities to ensure prospects of upward social mobility.

[31] Interview with Makmur Muhammad, chief organiser of PKS charitable activities in Solo, Solo, 11 July 2011.

[32] Interview with Anis Matta, president and former secretary general of the PKS, Jakarta, 28 January 2013.

[33] Interview with Anis Matta, president and former secretary general of the PKS, Jakarta, 28 January 2013; and Rama Pratama, PKS Economic Section, 14 July 2010.

student movement set up by activists who had returned from the Middle East at a time when Qutbist and Wahhabist tendencies had closely intermingled. In doing so, the PKS is clearly responding to the political exigencies encountered in democratic Indonesia, where ad hoc alliances are hardly driven by ideological purity or even common policy agenda, even if such responses may displease some of the party's rank-and-file activists, including at the university campus level, committed to the idea of an Islamic state as a way out of the morass in which the *ummah* has been entangled since colonial times.

Notwithstanding such reservations, the ideological permutations within the PKS have been rather far removed from issues of religious doctrine. They have been driven mainly by the imperatives of operating within a democracy infested with the practice of money politics rather than the internalisation of liberal values. As such, they are also less related to the sort of attitudinal softening and politically liberalising processes expected within the thesis of moderation through democratic institutional inclusion.

Democratic strategy and doctrinal rigidity

It is evident by now that the embrace of political (or economic) liberalism does not necessarily correlate with liberal attitudes and positions in the social sphere. Thus, it is possible to advocate democratic processes and global economic competitiveness while holding retrogressive views on a range of social issues, hence producing an illiberal form of democracy (Hamid: 207–208; also 188–189). But this is not just a matter of incomplete liberal transformation. In the case of the new Islamic populism, preserving these views is a matter of delineating the markers of Islamic identity, something which the conception of a homogenous *ummah* hinges upon, especially because of its contrast with the reality of the increasingly diverse social bases of Islamic politics.

The AKP in Turkey, for example, reinforces the markers of religious identity by periodically raising moral issues with reference to a huge reservoir of socially conservative values (Buruma 2013), which serves the function of distinguishing itself from secular and 'immoral' Kemalist rivals. In Indonesia, while the PKS has presented itself as being 'anti-establishment' by focussing its rhetoric on socio-economic reforms and on fighting corruption (Heiduk 2012: 37), it remains highly parochial in terms of the social values it upholds – much like the AKP that provided it with inspiration.[34] The party has thus promoted efforts to cleanse the Internet of pornographic material while party leader Anis Matta voices strong objections to homosexuality, even as he rhapsodises about the merits of

---

[34] Blocking pornographic sites was a pet project of Tifatul Sembiring, a senior PKS leader who served as minister of communications and informatics in the SBY government. See 'Tifatul: Pornografi Rusak Lima Sel Otak', *Republika Online*, 2 March 2014; Interview with Anis Matta, Jakarta, 28 January 2013.

democracy and the free market.[35] In this, his manner is similar to Muslim Brotherhood businessman and adviser to the Morsi government Diaa Farhad, who expresses the same views.[36] Additionally, the PKS-backed governor of West Java has supported the banning of the minority Ahmadiyah sect, thus allying himself with those, like the anti-democratic FPI, who argue that it is heretical.[37]

But there are limits to how Islamic political vehicles that have had to actually govern modern states can resort to the sort of social conservatism that relies on validation by doctrine.[38] For running such states in a highly globalised capitalist world ostensibly on the basis of religious precepts originating from a seventh-century society – and one that had a relatively simple social and economic structure – inevitably requires considerable human interpretation, reasoning and intervention even if such efforts may be geared to purify understandings of doctrine allegedly obfuscated by centuries of religious 'innovation' (Akbarzadeh 2011a: 3). Again, it matters what kind of social agents are endowed with the capacity to undertake interpretation and enforcement, and what their interests are, because the role can become as highly bureaucratised and power-laden as any other. Hence, writers like Bayat (2007) emphasise how in Iran, the Islamic Republic has had to evolve to address mundane, everyday matters of governance, giving rise to what Zubaida, adapting Weber's analysis of modern capitalism, has called 'routinisation' (Zubaida 2000:62–65).

Still, leaders such as MMI secretary general Sobirin Syakur consistently put their weight behind doctrinal rigidity. Criticising modern democratic precepts, they express the belief that it is not sensible to place equal value on the vote of a 'sinner', such as a prostitute, and that of *ulama*.[39] Others have even suggested that the vote of the average person cannot be considered equal in value to that of the learned cleric.[40] In some ways these views are reminiscent of those that existed in nineteenth-century Europe, which held that only people of high social standing, due to their ownership of property, were deemed deserving of the vote. Nonetheless, these are not uncontested positions, especially now that politically active members of the *ummah* have become so heterogeneous in their composition. For example, as a result of economic transformations

---

[35] Interview with Anis Matta, Jakarta, 28 January 2013.
[36] Interview, Cairo, 4 April 2011.
[37] The governor, Ahmad Heryawan, was to reiterate his support when running for election in 2013. See 'Gubernur Jabar Siap Bubarkan Ahmadiyah', *Republika Online*, 2 March 2011.
[38] Interview with Rached Ghannouchi, founder of the Tunisian En Nahda Party, Tunis, 18 April 2013. While underscoring that Islam is amenable to human rights, the market economy and equality of the sexes, he admits that governing has meant a process of experimentation, especially with regard to issues of eradicating corruption and establishing healthier state–business relations.
[39] Interview, Solo, 17 July 2007.
[40] Interview with Sudirman Marsudi, DDII Central Java branch leader, Solo, 19 July 2007; and with Sahbana, secretary general of the Alliance of North Sumatran Islamic Organisations, Medan, 22 September 2013.

placing more females into the workforce, they include ambitious middle-class professional women increasingly conscious of attaining rights in the private as well as public spheres.[41] It is no wonder that even the Salafi political parties in Egypt have agreed to the principle of women having a role in politics, though only in seemingly half-hearted fashion (Brown 2011: 10).

But it needs to be reiterated that the significance of the ideas expressed by religious 'hard-liners' in Indonesia does not lie in their content but in their deployment against those, like the PKS or PKB, more equipped to participate within the mechanics of democracy. For the former, the establishment of rule by Sharia in Indonesia provides a fanciful route to the sort of society where their continual marginalisation would be finally overcome, as it also appeared for their political predecessors, the Islamic petty bourgeoisie of the late colonial period.[42]

By the same token, those who dissociate themselves from such a tradition take virtually diametrically opposing views. Hence, activists linked to the Islamic Liberal Network (JIL) argue that commitment to Islam and to universal principles of individual freedom (Suratno 2011) – as well as the capitalist economy – can coexist cosily.[43] They do so, not surprisingly, to the chagrin of those ensconced in the militia groups and similar organisations discussed in previous chapters (see Fealy 2006). It is instructive that JIL activists typically have emerged from the top ranks of Jakarta's younger urban intellectual elites, adroit at navigating through the intricacies of democratic political and economic alliance building. Not having a broad social base of support of its own, JIL itself has had to latch on to some powerful secular nationalist vehicles in the continual absence of viable liberal ones. Its figurehead, Ulil Abshar-Abdalla, thus opted to join the Democrat Party of former president Susilo Bambang Yudhoyono and is also closely associated with the Freedom Institute, a think tank linked to Aburizal Bakrie, a major Soeharto-era crony and the leader of the Golkar Party.

Similarly liberal strands of Islamic politics have also struggled to attain more influence in other contexts in the absence of ready-made options (Kurzman 1998). In Egypt, support for the politically liberal Islamic political party Al-Wasat derives from younger, well-educated activists who had left the Muslim Brotherhood because it had not democratised enough internally.[44] Indeed many

---

[41] Interview with Mersni Sana, En Nahda member of Tunisian Constituent Assembly, Tunis, 18 April 2013. An academic, she claims that forty-four members of the assembly representing En Nahda are women.

[42] Thus, Sahbana, a dentist by profession and secretary general of the Alliance of North Sumatran Islamic Mass Organisations, suggests that rule by Sharia would resolve the issue of the continuing 'economic hegemony' of the ethnic Chinese community. Interview, Medan, 22 September 2013.

[43] See Abshar-Abdalla (2011, 2012).

[44] Interview with Yamen Nouh and Mohammad Ad-Dakhakni, Al-Wasat Youth Committee members, Cairo, 21 March 2011.

Muslim Brotherhood youths voluntarily departed from the organisation soon after the fall of Mubarak for the same reason.[45] Others were expelled when they attempted to form electoral vehicles in anticipation of the country's first free legislative elections, including the Egyptian Current Party, in defiance of directives to support the Freedom and Justice Party.[46] To take another example, Al-Wasat vice president Mohamed Mahsoub had left the Muslim Brotherhood many years before the start of the Arab Spring, after no less than two decades of membership, due to a similar kind of disenchantment with the organisation.[47]

It is also notable that some of these younger former members of the Muslim Brotherhood had been involved in the once highly touted Kefaya movement.[48] This movement had brought together a wide range of anti-Mubarak youths of different backgrounds in protests predating the outbreak of the Arab Spring (Bayat 2013a: 224). For such individuals, the experience provided a rare early opportunity to forge links with youths from outside of the close-knit Muslim Brotherhood community. It is instructive, however, that the mainstream leadership of the organisation tended to belittle Kefaya after Mubarak was deposed.[49] But the reason for this is clear: by that time it had developed a vested interest in a narrative of the 'Egyptian Revolution' that extolled the role of the organisation and which lent credibility to the idea that it alone deserved to rule after decades of heroic struggle. In the end, the overly vigorous pursuit of that narrative was inextricably linked to the Muslim Brotherhood's undoing.

The foregoing discussion suggests that there is more to the resilience of social conservatism within the new Islamic populism than merely intransigence on doctrinal matters. For vehicles engaging in democratic politics, the issue is not about incomplete liberal transformations. There are other matters at stake, such as the ability to mobilise mass support on the basis of common membership within an unjustly deprived *ummah*, which in turn induces emphasis on the markers of identity based on religious affiliation. This is so especially when opposing elites are conceived as being made up of the secular, oppressive and morally corrupt.

---

[45] Interview with Abdel Rahman Ayyash, former Muslim Brotherhood Youth member and computer science university student, Cairo, 23 March 2011.

[46] Interview with Mohamed Afan, Cairo, 28 March 2011. A lecturer at the Faculty of Medicine, Ain Shams University, he had been a member of the Muslim Brotherhood since 1991. He would later help found the Egyptian Current Party, which embraced critical Islamists as well as some liberals and leftists.

[47] Interview, Cairo, 2 April 2012. A noted legal scholar, Mahsoub nevertheless served on the committee charged with moulding Egypt's new Constitution and briefly in the Muslim Brotherhood-dominated cabinet, although he had withdrawn well before the Morsi government was overthrown.

[48] 'Kefaya' is often written with an exclamation point after the actual word – thus Kefaya! – in the transliteration from the Arabic word meaning 'enough'.

[49] Interview, Khaled Hamza, head of Muslim Brotherhood Media Bureau, Cairo, 29 March 2011. Hamza emphasised how each component of Kefaya has returned to its own grouping, and that they now have very little to do with each other.

The limits of Islamic party politics: Indonesia

In spite of the durability of organisations discussed in the previous chapter, the coalescing of Islamic and democratic politics in Indonesia after the Soeharto era should not be too surprising given that there is actually an established, though interrupted, history of democratic Islamic politics. It should be recalled that two Islamic politics were highly successful in Indonesia's relatively brief 1950s experience with parliamentary democracy, which took place when the post-colonial state was still in its long process of formation. These were the mutually competing Nahdlatul Ulama Party and the Masyumi Party. The experiences of such parties no doubt present some appealing historical reference points for today's crop of Indonesian Islamic parties, certainly ones that can compete with that provided by the Darul Islam rebellion. However, in the absence of broader and coherently organised multi-class alliances to underpin them, these Islamic parties remain unable to attain control over the state to the extent seen in recent times in Turkey and Egypt.

It is tantalising to think, nevertheless, that things might have evolved somewhat differently if the ICMI initiative had involved the forging of a more seriously cross-class constituency. Celebrated during its heyday as a symbol of reconciliation between the New Order and the *ummah*, ICMI was in fact merely a vehicle to recruit new apparatchiks from the ranks of Indonesia's newly emerging urban middle class (Ramage 1995: 7; also see Hefner 1993), many of whom had developed enhanced levels of religious piety. The fact that the organisation quickly became irrelevant due to fragmentation not long after the fall of Soeharto suggests that it had been merely glued together by New Order patronage. It was shown to have been an utter failure when the moment of truth came: the attempt to save the constantly besieged short presidency of B.J. Habibie, its main patron and the immediate successor to Soeharto. Rather than serving as an effective power base for Habibie when he faced opponents outside and within the regime (Robison and Hadiz 2004: 227–241), ICMI instead dissolved into competing factions backing different political horses.

Nevertheless, prior to this ICMI did carry out its function as an instrument of New Order rule quite usefully. The tensions caused by the *azas tunggal* controversy and such events as the Tanjung Priok massacre were to be significantly defused with its establishment in 1990, which provided the regime with a belated pro-Islamic facade. ICMI also handily provided Soeharto with a new base of support outside of the military and Golkar, extending his personal reach, especially to Muslim NGO activists and academics that had been critical of the New Order's development policy (Hefner 2000). Among them were public figures like Adi Sasono, Dawam Rahardjo, Imaduddin Abdulrachim and also Muhammadiyah leader Amien Rais, who would later break with the New Order again and become a leader of the 1998 anti-Soeharto movement. The existence of ICMI even forced the critical DDII to offer qualified support for Soeharto (Aspinall 2005: 69).

The main problem, however, remained: being thoroughly regimist at the core, ICMI was never intended to absorb all societal elements struggling for the advancement of the *ummah;* as we have seen, there was an array of such groups that remained 'out in the cold'. No big bourgeoisie was ever to emerge out of ICMI either, and moreover, attempts to organise the poor through it were never made because that would have contravened the New Order's floating mass politics.

ICMI only made efforts to reach out to those 'left out in the cold' for opportunistic reasons, triggering new kinds of political activism within the *ummah* that were focussed on such vehicles as militia organisations. Specifically, this new activism was triggered by the mobilisation of these new militia organisations on behalf of the weak Habibie presidency in 1998–1999 – a step made necessary because of the sheer ineffectiveness of ICMI itself in facing competitors within the regime and new challenges, in the form of wide-ranging student protests, outside of it. Thus, Islamic militia groups under an umbrella organisation called Pam Swakarsa were deployed to deal with anti-Habibie student demonstrators, in concert with the military. It was at this time that such previously unknown figures as Habib Rizieq, leader of the feared FPI, suddenly grew in prominence due to his sponsorship by top military and police leaders (Jones 2013: 111).

Nonetheless, in fact a precedent had been set by Soeharto's last-ditch efforts to preserve his own presidency. These involved manipulating nationalist as well as Islamic sentiment – portraying the challenge to his government as emanating from pawns of a Western-Christian-Zionist conspiracy. In this, Soeharto was obviously trying to capitalise on public resentment against the IMF-sponsored structural adjustment programme imposed on Indonesia during the Asian Crisis. An irony of history is that Soeharto, who had found the need to incapacitate Islamic movements at the start of the New Order, actually turned to some of their representatives for rescue during his last moments in power, albeit ultimately to little avail.

But once Soeharto had vacated the political stage, the impetus to form new political parties representing the *ummah* would come from politicians and activists incorporated into the New Order in a number of possible ways. First, they were among those who were cultivated within the network of patronage being developed within ICMI during the last years of the New Order, but which soon fragmented as the regime dissipated when Habibie failed to defend it. Platzdach notes (2009: 62), however, that key members of ICMI did not necessarily end up setting up overtly Islamic parties; the short-lived and unsuccessful Partai Daulat Rakyat (People's Sovereignty Party) was founded by the ambitious ICMI secretary general Adi Sasono, which did, nevertheless, make use of existing ICMI networks, including among students and activists. Another 'source' of leadership for Islamic party politics in the early post-New Order period was KISDI, an organisation ostensibly formed in solidarity with the plight of Bosnian Muslims. Its leaders, such as the late former anti-Soeharto activist Ahmad Sumargono, were instrumental in the forming of the socially conservative PBB (Crescent and Star Party), chaired by Yusril Ihza Mahendra, an ICMI figure and former Soeharto speech-writer. Mahendra often presents himself – with unconcealed hubris – as heir to the revered Mohammad Natsir, while the PBB he leads depicts itself, as mentioned in Chapter 3, as the direct continuation of Natsir's Masyumi.

In addition, individuals linked to either the Muhammadiyah or NU also took a leading role in forming new Islamic-oriented parties. Illustrating the prior accommodation they had reached with the Soeharto regime, both organisations had regularly contributed leading figures to the PPP, which, not surprisingly recasted itself as 'reformist' after 1998 too.[50]

It would seem then that the parties emerging out of these entrenched and large associations were set for considerable success. Not only did these associations command the loyalty of sections of the *ummah* based on networks of patronage that have been in place for decades, they also ran social or educational activities which were allowed to coexist with the institutions of the New Order. This is the case even for the period in which the NU was led by ICMI opponent Abdurrahman Wahid, who was closely associated in the 1990s with pro-democracy tendencies that incorporated a range of liberals and disenchanted former regimists within the so-called Democracy Forum (see Robison and Hadiz 2004: 128–129).

Wahid would go on to establish a party based on the support of rural clerics belonging to the NU, the PKB, and even managed a short and turbulent stint in the presidency (1999–2001). His erstwhile ally but much more frequent foe from the Muhammadiyah, Amien Rais, would form another party, the National Mandate Party (PAN). It is telling, however, that both parties came to emphasise their nationalist and inclusive credentials – as seen in their appellations – almost as much as their Islamic ones, partly by absorbing secular intellectual and activist figures. On one level, this may be seen as a conscious attempt to avoid outright sectarian politics. On another level, though, it showed awareness of the limits of a strictly *ummah*-based political strategy. It certainly appeared that leaders were conscious that their organisations fell far short of the coherence, discipline and mobilisation capacities of something like the Egyptian Muslim Brotherhood. Importantly, Hicks (2012) has shown too that parties associated with the NU and Muhammadiyah have been disadvantaged by

---

[50] Interview with Lukman Hakim Syaifuddin, PPP politician, deputy chair of the Indonesian People's Consultative Assembly (MPR) and, later, minister of religion, Jakarta, 12 July 2010.

reductions in state subsidies provided during the New Order, and which helped to run their social and educational activities.

Still, some of the most intriguing developments were taking place just beyond conventional elite politics. The PKS offered a somewhat different model in that the party was almost wholly underpinned by student groupings that had been semi-clandestinely cultivated within the Tarbiyah movement, initiated by a small collection of activists that had returned from studies in the Middle East and had been engaged with Muslim Brotherhood exiles.[51] It was significant, therefore, that the Muslim Brotherhood had exercised growing influence by this time outside of Egypt itself, largely because many of its members had been forced to seek refuge in other countries due to Nasserist repression in the 1960s. In Saudi Arabia, in particular, what transpired was a meeting of Wahhabist doctrinal rigidity and Muslim Brotherhood organisational capacity among the diaspora strewn across the Middle East. It was this historic combination that rippled through the Tarbiyah movement and eventually produced the PK and then the PKS in Indonesia. Like its counterparts in the Middle East, the Tarbiyah traditionally has had significant rank-and-file support among students of engineering and among similar disciplines found in secular institutions of higher learning.[52] Such students have remained among some of the most reliable of the movement's foot soldiers during election campaigns, ensuring votes especially from a significant portion of pious elements within the urban middle class.

That the Tarbiyah movement was to be influenced greatly by the Muslim Brotherhood – as seen in the copying of its cell-based clandestine structure – is not surprising. Like their model, Tarbiyah activists once had to cope with an authoritarian state that had a repeatedly proven capacity for sheer brutality. Furthermore, the Muslim Brotherhood had already given birth to 'branches' in numerous Muslim majority countries – and developed followings in European ones where immigrant populations from the Middle East and North Africa could be found. In Southeast Asia, ABIM (the Malaysian Islamic Youth Movement) – which produced future deputy prime minister and later opposition leader Anwar Ibrahim – was an important conveyor of Muslim Brotherhood ideas in the 1970s (Hamid 2009: 145–147).[53] As pointed out

---

[51] Interview with Jusuf Supendi, co-founder of Justice Party and of Tarbiyah movement, Jakarta, 6 July 2011. Supendi subsequently fell out with the leadership of the movement, however, and is a vigorous critic of the PKS.

[52] Interview with Arif Munandar, Tarbiyah researcher and activist, Depok, 14 July 2011. In addition, he suggests that many Tarbiyah cadres originate from such institutions as the elite State School of Accounting (STAN), explaining that accountants and engineers both find appeal in the precisely defined truths offered by religion because of their fields of study.

[53] A movement in the late 1970s to promote the donning of head coverings (*jilbab*) by females was initiated at the Istiqomah Mosque in Bandung, an important node of anti-New Order resistance at the time. A similar one undertaken by ABIM in Malaysia apparently inspired the movement. Interview with Bambang Pranggono and Syarif Hidayat, Istiqomah Mosque activists, Bandung, 14 July 2012.

earlier, it was a vital contact point for the highly influential Salman Mosque-Bandung Institute of Technology activist and lecturer Imaduddin Abdulrachim.

Yet it is self-evident that all of these Islamic parties have fared quite poorly in Indonesia. This was not happenstance, for it must be recalled that many of these parties quickly developed mutual animosity because of the defining logic of Indonesian democracy that was hardly conducive to countering fragmentation within the politics of the *ummah*. Within this logic, each Islamic political party claiming to represent the interests of the community of believers actually represents competing patronage networks within Indonesia's money politics-dominated electoral democracy.

Thus, vehicles that Alamsyah (2013) calls 'pure' Islamic parties – including the PKS – only garnered 18 per cent of the total vote in the 2004 elections. Five years later, all Islamic parties – if more broadly defined to include the PKB and PAN, which have emphasised their nationalist credentials almost as much as their religious ones – only received about a quarter of the total votes. The PKS has been marginally the star performer, winning between 7 and 8 per cent of the votes in both general elections, supplementing their results with victories in gubernatorial races in West Java in 2008 and in West Sumatera in 2010 (Alamsyah 2013). These outcomes clearly pale in comparison to the approximately half of the vote won by the AKP and half the seats won by the FJP, in general elections respectively taking place in 2011 and in 2011–2012. Such failure, which would be replicated in the 2014 general elections[54] – but with the PKS losing some ground – ultimately, highlights the comparative incapacity of the new Islamic populism in Indonesia to develop coherently and effectively organised multi-class support bases for its political vehicles.

Conclusion

Not surprisingly, the Arab Spring reignited old debates about whether the guiding principles of Islam are inherently incompatible with democracy or mutable enough to accommodate politics without an overtly exclusionary Islamic state (see Berman 2013; Jones, S.G. 2013). Such debates are inseparable from the question of whether political inclusion within democratic institutions would result in the internalisation of liberal and pluralist values among Islamic political actors.

This chapter, however, has explored the intricacies of the new Islamic populism's encounter with democratic politics in a way that suggests complexities going beyond the fairly simple thesis of political moderation through democratic inclusion. It confirms that acceptance of democratic politics is contingent on the position of those struggling for the social, economic and

---

[54] See the data provided in the next chapter.

political advancement of an *ummah* imagined to be unified through the experience of systemic and historically rooted marginalisation. The analysis of the new Islamic populist tendency shows that the relationship with democracy can fluctuate according to specific circumstances encountered in the terrain of political struggle. Of all the cases considered, the Egyptian one is perhaps the most intriguing in this regard given the failure of the Muslim Brotherhood to maintain power in spite of early spectacular successes through the democratic route.[55]

The chapter has also underlined the importance of the presence or absence of well-organised political vehicles that can claim to represent the *ummah* as a whole with credibility and forcefulness. This has been the case for the AKP in Turkey for most of its time in power, but less so for Egypt partly because of the Salafist challenge to the Muslim Brotherhood's claims. Indonesia's money politics-dominated democracy, however, has clearly further exacerbated historically already existing fragmentation within Islamic politics. Hence, it is more difficult in this case for the new Islamic populist tendency to successfully navigate through the democratic terrain in the absence of broad-enough social bases as well as coherent political vehicles that can lock in the allegiance of a sociologically diverse *ummah*.

---

[55] Though as yet unprovable, there is a sense among the Egyptian intelligentsia that certain sections of the Muslim Brotherhood have already resorted to violent acts from the Sinai to Cairo. There is also suspicion that they were responsible for numerous acts of sabotage of electric power grids in Egypt in 2014 to discredit the Al-Sisi government. Interview with Amira Howeidy, deputy editor-in-chief, *Al-Ahram Weekly* newspaper, Cairo, 17 December 2014.

8 Navigating through neoliberalism
A pathway to power?

Like the relationship between Islam and democracy, the relationship between Islam and capitalism has been a theme explored by succeeding generations of scholars. A varied group has come to critique the oft-made Weberian claim that the two are inherently incompatible due to cultural practices deriving from well-entrenched Islamic religious precepts that tend to create obstacles to private capital accumulation. Such scholars have done so from starkly dissimilar theoretical starting points: Rodinson (1966 [2007]), for example, explored this theme from a perspective steeped in the Marxist tradition of social and historical analysis, while Nasr (2009) more recently delved into it on the basis of neoliberal assumptions about the benefits of globalisation for those who engage with it.[1] Rudnyckyj (2010), by contrast, shows convergences between Islam and capitalism in Indonesia and elsewhere in the developing world through ethnographic analysis, especially with regard to developing workplace ethics and practices in modern firms. With references to religious values, these are geared to instil workers' self-discipline, sense of responsibility and, according to Rudnyckyj, to better prepare them for adaptation to the requirements of working in a globalised neoliberal economy.

The position taken in this book, however, reinforces an alternative view that there is nothing innate about the relationship between the purveyors of the Islamic religion and support for or rejection of various forms of capitalism and immersion in global markets. In this chapter, the theme is explored more specifically in connection with the shaping of new Islamic populist tendencies in Indonesia, as well as in Turkey and Egypt, particularly with regard to the inevitable requirement of navigating through existing constellations of power and interest.

It is shown that, like the relationship with democracy examined in the previous chapter, there is a great deal of contingency involved in the link between the evolution of the new Islamic populism and receptiveness to neoliberal globalisation. Once more, rather than just moral precepts, it is the broader context

---

[1] Alse see Gellner's (1981: 5–7) reflections on how Max Weber failed to recognise that the Islamic religion could have provided the ideational bases for capitalist development.

that moulds the responses of the social agents of Islamic populist politics towards capitalism and global markets. From this point of view, an important aspect of the problem is whether new Islamic populist alliances are strongly supported by capitalist elements that are well positioned to compete successfully in global markets and whether they can be conceived as being part of a broader *ummah* that had been systematically marginalised by past rulers of secular nationalist states. Furthermore, it matters whether the adoption of economically globalising strategies by the purveyors of the new Islamic populism is both viable and useful in the effort to establish their ascendancy.

Though the relationship between democratisation and the growth of capitalism, including in its neoliberal manifestation, is surely complex, it is clear that Muslim-majority societies like Indonesia, Egypt and Turkey have all experienced struggles over democratisation that are not independent of conflict over the distribution of wealth and power. Indeed, the struggle over the outcomes of political change ultimately cannot be separated from conflicts about the kinds of social interests that would be best positioned to take advantage of potential accompanying changes in the way that the economy is organised. These conflicts may involve a range of social agents residing within both the state apparatus and private business as well within broader civil society. Particular institutions within the state, such as the military in the cases at hand, can be prominently involved in these struggles due to the lingering influence of specific historical legacies.

Hanieh (2006) argues, however, that democratisation has been but the handmaiden of neoliberal globalisation in the Middle East. In his view, the promotion of democracy (Wittes 2008) is mainly suited to the interests of global capitalist interests and their allies within international development organisations and Western governments. These, he suggests, require only the facade of electoral politics in the Middle East to validate policies that harshly treat the poor and continually side with the already rich and powerful in the world.

But this sort of neat correspondence between democracy and the facilitation of neoliberal globalisation is surely too simplistic. It assumes that there are no sufficiently powerful and autonomous domestic social forces able to make use of democratisation as a means of advancing their own interests. In Hanieh's type of analysis, there is little room for domestic social forces that may be, in fact, hindered by state authoritarianisms closely intertwined with non-transparent links between big business and the managers of the state. However, this is the way that much of the Anatolian bourgeoisie, for example, saw its situation in Turkey for much of the period before the advent of AKP rule in Turkey.

What is certain is that the advent of structural adjustment policies across much of the Muslim world, which typically include the reduction of public spending and the privatisation of state functions, has significantly influenced the social and political terrain within which Islamic populism has evolved around the globe. In specific circumstances they might create the impetus for more thorough engagement with the processes of neoliberal globalisation. Significantly, market competition based on transparency and 'good governance' can be promoted as an antidote to the cronyism and corruption that Islamic political vehicles often profess to be against given their overt emphasis on safeguarding the moral quality of society. Such a propensity would be reinforced, furthermore, if cronyism and corruption have been evidently detrimental to economic interests associated with the *ummah*.[2]

It is therefore important to recall that the narrative of the *ummah* has evolved through the social memory of a collective experience of economic marginalisation going all the way back to the age of Western colonial domination, as explained in Chapter 3. When new nation states with their modernisation programmes emerged within the Muslim world, and new major economic players began to develop alongside them, within and outside of the apparatus of the state, the experience became infused in debates about arresting the further decline of the traditional Islamic petty bourgeoisie (Chapter 4). Hence, in Indonesia we saw the failed push to have the state play a major role in promoting the economic fortunes of businesses connected to *pribumi*-Muslim businesspeople. We also have alluded in earlier parts of this book to the aversion of major Islamic political leaders, such as Al-Banna in Egypt and Erbakan in Turkey – and some leaders of Indonesia's Sarekat Islam – to Western-dominated capitalism but not necessarily to capitalism as such. Nevertheless, we also know that some of the protectionist discourse traditionally associated with Islamic political movements of the twentieth century has been eroded subsequently by greater receptiveness to free market competition by some of their social agents.

This sort of transformation has been most prominent in Turkey where big Anatolian-based business groups have come increasingly to the fore since the Özal-era economic reforms and particularly under AKP rule. In Egypt, a similar attraction began developing within some business groups nurtured by the Muslim Brotherhood before the military-led coup against the Morsi government in 2013 struck a huge blow against their globalising dreams. From this point of view, Gumuscu (2010) was not quite correct when he claimed that an independent and pious bourgeoisie existed in Turkey but was absent in Egypt.

---

[2] For example, interview with Nafti Mahdi, En Nahda representative in Tunisian Constituent Assembly, 18 April 2013. He is painfully aware, however, that there is no Islamic bourgeoisie in his country ready to take over from the Ben Ali-era businesses that still dominate the economy. He says that this necessitates conciliatory measures towards the existing business community, which accounts for the small number of prosecutions mounted against top businessmen by the En Nahda-led government. Some leftist political activists are also aware that such a situation may lead to alliances between En Nahda and sections of the old Ben Ali-cultivated bourgeoisie – for example, interview with Zied Lakhdhar, secretary general of the Democratic Patriots Movement, Tunis, 18 April 2013.

As Tuğal (2012) points out, such bourgeoisie may have been comparatively less prominent in Egypt because of its association with the Muslim Brotherhood, which has had to exist as an underground movement for most of its political life. Tuğal also suggests that the bourgeois attraction to neoliberalism, and to democratic politics, in Turkey has been due to the close association of a culturally Islamic faction to a strong and practically monolithic vehicle of Islamic politics, the AKP. He suggests too that the same kind of confident assertion of such ideals has been hindered in Egypt because Islamic politics could not afford the same kind of political protection to big businesses emerging from within Islamic networks and groupings. Tuğal (2012: 34) refers specifically to political weaknesses arising from competition between the Muslim Brotherhood and various Salafi-related vehicles discussed in previous chapters of this book.

It is notable that Tuğal's observation can be easily transposed to Indonesia, where nothing approaching the Muslim Brotherhood, let alone the AKP, has existed at least since the end of the short golden age of the Sarekat Islam. It should not be surprising, therefore, that there exists in Indonesia a range of anti-democratic political vehicles dreaming of the day they might be rescued from political marginality by an Islamic state. It is no wonder too that businesses emerging out of the *ummah* here speak more hesitatingly (than in Egypt or Turkey) about the virtues of competition within neoliberal globalisation as opposed to a long-awaited benevolent state that would protect their interests.

Nevertheless, writers like Nasr have been making the argument that 'capitalism is alive and thriving' in the Middle East with great enthusiasm – referring to the 'signs of it everywhere' (Nasr 2009: 13). For him, these signs include everything from earnest efforts among businessmen to protect their property rights to the staggering rise in consumption levels that have made possible the erection of giant malls across the Muslim world, from Istanbul to Dubai and all the way to Kuala Lumpur. Throughout his book, he is keen to highlight an entrepreneurial spirit and an attraction to the profane among the pious that are plainly not out of step with the imperatives of global competition.

However, one should not get carried away with this sort of linear narrative, for it is also clear that the neoliberalising impulse is not always all-powerful. The impulse may be tempered, for example, by the necessity to address the economic interests of powerful institutions, such as well-established state- and quasi state-owned companies or that of the military, all of which have been prominent in Turkey and Egypt as well as in Indonesia. In this connection, it is useful to retain the emphasis on contingency in the discussion. If differences in responses to neoliberalisation (say in Indonesia and Turkey) are largely attributable to the absence or presence of significant elements of the bourgeoisie within their respective manifestations of new Islamic populist politics, then it is necessary to further examine the implications for navigating through the relevant constellations of power.

The challenge of neoliberal reform

It has been mentioned that aversion to Western-dominated capitalism, whether on the basis of its 'unethical' nature or premised on the need to offer protection to the traditional Muslim petty bourgeoisie, might have been expected to be the default stance taken by the social agents of Islamic populism. But more than this, there is also the assumption that the 'populist' label would connote opposition as well to 'market-oriented' institutional arrangements of economic life. As discussed in Chapter 2, 'irrational' economic policy opposed to the 'rationality' of the market is often thought to lie at the heart of populist governments. However, it was also pointed out that a 'neoliberal' form of populism had previously emerged in Latin America, where the Menem government in Argentina, for example, embarked on a 'populist road to market reform'. This form of populist politics was premised on the weakening of pre-existing corporatist organisations and the management of a shift towards neoliberal economic policy made possible by bringing together business and labour groups – both based on new internationally competitive economic sectors – into a newly developed social alliance (Gibson 1997: 355–356). In other words, just as affinity with the Islamic religion may not necessarily signal a rejection of free-market capitalism for reasons of morality, populist politics too is capable of similar adaptations in spite of its typically egalitarian rhetoric.

Once more, however, it is the case of Iran, lying outside of the main focus of this book, which provides some illuminating clues about the way in which the factor of contingency can work concretely to override doctrinal issues. In the early years of the Islamic Republic, and under the influence of the ideas of Ali Shariati and his disciples, the rhetoric of class struggle appeared to mesh with more traditional Islamic references to social justice favoured by those closer to Khomeini's inner circle. This is not surprising given the prior discussion of the varied social bases of the Iranian Revolution in Chapter 4. But clearly there was no real conception about how Islamic morality would be put into practice within a new economic system notionally siding with the good and the pious that felt oppressed and marginalised under the rule of the Shah and by his economic modernisation programme.

In the words of Nomani and Behdad (2006: 1), 'The Islamic state, with fictitiously lofty goals, began its quest for an Islamic utopia, with a hitherto undefined Islamic economic system.' However, according to these same authors, the burden of the war with Iraq and the fall of international oil prices eventually signalled a new phase in the economic policies of the Islamic Republic. By the late 1980s, the policies were aimed at structural adjustment and economic liberalisation involving the removal of price controls, subsidies, privatisation and currency devaluation typically counselled by international development organisations like the IMF. Nomani and Behdad also view the rise of Ahmadinejad in 2005 as representing a partial backlash against the social and economic consequences of such policies, put forward by the governments of Rafsanjani and Khatami. It also signified the reassertion of the power of the so-called *bonyad* – parastatal foundations in control of large business conglomerates – that had grown in wealth and power soon after the Iranian Revolution (Nomani and Behdad 2006: 36, 61–62).

In Indonesia, pressures for economic liberalisation also became acutely felt following the drastic fall of international oil prices in the 1980s. It resulted in a period characterised by export-led industrialisation based on labour-intensive manufacturing, the opening up of the trade and financial sectors, privatisation and greater encouragement of foreign investment (Robison and Hadiz 1993). But some of these same policies would later contribute to the extreme gravity of Indonesia's Asian Economic Crisis in the late 1990s. For instance, the deregulation of the banking sector in the late 1980s had allowed for the proliferation of banks that essentially served as a source of cheap capital for the same politically well-connected business conglomerates that had established them. In addressing the economic crisis, Indonesia had to cope with IMF conditions for assistance, which included yet another raft of structural adjustment policies, including cut-backs on state subsidies, as well as encouragement of further privatisation and a more investment-friendly climate, in addition to another set of financial sector reforms (see Robison and Hadiz 2004: Chapter 8).

In Egypt, economic reforms began under Sadat, who declared in 1974 that the country required *infitah*, liberalisation, in order to battle the inefficiency of a bloated public sector and to encourage private investment, especially from the newly cash-rich Gulf countries. However, this effort was stalled by the food riots of 1977, which saw large-scale protests against price increases due to the lifting of state subsidies. It has been noted earlier that Sadat's ad hoc alliance with the Muslim Brotherhood and other Islamic groupings against the Left dissipated under these circumstances, leading to the president's eventual assassination. A new economic liberalisation push was heralded in the mid-1980s, however, when the Mubarak government was forced to seek assistance from the IMF, the World Bank and various international creditors to address crippling domestic and international debt. More structural adjustment came following the first Gulf War, accompanying the debt relief that was extended to the country in return for its support for the Allied cause against Saddam Hussein. These included policies to facilitate the privatisation of state companies, new tax laws and the revocation of redistributive land regulations that had been put in place under Nasser (Owen 2004: 115–117).

Faced with severe balance-of-payments problems in the late 1970s, Turkey too had undertaken an economic liberalisation programme, which only gathered steam however under the Özal government of the 1980s that was supported by the military as well as the community of international development organisations. Its policies prominently included macroeconomic reforms geared to encourage exports and curb reliance on import substitution industries. Government austerity was encouraged too, as was the clearing of hurdles to foreign investment. In a related development, Turkey's military leaders took stronger measures to smash the power of leftist trade unions, which contributed to the development of a domestic cost structure that enabled industries to compete in the burgeoning markets of the Middle East and to make concerted inroads into Europe. In addition, more economic liberalisation policies were put in place in the wake of yet another economic crisis in 2001. This time the target was a decrepit banking sector, which had been used to funnel funds to politically well-connected businesses, eroding public confidence and causing a massive run on the banks as well as the drastic devaluation of the Turkish lira (Owen 2004: 123–125). Such an experience recalled some aspects of the crisis that had wreaked havoc on Indonesia's economy just a few years earlier. Like the Indonesian government before it, the AKP-led Turkish government worked closely with the IMF in handling this crisis (Dagi 2013: 97–98).

The Muslim response

In this connection, it is particularly significant that Islamic organisational vehicles in Indonesia, Turkey and Egypt did not mount concerted opposition to these economically liberalising reforms, for example, on the basis of the presumed moral depredations of capitalism. As mentioned, the AKP in Turkey in fact presided over close collaboration with the IMF and other international development institutions to solve the Turkish economic crisis it inherited upon coming to power. Perhaps all this is not so surprising given Tripp's (2006) observation that there has always been a great deal of adaptability in the way that Islamic scholars have dealt with the dictates of the modern capitalist economy. The most prominent example of such adaptability is probably shown in new ways of treating 'usury' to permit the development of a highly globalised and increasingly profitable world of 'Islamic banking' that is attractive to the pious. Islamic banking is appealing not only to religiously inclined individuals but also to business groups emerging out of Islamic networks, partly because it enables access to global financial markets with minimal costs in terms of the flaunting of religious identity.[3]

---

[3] Interview with Ustad Syuhada Bahri, chairman, Dakwah Islamiyah Indonesia (DDII), Jakarta, 3 January 2011; Ihab El-Fouly, Muslim Brotherhood-linked businessman and adviser to Khairat El-Shater, Heliopolis, 4 April 2012; interview with Amine Makkaoui and Slim Hajji, League of Young Engineers, Tunis 17 April 2013; interview with Abdeslam Ballaji, PJD (Justice and Development Party) member of the Moroccan parliament, Rabat, 23 April 2013. The PJD is allied with the monarchy and the leading party in parliament. Though it is rooted in a history of Islamic politics in Morocco going back to the 1960s, it is considered influenced by the AKP and the Egyptian Muslim Brotherhood (Zeghal 2008: xix–xx).

That such considerable malleability exists stands to reason if the battle over economic and political governance in Muslim-majority societies is more than about ideas and values, but also about the furtherance of the social position and interests of their bearers. In this regard, it is significant that there is no single institution in the Islamic world that has intrinsic monopoly over doctrinal interpretation and with the capacity to enforce it. This is in spite of the exalted position of Al-Azhar *ulama* in Egypt, the Shia clergy in Iran or of the claims to authority on religious matters made by the Indonesian Council of Ulama (MUI) – which has little basis actually because it was initially created as a mere instrument of control over the *ummah* under the New Order (Porter 2002: 47).

Tripp (2006: 142–149) also suggests, however, that such adaptability has meant the infusion of the logic of global finance into banking sub-sectors ostensibly runs according to religious injunctions but is equally driven by profit and the necessity of competition for clients. Although catering to a niche market made up of the economically well off and pious, the difference between conventional and Islamic banking has therefore become increasingly blurred. So rather than challenging global capitalism, Islamic banking has instead 'shown that the practices of global capitalism, whatever its origins or initially disruptive effects, can be incorporated into the world of meaning that is validated by reference to distinctive Islamic idioms' (Tripp 2006: 149; also see Halliday 2012: 216).

This sort of doctrinal elasticity has been clearly tied to the efforts by culturally Islamic businesspeople to seek out new roles other than of the traditional 'victims' of global capitalism. Nasr (2009), therefore, extols the role of a new generation of Islamic entrepreneurs and professionals who are more inclined to embrace the opportunities provided by global capitalism – and who are also immersed in things like global pop culture and its mostly Western artefacts. For Nasr (2009: 176–177), neoliberal globalisation is unambiguously providing the cultural resources for Muslims to become more pluralist, as well as capitalistic, without necessarily being less pious.[4]

But Tripp's observations, in particular, reinforce the point being made here that the embrace of neoliberal globalisation, replete with its narrative of progress through free trade, is more likely to occur when the social base of Islamic politics includes those who are equipped to derive benefit from it. Such social bases have been found within new Islamic populist alliances, most notably in Turkey, but also in Egypt, albeit perhaps less visibly so. They have been far less distinct in Indonesia, where the big bourgeoisie remains dominated by ethnic Chinese businesses for reasons that go all the way back to the structure of colonial capitalism in what was once the Dutch East Indies.

---

[4] While this may be true, it is nonetheless unclear why fondness for rap music or Western action-hero films, both mentioned by Nasr, could not be equally associated with individuals who support authoritarian regimes as they could with supporters of democratic systems.

In Egypt, therefore, even some adherents of the typically more conservative and social exclusionary Salafi strand, including medium-scale businessmen excited by the prospects offered by globalisation and, for a time, the possible sidelining of Mubarak business cronies, suggest that they are not necessarily against capitalism, as long as it is 'ethical'. What is emphasised in this view is that Islamic ethics functions to temper the depredations of capitalism instead of serving as the basis of opposition to it.[5] One major businessman close to the Muslim Brotherhood leadership when it was in power, therefore, states that adopting 'the pillars of the free market economy' would benefit businesses that had been long ignored by the state due to the cronyism of the Mubarak era – without forgetting to add the necessity of being mindful of 'Islamic values'.[6] The practical implications of such a position are greater access to power and the market for businesses that belong to, or identify with, the long marginalised *ummah* and which therefore form part of the multi-class alliance that enables the new Islamic populism.

Thus, like in Turkey under the AKP, and before it parts of Latin America, we see that populist politics do not necessarily contradict the impetus to embark on economic reforms in a neoliberal direction (Öniş 2012). Dagi points out, for example, that privatisation has brought in revenue for the Turkish state to the amount of $30.6 billion under the AKP government. Some of this privatisation has involved large entities, such as the state telecommunications company, Turktelekom, which was sold to a foreign company (Dagi 2013: 97), this time based in Saudi Arabia. Significantly, sometimes protests by workers who have lost their jobs as a result of privatisation have been brusquely dismissed as being hatched by the mysterious military-dominated 'deep state'. This was the situation in the case of the controversial sale of Tekel – a tobacco and alcoholic beverages company – to the international giant, British and American Tobacco.[7]

Such circumstances can be usefully understood in connection to Tripp's (2006: 103–124) observation of how many Muslim thinkers have attempted, over time, to basically appropriate capitalism while adding a layer of morality that could be regarded as being substantively Islamic on top of it. Thus, Tunisian En Nahda Party leader and respected Islamic thinker Rached Ghannouchi argues that free-market capitalism is wholly compatible with an economic system based on Islamic precepts although, in his view, the latter

---

[5] For example, interview with Mohamed Nour, Al-Nour Party spokesman and International Relations Coordinator, Cairo, 1 April 2012. He is also a software technologies entrepreneur.
[6] Interview with Ihab El Fouly, businessman, Heliopolis, 4 April 2012. But this usually means non-participation in areas of business where the elasticity of morals would be too sorely tested, such as those having to do with alcohol or gambling.
[7] Interview with Ali Tekin, Professor of International Relations, Bilkent University, Ankara, 10 October 2010.

would guarantee a high level of social justice as found in the Scandinavian countries rather than the unbridled capitalism of the United States.[8] The irony, of course, is that En Nahda's major foe is that historical pillar of Western social democracy, the trade union movement, which in Tunisia is stronger than its counterparts in other Arab countries because of the considerable state patronage that went all the way back to the days of Habib Bourguiba (see Alexander 2010; Bellin 2002; Anderson 1986).[9] According to Ghannouchi, nevertheless, the injunction to pay *zakat* symbolises no less than Islam's commitment to social justice.[10] Significantly, such a commitment will have broad appeal especially in societies like Tunisia where economic inequalities have been perceived as growing, notwithstanding En Nahda's running conflict with the unions. This is especially so because the latter had been so tainted by past close association with the authoritarian state.

It is true, however, that many prior Islamic thinkers have accommodated a range of anti-capitalist ideas in their critique of the marginalising effects of Western colonialism; some of these were even incorporated by regimes such as Nasser's in Egypt and practised in the form of redistributive policies (Tripp 2006: 95). Even today the Hizbut Tahrir strongly latches on to an anti-imperialist position to reject foreign investment in Muslim countries akin to that espoused by leftist movements, while its Indonesian branch is habitually at the forefront of denunciations of the privatisation of state utilities (Munabari 2010: 198–199).

Nevertheless, because much of the critique of the old Islamic petty bourgeoisie of capitalism was moralistic in nature – and infused as well by fear of the revolutionary agenda of the radical Left – there is considerable room for acceptance of capitalism, replete with its basic class structure, by their political descendants. Gilsenan, for example, reminds us that the Muslim Brotherhood in Egypt was 'resolutely antileft and certainly saw no salvation in a revolution of Egypt's social structure' (2008: 221), as was also pointed out in Chapter 3. This is the case even if a range of ethical caveats were to be regularly pronounced by Muslim social and political activists, such as avoidance of industries that revolve around alcohol consumption or gambling. Class inequalities, by the same token, can also be accepted as long as the payment of *zakat* is ensured to enable activities that alleviate the suffering of the poor.[11]

---

[8] Greatly influenced by the traditions of the Muslim Brotherhood, Ghannouchi would, during his political evolution, come to be one of the great symbols of the claim that Islam and democracy were wholly compatible (Tamimi 2001).
[9] Another irony is that, precisely because of this relative strength, it was actually the trade union movement that was capable of taking the leading role in instigating the uprising against Ben Ali at the end of 2010 (Zemni 2013).
[10] Interview, Tunis, 18 April 2013. Rama Pratama, a leading figure of the PKS in Indonesia made a similarly positive reference to Northern European-style capitalism in an interview in Jakarta, 14 July 2010.
[11] Interview with Amine Makkaoui and Slim Hajji, League of Young Engineers, Tunis, 17 April 2013.

In the case of Turkey, it has been shown already that the AKP's pro-neoliberal reform position provides it with an instrument to cultivate support from the more global market-oriented Anatolian bourgeoisie that had been previously shunned in favour of the so-called Istanbul bourgeoisie – big business groups nurtured under previously dominant protectionist and largely import substitution industries-oriented policies (see Bugra 1998). This is indicated in the running conflict between the AKP and TUSIAD, the business association which claims that its members account for half of Turkey's gross domestic product (GDP) and that is widely regarded to represent Istanbul's more established industrial elite.[12] TUSIAD businesses are also regarded as rivals of business groups closer to the AKP, which assemble mostly under the auspices of a different business federation, the aforementioned MUSIAD.

The latter organisation is considered by Başkan (2010: 410–415) to enjoy such strong organic links to the AKP that its members provide not only financial resources but also actual personnel to work for local party branches across the nation. Interestingly, an attempt to emulate MUSIAD took place in Egypt during the short period in which the Muslim Brotherhood was in power. An Egyptian Business Development Association (EBDA) was brought into being by businesspeople connected to the then ascendant organisation with the aim of developing a business community untainted by the sort of cronyism associated with the Mubarak era.[13]

That such an organic relationship came to develop in Turkey appears to have been the outcome of developments that began with the economic reforms of the Özal government and which culminated in those undertaken subsequently by the AKP. These policy reforms facilitated the Anatolian bourgeoisie's consolidation as major exporters to European, Middle Eastern and Central Asian markets and its development into a powerful faction of the capitalist class. For the AKP itself, the embrace of pro-EU policies, in particular, conferred a degree of international protection from its domestic foes given their indirect association with politically liberal values. For example, more – and not less – civilian control over the military apparatus would be required for Turkey to fall in line with European standard practices (Rabasa and Larrabee 2008: 80). This is so in spite of the EU's continual refusal to accept Turkey as a full member country.

MUSIAD officials are thus aware that the attempted push into the EU has gone together with the 'democratisation and economic reform' agenda that has

---

[12] See 'Turkish Business Chief Criticises Erdogan' 2012.
[13] Interview with Ihab El Fouly, Muslim Brotherhood-linked businessman and adviser to Khairat El-Shater, Heliopolis, 4 April 2012. He points to the prominent businessman Hassan Malek, whose family owns companies in such diverse areas as textiles, trade, information technology and furniture manufacturing, as the main initiator of the organisation. Malek, who is also closely associated with the Muslim Brotherhood, had been put behind bars for a short period under the Mubarak government.

served them so well. They also note with enthusiasm that the top 200 companies in Turkey in the 1990s did not include any 'conservative' ones – shorthand for culturally Islamic and regionally Anatolian – but that 'the monopoly has now been broken'.[14] Interestingly, however, Başkan (2010: 408) observed that MUSIAD did not have the same zeal for the AKP's immediate predecessor, the Welfare Party led by Erbakan, which was thought to be too old-fashioned and lagging 'behind global trends'. The concern was apparently that Erbakan had a preference for economic protectionist policies that reflected more traditionally petty bourgeois sensibilities that used to dominate the older form of Islamic populism rather than those that represented the growing wealth and self-confidence, in particular, of the Anatolian bourgeoisie.

In Indonesia, however, it has been said that the relationship between the new Islamic populism and support for neoliberal globalisation remains much more ambiguous. Certainly, the sort of self-assured embrace of neoliberalism by culturally Islamic businesspeople, such as in Turkey, and even Egypt, is harder to come across. Rather than overt acceptance, what is more likely to be encountered are bywords like 'good governance', 'economic efficiency' and 'civil society participation', which are then linked to the ideas of 'social justice' and 'moral society' associated traditionally with Islamic politics since at least the early twentieth century.[15] This is in spite of the PKS chief Anis Matta's unusually uninhibited expression of support for full engagement in the world capitalist economy, which he says would be achieved by enhancing the entrepreneurial talents of the *ummah*.[16]

But such confidence is not always reflected among the actual businessmen that support his and other Islamic parties, for they remain too small and ill equipped to thrive in a free-market economy in which they would have to face well-established business conglomerates. Solo-based Muslim businessman and rice distributor Joko Setiono, for example, is well aware that he and his colleagues are not in any position to rival the more experienced Chinese conglomerates in such a free market.[17] Thus, he expresses the hope that support for Islamic political parties would translate into direct benefits to his businesses. He also makes few claims about readiness to plunge into a market free of political connections even if those he already enjoys have not propelled him into the big leagues of the business world. Similarly, another Solo-based

---

[14] Interview with Eyup Vural Aydin (secretary general) and Dr Hatice Karahan Pişkin (deputy secretary general) of MUSIAD, Istanbul, 20 September 2011.

[15] See 'Akhir Tahun, PKS Evaluasi Kinerja Dewan' 2011; 'OKJ Harus Laksanakan Prinsip Good Governance' 2011; 'Visi dan Misi' 2013; and 'Falsafah Dasar Perjuangan dan Platform Kebijakan Pembangunan PKS' 2013.

[16] Interview, Jakarta, 28 January 2013.

[17] Joko Setiono, who is widely known as 'Joko Beras' or 'Joko Rice', comes from a Muslim, small-business family background – his father was a financial backer of the local branch of the Masyumi. Interview, Solo, 9 July 2011.

businessman, a member of the PKS, recognises that supporting the party has brought him such benefits as access to a wider circle of business contacts. He is fully aware, however, that the party he supports lacks the clout, capacity and 'machinery' to help businesses owned by Muslims to compete with far more established ones, including those owned by ethnic Chinese Indonesians.[18]

In addition, because of the relative absence of a big bourgeoisie within the *ummah* and the lack of a cohesive political vehicle to represent it in democratic competition, there is much emphasis in Indonesia on the desirability of state control over key (mainly natural resource-based) industries, to be utilised for the common good rather than for private interests. Thus, support for extensive privatisation of state-owned companies that have been powerful since the New Order era rarely emanates from Indonesia's manifestation of the new Islamic populism. The focus on the aforementioned industries – usually validated by reference to appropriate verses in the Koran or to selected Hadith – is not surprising given Indonesia's rich endowment in natural resources. Moreover, Indonesia was one of the OPEC member countries that benefited from windfall revenue brought about by the oil booms of the 1970s and early 1980s, though it has been subsequently reduced to the status of net oil exporter due to dwindling production and reserves as well as increased domestic consumption. The idea that Indonesia's oil wealth had been squandered during the Soeharto era, through graft and economic mismanagement, is commonly encountered and provides impetus for the assertion that Islam necessitates state control over public resources, although with the familiar qualification that it should be exercised on the basis of Islamic morality.

It is not always smooth sailing towards global capitalism, however, outside of the Indonesian case. For example, the venerable Al-Azhar had pointedly rejected the Morsi government's issuance of 'Islamic bonds' for contravening religious injunctions against usury. Under strong pressure to achieve concrete results in reviving the economy, that government had produced a draft law allowing it to sell sovereign bonds representing shares in government assets and utilities through public offerings. Interestingly, Al-Azhar also rebuked the government for attempting to take up the authority to dispense with state property without the approval of parliament. In this, Al-Azhar appeared to be underlining its support for the democratic process – and distancing itself from past association with authoritarian governments, as well as their neoliberal economic policies.[19]

However, displaying the contextual nature of doctrinal interpretation, Al-Azhar has been, in fact, inconsistent in its views on the compatibility of modern

---

[18] Interview with Abdul Khoris, PT Intermedia publishers, Solo, 11 July 2011.
[19] See 'Al-Azhar Rejects Draft Law on Islamic Bonds' 2012. Al-Azhar representatives have been involved closely in the shaping of Egypt's post-Mubarak institutions of governance, being active, for example, in the body that drafted the new constitution.

financial instruments and Islam. In 1989, when Mubarak's position was virtually unassailable, the Grand Mufti had actually issued a *fatwa* approving the issuance of interest-bearing bonds by the government, while citing development needs (Tripp 2006: 129). Given Al Azhar's subsequent support for the military coup that deposed Morsi, it may be that the age-old and internationally respected Al-Azhar was simply signalling its unwillingness to subordinate itself to the Muslim Brotherhood rather than substantive opposition to its economic policies.

In any case, it would be unwise to consider enchantment with global capitalism as translating into the elimination of the state's role in the economy. What it does entail, of course, is a recalibration of that role – after all, even neoliberal thinking at its source has dispensed with the idea that simply dismantling the state or ensuring its economic retreat would produce efficiently working markets (World Bank 1991, 2002). In other words, it is well accepted within the neoliberal orthodoxy now that institutions need to be established to facilitate the operations of these markets. As would be expected, this is always an eminently political process in which control over the levers of state power is a vital factor.

This is why it is important to recall that the appropriation of the neoliberal agenda by powerful, even predatory, groups within countries moving towards greater engagement with economic globalisation is nothing new. Much has been written about this in the Indonesian context, for example, where neoliberal reforms since the 1980s have repeatedly provided new instruments to sustain the ascendancy of entrenched predatory forces, whether in relation to the banking and financial sector or decentralisation policy, as embarked upon after the fall of Soeharto (Robison and Hadiz 2004; Hadiz 2010). The issue has been also discussed in great depth in very different contexts, such as that of post-Soviet Russia (Rutland 2013). Significantly, there is much space in any shift to pro-economic globalisation policies for conflict over the form they would take and whom they would benefit most. The problem for new Islamic populist forces is how well positioned they are to gain the advantage from such conflicts in specific circumstances.

Neoliberalising Islam and the military

In this regard, it is noteworthy that the military as an institution has been among the most serious sources of threat to the social alliances underpinning the new Islamic populism, although such an observation particularly holds true for Turkey and Egypt rather than for Indonesia. Importantly, the militaries in all these countries have had a major role in suppressing various manifestations of Islamic populism in the past. Such is the case in spite of the Turkish 'synthesis' of the 1980s, concerted attempts by the Muslim Brotherhood in Egypt to infiltrate the military going back to the 1940s, as well as the temporary alliance forged between ICMI and military elements in Indonesia in the late Soeharto era (Mietzner 2009). In all of these experiences, the relationship between the social agents of the new Islamic populism and the military as an institution – and as a particularly powerful receptacle of old regime interests – has been critical.

In all of these cases, it is also significant that the military had carved out a privileged place for itself within the existing social order, to the extent of occupying important positions within national economies and developing significant stakes in them. In the Indonesian context, however, it is notable that ethnic Chinese business conglomerates and other Soeharto-era cronies had long dwarfed the military's interests well before the advent of democratisation in 1998. This may actually explain why the military has been relatively restrained in confronting coalitions of power that come together today through political parties and parliaments, and which now dominate Indonesia's highly corruption-ridden democracy. Rather than curtailing the scope of these democratic institutions, retired military officers have instead opted to join in and become key figures in many of them, thus developing a way to indirectly protect the interests of the military and its personnel within the hurly-burly of Indonesian democratic life (Mietzner 2013: 103).

In contrast to Turkey and Egypt, it is also notable there has been no meaningful threat of a military clampdown on Indonesian Islamic political vehicles since the advent of democratisation.[20] Neither are there the kind of potential associated conflicts having to do with economic reorganisation between these political vehicles and the military given that neither can be counted among the major economic players of the post-authoritarian period. In fact, it is noteworthy that the economic base of Indonesian Islamic parties does not lie in existing or would-be business empires but in their entanglement in the murky world of Indonesia's distinctly money politics-driven democracy, where political and business deals are made behind closed doors. This has meant that they have developed a strong interest to ensure the survival of Indonesian democracy regardless of attacks against them launched by compatriots who are not on the democratic route, often conveyed with reference to strict devotion to religious doctrine.

---

[20] In fact the Tarbiyah movement from its earliest days had quietly forged links with the security agencies. These links were mainly initiated through Soeripto, a veteran state intelligence operative who was active in the movement and co-founded the PK that eventually evolved into the PKS. A former minister of forestry in the Wahid government, he was deposed from that powerful position due to his implication in a corruption case. Reflecting the concerns of security officials, Soeripto recalls thinking all the way back in the 1970s that harsh suppression of Islamic organisations might result in the resurgence of communism. Hence, he claims that he was always advocating a policy of partial accommodation of such organisations among state policy makers and security officials. Interview, Jakarta, 18 January 2013.

In all of these cases as well, it is useful to recall that the role of the military in the economy was initially the by-product of statist-nationalist modernisation projects undertaken in prior phases of economic development. This sort of military economic involvement was often proxy for the state role and thereby given legitimacy in nationalist terms. In Indonesia, for example, the nationalisation of foreign companies in the late 1950s – which came to be managed by the military – provided a strong historical basis for the involvement of men in uniform in economic activities for decades to come. Like the militaries of Egypt and Turkey, the Indonesian military also developed a highly anti-organised labour outlook because working-class movements came to undermine its own interests as managers and employers (Hadiz 1997).[21]

Mohammad Ayoob's (2007: 107) discussion of military politics in Indonesia and Turkey is pertinent in this respect. He suggests that the armed forces of both countries have been viewed as guardians of state secularism. Though there has been no overt principle of 'secularism' as something 'sacred' in Indonesia, its military has perpetually projected the image of an institution sworn to uphold the state ideology of Pancasila, an eclectic product of the Indonesian anti-colonial struggle that Darul Islamists and like-minded groupings have rejected because it has no basis in the Islamic religion. In both countries, as well as in Egypt, where the integration of Islam within the nationalist state's ideological constructions has proceeded further for reasons discussed in Chapter 3,[22] the military is also prone to present itself as the real embodiment of the interests of the nation as a whole.

Well-worn historical narratives lend credibility to these claims. In Indonesia, the military has traditionally enjoyed privileges because of its role in the very creation of the Indonesian nation-state in a bloody struggle against the Dutch after World War II. The Turkish military is revered for 'saving' the country from Western occupation and perhaps colonisation following the demise of the Ottoman Empire in the aftermath of World War I. In the case of Egypt, the social prestige of the military has been undoubtedly enhanced by heroic depictions of its role in wars against Israel, particularly that of 1973.

Nevertheless, the claim to represent the 'nation' masks the fact that all these militaries have developed a range of interests of their own that are underpinned by a huge presence in the national economy. To what extent Egyptian GDP is attributable to military-related economic activities is debatable, but the latter is

---

[21] Pro-AKP human rights activists in Turkey thus suggest that economic and political developments in Turkey cannot be separated from each other and that the military's ardent protection of state secularism is based on a more basic requirement to protect its economic interests. Interview with Murat Özer, branch manager, Mazlumder (Istanbul) and Cihat Gökdemir, chairman of the Board of Mazlumder (National), Istanbul, 19 October 2010.

[22] According to Bayat (2013: 216), for example, 'the state had adopted laws with roots in both religious and secular values' and 'based its authority in both discourses...'

certainly sizeable by most accounts.[23] It is well known that military-run companies in that country are involved in producing a bewildering range of consumer goods as well as in property and retail, which have little to do with defence or security matters. These economic interests go a long way in securing the privileged lifestyles of senior Egyptian military officers.[24] In Turkey, the military's business interests are largely organised through Oyak (Richards and Waterbury 2007: 356), a holding company that began life as a pension fund for military personnel. It has been involved in a range of businesses, not just in the production of military goods, but also in banking and finance, as well as in commerce and industry. It is has developed international partnerships too, the most famous being Oyak's collaboration with Renault in automobile manufacturing. Similar to Egypt, the lack of civilian oversight over these businesses extends to official budgetary matters, over which the military has traditionally enjoyed considerable autonomy (Akça 2010).

In Indonesia, as already mentioned, military personnel have been formally involved in formal business activity since the 1950s. In the decade prior to this, soldiers had partaken in smuggling activities to fund the war against the Dutch, which necessitated newly formed alliances with fledgling businesspeople. In the early New Order, however, military involvement in business entered a new phase as numerous military-owned enterprises expanded into various sectors of the economy, from construction and property, to commerce and industry (Robison 1986; Crouch 1988). Although mostly ethnic Chinese-owned conglomerates would come to overtake military-owned enterprises, the military-as-institution clearly retained a considerable economic stake in the longevity of the New Order. This was so notwithstanding its slowly diminishing influence within the regime itself because of the increasing integration of bureaucratic and business families at the head of a close-knit oligarchy centred on the Soeharto family (Robison and Hadiz 2004).

In the democratic era, governments have made attempts to break up these military enterprises, though with dubious success (Michaels and Haryanto 2012). These efforts have nonetheless made military involvement in the economy even more opaque, with local military commands being involved in localised alliances that enable such activity as security provision for businesses, illegal logging and the like. Thus, a range of off-budget activities continue to supplement state funding for the military in Indonesia too, which is officially quite meagre, even though the contribution of military-owned official businesses as such appears to be more limited than in the past (Rieffel and Pramodhawardani 2007).

---

[23] See 'Egypt's Army: Ambitious Men in Uniform' 2013.
[24] For some of the relevant details, see Clover and Khalaf (2011).

Because of the specific attributes of military forces, however – mainly their access to guns and other weaponry – new Islamic populist alliances have largely left the 'material base' of military institutions intact even as they have attempted to establish their dominance within the state. We have seen earlier how the prior Muslim Brotherhood-led government in Egypt attempted to appease the military by constitutionally guaranteeing its privileges, including in the economic field. This has been the case similarly in Turkey where the AKP has scored major victories over the military, significantly diminishing its political influence. Rather than to disengage the Turkish military from its vast economic empire, however, the major concern of the AKP has been to avoid the fate of the Welfare (Refah) Party that was ousted from power in 1997 and then banned through the machinations of its military foes on the premise that it had posed a threat to the secularist principles of the Turkish state (Nasr 2009: 240). Such concern about the military's intentions has been shown to be justified: in 2008, the AKP's adversaries attempted to use a hostile judiciary again to ban the AKP on the basis that it was plotting change towards an Islamic system of government.[25] This move was ostensibly triggered by the AKP's support for lifting the ban on headscarves in universities, an issue that has particularly polarised Turkish society.[26]

Since then, however, the AKP has displayed its own swagger by subsequently placing hundreds of military officers, including leading generals, behind bars, accusing them of inhabiting a mysterious 'deep state' – dubbed Ergenekon.[27] In fact, the spectre of Ergenekon has been regularly invoked by the AKP to validate harsh measures against political opponents more generally,[28] including among trade unions opposed to its privatisation policies.

Yet it is significant that Oyak has been able to maintain control over its affiliated companies. As recently as 2009, it still had assets reportedly amounting to over $13.5 billion (See 'Turkey's Military Has a Stake in 60 Companies' 2010). One rare scholarly analysis ranked Oyak consistently within the top three largest business conglomerates in Turkey for a decade (Demir 2010).

---

[25] The military has often worked in concert with the judiciary. As Taşpınar summarised (2012):

> All previous Islamist parties in Turkey had been shut down by either military intervention or rulings by the constitutional court: The National Order Party, founded in 1970, was banned by the Constitutional Court in 1971. The National Salvation Party, founded in 1972, was outlawed after the 1980 military coup. The Welfare Party, founded in 1983, was banned by the Constitutional Court in 1998. The Virtue Party, founded in 1997, was banned in 2001.

[26] See 'Turkish Court Considers AKP Ban' 2008.
[27] This is the name given to a deeply hidden valley referenced in ancient Turkish mythology. See Esayan, 'What is Deep State?'.
[28] See 'Ergenekon Case an Excuse to Try Anti-Government Figures: CHP Leader' 2013. See also, 'Analysis: Turkey's Divisive Ergenekon Trial' 2013. The rift, which was soon to grow dramatically, was discussed by key Gülen movement personality Husseyn Gulerce, in an interview in Istanbul, 16 September 2011.

Furthermore, Turkish columnist Lale Kemal (2014) has predicted that if a weaker AKP government were to result from a rift between Erdogan and the Gülen movement that widened after the Gezi Park demonstrations, then the military and its businesses would be the main beneficiary.

Nevertheless, it should be emphasised that what we are seeing is not a clear-cut case of inward looking military business protectionism versus Islamic business neoliberalism in any of these cases. In fact in Turkey, military businesses have been able to manoeuvre their way through economic liberalisation processes since the 1980s, looking outwardly to new foreign partners, while maintaining their standing in the domestic economy (Demir 2010). Ties between military businesses and those that form a support base for the AKP appear to have been developing behind the scenes as well, spurred by common ground found in economic activity. For example, according to a major report on the economic interests of the Turkish military, a number of MUSIAD-linked companies already have such ties due to their participation in the huge 'military-industrial sector' dominated by military-affiliated companies (Akça 2010: 27). The possible future implications of these kinds of business ties on the political relationship between the military and the AKP are intriguing, especially given the subsequent rift between the leadership of the latter and its former key ally, the Gülen movement. Because of the brief tenure of the Muslim Brotherhood at the helm of state power in Egypt, whether businesses connected to it would have been tempted to make inroads into areas dominated by military businesses is unknown. Suffice it to say, they would have tried not to squander their newfound access to state power.

In the absence of a self-identifying Islamic faction of the big bourgeoisie, these sorts of matters do not feature strongly in Indonesia, however. What is more important here is a particularly predatory form of democratic politics that has sucked Islamic political parties into its defining logic. This is shown best in the implication of key PKS figures, including a sitting party president in 2013, in widely publicised corruption scandals involving kickbacks and meat importation quotas. Moreover, the PKS was earlier startlingly active in supporting the move to name Soeharto a 'national hero' (Damanik 2010), which inevitably invited accusations that the dead dictator's wealthy family had paid the party for such backing in an attempt at political rehabilitation.

Nevertheless, new Islamic populists in Indonesia who have taken the route of electoral democracy still have in common with their counterparts elsewhere the fact that a return to authoritarian rule is more likely than not to harm their immediate material interests as well as future prospects for advancement. The case of Egypt provides a good example, of course, notwithstanding the deal that Salafis seem to have, at least temporarily, struck with the country's post-Morsi military rulers. Here, it is highly doubtful that the globalising triumphalism of the businesses that had backed the Muslim Brotherhood will be realised any time soon given the coup of 2013, while the return of Mubarak-era cronies to positions of dominance in the economy seems much more than likely.

But even without the Egyptian example, all political parties in Indonesia are aware that they would have to share more of the spoils of power if, for example, the military were to re-enter the formal sphere of politics because Indonesia's money politics-driven electoral democracy had become too unwieldy or fundamentally de-legitimised. Islamic political parties, so immersed in the Indonesian system of money politics by now, are no exception. This is the case even if the military in this country appears less well positioned to make a political comeback than its counterpart in Egypt, having been stripped, for example, of a previously sacrosanct right to automatic parliamentary representation as early as in 2004 (Mietzner 2013: 90).

The contradictions of development

In every social context within which it has emerged, the new Islamic populism faces the challenge of addressing quite a number of socially combustible issues arising from the contradictions of development that are not so easily resolvable.[29] All across the Muslim world, these have been, at the very least, accentuated in the present neoliberal phase of capitalist development. Undoubtedly the most prominent of such issues is that of growing inequality, which continues to be combined with chronic unemployment and underemployment, as well as persisting significant levels of poverty in a large number of cases. Most of these issues are likely to have the most volatile effects when they concern youths, especially those whose aspirations have grown with greater access to education. As to be expected, lying at the core of social grievances in such contexts is the matter not only of material deprivation, if only relative, but also of the dashed hopes and broken promises of modernisation for a considerable cross-section of society. This includes parts of the population who are urban middle class in terms of their social status and consumerist lifestyle but only in the most tenuous of senses.

While some of these contradictions had provided the setting for the very development of new Islamic populist alliances in the first place, they also provide opportunities for challenges from other forms of populism, including more secular nationalist ones. In other words, while the new Islamic populism has been a growing social phenomenon it is not necessarily the only game in town.

This has been shown clearly once again in Indonesia, where secular nationalist political parties were victorious in the general elections of 2014 and where the new Islamic populism has been the least successful. The top three parties

---

[29] This should be distinguished from the idea of the outright 'failure' of development, which formed the basis of Rahnema's (2008) analysis of Islamic politics.

emerging from these elections were the PDI-P, Golkar and Gerindra – the last of which only goes back to the 2009 parliamentary poll. Repeating the pattern of past general elections, their collective performance in 2014 was far better than that of parties overtly presenting themselves as 'Islamic', or which have been closely associated with Islamic social and political networks. This time around, Alamsyah's 'pure' Islamic parties (the PKS – in spite of its 'opening up' to non-Muslims – PPP and PBB) combined for less than 15 per cent of the vote. Even if the NU-backed PKB (which experienced a minor resurgence) and Muhammadiyah-associated PAN were to be added to this tally – in spite of internal alliances that stretch far beyond these organisations – it would still amount to a relatively weak 31.5 per cent of the vote (KPU 2014).

It should be pointed out that Gerindra, led by New Order-era retired general and former Soeharto son-in-law Prabowo Subianto, like the PDI-P, clearly offered more conventionally populist political imagery based on the notion of improving the lot of the 'common people' rather than on a long-suffering *ummah*. This is the case even if its election manifesto proclaimed the objective of 'purifying' religious practice in the country in a clearly opportunistic attempt to link up with Islamic parties in anticipation of presidential elections that were due to follow later in the same year.[30]

In Turkey there is the continuing challenge of the CHP, of course, which has its own entrenched nationalist-populist appeal, but also the ultra-right wing MHP (Nationalist Movement Party). Both of these may yet take some advantage of a development process that retains strong elements of social inequality while lately being associated with corruption and greed among the once almost unimpeachably pious. Yet the AKP defied prognostications of its doom when it still managed a convincing victory in nationwide municipal elections held in 2014. This is in spite of the Gezi Park protests in the previous year, a serious rift with the powerful Gülen movement and the unwanted scrutiny brought about by a sudden spate of corruption scandals surrounding cabinet ministers and even the Erdogan family.[31] Erdogan was even able to 'climb' into a more interventionist presidency later the same year while Ahmet Davutoğlu took over as prime minister.

In the case of Egypt, it has been mentioned that the Nasserist tradition has been much diminished over the decades. Nonetheless, the forced

---

[30] Here the relatively weak manifestation of the new Islamic populism in Indonesia became evident again when the PKS – floundering at the polls due to a newly developed reputation for poor levels of integrity – indicated that it was willing to subordinate itself once more within a large coalition of parties. Prabowo Subianto's Gerindra would lead such a coalition this time. See various news reports, including Ihsanuddin (2014). The PPP, closely associated with New Order rule in spite of its reformist reinvention, took the same route, as did the PBB.

[31] Nationwide, the AKP won 43 per cent of the vote, better than the party's showing in the 2009 municipal elections when it won 38 per cent. The ultra nationalists posted a slight gain from 16 to 17 per cent (see 'Erdogan's Victory, the Country's Loss' 2014).

retreat of the Muslim Brotherhood from the formal political arena may conceivably open new spaces for similarly nationalist forms of populism in Egypt. This is in spite of the undoubted Salafi intent to make the most of the post-Morsi political constellation – where the Muslim Brotherhood is notionally absent – including through a new alliance and cooperation with the powerful military.

For these reasons, the sorts of contradictions of development that are indicated by the following data are important to acknowledge when considering the broader context within which the new Islamic populism will continue to operate in each of these countries. In Indonesia, though the official unemployment rate hovers at around only 6 per cent (BPS 2013: 1), what is more important is an underemployment rate that stands closer to 33 per cent (Tadjoeddin 2014). Furthermore, no less than a quarter of Indonesian youths, better educated and more literate than their predecessors, are classified as being unemployed.[32] Such is the case even if the poverty rate in Indonesia has fallen to around 12.5 per cent according to recent estimates.[33] Undoubtedly providing fertile ground for populist responses to development problems, Indonesia went through a period of growth in inequality between 1990 and 2012 that led to the greatest level recorded in its history – this during a time span that covers the late authoritarian period as well as democratisation (CEDS-USAID 2013: 4; according to this document, the Gini coefficient grew from .33 in 1990 to .41 in 2012). It is notable, therefore, given the limitations of what can be conveyed by Gini coefficients, that Winters has found 'the average net worth of Indonesia's forty richest oligarchs' to be 'over 630,000 times the country's GDP per capita'. He also found that although these wealthy individuals 'constitute less than 2/1,000,000ths of the population, their combined assets equal 10 per cent of GDP' (Winters 2013:1).[34]

Not surprisingly, more obviously dire conditions are present in Egypt, where 13.4 per cent of the workforce was reported to be unemployed in 2013.[35] While underemployment is also a much more serious problem here, approximately a quarter of Egyptian youths are categorised as jobless.[36] Furthermore, although the Gini Index in Egypt was a relatively low 30.8 in 2008,[37] the poverty rate was reported to be at over 25 per cent in 2011, and this is likely to have

---

[32] See World Bank data in www.tradingeconomics.com/indonesia/unemployment-youth-total-per cent-of-total-labor-force-ages-15–24-wb-data.html.

[33] See World Bank data in www.tradingeconomics.com/indonesia/poverty-headcount-ratio-at-national-poverty-line-percent-of-population-wb-data.html.

[34] According to Winters (2013: 1), 'in Thailand and South Korea the gap is 190,000 and 69,000 times, respectively'.

[35] See the World Bank data presented in www.tradingeconomics.com/egypt/unemployment-rate.

[36] See the World Bank data presented in www.tradingeconomics.com/egypt/unemployment-youth-total-percent-of-total-labor-force-ages-15–24-wb-data.html.

[37] See the World Bank data presented in www.tradingeconomics.com/egypt/gini-index-wb-data.html.

increased following the turmoil and economic uncertainty of much of the immediate post-Mubarak period.[38]

Furthermore, it is often forgotten that the Tahrir Square-led uprising was preceded from roughly 2006 to 2009 by escalating labour protests in such industrial centres as Mahalla and Suez, which took place under conditions of extreme state repression. Even then workers were evidently already responding to the 'relentless neoliberal onslaught' that had brought in privatisation, downsizing and diminishing entitlements (Bayat 2013a: 227). After 2011, another wave of labour strikes in fact emerged, spreading to poorer white-collar workers such as schoolteachers and a range of government employees. But importantly, neither wave of industrial unrest was due primarily to official trade union activism, already so domesticated since the Nasser era, nor instigated by Left-of-centre parties that were preparing for elections but had no base of support among workers. They were instead largely self-organised or took place in conjunction with a range of small middle-class-based human rights or legal aid organisations.[39]

Even in Turkey – often regarded, like Indonesia, to be a future economic high flyer[40] – official unemployment stood at a hefty 9.2 per cent in 2013, while more than one fifth of Turkish youths are deemed to be unemployed.[41] This has been the situation in spite of the AKP's celebrated economic achievements. In 2009, a substantial 18 per cent of the Turkish population was still living below the national poverty line,[42] while the Gini Index was reported to be at 40.4 in 2010, although this actually represented a decline from five years earlier (Gursel 2012). It should be reiterated that available statistics also show sizeable middle classes present in all these societies.[43] What they tend not to show, however, is

---

[38] See the World Bank data presented in www.tradingeconomics.com/egypt/poverty-headcount-ratio-at-national-poverty-line-percent-of-population-wb-data.html.

[39] Interview with Nadeem Mansour, director, Egyptian Centre for Economic and Social Rights, Cairo, 3 April 2012. Evidently, labour activists view political parties with distrust and tend to refuse involvement in party politics. Furthermore, the emergence of the Al-Sisi government might see the reconsolidation of the old organisational structure that had been largely viewed as ineffectual in terms of upholding labour rights. Interview with Nadine Abdalla, Egyptian labour researcher, Cairo, 14 December 2014.

[40] See the McKinsey Global Institute (2012) report on Indonesia. It predicts that Indonesia will be the seventh largest economy in the world by 2030. Also see ING Economics Department (2012) on Turkey, which predicts that it will be Europe's fifth largest economy by the same year.

[41] See World Bank data presented in www.tradingeconomics.com/turkey/unemployment-rate; and in www.tradingeconomics.com/turkey/unemployment-youth-total-percent-of-total-labor-force-ages-15–24-wb-data.html.

[42] See World Bank data presented in www.tradingeconomics.com/turkey/poverty-headcount-ratio-at-national-poverty-line-percent-of-population-wb-data.html.

[43] The Asian Development Bank (2011:11) estimates that the middle class constitutes 43 per cent of the Indonesian population. The African Development Bank Group (2011: 5) puts the middle class at 31.6 per cent of the population of Egypt. A study by Yilmaz (2008: 7) estimates that 45 per cent of the Turkish population are middle class. It should be noted that these sources provide their estimates on the basis of divergent criteria and so the figures should be taken only as indicative.

the precarious nature of middle-class status for many and, therefore, the very real anxieties ensuing from everyday life struggles to maintain such status and associated lifestyles and aspirations. Snapshots of contemporary professional urban middle-class life, such as provided by Bayat for Egypt (2013: 210–212), are able to fill in some of this gap.

Such contradictions of development surely provide ample fertile ground for populist politics to continue to thrive, whether of the Islamic or secular nationalist variety. They can all potentially bring together an amalgam of those absolutely or relatively marginalised within social alliances formed in the continuing general absence of viable leftist forces – and even politically liberal ones as a result of prior conflicts over state modernising projects discussed in Chapter 4. While the Turkish case has displayed a scenario of thus-far triumphant new Islamic populism as a particular kind of response to the contradictions of development – though by no means unchallenged – the dramatic backlash in Egypt and continuing stagnation in Indonesia show that this is not the only kind of scenario that is possible.

Conclusion

This chapter has further elaborated on the factor of contingency raised in earlier sections of this book, but with special reference to the connection between the new Islamic populism and the neoliberal phase of capitalist development within specific contexts. It has explored the conditions under which the purveyors of the new Islamic populism may develop an interest in providing political support for neoliberal reforms and those that may ensure that such support remains much more ambiguous. But such an interest will not evolve simply as a matter of course, as the Indonesian case shows. In the process, the chapter has reinforced the idea that the social interests embedded within the new Islamic populism are instrumental in shaping its social and political agenda, as is its development within broader constellations of social power.

The crucial point, quite plainly, is whether support for neoliberal reform can advance the social interests of those that form the broad alliances that hinge on the notion of a homogenous and historically marginalised *ummah* and, ultimately, whether or not such reforms can plausibly bring them closer to the corridors of state power and to the commanding heights of the national economy. Of course, in reality, not all the components of these alliances will benefit equally from such advances. This is why the capacity of the AKP and its networks to step in with charitable activities and social services for the poor (see Chapter 2), in a manner that recalls the strategy developed initially by the Muslim Brotherhood in Egypt – and which acolytes in Indonesia cannot emulate effectively – is a crucial matter.[44] These developments suggest that the AKP, as the manifestation of the new Islamic populist tendency in Turkey, has been able to maintain the multi-class alliance that has sustained its strong embrace of the poor. Such is the case in spite of its own neoliberal policies that have, for example, prominently involved privatisation leading to job losses, but which have in turn, ensured continual demand for its charitable activities (Öniş 2012).[45]

---

[44] The AKP's control over the majority of municipal governments also allows it to undertake local budgetary measures to bolster its credibility among the poor. Musaffer Saraç, head of social services of the Istanbul government, suggests that improvement of the budgetary infrastructure for social services aimed at the poor in the city first took place when Erdogan was mayor in the 1990s (as a member of the Refah Party). Interview, Istanbul, 23 August 2013.

[45] According to one estimate, the AKP can count on support from 'more than 10 million "green card" holders who receive social security insurance because of their low-income status; and disabled, poor, elderly and widowed citizens who receive millions ... in direct and indirect aid, cash and in-kind benefits from the state and AK Party municipalities' (See 'Erdogan's Victory, the Country's Loss' 2014).

9   Conclusion

This book has examined responses to problems rooted in social transformations and their associated dislocations expressed in the emergence of a new Islamic populism in important parts of the Muslim world. It has been put forward that any specific response taking the form of economic and political agendas must be understood in relation to the relevant historical and sociological context that made it possible in the first place. So too must the related strategies and organisational vehicles adopted by specific social agents. Indeed, as pointed out by Lynch (2012: 2011), in reality there is no 'Islamist monolith' in spite of popular depictions that became prevalent after 9/11 about a kind of global Islamic politics best represented by the supranational ambitions of Al-Qaeda and, more lately, ISIS.[1] In reality, these may resonate with national-level struggles only to a limited extent (Roy 2009; also 2004), thus hindering the more outright and fully transnational kinds of militancy envisaged by Vertigans (2009: 74–80).

But what kind of national-level struggles are they and what could be their long-term effects in terms of possible social and political trajectories? Not long ago, a volume co-edited by one of the most well-known theorists of democratic transitions, Larry Diamond, questioned why the Middle East had remained relatively untouched by the so-called third wave of democratisation – considered to have occurred globally in the 1970s and 1980s (Diamond, Plattner and Brumberg 2003). Before the tumult of the Arab Spring, this was in fact likely to have been the most asked question by scholars of Middle Eastern countries with predominantly Muslim populations (e.g. Entelis 1997; King 2007).[2]

---

[1] For example, see the diverse case studies in Khoo, Hadiz and Nakanishi (2014).
[2] One of the contributing authors to the volume answered the question by identifying a deeply ingrained 'Arab-Muslim' tradition of 'oriental despotism' (Tibi 2003: 4), while another, though critical of the thesis of 'Muslim exceptionalism' (Filaly-Ansari 2003: 202), asserted that the problem at hand is a cultural one of getting Muslims to accept the benefits of democracy. Sadiki (2011) is one of the relatively few scholars who consciously used the lexicon of the democratic transitions literature to 'rescue' the possibility of democratisation in these Arab-Muslim countries. But he did so in somewhat heterodox fashion by focussing on the interests of non-elite political actors and identifying cultural references, including those found in the Islamic religion, which may contribute to rather than hinder democratic change.

One type of ready-made answer was never actually in short supply. Echoing Lewis's views, the noted British historian and political scientist Kedourie (1992: 1), for example, emphatically argued that 'the idea of democracy is quite alien in the mind-set of Islam'. Still, the criticism that Said (2001) famously directed at Huntington (1993, 1996) – that his view of the world was too culturally reductionist to be plausible – could have been easily posed to Kedourie too. Indeed, the approach that has guided this book implies a basic agreement with Said's trenchant critique of overly cultural deterministic approaches to modern Islamic politics.[3]

Two decades on, and in spite of the period of marked neoconservative ascendancy in the United States that practically converged with the 9/11 attacks, the sort of arguments proffered by Huntington, Kedourie, Lewis and others may seem markedly outdated to other analysts (see the contributions in Wright 2012). Roy (2012: 13–14), for example, puts forward the view that Islamic and democratic politics have often intersected because of the reality that many Islamic vehicles have come to depend on the mechanisms of electoral politics for their own survival, not least to protect themselves from continual authoritarian repression (Hamid 2014: 51–52).

But even this was not a completely new observation. After all, Esposito and Voll (1996:16), among others, had recognised that the reassertion of Islamic identity in the Muslim world has been deeply intertwined with discontent with authoritarian rule, and therefore contains at least latent democratising impulses. Building on such an observation, and in response to growing Islamophobia in the West, Esposito (2010) went on to subsequently argue against the very notion of Muslim political exceptionalism in the same manner as Said.

Together with Turkey, Indonesia has now been championed as a model of democratic possibility within the Muslim world. As mentioned, it is the country with the largest Muslim population and yet is a functioning, albeit corruption-ridden, democracy in spite of prior decades of authoritarian rule – during which the social agents of Islamic politics were among the most prominent victims. The Indonesian experience with democratic reform was even put forward as a benchmark for Egypt after the ousting of Mubarak, at least prior to the ensuing military coup of 2013 (Solomon 2011).

Nevertheless, there has been a much 'darker' understanding of the relationship between Islam and Indonesian democracy, which tends to resurface when violence in the name of religion comes to the fore. Commenting on the emergence of the Jemaah Islamiyah and of communal conflict in the early post-Soeharto period, Abuza was among several scholars who highlighted the idea that the fall of the New Order and subsequent democratisation had

---

[3] Said, in fact, dismissed the clash of civilisations thesis as a mere 'gimmick'.

'sanctioned the extremists, giving them political platforms to express their pent-up grievances' (Abuza 2003: 17). In this linear narrative, as the authority of the feared Indonesian military declined out in the regions,[4] Al-Qaeda was gifted with a new site to project its influence (Abuza 2003: 18–19).

Therefore, it was not too long ago that the focus of the world's attention when it came to Indonesia, particularly in the initial post-Soeharto years, was the outbreak of communal violence (Van Klinken 2007) as well as sporadic but destructive occurrences of terrorist activity (ICG 2002, 2005b). These developments, emanating after three decades of strict authoritarian rule, gave rise to fears about Indonesia as a fertile breeding ground for new generations of terrorists. But while terror groups undoubtedly still operate in Indonesia, they have been evidently reduced within a decade after the first Bali bombing to small bands with little central coordination or leadership. Though this brings a new set of problems, given that such small groups are harder to detect and monitor, it is obvious that their acts of violence have brought little advancement to the causes of those who commit them.

A prominent fact, moreover, is that credible challenges to secular state authority under the banner of Islam, whether during the authoritarian New Order period (1966–1998) or in the current democratic era, have yet to be mounted through either the formal mechanisms of politics or violent action. Instead, internal transformations within Islamic movements and political vehicles have resulted in new accommodations with secular electoral politics and, to some extent, with neoliberal globalisation. Organisations like the FPI, which notionally opposes democratic politics as un-Islamic on doctrinal grounds (Al-Battar 2013), have become more closely involved in it, as seen in the support it gave to the presidential ambitions of former Soeharto son-in-law Prabowo Subianto in 2014. While it is true that secular nationalist vehicles have adopted Islamic posturing to make but flimsy claims on morality and integrity (see Chapter 7), this appears to have pre-empted more inroads into state power by Islamic political vehicles. Furthermore, in order to partake in competition over power and resources significantly shaped by the requirements of money politics, Islamic political vehicles have found it convenient to play the democratic game. Not to do so would result in more or less permanent consignment to the fringes of state and society, as many have also found to their chagrin (Chapters 5 and 6).

Still, this book has elaborated on the broader view taken that there is no intrinsic link between a resurgence in Islamic politics and democratic or authoritarian trajectories. Such is the case in spite of Nasr's (2009) deep confidence that engagement with globalisation and democracy innately go

---

[4] Here he refers specifically to the abnegation of *dwifungsi*, the dubious principle that had been held in Indonesia since the 1950s, but was emphasised by the New Order, through which the military claimed functions beyond that of defence, and spanned the realms of government and the economy. For decades, this principle had helped to legitimise military violence and corruption.

together, and that the Muslim world is no exception to this rule. This view is also maintained in spite of the hardiness of the heirs of the Darul Islam movement in Indonesia and the ubiquity of militia organisations in many Indonesian cities that specialise in thuggery and intimidation, including against religious minorities – as well as the Jemaah Islamiyah and its various possible splinter groups. However, there clearly has been no correlation between Indonesian democratisation and a descent into the abyss of chaos and religious violence.

The aspect of contingency has been, instead, highlighted in this book. Focussing on the case of Indonesia, but making use of deep comparisons with others, especially Egypt and Turkey, the book has developed the argument that democracy tends to be embraced when broad-ranging social alliances forged under the banner of Islam can credibly latch on to it to advance the social, economic and political position of a disparate *ummah* unified by the idea of a common experience of marginalisation. A similarly contingent relationship exists between Islamic politics and the embrace or rejection of capitalism and of neoliberal globalisation.

The findings of this book are also suggestive of the idea that there is no direct relationship between either the rise of piety or religious consciousness and the Islamisation of politics, certainly not in the sense of the dominance of political movements urging the establishment of states based on strict observance of Sharia. Like much of the Muslim world, Indonesian society can be easily portrayed as more 'Islamic' than half a century ago (Ota, Masaaki and Suaedy 2010: 3). This can be witnessed on the level of everyday life, such as in the greater preponderance of garments associated with religious identity worn by females in different social settings: on university campuses as well as in rural villages (including in the famously syncretic region of Central Java). This is easily seen too in such areas as pop culture, as discussed in Rachmani's (2014) research on Indonesian television melodramas, which demonstrates that television producers have discovered the commercial potential of programming that is heavy on religious morality due to its appeal to a broad mass audience. Heryanto (2011) more specifically traces new Islamic expressions of pop culture to the tastes and sensibilities of the pious and religiously self-conscious, as well as more economically successful, members of the urban middle class.

Nevertheless, these do not translate directly to the sort of successes in accessing state power found in Turkey. Unlike in Egypt too, Islamic political and organisational vehicles in Indonesia have never achieved the sort of grip on civil society activity that was associated with the Muslim Brotherhood. In that case, a strong civil society presence effectively became a backdoor to state power, however temporary.

The explanation for these different trajectories has not been pursued through cultural lenses or through one that privileges only institutional incentives to the modification of political behaviour. Rather, it has been pursued by utilising the conception of a new Islamic populism, which has been presented as gaining impetus through the merging of grievances and frustrations as well as aspirations of a potentially large cross-section of society. In this form of populism, the masses of 'good' and 'virtuous' people are defined primarily by their faith – that is, by conceiving of their common membership within a long-suffering and marginalised *ummah*.

Here, the aspect of populism that involves actual or potential multi-class alliances has been emphasised, instead of its ideational or organisational aspects. It has been maintained, furthermore, that the new Islamic populism in the Indonesian case has been much less dynamic compared to manifestations in Turkey and Egypt due to failure to develop far-reaching and coherent cross-class alliances. Such failure has been traced to struggles going all the way back to the period in world history characterised by Western colonial domination, through to the advent of post-colonial modernisation projects, to the outcomes of the Cold War and effects of capitalist transformation and neoliberal engagement. It has been suggested that a major factor has been the historical absence of a strong, big business component within the Indonesian new Islamic populism, in contrast to Turkey and even Egypt, as well as the lack of vehicles capable of credibly monopolising the claim of representing an internally diverse *ummah*.

The book has put forward the idea too that, like all populisms, the evolution of the 'new Islamic' variant is closely linked to the preponderance of marginality, social dislocation and uncertainty. Today, it cannot be separated especially from the precariousness associated with neoliberal globalisation. From this vantage point, it is useful to reiterate that the appeal of various kinds of populist 'alternatives' in present-day Europe is directly related to the post-Cold War end of viable leftist challenges to the existing social order, and the continual decline of social democracy under seemingly relentless pressures from neoliberal globalisation (Berezin 2009: 1–8). As is widely accepted by now, the neoliberal transformation in the West, as in other parts of the world, has had the general effect of widening social disparities, hence producing new and pervasive anxieties among a wide range of people, exacerbated by a host of unfulfilled expectations regarding social and economic mobility. Moreover, with the decline of vehicles such as socialist and social democratic parties and trade unions, a vacuum has been partially filled by right-wing populist parties and associations that have become increasingly appealing to some sections of the former constituencies of vehicles traditionally belonging to the Left.

Viewed in this way, the rise of the new Islamic populism in the Muslim world is but a mirror image of the rise of populist tendencies in the West. Bereft of a viable Left alternative in most cases, and also with only weak liberal or social democratic impulses after decades of authoritarianism by nationalist secular states, the evolution of a form of Islamic politics responding to the manifold contradictions of the economic development process was, in many ways, to be expected.

A key question raised in the book concerns the circumstances that are more conducive to the evolution of particular kinds of political agendas, strategies and outcomes. Once again, the book has emphatically argued that the answer cannot be found simply through an analysis of the ascendancy of certain kinds of interpretations of Islamic doctrine among the *ummah* over others – such as 'moderate' over 'radical' ones – and thus leading to certain ingrained, immutable cultural dispositions. First of all, the social position and interests of the interpreters of doctrine would need to be accounted for, as well as constellations of power that allow some interpretations to resonate more greatly than others within specific contexts.

Finally, it should be pointed out that the approach taken in this book has enabled an analysis that establishes considerable distance from either the depiction of Indonesia as 'proof' that Islam can go together with democracy, or conversely, that the presence of 'radical' and even violent groupings waiting in the wings for their opportunity to strike is evidence that it can not. This is because the book has remained focussed on the historical and sociological contexts that shape the development of Islamic politics – rather than culturally or doctrinally determined political behaviour – and hence, the kinds of agendas and strategies more readily available to its social agents in advancing the position of an *ummah* whose interests are imagined to be homogenised by marginality and common faith. Applying such analysis to other cases in the Muslim world would no doubt result in different kinds of outcomes, as might be imagined – for example – in societies where social transformations and engagement with neoliberal globalisation have been less intensive or those that have become the site of long-term international war zones. The latter condition would conceivably affect the availability of social foundations for the development of multi-class alliances that could forcefully pursue their interests through the democratic route or by plunging into the world of neoliberal free markets. Insights gained from contrasting the case of Indonesia with those of Turkey and Egypt, however, have helped to develop a complex narrative that steers away from both liberal democratic triumphalism and the more Hobbesian, security-oriented, hyper-alarmism that had recently featured quite prominently in the literature on its Islamic politics.

Bibliography

Abdullah, C.D. (2005). *Memoir Abdullah C.D.: Zaman Pergerakan Sehingga 1948*, Part 1. Selangor: SIRD.
Abinales, Patricio N. (2010). *Orthodoxy and History in the Muslim-Mindanao Narrative*. Quezon City: Ateneo de Manila University Press.
Abrahamian, Ervand. (1991). 'Khomeini: Fundamentalist or Populist?', *New Left Review*, 186, 102–119.
Abrahamian, Ervand. (2009). 'Why the Islamic Republic Has Survived', *Middle East Research and Information Project*, 250. www.merip.org/mer/mer250/why-islamic-republic-has-survived, accessed on 28 July 2012.
Abshar-Abdalla, Ulil. (n.d.). 'Islam dan Kapitalisme', *Jaringan Islam Liberal*. http://islamlib.com/id/artikel/islam-dan-kapitalisme1, accessed on 20 February 2012.
Abshar-Abdalla, Ulil. (n.d.). 'Revolusi Post-Islamis di Dunia Islam', *Jaringan Islam Liberal*, http://islamlib.com/id/artikel/revolusi-post-islamis-di-dunia-islam, accessed on 21 November 2011.
Abuza, Zachary. (2003). *Militant Islam in Southeast Asia: Crucible of Terror*. Boulder, CO: Lynne Rienner.
Abuza, Zachary. (2007). *Political Islam and Violence in Indonesia*. New York: Routledge.
Achcar, Gilbert. (2004). 'Maxime Rodinson on Islamic "Fundamentalism": An Unpublished Interview with Gilbert Achcar', *Middle East Report*, 233, 2–4.
African Development Bank. (2011). 'The Middle of the Pyramid: Dynamics of the Middle Class in Africa', *Market Brief*, April 20, www.afdb.org/fileadmin/uploads/afdb/Documents/Publications/The%20Middle%20of%20the%20Pyramid_The%20Middle%20of%20the%20Pyramid.pdf, accessed on 2 May 2011.
Akbarzadeh, Shahram. (2011a). 'The Paradox of Political Islam', in Shahram Akbarzadeh (ed.), *Routledge Handbook of Political Islam*. Abingdon: Routledge, pp. 1–8.
Akbarzadeh, Shahram. (2011b). 'Islamism Reaches Central Asia', in Shahram Akbarzadeh (ed.), *Routledge Handbook of Political Islam*. Abingdon: Routledge, pp. 119–128.
Akça, Ismet. (2010). *Military-Economic Structure in Turkey: Present Situation, Problems, and Solutions*. Istanbul: Tesev Publications.

Akçam, Taner. (2004). *From Empire to Republic: Turkish Nationalism and the Armenian Genocide*. London: Zed Books.

'Akhir Tahun, PKS Evaluasi Kinerja Dewan', *vivanews*, 24 December 2011, http://us.nasional.news.viva.co.id/news/read/274677-akhir-tahun–pks-evaluasi-kinerja-dewan, accessed on 25 November 2013.

Alamsyah, Andi Rahman. (2013). 'Islamic Parties at an Impasse, Need Reform to Avoid the Worst', *Jakarta Post*, February 25, www.thejakartapost.com/news/2013/02/25/islamic-parties-impasse-need-reform-avoid-worst.html, accessed on 26 February 2013.

Al-Anani, Khalil. (2012). 'Egypt: the New Puritans', in Robin Wright (ed.), *The Islamists Are Coming*. Washington, DC: Wilson Centre, pp. 31–37.

'Al-Azhar Rejects Draft Law on Islamic Bonds', *Ahram Online*, 3 January 2012, http://english.ahram.org.eg/NewsContent/3/12/61703/Business/Economy/AlAzhar-rejects-draft-law-on-Islamic-bonds.aspx, accessed on 15 January 2012.

Al-Azmeh, Aziz S. (2003). 'Postmodern Obscurantism and the "Muslim Question" ', in Leo Panitch and Colin Leys (eds.), *Fighting Identities: Race, Religion and Ethnonationalism*. London: Merlin Press, pp. 28–50.

Al-Battar, Saif. (2013). 'Habib Rizieq: Demokrasi Lebih Bahaya dari Babi', *Arrahmah.com*, 2 April, www.arrahmah.com/news/2013/04/02/habib-rizieq-demokrasi-lebih-bahaya-dari-babi.html, accessed on 5 May 2014.

Albertazzi, Daniele and Duncan McDonnell (eds.). (2008a). *Twenty-First Century Populism: The Spectre of Western European Democracy*. London: Palgrave MacMillan.

Albertazzi, Daniele and Duncan McDonnell. (2008b). 'Introduction: The Sceptre and the Spectre', in Daniele Albertazzi and Duncan McDonnell (eds.), *Twenty-First Century Populism: The Spectre of Western European Democracy*. London: Palgrave MacMillan, pp. 1–11.

Al Chaidar. (2006). 'Perpecahan dan Integrasi: Perkembangan Darul Islam di Indonesia dan Jaringannya di Asia Tenggara 1962–2006', Unpublished paper.

Alexander, Christopher. (2010). *Tunisia: Stability and Reform in the Modern Maghreb*. London and New York: Routledge.

Alexander, Christopher. (2012). 'Tunisia: The Best Bet', in Robin Wright (ed.), *The Islamists are Coming*. Washington, DC: Woodrow Wilson International Center for Scholars, pp. 39–48.

'Analysis: Turkey's Divisive Ergenekon Trial', *Al Jazeera*, 12 August 2013, www.aljazeera.com/indepth/features/2013/08/201381175743430360.html, accessed on 7 September 2013.

Anderson, Benedict. (1983). 'Old State, New Society: Indonesia's New Order in Comparative Historical Perspective', *The Journal of Asian Studies*, 42 (3), 477–496.

Anderson, Benedict. (2009). 'Afterword', in Kosuke Mizuno and Pasuk Phongpaichit (eds.), *Populism in Asia*. Singapore: NUS Press in association with Kyoto University Press.

Anderson, Lisa. (1986). *The State and Social Transformation in Tunisia and Libya, 1830–1980*. Princeton, NJ: Princeton University Press.

Ansari, Ali. (2008). 'Iran under Ahmadinejad: Populism and Its Malcontents', *International Affairs*, 84 (4), 683–700.

Anwar, Rosihan. (2004). *Sejarah Kecil 'Petite Histoire' Indonesia*. Jakarta: Penerbit Buku Kompas.
Aragon, Lorraine. (2001). 'Communal Violence in Poso: Where People Eat Fish and Fish Eat People', *Indonesia*, 72, 45–79.
Asian Development Bank. (2010). *Key Indicators for Asia and the Pacific*. Manila: Asian Development Bank.
Aspinall, Edward. (2005). *Opposing Suharto: Compromise, Resistance, and Regime Change in Indonesia*. Stanford: Stanford University Press.
Aspinall, Edward. (2009). *Islam and Nation Separatist Rebellion in Aceh, Indonesia*. Stanford: Stanford University Press.
Awad, Marwa. (2011). 'Egypt Brotherhood Businessman: Manufacturing is the Key', *Reuters*, 28 October, www.reuters.com/article/2011/10/28/us-egypt-brotherhood-investment-idUSTRE79R1NQ20111028, accessed on 30 October 2011.
Ayoob, Mohammed. (2007). *The Many Faces of Political Islam: Religion and Politics in the Muslim World*. Ann Arbor: University of Michigan Press.
Ayubi, Nazih. (1993). *Political Islam: Religion and Politics in the Arab World*. London: Routledge.
Ayubi, Nazih. (1995). *Over-stating the Arab State: Politics and Society in the Middle East*. London: I.B.Tauris.
Badan Pusat Statistik (BPS). (2013). 'Berita Resmi Statistik No.78/11/Th.XVI', 6 November 2013, www.bps.go.id/brs_file/naker_06nov13.pdf, accessed on 10 January 2014.
Badran, Margot. (2013). 'Egypt's Muslim Brotherhood: A Project of Patriarchal Extremism', *Ahram Online*, 28 March, http://english.ahram.org.eg/NewsContent P/4/67939/Opinion/Egypt%E2%80%99s-Muslim-Brotherhood-A-project-of-patri archa.aspx, accessed on 16 April 2013.
Barros, Sebastian. (2005). 'The Discursive Continuities of the Menemist Rupture', in Francisco Panizza (ed.), *Populism and the Mirror of Democracy*. London: Verso, pp. 250–274.
Barton, Greg. (2002). *Abdurrahman Wahid: Muslim Democrat, Indonesian President*. Sydney: UNSW Press.
Barton, Greg. (2004). *Jemaah Islamiyah: Radical Islamism in Indonesia*. Sydney: UNSW Press.
Başkan, Filiz. (2010). 'The Rising Islamic Business Elite and Democratization in Turkey', *Journal of Balkan and Near Eastern Studies*, 12 (4), 399–416.
Bayat, Asef. (2007). *Making Islam Democratic: Social Movements and the Post-Islamist Turn*. Stanford: Stanford University Press.
Bayat, Asef. (2010). *Life as Politics: How Ordinary People Change the Middle East*. Stanford: Stanford University Press.
Bayat, Asef. (2013a). 'Egypt and its Unsettled Islamism', in Asef Bayat (ed.) *Post-Islamism: The Changing Faces of Political Islam*. Oxford: Oxford University Press, pp. 185–239.
Bayat, Asef. (2013b). 'Post-Islamism at Large' in Asef Bayat (ed.) *Post-Islamism: The Changing Faces of Political Islam*. Oxford: Oxford University Press, pp. 3–32.
Beinin, Joel and Zachary Lockman. (1998). *Workers on the Nile: Nationalism, Communism, Islam and the Egyptian Working Class 1882–1954*. Cairo: The American University in Cairo Press.

Bellin, Eva. (2000). 'Contingent Democrats: Industrialists, Labor, and Democratization in Late-Developing Countries', *World Politics*, 52 (2), 175–205.
Bellin, Eva. (2002). *Stalled Democracy: Capital, Labor, and the Paradox of State-Sponsored Development*. Ithaca: Cornell University Press.
Bellin, Eva. (2004). 'The Robustness of Authoritarianism in the Middle East: Exceptionalist in Comparative Perspective', *Comparative Politics*, 36 (2), 139–157.
Bellin, Eva. (2008). 'Faith in Politics: New Trends in the Study of Religion and Politics', *World Politics*, 60, 315–347.
Berezin, Mabel. (2009). *Illiberal Politics in Neoliberal Times: Culture, Security and Populism in the New Europe*. Cambridge: Cambridge University Press.
Berman, Sheri. (2003). 'Islamism, Revolution and Civil Society', *Perspectives on Politics*, 1 (2), 11–26.
Berman, Sheri. (2013). 'The Promise of the Arab Spring: In Political Development, No Gain Without Pain', *Foreign Affairs*, 92.1 (January/February), 64–74.
Berman, Sheri and Gideon Rose. (2006). 'Hizbollah is Rearing an Uncivil Society', *Financial Times*, 1 September, p. 13.
Bertrand, Jacques. (2004). *Nationalism and Ethnic Conflict in Indonesia*. Cambridge: Cambridge University Press.
Biki, Amir. (2003). 'Let Me Die for the Islamic World!', in David Bourchier and Vedi R. Hadiz (eds.), *Indonesian Politics and Society: A Reader*. London and New York: RoutledgeCurzon, pp. 151–155.
Boland, Bernhard J. (1971). *The Struggle of Islam in Modern Indonesia*. The Hague: Martinus Nijhoff.
Bourchier, David. (1996). 'Lineages of Organicist Political Thought in Indonesia', PhD thesis. Melbourne: Monash University.
Bourchier, David M. and Vedi R. Hadiz. (2003). *Indonesian Politics and Society: A Reader*. London and New York: RoutledgeCurzon.
Brachman, Jarret M. (2009). *Global Jihadism: Theory and Practice*. London: Routledge.
Bradley, John R. (2012). *After the Arab Spring: How Islamists Hijacked The Middle East Revolts*. New York: Palgrave Macmillan.
Brown, David and Ian Wilson. (2007). 'Ethnicized Violence in Indonesia: Where Criminals and Fanatics Meet', *Nationalism and Ethnic Politics*, 13 (3), 367–403.
Brown, Jonathan. (2011). *Salafis and Sufis in Egypt*. Washington, DC: Carnegie Endowment for International Peace.
Bubalo, Anthony, Greg Fealy and Whit Mason. (2008). 'Zealous Democrats: Islamism and Democracy in Egypt, Indonesia and Turkey', Lowy Institute Paper 25. Sydney: The Lowy Institute for International Policy.
Buehler, Michael. (2012). 'Revisiting the Inclusion-Moderation Thesis in the Context of Decentralized Institutions: The Behavior of Indonesia's Prosperous Justice Party in National and Local Politics', *Party Politics*, 19 (2), 210–229.
Bugra, Ayse. (1998). 'Class, Culture and State: An Analysis of Interest Representation by Two Turkish Business Associations', *International Journal of Middle East Studies*, 30 (4), 521–539.
Bukay, David. (2009). 'Is the Military Bulwark Against Islamism Collapsing', *Middle East Quarterly*, xvi (3), 25–32.

Buruma, Ian. (2013). 'There's a Class Struggle behind "Turkish Spring"' *The Australian*, 8 June, www.theaustralian.com.au/news/world/theres-a-class-struggle-behind-turkish-spring/story-fnfi3iga-1226659527879#, accessed on 16 June 2013.

Bush, Robin (2008). 'Regional Shariah Regulations in Indonesia: Anomaly or Symptom?' in Greg Fealy and Sally White (eds.) *Expressing Islam: Religious Life and Politics in Indonesia*. Singapore: ISEAS, pp. 174–191.

Butler, Judith, Ernesto Laclau and Slavoj Žižek. (2000). *Contingency, Hegemony, Universality: Contemporary Dialogues on the Left*. London: Verso.

Calvert, John. (2010). *Sayyid Qutb and the Origins of Radical Islamism*. New York: Columbia University Press.

Canovan, Margaret. (1981). *Populism*. New York: Harcourt Brace Javonovich.

Canovan, Margaret. (2005). *The People*. Cambridge: Polity Press.

Capoccia, Giovanni and R. Daniel Kelemen. (2007), 'The Study of Critical Junctures', *World Politics*, 59, 341–369.

Casier, Marlies and Joost Jongerden. (2011). *Nationalisms and Politics in Turkey: Political Islam, Kemalism, and the Kurdish Issue*. Milton Park, Abingdon, Oxon: Routledge.

CEDS-USAID (Centre for Economics and Development Studies, Padjadjaran University and United States Agency for International Development). (2013). 'Evolution of Inequality in Indonesia, 1990–2012', SEADI Discussion Paper No.17, 1–15.

Chua, Christian. (2008). *Chinese Big Business in Indonesia: The State of Capital*. Abingdon: Routledge.

Clarke, Janine A. (2004). *Islam, Charity and Activism*. Bloomington and Indianapolis: Indiana University Press.

Clover, Charles and Roula Khalaf. (2011). 'Egypt Military Uneasy Over Business Ties', FT.com, 28 February, www.ft.com/intl/cms/s/0/a301b6ec-435b-11e0-8f0d-00144feabdc0.html#axzz2Lu85k3Bc, accessed on 16 March 2011.

Colas, Alejandro. (2004). 'The Reinvention of Populism: Islamicist Responses to Capitalist Development in the Contemporary Maghreb', *Historical Materialism*, 12 (4), 231–260.

Conniff, Michael. (1999). *Populism in Latin America*. Tuscaloosa: University of Alabama Press.

Connors, Michael K. (2007). 'War on Error and the Southern Fire: How Terrorism Analysts Get it Wrong', in Duncan McCargo (ed.), *Rethinking Thailand's Southern Violence*. Singapore: NUS Press, pp. 145–164.

'Court Postpones Retrial of Egypt Steel Tycoon Ezz', *Al Ahram Online*, 5 August 2013, http://english.ahram.org.eg/NewsContent/3/12/78353/Business/Economy/Court-postpones-retrial-of-Egypt-steel-tycoon-Ezz.aspx, accessed on 5 August 2013.

Crouch, Harold. (1988). *The Army and Politics in Indonesia*. Ithaca: Cornell University Press.

Dagi, Ihsan. (2013). 'Post-Islamism à la Turca', in Asef Bayat (ed.), *Post-Islamism: The Changing Faces of Political Islam*. Oxford: Oxford University Press, pp. 71–108.

Dalacoura, Katerina. (2006). 'Islamist Terrorism and the Middle East Democratic Deficit: Political Exclusion, Repression and the Causes of Extremism', *Democratization*, 13 (3), 508–525.

Damanik, Caroline. (2010). 'Nanti, PKS Usulkan Lagi', Kompas.com, 12 November, http://nasional.kompas.com/read/2010/11/12/1529009/Nanti.PKS.Usulkan.Soeharto.Lagi, accessed on 20 November 2010.
Deiwiks, Christa. (2009). 'Populism', *Living Reviews in Democracy*, www.livingreviews.org/lrd-2009-3, accessed on 12 June 2012.
Demir, Firat. (2010). 'A Political Economy Analysis of the Turkish Military's Split Personality: Patriarchal Master or Crony Capitalist?' in Tamer Çetin and Feridum Yilmaz (eds.), *Understanding the Process of Economic Change in Turkey: An Institutional Approach*. New York: Nova Science Publishers.
Demir, Omer, Mustafa Acar and Metin Toprak. (2004). 'Anatolian Tigers and Islamic Capital', *Middle Eastern Studies*, 40 (6), 166–188.
Desai, Radhika. (2004). 'Forward March of Hindutva Halted?' *New Left Review*, 30, 49–67.
Diamond, Larry, Marc F. Platnner and Daniel Brumberg (eds.). (2003). *Islam and Democracy in the Middle East*. Baltimore: the Johns Hopkins University Press.
Dinçşahin, Şakir. (2012) 'A Symptomatic Analysis of the Justice and Development Party's Populism in Turkey, 2007–2010', *Government and Opposition*, 47 (4): 618–640.
'Dituntut Hukuman Mati, Sang Imam Pun Menangis', *Tempo*, Edisi 52/11, 27 Februari 1982.
Dorraj, Manochehr. (1990). *From Zarathustra to Khomeini: Populism and Dissent in Iran*. Boulder: Lynne Rienner Publishers.
Ebaugh, Helen Rose. (2010). *The Gülen Movement: A Sociological Analysis of a Civic Movement Rooted in Moderate Islam*. Dordrecht: Springer.
Effendy, Bachtiar. (2003). *Islam and the State in Indonesia*. Singapore: Institute of Southeast Asian Studies.
'Egypt Court Bans all Brotherhood Activities, *Reuters*, 23 September 2013, www.reuters.com/article/2013/09/23/us-egypt-brotherhood-urgent-idUSBRE98M0HL20130923, accessed on 23 November 2013
'Egypt Opposition Says Islamists Trying to Stifle Dissent', *Reuters*, 28 December 2012, http://english.ahram.org.eg/NewsContentP/1/61441/Egypt/Egypt-opposition-says-Islamists-trying-to-stifle-d.aspx, accessed on 10 January 2013.
'Egypt's Army: Ambitious Men in Uniform', *The Economist*, 3 August 2013, www.economist.com/news/middle-east-and-africa/21582564-generals-who-deposed-muslim-brotherhood-are-keener-power-they-let, accessed on 17 August 2013.
'Elections Violate Islamic Law: Egypt's Mohamed El-Zawahiri', *Ahram Online*, 4 March 2013, http://english.ahram.org.eg/NewsContent/1/64/66087/Egypt/Politics-/Elections-violate-Islamic-Law-Egypts-Mohamed-ElZaw.aspx, accessed on 21 April 2013.
El-Hodaiby, Ibrahim. (2013). 'Egypt: in the Shadow of the State', *Ahram Online*, 13 April, http://english.ahram.org.eg/NewsContentP/4/69133/Opinion/Egypt-In-the-shadow-of-the-state.aspx, accessed on 7 October 2013.
Eligur, Banu. (2010). *The Mobilization of Political Islam in Turkey*. Cambridge: Cambridge University Press.
El-Kouedi, Mona. (2013). 'Live and Let Die: The Military and the Brotherhood', *Ahram Online*, 18 February, http://english.ahram.org.eg/NewsContent/4/0/65082/Opinion/Live-and-let-die-The-military-and-the-Brotherhood.aspx, accessed on 20 February 2013.

El-Rashidi, Sarah. (2012). 'Egypt's Sinai Peninsula: Fertile Ground for Discontent', *Al Ahram Online*, 2 September, http://english.ahram.org.eg/NewsContent/1/64/51578/Egypt/Politics-/Egypts-Sinai-Peninsula-Fertile-ground-for-disconte.aspx, accessed on 21 Desember 2012.

El-Wardani, Lina. (2011) 'Ahram Online's Idiot's Guide to Egypt's Emergent Political Landscape', *Ahram Online*, 20 April, http://english.ahram.org.eg/~/NewsContent/1/64/10342/Egypt/Politics-/Ahram-Onlines-idiots-guide-to-Egypts-emergent-pol i.aspx, accessed on 25 April 2011.

Emmerson, Donald K. (2002). 'Whose Eleventh? Indonesia and the United States Since 11 September', *Brown Journal of World Affairs*, IX (1), 115–126.

Entelis, John P. (1997). *Islam, Democracy, and the State in North Africa*. Bloomington: Indiana University Press.

'Erdogan's Victory, the Country's Loss', todayszaman.com, www.todayszaman.com/blog/oguzhan-tekin_344355_erdogans-victory-the-countrys-loss.html, accessed on 11 April 2014.

'Ergenekon Case an Excuse to Try Anti-Government Figures: CHP Leader', *Hurriyet Daily News*, 12 August 2013, www.hurriyetdailynews.com/ergenekon-case-an-excuse-to-try-anti-government-figures-chp-leader.aspx?pageID=238&nID=52424&NewsCatID=338, accessed on 10 January 2014.

Esayan, Markar. (n.d). 'What is Deep State?', *Today's Zaman*, www.todayszaman.com/columnist-302319-what-is-deep-state.html, accessed on 15th April 2014.

Esposito, John L. (2010). *The Future of Islam*. New York: Oxford University Press.

Esposito, John L., and John Obert Voll. (1996). *Islam and Democracy*. New York: Oxford University Press.

'Falsafah Dasar Perjuangan dan Platform Kebijakan Pembangunan PKS', *pks.or.id*, 28 May 2013, www.pks.or.id/content/falsafah-dasar-perjuangan-dan-platform-kebija kan-pembangunan-pks, accessed on 16 June 2013.

Farah, Nadia Ramsis. (2009). *Egypt's Political Economy: Power Relations in Development*. Cairo: American University in Cairo Press.

Fealy, Greg. (2004). *Islamic Radicalism in Indonesia: The Faltering Revival?, Southeast Asian Affairs*. Singapore: ISEAS, pp. 104–121.

Fealy, Greg. (2006). 'A Conservative Turn: Liberal Islamic Groups Have Prompted a Backlash', *Inside Indonesia*, 87, July–September, www.insideindonesia.org/weekly-articles-87-jul-sep-2006/a-conservative-turn-15071555, accessed on 8 October 2010.

Fealy, Greg and Sally White (eds.). (2008). *Expressing Islam: Religious Life and Politics in Indonesia*. Singapore: ISEAS.

Feillard, Andree and Rémy Madinier. (2010). *The End of Innocence?: Indonesian Islam and the Temptation of Radicalism*. Honolulu: University of Hawaii Press.

Feith, Herbeth. (1962). *Decline of Constitutional Democracy in Indonesia*. Ihtaca: Cornell University Press.

Filaly-Ansari, Abdou. (2003). 'Muslims and Democracy', in Larry Diamond, Marc F. Plattner and Daniel Brumberg (eds.), *Islam and Democracy in the Middle East*. Baltimore: The Johns Hopkins University Press, pp. 193–207.

Formichi, Chiara. (2010). 'Pan-Islam and Religious Nationalism: The Case of Kartosuwiryo and the Negara Islam Indonesia', *Indonesia*, 90 (October), 1–23.

Formichi, Chiara. (2012). *Islam and the Making of the Nation: Kartosuwiryo and Political Islam in 20th Century Indonesia*. Leiden: KITLV Press.

Frisch, Hillel and Efraim Inbar (eds.). (2008). *Radical Islam and International Security: Challenges and Responses*. London: Routledge.
Gabriel, Satyananda J. (2001). 'Class Analysis of the Iranian Revolution of 1979', in J.K. Gibson-Graham, Stephen Resnick and Richard Wolff (eds.), *Re/presenting Class: Essays in Postmodern Marxism*. Durham: Duke University Press, pp. 206–226.
Gambetta, Diego and Steffen Hertog. (2009). 'Why Are There So Many Engineers Among Islamic Radicals?', *European Journal of Sociology*, 50 (2), 201–230.
Gatra, Sandro. (2012). 'Mendagri: Perda Syariah di Tasikmalaya Tak Mungkin Disetujui', Kompas.com, 6 June, http://nasional.kompas.com/read/2012/06/06/19 11180/Mendagri.Perda.Syariah.di.Tasikmalaya.Tak.Mungkin.Disetujui, accessed on 16 June 2012.
'GDP Growth (annual%)', *The World Bank*, http://data.worldbank.org/indicator/NY.G DP.MKTP.KD.ZG, accessed on 20 April 2012.
Geertz, Clifford. (1960). *Religion of Java*. Glencoe, IL: The Free Press.
Geertz, Clifford. (1971). *Islam Observed: Religious Development in Morocco and Indonesia*. Chicago: Chicago University Press.
Gellner, Ernest. (1981). *Muslim Society*. Cambridge: Cambridge University Press.
Gerges, Fawaz A. (2013). 'The Islamist Moment: From Islamic State to Civil Islam? *Political Science Quarterly*, 128 (3), 389–426.
Gershman, John. (2002). 'Is Southeast Asia the Second Front?', *Foreign Affairs*, July–August, 60–74.
Gheissari, Ali and Seyyed Vali Reza Nasr. (2006). *Democracy in Iran: History and the Quest for Liberty*. Oxford: Oxford University Press.
Gibson, Edward. (1997). 'The Populist Road to Reform. Policy and Electoral Coalitions in Mexico and Argentina', *World Politics*, 49 (2): 339–370.
Gilsenan, Michael. (1988). 'The Apprehensions of Islam', *Middle East Report*, July–August.
Gilsenan, Michael. (2008). *Recognizing Islam: Religion and Society in the Modern Middle East*. London: I.B. Taurus.
Gocek, Fatma Müge. (2011). *The Transformation of Turkey. Redefining State and Society from the Ottoman Empire to the Modern Era*. London and New York: I. B. Tauris.
Gökmen, Özgür. (2004). 'The State of Labour in Turkey, 1919–1938', *Mitteilungsblatt des Instituts für soziale Bewegungen* Heft 33, 123–136.
'Gubernur Jabar Siap Bubarkan Ahmadiyah', *Republika Online*, www.republika.co.id/ berita/breaking-news/nasional/11/03/02/166873-gubernur-jabar-siap-bubarkan-ah madiyah, accessed on 2 March 2011.
Gumuscu, Sebnem. (2010). 'Class, Status and Party: The Changing Face of Political Islam in Turkey and Egypt', *Comparative Historical Studies*, 43 (7), 835–861.
Gunaratna, Rohan. (2002). *Inside Al Qaeda: Global Network of Terror*. New York: Columbia University Press.
Gunaratna, Rohan. (2004). 'Understanding Al Qaeda and its Network in Southeast Asia', in Kumar Ramakrishna and Tan See Seng (eds.) (2003) *After Bali: The Threat of Terrorism in Southeast Asia*. Singapore: World Scientific, pp. 117–132.
Gunaratna, Rohan, Arabinda Acharya and Sabrina Chua (eds.). (2005). *Conflict and Terrorism in Southern Thailand*. Singapore: Marshall Cavendish Academic.

Gursel, Seyfettin. (2012). 'Income Inequality in Turkey', Todayszaman.com. 12 November, www.todayszaman.com/columnists/seyfettin-gursel_297924-income-inequality-in-turkey.html, accessed on 15 November 2012.
Hadiz, Vedi R. (1997). *Workers and the State in New Order Indonesia*. London: Routledge.
Hadiz, Vedi R. (2010). *Localising Power in Post-Authoritarian Indonesia: A Southeast Asia Perspective*. Stanford: Stanford University Press.
Hadiz, Vedi R. (2011). 'Indonesian Political Islam: Capitalist Development and the Legacies of the Cold War', *Journal of Current Southeast Asian Affairs*, 30 (1), 3–38.
Hadiz, Vedi R. (2014). 'The New Islamic Populism and the Contradictions of Development', *Journal of Contemporary Asia*, 44 (1), 125–143.
Hadiz, Vedi R. and Khoo Boo Teik. (2011). 'Approaching Islam and Politics from Political Economy: A Comparative Study of Indonesia and Malaysia', *Pacific Review*, 24 (4), 463–485.
Hadiz, Vedi R. and Richard Robison. (2012). 'Political Economy and Islamic Politics: Insights from the Indonesian Case', *New Political Economy*, 17 (2), 137–155.
Haklai, Oded. (2009). 'Authoritarianism and Islamic Movements in the Middle East: Research and Theory-building in the Twenty-first century', *International Studies Review* 11 (1): 27–45.
Halliday, Fred. (1978). 'Trade Unions and the Working Class Opposition', *MERIP Reports*, No. 71 (October), pp. 7–13.
Halliday, Fred. (1988). 'The Iranian Revolution: Uneven Development and Religious Populism', in Fred Halliday and Hamza Alavi (eds.), *State and Ideology in the Middle East and Pakistan*. Basingstoke: Macmillan, pp. 31–63.
Halliday, Fred. (1995). 'Islam is in Danger: Authority, Rushdie and the Struggle for the Migrant Soul', in Jochen Hippler and Andrea Lueg (eds.), *The Next Threat: Western Perceptions of Islam*. London: Pluto Press, pp. 71–81.
Halliday, Fred. (1996). *Islam and the Myth of Confrontation: Religion and Politics in the Middle East*. London and New York: IB Tauris & Co Ltd.
Halliday, Fred. (2000). *Nation and Religion in the Middle East*. London: Saqi Books.
Halliday, Fred. (2002). *Islam and the Myth of Confrontation: Religion and Politics in the Middle East*. London: I.B. Tauris.
Halliday, Fred. (2004). 'The Iranian Left in International Perspective', in Stephanie Cronin (ed.), *Reformers and Revolutionaries in Modern Iran: New Perspective on the Iranian Left*. London: RoutledgeCurzon, pp. 19–36.
Halliday, Fred. (2012). *Political Journeys: The openDemocracy Essays*. New Haven: Yale University Press.
Halperin, Sandra. (2005). 'The Post-Cold War Political Topography of the Middle East: Prospects for Democracy', *Third World Quarterly*, 26 (7), 1135–1156.
Hamayotsu, Kikue. (2002). 'Islam and Nation Building in Southeast Asia: Malaysia and Indonesia in Comparative Perspective', *Pacific Affairs*, 75 (3), 353–375.
Hamayotsu, Kikue. (2011). 'The End of Political Islam? A Comparative Analysis of Religious Parties in the Muslim Democracy of Indonesia', *Journal of Current Southeast Asian Affairs*, 30 (3) (December), 133–159.
Hamid, Ahmad Fauzi Abdul. (2009). *The New Challenges of Political Islam in Malaysia*, Perth, Murdoch University, Asia Research Centre, Working Paper No. 154, wwwarc.murdoch.edu.au/wp/wp154.pdf, accessed on 14 August 2009.

Hamid, Shadi (2014). *Temptations of Power: Islamists & Illiberal Democracy in the New Middle East*, Oxford: Oxford University Press.
Hamilton-Hart, Natasha. (2005). 'Terrorism in Southeast Asia: Expert Analysis, Myopia and Fantasy', *Pacific Review*, 18 (3), 303–325.
Hamzawi, Amr, Marina Ottaway and Nathan J. Brown. (2009). 'What Islamicists Need to be Clear About: The Case of the Egyptian Brotherhood', *Policy Outlook*. Washington, DC: Carnegie Endowment for International Peace.
Hanieh, Adam. (2006). "Democracy Promotion" and Neoliberalism in the Middle East', *Links: International Journal of Socialist Renewal*, Issue 29. Available: http://links.org.au/node/224.
Hara, Abubakar Eby. (2010). 'Pancasila and the Perda Syari'ah' Debates in the Post-Suharto Era: Toward a New Political Consensus', in Ota Atsushi, Okamoto Masaaki and Ahmad Sueady (eds.), *Islam in Contention: Rethinking Islam and State in Indonesia*. Jakarta: Wahid Institute, CSEAS and CAPAS, pp. 36–75.
Harvey, Barbara S. (1977). *Permesta: Half a Rebellion*. Ithaca: Cornell University Southeast Asia Programme, Monograph No. 57.
Hasan, Noorhaidi. (2006). *Laskar Jihad: Islam, Militancy, and the Quest for Identity in Post-New Order Indonesia*. Ithaca, NY: Southeast Asia Program Publications, Cornell University.
Hashemi, Nader and Danny Postel (eds.). (2010). *The People Reloaded, The Green Movement and the Struggle for Iran's Future*. Brooklyn: Melville House.
Hastings, Justin V. (2010). *No Man's Land: Globalization, Territory and Clandestine Groups in Southeast Asia*. Ithaca, NY: Cornell University Press.
Hauslohner, Abigail. (2013). 'After Morsi's Ouster, Egypt's Old Guard is Back', *Washington Post*, 19 July, http://articles.washingtonpost.com/2013-07-19/world/40680255_1_muslim-brotherhood-old-guard-regime, accessed on 25 August 2013.
Hawkins, Everett D. (1963). 'Labour in Transition', in Ruth McVey (ed.), *Indonesia*. New Haven: Yale University Press, pp. 248–271.
Hawkins, Kirk. (2003). 'Populism in Venezuela: The Rise of Chavismo', *Third World Quarterly*, 24 (6): 1137–1160.
Hawkins, Kirk A. (2010). *Venezuela's Chavismo and Populism in Comparative Perspective*. Cambridge: Cambridge University Press.
Haynes, Jeffrey and Guy Ben Porat. (2010). Globalisation, Religion and Secularisation – Different States, Same Trajectories?, *Totalitarian Movements and Political Religions*, 11 (2), 125–132.
Hefner, Robert W. (1993). 'Islam, State and Civil Society: ICMI and the Struggle for the Indonesian Middle Class', *Indonesia*, 56, 1–35.
Hefner, Robert W. (2000). *Civil Islam: Muslims and Democratisation in Indonesia*. Princeton: Princeton University Press.
Hefner, Robert W. (2001). 'Introduction', in Robert W. Hefner (ed.), *The Politics of Multiculturalism: Pluralism and Citizenship in Malaysia, Singapore, and Indonesia*. Honolulu: University of Hawaii Press, pp. 1–56.
Hefner, Robert W. (2004). 'Introduction: Modernity and the Remaking of Muslim Politics', in R.W. Hefner (ed.), *Remaking Muslim Politics: Pluralism, Contestation, Democratization*. Princeton, NJ: Princeton University Press, pp. 1–28.

Hefner, Robert W. (2005a). 'Introduction: Modernity and the Remaking of Muslim Politics', in Robert W. Hefner (ed.), *Remaking Muslim Politics: Pluralism, Contestation, Democratization*. Princeton: Princeton University Press, pp. 1–28.

Hefner, Robert W. (ed.). (2005b). 'Muslim Democrats and Islamist Violence in Post-Suharto Indonesia', in Robert W. Hefner (ed.), *Remaking Muslim Politics: Pluralism, Contestation, Democratization*. Princeton: Princeton University Press, pp. 273–301.

Hefner, Robert W. (2009a). *Making Modern Muslims: the Politics of Islamic Education in Southeast Asia*. Honolulu: University of Hawaii Press.

Hefner, Robert W. (2009b). 'September 11 and the Struggle for Islam', *Social Science Research Council/After Sept. 11*, http://essays.ssrc.org/sept11/essays/hefner_text_only.htm, accessed on 2 October 2009.

Hefner, Robert W. (2011). 'Human Rights and Democracy in Islam: The Indonesian Case in Global Perspective', in Thomas Banchoff and Robert Wuthnow (eds.), *Religion and the Global Politics of Human Rights*. Oxford: Oxford University Press, pp. 39–69.

Heiduk, Felix. (2012). 'Between a Rock and a Hard Place: Radical Islam in Post-Suharto Indonesia', *International Journal of Conflict and Violence*, 6 (1), 26–40.

Hennessy, Alistair. (1969). 'Latin America', in Ghiţa Ionescu and Ernest Gellner (eds.), *Populism, Its Meanings and National Characteristics*. New York: Macmillan, pp. 28–61.

Henry, Clement and Robert Springborg. (2001). *Globalization and the Politics of Development in the Middle East*. New York: Cambridge University Press.

Heryanto, Ariel. (2011). 'Upgraded Piety and Pleasure: The New Middle Class and Islam in Indonesian Popular Culture', in Andrew Weintraub (ed.), *Islam and Popular Culture in Indonesia and Malaysia*. London: Routledge.

Hicks, Jacqueline. (2012). '"The Missing Link": Explaining the Political Mobilisation of Islam in Indonesia', *Journal of Contemporary Asia*, 42 (1), 39–66.

Hilmy, Masdar. (2010). *Islamism and Democracy in Indonesia: Piety and Pragmatism*. Singapore: Institute of Southeast Asian Studies.

Hinnebusch, Raymond. (1984). 'The Reemergence of the Wafd Party: Glimpses of the Liberal Opposition in Egypt', *International Journal of Middle Eastern Studies*, 16, 99–121.

Hirschkind, Charles. (1997). 'What is Political Islam?', *Middle East Report*, 205, 12–14.

Hofstadter, Richard. (1969). 'North America', in G. Ionescu and E. Gellner (eds.), *Populism Its Meanings and National Characteristics*. London: Weidenfeld and Nicolson, pp. 9–27.

Hooglund, Eric. (1992). 'Iranian Populism and Political Change in the Gulf', *Middle East Report*, No. 174 (January–February), 19–21

Horowitz, David. (2011). 'A Mass Expression of Outrage Against Injustice' (interview with Bernard Lewis), *Jerusalem Post*, 25 February, www.jpost.com/Opinion/Columnists/Article.aspx?id=209770, accessed on 15 April 2011.

Hui Yew-Feng (ed.). (2013). *Encountering Islam: the Politics of Religious Identities in Southeast Asia*. Singapore: Institute of Southeast Asian Studies.

Huntington, Samuel P. (1993). 'The Clash of Civilizations', *Foreign Affairs*, 72 (3), 22–49.

Huntington, Samuel P. (1996). *The Clash of Civilizations and the Remaking of World Order*. New York: Simon and Schuster.
ICG (International Crisis Group). (2002). 'Al Qaeda in Southeast Asia: The Case of the "Ngruki Network" in Indonesia', *Asia Briefing*, No. 20, 8 August, corrected on 10 January 2003, www.crisisgroup.org/en/regions/asia/south-east-asia/indonesia/B0 20-al-qaeda-in-southeast-asia-the-case-of-the-ngruki-network-in-indonesia-cor rected-on-10-January-2003.aspx, accessed on 29 July 2009.
ICG (International Crisis Group). (2005a). 'Southern Thailand: Insurgency, Not Jihad', *Asia Report*, No. 98, 18 May, www.crisisgroup.org/en/regions/asia/sout h-east-asia/thailand/098-southern-thailand-insurgency-not-jihad.aspx, accessed on 18 September 2005.
ICG (International Crisis Group). (2005b). 'Recycling Militants in Indonesia: Darul Islam and the Australian Embassy Bombing', *Asia Report*, No. 92, 22 February, www.crisisgroup.org/en/regions/asia/south-east-asia/indonesia/092-recycling-mil itants-in-indonesia-darul-islam-and-the-australian-embassy-bombing.aspx, accessed on 29 July 2009.
ICG (International Crisis Group). (2010). 'Indonesia: The Dark Side of Jama'ah Ansharut Tauhid (JAT)', *Asia Briefing*, No. 107, 6 July, www.crisisgroup.org/en/ regions/asia/south-east-asia/indonesia/B107-indonesia-the-dark-side-of-jamaah-a nsharut-tauhid-jat.aspx, accessed on 17 August 2010.
Ihsanuddin. (2014). 'PKS Optimistis Koalisi dengan Gerindra Bisa Kalahkan Jokowi'. Kompas.com. 28 April, http://nasional.kompas.com/read/2014/04/28/0033159/P KS.Optimistis.Koalisi.dengan.Gerindra.Bisa.Kalahkan.Jokowi, accessed on 28 April 2014.
'Imran, Imran Sampai di Sini,' *Tempo*, Edisi 08/13, 23 April 1983.
ING Economics Department. (2012). 'Turkey: An Economic Pearl on the Bosphorus', 17 April, www.ing.nl/Images/ING%20report%20Turkey,%20an%20economic%20pea rl%20on%20the%20Bosphorus_tcm14-109367.pdf, accessed on 31 July 2012.
Introvigne, Massimo. (2006). 'Turkish Religious Market(s): A View Based on the Religious Economy Theory', in Hakan Yavuz (ed.), *The Emergence of A New Turkey: Democracy and the AK Parti*, pp. 23–48.
Ionescu, Ghita. (1969). 'Eastern Europe', in Ghita Ionescu and Ernest Gellner (eds.), *Populism. Its Meanings and National Characteristics*. London: Weidenfeld and Nicolson, pp. 97–121.
Ionescu, Ghita and Ernest Gellner (eds.). (1969). *Populism: Its Meanings and National Characteristics*. London: Weidenfeld and Nicolson.
Ismail, Noor Huda. (2010). *Temanku Teroris? Saat Dua Santri Ngruki Menempuh Jalan Berbeda*. Jakarta: Hikmah.
Jackson, Karl D. (1980). *Traditional Authority, Islam, and Rebellion: A Study of Indonesian Political Behavior*. Berkeley and Los Angeles: University of California Press.
Jahroni, Jajang. (2008). *Defending the Majesty of Islam: Indonesia's Front Pembela Islam, 1998–2003*. Bangkok: Asian Muslim Action Network.
Jansen, Robert S. (2011). 'Populist Mobilization: A New Theoretical Approach to Populism', *Sociological Theory*, 29, 2: 75–96.
Jenkins, David. (2002). 'Soeharto's Komando Jihad, Chickens Come Home to Roost', *Sydney Morning Herald*, 14 October, www.smh.com.au/articles/2002/10/14/1034 222686274.html, accessed on 5 January 2010.

Johnson, Carol. (1998). 'Pauline Hanson and One Nation', in Hans-Georg Betz and Stefan Immerfall (eds.), *The New Politics of the Right: Neo-Populist Parties and Movements in Established Democracies.* New York: St. Martin's Press, pp. 211–218.

Jones, Seth G. (2013). 'The Mirage of the Arab Spring: Deal with the Region You Have, Not the Region You Want', *Foreign Affairs*, 92 (1) (January/February), 55–63.

Jones, Sidney. (2013). 'Indonesian Government Approaches to Radical Islam Since 1998', in Mirjam Künkler and Alfred Stepan (eds.), *Democracy & Islam in Indonesia.* New York: Columbia University Press, pp. 109–125.

Jongerden, Joost and Ahmet Hamdi Akkaya. (2011). 'Born from the Left: the Making of the PKK', in Marlies Casier and Joost Jongerden (eds.), *Nationalims and Politics in Turkey: Political Islam, Kemalism and the Kurdish Issue.* Abingdon: Routledge, pp. 123–142.

Juergensmeyer, Mark. (2008). *Global Rebellion: Religious Challenges to the Secular State, from Christian Militias to al Qaeda.* Berkeley: University of California Press.

Kahin, Audrey. R. and George M. Kahin. (1995). *Subversion as Foreign Policy: The Secret Eisenhower and Dulles Debacle in Indonesia.* New York: The New Press.

Kalaycıoğlu, Ersin. (2010). 'Turkish Referendum: Divided We Stand', *Today's Zaman*, September 19, www.todayszaman.com/news-222065-turkish-referendum-divided-we-stand.html, accessed on 20 November 2010.

Kandil, Hazem. (2011). 'Islamizing Egypt? Testing the limits of Gramscian counterhegemonic strategies', *Theory and Society*, 40, (1) (January 2011), 37–62.

Karakas, Cemal. (2007). 'Turkey: Islam and Laicism Between the Interests of State, Politics, and Society', *PRIF Reports* No. 78. Frankfurt: Peace Research Institute.

Karmon, Ely. (1997). 'Radical Islamic Political Groups in Turkey', *Middle East Review of International Affairs*, 1, 4 December, http://meria.idc.ac.il/journal/1997/issue4/jv1n4a2.html, accessed on 14 February 2012.

Keddie, Nikki R. (1994). 'The Revolt of Islam, 1700 to 1993: Comparative Considerations and Relations to Imperialism', *Comparative Studies in Society and History*, 36 (3) (July), 463–487.

Kedourie, Ellie. (1992). *Democracy and Arab Political Culture.* Washington, DC: Washington Institute for Near East Policy.

Kemal, Lale. (2014). 'Turkish Military Only Winner in Current Turmoil', *Today's Zaman*, 3 February, www.todayszaman.com/columnists/lale-kemal_338391-turkish-military-only-winner-in-current-turmoil.html, accessed on 1 March 2014.

Kepel, Gilles. (1984). *The Prophet and the Pharaoh: Muslim Extremism in Egypt.* London: Al Saqi Books.

Kepel, Gilles. (2003a). *Jihad: The Trail of Political Islam.* Cambridge: Belknap Press.

Kepel, Gilles. (2003b). *Muslim Extremism in Egypt: The Prophet and Pharaoh.* Berkeley: University of California Press.

Keshavarzian, Arang. (2010). 'Iran', in Michele Penner Angrist (ed.), *Politics & Society in the Contemporary Middle East.* Boulder, CO: Lynne Rienner Publishers, 2010, pp. 229–260.

Kessler, Clive. (1978). *Islam and Politics in a Malay State: Kelantan 1938–1969.* Ithaca: Cornell University Press.

Keyder, Çağlar. (1987). *State and Class in Turkey: A Study in Capitalist Development*. London: Verso.
Khalifa, Doaa. (2013). 'Egypt's Slum Crisis Persists amid Housing Abundance', *Ahram Online*, 12 January, http://english.ahram.org.eg/NewsContent/1/64/62321/Egypt/Politics-/Egypts-slum-crisis-persists-amid-housing-abundance.aspx, accessed on 16 February 2013.
Khoo Boo Teik. (2006). 'Islamic Opposition in Malaysia: Political Idiom, Moral Economy and Religious Governance', in Vedi R. Hadiz (ed.), *Empire and Neoliberalism in Asia*. London: Routledge, pp. 139–155.
Khoo Boo, Teik, Vedi R. Hadiz and Yoshihiro Nakanishi (eds.). (2014). *Between Dissent and Power: The Transformation of Islamic Politics in the Middle East and Asia*. London: Palgrave Macmillan
King, Stephen J. (2007). 'Sustaining Authoritarianism in the Middle East and North Africa', *Political Science Quarterly*, 122 (3), 433–459.
Kingsley, Patrick. (2013). 'Egypt in Turmoil as Defiant Morsi Stands Firm over "Coup" Threat', *The Guardian*, 2 July, www.guardian.co.uk/world/2013/jul/01/egypt-army-mohamed-morsi-coup, accessed on 16 October 2013.
KPU (Komisi Pemilihan Umum). (2014). 'Persentasi Hasil Suara Partai', www.kpu.go.id/index.php/persentasepartai.
KPG and Tempo. (2011). *Kartosuwiryo: Mimpi Negara Islam*. Jakarta: Kepustakaan Populer Gramedia and Tempo.
Kurzman, Charles. (1998). *Liberal Islam: A Sourcebook*. Oxford: Oxford University Press.
Kuzminski, Adrian. (2008). *Fixing the System: A History of Populism, Ancient and Modern*. New York: Continuum.
Laclau, Ernesto. (2005). *On Populist Reason*. London: Verso.
Laclau, Ernesto. (2006). 'Populism: What's in a Name', in Panizza, Francisco (ed.) (2005) *Populism and the Mirror of Democracy*. London: Verso, pp. 32–49.
Lane, Max. (2008). *Unfinished Nation: Indonesia before and after Suharto*. London: Verso Books.
Lapidus, Ira. (2002). *A History of Islamic Societies*. Cambridge: Cambridge University Press.
Laskier, Michael M. (2008). 'Islamic Radicalism and Terrorism in the European Union: The Maghrebi Factor', in Hillel Frisch and Efraim Inbar (eds.), *Radical Islam and International Security: Challenges and Response*. London: Routledge, pp. 93–120.
Lee, Robert D. (2010). *Religion and Politics in the Middle East: Identity, Ideology, Institutions, and Attitudes*. Boulder, CO: Westview Press.
Leezenberg, Michiel. (2001). 'Political Islam Among the Kurds', paper prepared for the International Conference 'Kurdistan: The Unwanted State', 29–31 March, Jagiellonian University/Polish-Kurdish Society, Cracow, Poland.
Lewis, Bernard. (1990). 'The Roots of Muslim Rage', *The Atlantic*, September, www.theatlantic.com/doc/199009/muslim-rage, accessed on 15 April 2009.
Lewis, Bernard. (1994). 'Why Turkey is the Only Muslim Democracy', *Middle East Quarterly*, 1 (1), 41–49.
Liddle, William R. (1996). 'The Islamic Turn in Indonesia', *The Journal of Asian Studies*, 55 (3), 613–634.

Liow, Joseph Chinyong. (2006). *Muslim Resistance in Southern Thailand and Southern Philippines: Religion, Ideology, and Politics*, Policy Studies No. 24. Washington, DC: East-West Centre.

Lubeck, Paul M. (1998). 'Islamist Responses to Globalization: Cultural Conflict in Egypt, Algeria, and Malaysia', in Beverly Crawford and Ronnie D. Lipschutz (eds.), *The Myth of 'Ethnic Conflict': Politics, Economics, and 'Cultural' Violence*. Berkeley: University of California Press, pp. 293–319.

Lucardie, Paul. (2008). 'The Netherlands: Populism versus Pillarization', in Daniele Albertazzi and Duncan McDonnell, *Twenty-first Century Populism: The Spectre of Western European Democracy*. Basingstoke: Palgrave Macmillan, pp. 151–165.

Lynch, Marc. (2012). *The Arab Uprising: The Unfinished Revolutions of the New Middle East*. New York: Public Affairs.

Lyon, Margo L. (1970). *Bases of Conflict in Rural Java*. Berkeley, CA: Center for South and Southeast Asia Studies, University of California.

Machmudi, Yon. (2006). 'Islamising Indonesia: The Rise of the Jemaah Tarbiyah and the Prosperous Justice Party (PKS)', PhD dissertation, Australian National University.

Maidin, Rashid. (2005). *Daripada Perjuangan Bersenjata Kepada Perdamaian*. Selangor: SIRD.

Malaka, Tan. (1922). 'Communism and Pan-Islamism', www.marxists.org/archive/malaka/1922-Panislamism.htm, accessed on 30 December 2009.

Mamdani, Mahmood. (2002). 'Good Muslim, Bad Muslim: A Political Perspective on Culture and Terrorism', *American Anthropologist*, 104 (3), 766–775.

Mamdani, Mahmood. (2004). *Good Muslim, Bad Muslim: America, the Cold War, and the Roots of Terror*. New York: Pantheon Books.

Mann, Michael. (1984). 'The Autonomous Power of The State: Its Origins, Mechanisms, and Results', *European Archive Of Sociology*, 25, 185–212.

Mann, Michael. (1986). 'The Autonomous Power of the State: Its Origins, Mechanisms, and Results', in John A. Hall (ed.), *States in History*. Oxford: Blackwell.

Mardin, Serif. (2006). *Religion, Society, and Modernity in Turkey*. Syracuse: Syracuse University Press.

Marliere, Philippe. (2013). 'From Le Pen to Beppe Grillo: The Spectre of Populism', *Counter Punch*, Weekend Edition June 14–16, www.counterpunch.org/2013/06/14/the-spectre-of-populism/, accessed on 16 July 2014.

Martin, Richard C. and Abbas Barzegar (eds.). (2010). *Islamism: Contested Perspectives on Political Islam*. Stanford, CA: Stanford University Press.

Matin-Asgari, Afshin. (2004). 'From Social Democracy to Social Democracy: the Twentieth Century Odyssey of the Iranian Left', in Stephanie Cronin (ed.), *Reformers and Revolutionaries in Modern Iran: New Perspective on the Iranian Left*. London: RoutledgeCurzon, pp. 37–64.

Matsunaga, Yasuyuki. (2009). 'Struggles for Democratic Consolidation in the Islamic Republic of Iran, 1979–2004', PhD dissertation, New York: Department of Politics, New York University.

McCargo, Duncan. (2008). *Tearing Apart the Land: Islam and Legitimacy in Southern Thailand*. Ithaca: Cornell University Press.

McKinsey Global Institute. (2012). *The Archipelago Economy: Unleashing Indonesia's Potential*, September.

McVey, Ruth T.(1965 [2006]). *The Rise of Indonesian Communism*. Ithaca: Cornell University Press.

McVey, Ruth T. (2009). 'Datuk Batuah', in Gudrun Krämer, Denis Matringe, John Nawas and Everett Rowson (eds.), *Encyclopaedia of Islam*. Brill Online, 2013. Reference. 9 November 2013, www.paulyonline.brill.nl/entries/encyclopaedia-of-islam-3/batuah-datuk-COM_23120, accessed on 9 November 2013.

Means, Gordon. (2009). *Political Islam in Southeast Asia*. Boulder: Lynne Rienner.

Meijer, Roel. (2011). 'The Jama'at al-Islamiyya as a Social Movement', in Joel Beinin and Frédéric Vairel (eds.), *Social Movements, Mobilization and Contestation in the Middle East and North Africa*. Stanford, CA: Stanford University Press, pp. 143–162.

Michaels, Samantha and Ulma Haryanto. (2012). 'What's the Indonesian Military's Business?', *Jakarta Globe*, 11 May.

Mietzner, Marcus. (2009). *Military Politics, Islam, and the State in Indonesia: From Turbulent Transition to Democratic Consolidation*. Singapore: Institute of Southeast Asian Studies.

Mietzner, Marcus. (2013). 'Veto Player No More? The Declining Political Influence of the Military in Post-Authoritarian Indonesia', in Mirjam Künkler and Alfred Stepan (eds.), *Democracy & Islam in Indonesia*. New York: Columbia University Press, pp. 89–108.

Mirsepassi, Ali. (2004). 'The Tragedy of the Iranian Left', in Stephanie Cronin (ed.), *Reformers and Revolutionaries in Modern Iran: New Perspective on the Iranian Left*. London: RoutledgeCurzon, pp. 229–249.

Misbach, Haji Mohammad. (1925). 'Islamisme dan Kommunisme', *Medan Moeslimin*, 11 (4).

Mitchell, Richard P. (1993). *The Society of the Muslim Brothers*. New York and Oxford: Oxford University Press.

Mizuno, Kosuke and Pasuk Phongpaichit (eds.). (2009). *Populism in Asia*. Singapore: NUS Press in association with Kyoto University Press.

Moertopo, Ali. (1973). *Some Basic Thoughts on the Acceleration and Modernization of 25 Years Development*. Jakarta: Yayasan Proklamasi and Center for Strategic and International Studies.

Moghadam, Val. (1987). 'Socialism or Anti-Imperialism? The Left and the Revolution in Iran', *NLR I/166*, November–December, 5–28.

Moore, Barrington. (1966). *The Social Origins of Dictatorship and Democracy: Lord and Peasant in the Making of the Modern World*. Boston: Beacon Press.

Mortimer, Rex. (1974). *Indonesian Communism under Sukarno: Ideology and Politics 1959–1965*. Ithaca, NY: Cornell University Press.

Mouffe, Chantal. (2005). 'The "End of Politics" and the Challenge of Right-Wing Populism', in Francisco Panizza (ed.), *Populism and the Mirror of Democracy*. London: Verso, pp. 50–71.

Moussalli, Ahmad S. (2010). 'Sayyid Qutb: Founder of Radical Islamic Ideology', in Shahram Akbarzadeh (ed.), *Routledge Handbook of Political Islam*. Abingdon: Routledge, pp. 9–26.

Mouzelis, Nicos. (1985). 'On the Concept of Populism: Populist and Clientelist Modes of Incorporation in Semi-peripheral Polities', *Politics & Society*, 14, 329–348.

Mudde, Cas. (2004). 'The Populist Zeitgeist', *Government and Opposition*, 39 (4), 541–563.

Mudde, Cas and Cristobal Rovira Kaltwasser (eds.). (2012). *Populism in Europe and the Americas: Threat or Corrective for Democracy*. Cambridge: Cambridge University Press.

Mulyadi, Hari and Soedarmono. (1999). *Runtuhnya Kekuasaan 'Kraton Alit', Studi Radikalisasi Sosial 'Wong Sala' dan Kerusuhan Mei 1998 di Surakarta*. Solo: LPTP.

Munabari, Fahlesa. (2010). 'Hizbut Tahrir Indonesia: The Rhetorical Struggle for Survival', in Ota Atsushi, Okamoto Masaaki and Ahmad Sueady (eds.), *Islam in Contention: Rethinking Islam and State in Indonesia*. Jakarta: Wahid Institute, CSEAS and CAPAS, pp. 169–213.

Munandar, Arief. (2011). 'Antara Jemaah dan Partai Politik: Dinamika Habitus Kader Partai Keadilan Sejahtera (PKS) dalam Arena Politik Indonesia Pasca Pemilu 2004', PhD Thesis, Universitas Indonesia.

'Muslim Inc: How Rich is Khairat El-Shater?', *Ahram Online*, 2 April 2012, http://english.ahram.org.eg/News/38278.aspx, accessed on 30 April 2012.

Mutalib, Hussin. (1990). *Islam and Ethnicity in Malay Politics*. Singapore: Oxford University Press.

Nagata, Judith. (1984). *The Reflowering of Malaysian Islam: Modern Religious Radical and Their Roots*. Vancouver: University of British Columbia Press.

Nasr, Vali. (2005). 'The Rise of "Muslim Democracy"', *Journal of Democracy*, 16 (2): 13–27.

Nasr, Vali. (2009). *Forces of Fortune: The Rise of the New Muslim Middle Class and What It Will Mean for Our World*. New York: Free Press.

Nasution, Adnan Buyung. (1995). *Aspirasi Pemerintah Konstitutional di Indonesia: Studi Sosio-Legal atas Konstituante 1956–1959*. Jakarta: Pustaka Utama Grafiti.

Newland, Lynda. (2000). 'Under the Banner of Islam: Mobilising Religious Identities in West Java', *The Australian Journal of Anthropology*, 11 (3), 199–222.

Noer, Deliar. (1963). 'The Rise and Development of the Modernist Muslim Movement in Indonesia during the Dutch Colonial Period (1900–1942)', PhD Dissertation, Cornell University.

Nomani, Farhad and Sohrab Behdad. (2006). *Class and Labor in Iran: Did the Revolution Matter?* Syracuse: Syracuse University Press.

Noor, Farish A. (2004). *Islam Embedded: The Historical Development of the Pan-Malaysian Islamic Party PAS (1951–2003)*, 2 vols. Kuala Lumpur: Malaysian Sociological Research Institute.

'OKJ Harus Laksanakan Prinsip Good Governance', *Investor Daily Indonesia*, 27 October 2011, www.investor.co.id/home/okj-harus-laksanakan-prinsip-good-governance/22998, accessed on 25 November 2013.

'One Suspect Released in Oda TV Sase', *Hurriyet Daily News*, 28 December 2012, www.hurriyetdailynews.com/one-suspect-released-in-oda-tv-case.aspx?pageID=238&nID=37839&NewsCatID=339, accessed on 14 February 2013.

Öniş, Ziya. (1997). 'The Political Economy of Islamic Resurgence in Turkey: The Rise of the Welfare Party in Perspective', *Third World Quarterly*, 18 (4), 743–767.

Öniş, Ziya. (2012). 'The Triumph of Conservative Globalism: The Political Economy of the AKP Era', *SSRN*, 10 February, http://ssrn.com/abstract=2003026 or http://dx.doi.org/10.2139/ssrn.2003026, accessed on 5 April 2012.

Öniş, Ziya and Emin Fuat Keyman. (2003). 'A New Path Emerges', *Journal of Democracy*, 14 (2), 95–107.

Osman, Mohamed Nawab Mohamed. (2012). 'The Future of Islamism in Indonesia: Neo- or post- Islamism?', *RSIS Commentaries*, No. 124, Singapore.
Ota Atsushi, Masaaki Okamoto Masaaki and Ahmad Suaedy. (2010). 'Introduction', in Ota Atushi, Okamoto Masaaki and Ahmad Suaedy (eds.), *Islam in Contention: Rethinking Islam and the State in Indonesia*. Jakarta: Wahid Institute, CSEAS and CAPAS, pp. 1–12.
Ottaway, Marina and Julia Choucair-Vizoso. (2008). *Beyond the Façade: Political Reform in the Arab World*. Washington, DC: Carnegie Endowment for International Peace.
Owen, Roger. (2004). *State, Power and Politics in the Making of the Modern Middle East*. London: Routledge.
Oxhorn, Philip. (1998). 'The Social Foundations of Latin America's Recurrent Populism: Problems of Popular Sector Class Formation and Collective Action', *Journal of Historical Sociology*, 11 (2) (June), pp. 212–246.
Panizza, Francisco (ed.). (2005). *Populism and the Mirror of Democracy*. London: Verso.
Pargeter, Alison. (2010). *The Muslim Brotherhood: The Burden of Tradition*. London: Saqi.
'Parliament to Make Last-Ditch Charter Bid', *Hurriyet Daily News*, 29 December 2012, www.hurriyetdailynews.com/parliament-to-make-last-ditch-charter-bid.aspx?pageID=238&nID=37916&NewsCatID=338, accessed on 16 June 2013.
'*Perguruan Thawalib Padang Panjang*', http://thawalibppanjang1911.blogspot.com/, accessed on 10 May 2014.
Permata, Ahmad Norma. (2008). 'Islamist Party and Democratic Participation: Prosperous Justice Party (PKS) in Indonesia 1998–2006', PhD dissertation, University of Münster.
Peters, Ralph. (2002). 'Rolling Back Radical Islam', *Parameters: US Army War College Quarterly* (Autumn), 4–16.
Platzdasch, Bernhard. (2009). *Islamism in Indonesia: Politics in the Emerging Democracy*. Singapore: Institute of Southeast Asian Studies.
Poeze, Harry A. (1999). *Tan Malaka: Pergulatan Menuju Republik 1925–1945*. Jakarta: Pustaka Utama Grafiti.
Porter, Daniel. (2002). *Managing Politics and Islam in Indonesia*. London: RoutledgeCurzon.
Postel, Charles. (2007). *The Populist Vision*. Oxford: Oxford University Press.
Posusney, Marsha Pripstein and Michele Penner Angrist (eds.). (2005). *Authoritarianism in The Middle East: Regimes And Resistance*. Boulder, CO: Lynne Rienner Publishers.
Pratt, Nicola Christine. (2007). *Democracy and Authoritarianism in the Arab World*, Boulder: Lynne Rienner.
Pringle, Robert. (2010). *Understanding Islam in Indonesia: Politics and Diversity*. Singapore: Editions Didier Millet.
Qutb, Sayyid. (2000). *Social Justice in Islam*. Teaneck, NJ: Islamic Publications International.
Qutb, Sayyid. (2007). *Milestones*. Chicago: Kazi Publications.
Rabasa, Angel. (2005). 'Moderate and Radical Islam', Testimony presented before the House Armed Services Committee Defense Review of Terrorism and Radical Islam Gap Panel, 3 November. Santa Monica: Rand Corporation.

Rabasa, Angel and Stephen F. Larrabee. (2008). *The Rise of Political Islam in Turkey*. Santa Monica, CA: Rand.
Rachmani, Inaya. (2014). 'The Commercialisation of *Da'wah*: Understanding Indonesian *Sinetron* and Their Understanding of Islam', *International Communication Gazette*, 76 (4–5) (June–August), 340–359.
Rahmat, Imdadun M. (2008). *Ideologi Politik PKS: Dari Masjid Kampus ke Gedung Parlemen*. Yogyakarta: LKIS.
Rahnema, Saeed. (2008). 'Radical Islamism and Failed Developmentalism', *Third World Quarterly*, 29 (3), 483–496.
Raid, Hasan. (2001). *Pergulatan Muslim Komunis: Otobiografi Hasan Raid*. Yogyakarta: LKPSM Syarikat.
Raillon, Francois. (1994). 'The New Order and Islam, or the Imbroglio of Faith and Politics', *Indonesia*, 57, 197–217.
Ramage, Douglas E. (1995). *Politics in Indonesia: Democracy, Islam, and the Ideology of Tolerance*. London: Routledge.
Ramakrishna, Kumar. (2009). *Radical Pathways: Understanding Muslim Radicalization in Indonesia*. New York: Praeger.
Ramakrishna, Kumar and Tan See Seng. (eds.). (2003). *After Bali: The Threat of Terrorism in Southeast Asia*. Singapore: World Scientific.
Ramakrishna, Kumar and Tan See Seng. (2004). 'Interstate and Intrastate Dynamics in Southeast Asia's War on Terror', *SAIS Review*, 24 (1), 91–105.
'Ribuan Pejabat Daerah Terlibat Kasus Korupsi', *Tempo.co*, 29 August 2013, www.tempo.co/read/news/2012/08/29/078426251/Ribuan-Pejabat-Daerah-Terlibat-Kasus-Korupsi, accessed on 23 November 2013.
Richards, Alan and John Waterbury. (2007). *A Political Economy of the Middle East*. Boulder, CO: Westview Press.
Ricklefs, Merle C. (2012). *Islamisation and Its Opponents in Java*. Singapore: NUS Press.
Rieffel, Lex and Jaleswari Pramodhawardani. (2007). *Out of Business and On Budget: The Challenge of Military Financing in Indonesia*. Washington, DC: Brookings Institution Press.
Robinson, Kathryn. (2009). *Gender, Islam and Democracy in Indonesia*, London: Routledge.
Robison, Richard. (1986). *Indonesia: The Rise of Capital*. Sydney: Allen and Unwin.
Robison, Richard. (2014). 'Political Economy and the Explanation of the Islamic Politics in the Contemporary World', in Khoo Boo Teik, Vedi R. Hadiz and Yoshihiro Nakanishi (eds.), *Between Dissent and Power: The Transformation of Islamic Politics in the Middle East and Asia*. London: Palgrave Macmillan, pp. 19–41.
Robison, Richard and Vedi R. Hadiz. (1993). 'Privatisation or the Reorganisation of Dirigism?: Indonesian Economic Policy in the 1990s', *Canadian Journal of Development Studies*, Special Edition, pp. 13–32
Robison, Richard and Vedi R. Hadiz. (2004). *Reorganising Power in Indonesia: The Politics of Oligarchy in an Age of Markets*. London: RoutledgeCurzon.
Rodan, Garry, Kevin Hewison and Richard Robison (eds.). (2006). *Political Economy of South-East Asia: Market, Power and Contestation*, Oxford: Oxford University Press.
Rodinson, Maxime. (1966 [2007]). *Islam and Capitalism*. London: Saqi.

Roff, William R. (1967). *The Origins of Malay Nationalism*. Kuala Lumpur: University of Malaya Press.
Roff, William R. (2009). *Studies on Islam and Society in Southeast Asia*. Singapore: NUS Press.
Roosa, John. (2006). *Pretext for Mass Murder: The September 30th Movement and Suharto's Coup d'État in Indonesia*. Madison: The University of Wisconsin Press.
Roth, Dik. (2007). 'Many Governors, No Province: The Struggle for a Province in the Luwu-Tana Toraja Area in South Sulawesi', in Henk Schulte Nordholt and Gerry van Klinken (eds.), *Renegotiating Boundaries: Local Politics in Post-Suharto Indonesia*. Leiden: KITLV Press, pp. 121–147.
Roy, Olivier. (1994). *The Failure of Political Islam*. Cambridge: Harvard University Press.
Roy, Olivier. (2004). *Globalised Islam: The Search for a New Ummah*. London: Hurst.
Roy, Olivier. (2009). 'Neo-Fundamentalism', *Social Science Research Council/After Sept.11*, http://essays.ssrc.org/sept11/essays/roy_text_only.htm, accessed on 2 October 2009.
Roy, Olivier. (2012). 'Islam: the Democracy Dilemma', in Robin Wright (ed.), *The Islamists are Coming: Who They Really Are*. Washington, DC: Woodrow Wilson International Center for Scholars, pp. 13–20.
Rubin, Barry M. (2010). 'Introduction', in Barry M. Rubin (ed.), *The Muslim Brotherhood: The Organization and Policies of a Global Islamist Movement*. New York: Palgrave Macmillan, pp. 1–6.
Rudnyckyj, Daromir. (2010). *Spiritual Economies: Islam, Globalization, and the Afterlife of Development*. Ithaca and London: Cornell University Press.
Rueschemeyer, Dietrich, Evelyne Huber Stephens and John D. Stephens (eds.). (1992). *Capitalist Development and Democracy*. Chicago: University of Chicago Press.
Rutherford, Bruce K. (2008). *Egypt after Mubarak: Liberalism, Islam, and Democracy in the Arab World*. Princeton: Princeton University Press.
Rutland, Peter (2013). 'Neoliberalism and the Russian Transition', *Review of International Political Economy*, 20 (2), 322–362.
Sadiki, Larbi. (2009). *Rethinking Arab Democratization: Elections Without Democracy*. New York: Oxford University Press.
Sahid, H.M. (2012). 'Rekonstruksi Fiqh Jinayah Terhadap Perda Syariat Islam', *Islamica*, 6 (2), Maret, 329–343
Said, Edward. (2001). 'The Clash of Ignorance', *The Nation*, 22 October.
Saravanamuttu, Johan (ed.). (2010). *Islam and Politics in Southeast Asia*. London: Routledge.
Saul, John. (1969). 'Africa', in Ghiṭa Ionescu and Ernest Gellner (eds.), *Populism. Its Meanings and National. Characteristics*. London: Weidenfeld and Nicolson, pp. 124–127.
'Sebuah Pengadilan untuk Imam IM', *Tempo*, Edisi 45, 9 January 1982.
Shadid, Anthony. (1997). 'Marxism Makes Way for Islam', *BIC News*, 8 July.
Shehata, Samer. (2012). 'Egypt: the Founders', in Robin Wright (ed.), *The Islamists Are Coming: Who They Really Are*. Washington, DC: The Woodrow Wilson Center Press, pp. 21–30.
Shils, Edward. (1956). *The Torment of Secrecy*. Glencoe, IL: The Free Press.

Shiraishi, Takashi. (1990). *An Age in Motion: Popular Radicalism in Java, 1912–1926.* Ithaca: Cornell University Press.
Sidel, John T. (2006). *Riots, Pogroms, Jihad: Religious Violence in Indonesia.* Ithaca: Cornell University Press.
Sidel, John T. (2007). *The Islamist Threat in Southeast Asia: A Reassessment.* Washington, DC: East-West Centre.
Silaen, Victor. (2007). 'Tinjauan kritis atas perda-perda bermasalah', *Sociae Polites: Jurnal Ilmiah Ilmu Sosial dan Ilmu Politik,* 5 (25), 11–24.
Simpson, Bradley Robert. (2008). *Economists with Guns: Authoritarian Development and US-Indonesian Relations, 1960–1968.* Stanford, CA: Stanford University Press.
Singh, Bilveer. (2007). *The Talibanization of Southeast Asia: Losing the War on Terror to Islamist Extremists.* Westport: Praeger.
Sivan, Emmanuel. (2003). 'Illusions of Change', in Larry Diamond, Marc F. Plattner and Daniel Brumberg (eds.), *Islam and Democracy in the Middle East.* Baltimore: Johns Hopkins University Press, pp. 13–27.
Skocpol, Theda. (1982). 'Rentier State and Shi'a Islam in the Iranian Revolution', *Theory and Society,* 11 (3), 265–283.
Soage, Ana Belén and Jorge Fuentelesaz Franganillo. (2010). 'The Muslim Brothers in Egypt', in Barry M. Rubin (ed.), *The Muslim Brotherhood: The Organization and Policies of a Global Islamist Movement.* New York: Palgrave McMillan, pp. 39–56.
Soebardi, S. (1983). 'Kartosuwiryo and the Darul Islam Rebellion in Indonesia', *Journal of Southeast Asian Studies,* 14 (1), 109–133.
Soedarmanta, J.B. (2008). *Pater Beek, SJ: Larut Tetapi Tidak Hanyut.* Jakarta: Obor.
Solahudin. (2011). *NII Sampai JI : Salafy Jihadisme di Indonesia.* Jakarta: Komunitas Bambu.
Soliman, Samer. (2011). *The Autumn of Dictatorship: Fiscal Crisis and Political Change in Egypt under Mubarak.* Stanford: Stanford University Press.
Solomon, Jay. (2011). 'In Indonesia, a Model for Egypt's Transition', *Wall Street Journal,* 12 February, http://online.wsj.com/article/SB10001424052748704329104576138490822239336.html, accessed on 19 January 2013.
Springer, Devin R., James L. Regens and David N. Edger (2009). *Islamic Radicalism and Global Jihad.* Georgetown: Georgetown University Press.
Stacher, Joshua. (2012). *Adaptable Autocrats: Regime Power in Egypt and Syria.* Stanford: Stanford University Press.
Stark, Jan. (2004). 'Contesting Models of Islamic Governance in Malaysia and Indonesia', *Global Change, Peace & Security,* 16 (2), 115–131.
Starrett, Gregory. (1998). *Putting Islam to Work: Education, Politics and Religious Transformation in Egypt.* Berkeley: University of California Press.
Stewart, Angus. (1969). 'The Social Roots', in Ghita Ionescu and Ernest Gellner (eds.), *Populism: Its Meanings and National Characteristics.* London: Weidenfeld and Nicolson, pp. 180–196.
Sullivan, Dennis Joseph and Sana Abed-Kotob (1999). *Islam in Contemporary Egypt: Civil Society Vs. the State.* Boulder, CO: Lynne Rienner Publishers.
Sunar, Ilkay and Binnaz Toprak (1983). 'Islam in Politics: The Case of Turkey', *Government and Opposition,* 18 (4), 421–441.

Suratno. (2011). 'The Flowering of Islamic Thought: Liberal-Progressive Discourse and Activism in Contemporary Indonesia', Irasec Discussion Papers no. 8, February.
Swift, Ann. (2010). *The Road to Madiun: The Indonesian Communist Uprising of 1948*. Singapore: Equinox Publishing.
Tadjoeddin, Mohammad Zulfan. (2014). 'Decent Work: On the Quality of Employment in Indonesia', *Asian Journal of Social Science*, 42 (1–2), 9–44.
Taggart, Paul. (2000). *Populism*. Buckingham: Open University Press.
Tagma, Halit Mustafa. (2011). 'Model, Event, Context: Globalization, Arab Social Movements, and the Modeling of Global Order', *Globalizations*, 8 (5), 623–628.
Tamimi, Azzam S. (2001). *Rachid Ghannouchi: A Democrat within Islamism*. Oxford: Oxford University Press.
Tan, Charlene. (2011). *Islamic Education and Indoctrination: The Case in Indonesia*. New York and Abingdon: Routledge.
Taspinar, Omar. (2012). 'Turkey: the New Model?', in Robin Wright (ed.), *The Islamists are Coming: Who They Really Are*. Washington, DC: The Woodrow Wilson Center Press), pp. 127–136
Tedjasukmana, Iskandar. (1957). *The Political Character of the Indonesian Trade Union Movement*. Ithaca: Cornell University, Southeast Asia Program.
Temby, Quinton. (2010). 'Imagining an Islamic State in Indonesia: From Darul Islam to Jemaah Islamiyah', *Indonesia*, 89, April, 1–36.
'The Odatv and Ergenekon Cases', *Today's Zaman Online*, 29 January 2012, www.todayszaman.com/columnist-269929-the-odatv-and-ergenekon-cases.html, accessed on 14 February 2012.
Therborn, Goran. (1977). 'The Rule of Capital and the Rise of Democracy', New Left Review I/103, May–June, 3–41.
Tibi, Bassam. (2002). *The Challenge of Fundamentalism: Political Islam and the New World Disorder*. Berkeley: University of California Press.
Tifatul: Pornografi Rusak Lima Sel Otak', *Republika Online*, 2 March 2014, www.republika.co.id/berita/nasional/umum/14/03/02/n1rqiq-tifatul-pornografi-rusak-lima-sel-otak.
Tomsa, Dirk. (2012). 'Moderating Islamism in Indonesia: Tracing Patterns of Party Change in the Prosperous Justice Party', *Political Research Quarterly*, 65 (3), 486–498.
Trager, Eric. (2013). 'The Unbreakable Muslim Brotherhood: Grim Prospects for a Liberal Egypt', *Foreign Affairs*, September/October Issue, www.foreignaffairs.com/articles/68211/eric-trager/the-unbreakable-muslim-brotherhood, accessed on 31 December 2013.
Tripp, Charles. (2006). *Islam and the Moral Economy: The Challenge of Capitalism*. Cambridge: Cambridge University Press.
Tuğal, Cihan. (2009). *Passive Revolution: Absorbing the Islamic Challenge to Capitalism*. Stanford, CA: Stanford University Press.
Tuğal, Cihan. (2012). 'Fight or Acquisce? Religion and Political Process in Turkey's and Egypt's Neoliberalizations', *Development and Change*, 43 (1), 23–51.
Tuğal, Cihan. (2013). 'Islam and the Retrenchment of Turkish Conservatism', in Asef Bayat (ed.), *Post-Islamism: The Changing Faces of Political Islam*. Oxford: Oxford University Press, pp. 109–133.

Turam, Berna. (2007). *Between Islam and the State: The Politics of Engagement*. Stanford: Stanford University Press.

'Turkey's Military Has a Stake in 60 Companies', *The National*, 19 October 2010, www.thenational.ae/news/world/Europe/turkey-military-has-a-stake-in-60-companies, accessed on 20 November 2010.

'Turkey's Religious Schools Being Used as Model to Fight Islamic Extremism', *Voice of America*, 14 April 2010, www.voanews.com/english/news/europe/Turkeys-Religious-Schools-Being-Used-as-Model-to-Fight-Islamic-Extremism-90856834.html, accessed on 16 June 2011.

'*Turkish Business Chief Criticises Erdogan*', FT.com, 17 September 2012, www.ft.com/cms/s/0/42db534a-00e2-11e2-9dfc-00144feabdc0.html#axzz2HIGqY6Zf, accessed on 30 November 2012.

'Turkish Court Considers AKP Ban', *OnIslam*, 31 March 2008, www.onislam.net/english/news/europe/443777.html, accessed on 28 November 2013.

Türsan, Huri. (2004). *Democratisation in Turkey: The Role of Political Parties*. Brussels: Peter Lang.

Ufen, Andreas. (2011). 'Political Islam and Democratization in Southeast Asia', in Marco Bünte and Aurel Croissant (eds.), *The Crisis of Democratic Governance in Southeast Asia*. Houndmills, Basingstoke, Hampshire: Palgrave MacMillan, pp. 75–92

Ul Haq, Fajar Riza. (2008). 'Islam dan Gerakan Sosial: Studi Kasus Gerakan Jamaah Al Islam di Gumuk Surakarta', Master's Thesis, Gadjah Mada University.

Uslu, Emre. (2011). 'Erbakan's Contributions to Turkish Politics', *Today's Zaman*, 1 March, www.todayszaman.com/columnists/emre-uslu_236902-erbakans-contributions-to-turkish-politics.html, accessed on 16 June 2011.

Van Bruinessen, Martin. (1996). 'Islamic State or State Islam? Fifty Years of State–Islam Relations in Indonesia', in Ingrid Wessel (ed.), *Indonesien am Ende des 20. Jahrhunderts*. Hamburg: Abera-Verlag, pp. 19–34.

Van Bruinessen, Martin. (2002). 'Genealogies of Islamic Radicalism in Post-Suharto Indonesia', *South East Asia Research*, 10 (2), 117–154.

Vanderlippe, John M. (2005). *The Politics of Turkish Democracy: Ismet Inonu and the Formation of the Multi-Party System 1938–1950*. Albany: State University of New York Press.

Van Dijk, Cornelis. (1981). *Rebellion under the Banner of Islam: The Darul Islam in Indonesia*. The Hague: M. Nijhoff.

Van Klinken, Gerry. (2007). *Communal Violence and Democratization in Indonesia: Small Town Wars*. London: Routledge.

Vertigans, Stephen. (2009). *Militant Islam: A Sociology of Characteristics, Causes and Consequences*. London: Routledge.

'Visi dan Misi', *pks.or.id*, 28 May 2013, www.pks.or.id/content/visi-dan-misi, accessed on 31 July 2013.

Ward, Ken. (2008). 'Indonesian Terrorism: From Jihad to Dakwah', in Greg Fealy and Sally White (eds.), *Expressing Islam: Religious Life and Politics in Indonesia*. Singapore: Institute of Southeast Asian Studies, pp. 211–229.

Weber, Max. (1978). *Economy and Society: An Outline of Interpretive Sociology*. Berkeley: University of California Press.

Weyland, Kurt. (2003). 'Neopopulism and Neoliberalism in Latin America: How Much Affinity?', *Third World Quarterly*, 24, 1095–1115.

White, Jenny. (2002). *Islamist Mobilization in Turkey: A Study in Vernacular Politics*. Seattle: University of Washington Press.
Wickham, Carrie Rosefsky. (2002). *Mobilizing Islam: Religion, Activism, and Political Change in Egypt*. New York: Columbia University Press.
Wictorowicz, Quintan (ed.). (2004). *Islamic Activism: A Social Movement Theory Approach*. Bloomington: Indiana University Press.
Wildan, Muhammad. (2013). 'Mapping Radical Islam: A Study of the Proliferation of Radical Islam in Solo, Central Java', in Martin van Bruinessen (ed.), *Contemporary Developments in Indonesian Islam: Explaining the Conservative Turn*. Singapore: ISEAS, pp. 190–223
Williams, Michael C. (2009). *Sickle and Crescent: The Communist Revolt of 1926 in Banten*. Singapore: Equinox Publishing.
Wilson, Ian Douglas. (2008). 'As Long as It's *Halal*: Islamic *Preman* in Jakarta', in Greg Fealy and Sally White (eds.), *Expressing Islam: Religious Life and Politics in Indonesia*. Singapore: Institute of Southeast Asian Studies, pp. 192–211.
Winters, Jeffrey A. (1995). *Power in Motion: Capital Mobility and the Indonesian State*. Ithaca: Cornell University Press.
Winters, Jeffrey A. (2013). 'Oligarchy and Democracy in Indonesia', *Indonesia* 96, 11–33.
Wittes, Tamara Cofman. (2008). *Freedom's Unsteady March: America's Role in Building Arab Democracy*. Washington, DC: Brookings Institution Press.
Witular, Rendy A. and Hasyim Widhiarto. (2010). 'Next in Line: Potential Leaders of Underground Jihadist Movement', *The Jakarta Post, Special Report*, 11 August, www.thejakartapost.com/news/2010/08/11/next-line-potential-leaders-underground-jihadist-movement.html, accessed on 11 August 2011.
World Bank. (1991). 'Managing Development: The Governance Dimension, A Discussion Paper'. Washington DC: The World Bank.
World Bank. (2001). 'World Development Report 2002: Building Institutions for Markets'. Washington, DC: The World Bank.
Yavuz, M. Hakan. (2006). 'Introduction: The Role of the New Bourgeoisie in the Transformation of the Turkish Islamic Movement', in M. Hakan Yavuz (ed.), *The Emergence of a New Turkey: Democracy and the AK Parti*. Salt Lake City: University of Utah Press, pp. 1–19.
Yavuz, M. Hakan. (2009). *Secularism and Muslim Democracy in Turkey*. Cambridge: Cambridge University Press.
Yavuz, M. Hakan and John L. Esposito (eds.). (2003). *Turkish Islam and the Secular State: The Gülen Movement*. Syracuse: Syracuse University Press.
Yegen, Mesut. (2011). 'The Kurdish Question in Turkey: Denial to Recognition', in Marlies Casier and Joost Jongerden (eds.), *Nationalisms and Politics in Turkey: Political Islam, Kemalism and the Kurdish Issue*. Abingdon: Routledge, pp. 67–84.
Yilmaz, Hakan. (2008). *In Search of a Turkish Middle Class: Economic Occupations, Political Orientations, Social Life-Styles, Moral Values*. Istanbul: Bogazici University.
Young, Kenneth. (1994). 'A New Political Context: The Urbanization of the Rural', in David Bourchier and John Legge (eds.), *Democracy in Indonesia, 1950s and 1990s*. Clayton, VIC: Centre of Southeast Asian Studies, Monash University.
Zed, Mestika. (2004). *Pemberontakan Komunis Silungkang 1927: Studi Gerakan Sosial Di Sumatera Barat*. Yogyakarta: Syarikat Indonesia.

Zeghal, Malika. (2008). *Islamism in Morocco: Religion, Authoritarianism, and Electoral Politics*. Princeton, NJ: Markus Wiener Publishers.

Zemni, Sami. (2013) 'From Socio-Economic Protest to National Revolt: The Labor Origins of the Tunisian Revolution', in Nouri Gana (ed.), *The Making of The Tunisian Revolution: Contexts, Architects, Prospects*. Edinburgh: Edinburgh University Press, pp. 127–146.

Zubaida, Sami. (2000). 'Trajectories of Political Islam: Egypt, Iran and Turkey', *The Political Quarterly*, 71, (Supplement s1), August, 60–78.

Zubaida, Sami. (2009). 'Political Modernity', in Muhammad Khalid Masud, Armando Salvatore and Martin van Bruinessen (eds.), *Islam and Modernity: Key Issues and Debates*. Edinburgh: Edinburgh University Press, pp. 57–90.

Zubaida, Sami. (2011). *Beyond Islam: A New Understanding of the Middle East*. London: I.B. Tauris.

Index

9/11, 1, 18, 184–185

abangan, 105, 128
Abdalla, Ulil Abshar, 151. *See also* Islamic Liberal Network (JIL)
Abduh, Muhammad, 59–60, 118
Abdulrachim, Imaduddin, 122, 153, 157
Abdurrahman, Maman, 122
ABIM (The Malaysian Islamic Youth Movement), 122, 156
Abrahamian, Ervand, 33–34
Abuza, Zachary, 18, 185–186
Aceh, 119
Adam, Marwa, 5
Afghanistan, 108, 121, 124
Ahmadinejad, Mahmud, 21, 31. *See also* Iran
Ahmadiyah
  sect, 150. *See also* religious minority
Aidit, Dipa Nusantara
  PKI leader. *See* PKI (Indonesian Communist Party)
AKP (Justice and Development Party) in Turkey, 3, 13, 24, 26, 44, 67, 69, 103, 110–111, 114, 145, 158, 165, 167, 169, 176–177
  against Turkish establishment, 139
  agenda of neoliberal reform, 22
  and neoliberal economic policies, 39
  and the IMF, 165
  as 'conservative' party, 69
  break with Gülen movement, 146
  business groups, 169
  charitable activities, 182
  commitment to democracy, 141
  conflict with TUSIAD, 169
  corruption within, 141
  economic and electoral success in Turkey, 5
  electoral victory, 85
  government, 39, 71, 167, 177
  leadership in Turkey, 37
  marginalisation by Kemalists, 99, 176
  Muslim Brotherhood as model, 111

  political precursors, 110
  religious identity, 149
  religious morality, 40
  route to power, 42
  social and political networks, 44
  support base, 177
Al-Afghani, 59–60, 118
Al Azhar, 79, 172
  doctrinal interpretation, 171
  Grand Mufti's *fatwa*, 172
  political involvement in post-Mubarak era, 171
  rejection of 'Islamic bonds', 171
  religious authority, 61
  support of democratic process, 171
  ulama, 60, 166
  university, 58, 59
Al-Baghdadi, Abdurrahman. *See* Hizbut Tahrir
Al-Banna, Hassan, 11, 36, 59, 161. *See also* Muslim Brotherhood
  anti-British, 55
  assassination of, 57
  early followers, 55
  Muslim Brotherhood founder, 11
  Sufi Orders and, 60
Al-Beltagy, Mohammed, 138
Al-Da'wa Al Salafiyaa, 101
Algeria, 33, 85
Ali, Asad. *See* BIN
Ali, Mohamed, 57–59, 79
aliran kepercayaan. *See kejawen*
Al-Islam, 132, See also Mudzakir
Alliance of North Sumatran Islamic Organisations, 150
Al-Mukmin, 125, 128
  establishment, 127
  in Ngruki, 128
  pesantren, 108, 123, 125
Al-Nour Party in Egypt, 102, 167
Al Qaeda, 5, 18, 101, 184, 186
  fighters from Southeast Asia, 108
  infiltration by, 16

215

Al-Sisi, Abdel Fattah, 10. *See also* Egypt government, 158, 181
Al-*Urwat al-Wutsqa*. *See also* Al-Afghani
Al Wasat, 152
   liberal Islamic political party, 151
   Youth Committee, 151, *See also* Egypt
Al-Zaytun
   Islamic boarding school, 130, *See also pesantren*
Amarullah (Buya Hamka), Haji Abdul Karim, 53
Ambon, 126, 129
American aid
   Indonesian politics, 90
   military, 90
American populism, 24
Aminuddin, Hilmy, 140
   son of DI veteran. *See also* Hasan
Amir, H.M., 128
anarchists, 50
Anatolia, 65
Anatolian bourgeoisie, 38–39, 111, 161, 169–170
Ansari, Ali, 31
anti-Chinese sentiments, 62
anti-colonial movements, 10, 49, 51, 72–73
   in Indonesia, 9
   in Muslim-majority societies, 49
   sentiment, 72
anti-communist, 70, 133
   campaign, 76, 117
anti-coup students alliance. *See* Egypt
anti-immigration, 21
anti-Mubarak protesters, 2, 152
anti-New Order resistance. *See* anti-Soeharto
anti-PKI. *See* anti-communist
anti-Soeharto
   demonstrations of 1998, 36
   movement, 133, 153
anti-Soekarno
   protests, 76
approaches to populism
   political economy and historical sociology, 20
Arab
   authoritarianism, 83, 138
   Bedouin tribes, 98
   countries, 7, 168
   homelands of Islam, 15
   peninsula, 11
   regimes, 84
   ruling elites and networks of patronage, 83
Arab-Muslim countries, 184. *See* Muslim majority societies
Arab Socialist Union in Egypt, 10

Arab Spring, 1–2, 10, 13, 30, 40, 85, 100, 140, 152, 157, 184
   in Egypt, 37
Arab world, 2, 77, 85
Argentina, 21
Asian Economic Crisis in 1997–98, 22, 35, 84–85, 154, 164
Asian 'miracle' economy, 84
Assad, Bashar
   regime, 144. *See also* Syria
Ataturk, Mustafa Kemal, 82
   agenda of secularisation, 40
   founder of the Republic (Turkey), 66
   military hero, 66
   mobilisation of religious identity, 67
   westernising Turkey, 63
Ataturk's revolution, 79
authoritarian, 36, 82, 85–86, 95
   governments, 171
   regimes, 100, 117, 137
   repression, 185
   rule, 16, 77, 93, 106, 177
   secular state, 68
   state, 5, 11, 37, 58, 78, 94, 156
   statism, 68
Ayoob, Mohammad, 174
Ayubi, Nazih, 29, 83, 84
azas tunggal, 95, 106, 109. *See also* Pancasila

Ba'asyir, Abubakar, 49, 108, 113, 123, 126, 128, 134, 143
   Jemaah Islamiyah spiritual leader, 113
Ba'athists in Syria and Iraq, 10
Badia, Mohamed, 97, 138
Bahri, Syuhada, 105, 165
   Chairman of DDII, 81
Bakrie, Abu Rizal, 161. *See also* Golkar Party
Bali Bombings, 18, 186
Balkans, 26
Bandung, 120
Bandung Institute of Technology, 122, 157
Bangkok, 107
Bank Central Asia, 124. *See also* Liem Sioe Liong
Baraja, Abdul Qadir, 126
Başkan, Filiz, 169–170
Batuah, Haji Datuk, 53
Bayat, Asef, 5, 7, 30, 32, 35, 150, 182
bazaari, 78
BDP (Peace and Democracy Party), 141. *See also* Kurdish Movement
Beek, Josephus Gerardus, 109
   Dutch anti-communist, 105
   Parmusi, 105

Bekaroğlu, Mehmet, 69
Bellin, Eva, 28, 32, 83
   'Contingent Democrats', 4
   Middle Eastern authoritarianism, 83
Ben Ali, Zine El-Abidine, 2
   after the fall of, 145
   cultivation of bourgeoisie, 161
   opposition to, 77, 168
   predecessor, 145
   uprising against. *See also* trade union movement (Tunisia)
Benjedid, Chedli
   'political-financial mafia', 43
   government in Algeria (1979–1992), 43
Benteng programme, 56, 81, 92
Biki, Amir. *See also* Tanjung Priok massacre
   Islamic petty bourgeoisie, 109
Bogor Institute of Agriculture (IPB), 143
Bolshevik Revolution of 1917, 49
bonyad, 164
Borobudur Temple
   bombing of, 124
Bosnian Muslims, 155
bourgeoisie, 3, 9, 33, 37, 42, 45, 48, 50, 63, 71–72, 92, 97, 103
   an independent and pious, 161
   Chinese, 137
   Christian, 71
   colonial era, 55, 118, 131
   Indonesian, 72, 94
   Indonesian Muslim, 66, 68
   marginalisation of, 10
   Muslim petty, 63, 66, 68, 72–73, 82, 86, 93, 109, 132, 163, 168
   Turkey and Egypt, 38, 74
Bourguiba, Habib, 140, 168. *See also* Tunisia
   cultural backwardness and Islam, 145
Boyolali, 125
Brazil, 21
Brebes, 119
British and American Tobacco
   sale of Tekel, 167
British colonialism, 9
British domination of Egypt, 10–11, 58–59
BTI (Indonesian Peasants' Front), 89
Buehler, Michael
   thesis of 'moderation' and 'inclusion', 17
Building and Development Party in Egypt, 101
Buruma, Ian, 5
business conglomerates
   in Egypt, 41
   in Indonesia, 164
   in Turkey, 176
   post-Iranian Revolution, 164

Caliphate, 10, 143. *See also* Islamic state
   abolishment, 67
   Caliph, 64, 73
   establishment of a new, 49
   Ottoman, 9, 49
Canovan, Margaret, 23, 30
capitalism, 32–33, 50–52, 55, 86, 160, 168
   and Muslim thinkers, 167
   and neoliberal globalisation, 187
   democratisation and, 160
   depredations of, 167
   free market, 14, 41, 69, 161, 163, 167, 170
   free trade, 59, 166
   Islamic religion and various forms of, 159
   Salafi acceptance of, 167
   Western-dominated, 161, 163
capitalist accumulation, 38
capitalist class, 169. *See also* bourgeoisie
capitalist development, 28, 33, 77
   during the New Order, 107
   model, 73
   neoliberal phase of, 178, 182
capitalist economy, 4, 6, 13, 38
capitalist modernisation, 25, 42
capitalist oligarchy
   political and economic power, 86
capitalist transformation, 25, 30, 188
   and integration, 10
   during the New Order, 126
Catholic, 95
   political cadres, 105
Central Asia, 26, 63, 143
Central Java, 52, 106, 108, 112, 117, 119, 125
   religious transformation of, 129
   Tegal, Brebes, Pekalongan, Kebumen, 119
chains of 'equivalence', 27, 30, 35
Chavez, Hugo, 21
Chavismo in Venezuela, 23
Cheffi, Samir, 140
Chinese, 38, 45, 48
   merchants, 132
   'middlemen' in the East Indies economy, 62
CHP (Republican People's Party) in Turkey, 68–69, 82, 141
   nationalist populist appeal, 179
Christians, 45, 62, 65, 72, 105
   Armenians, 65
   socialists, 50
CIA, *see also* MI5
   coup against Mossadegh government, 78
civil society, 12–13, 43, 46, 86, 90
   activism, 100
   based opposition, 3
   organisations, 99
   participation, 170

clash of civilisations thesis, 1, 138, 185
class and ethnicity, 45
class-based political movements, 33
class conflict, 55, 58, 64, 93
class inequalities, 168
class struggle, 163
Colas, Alejandro, 33–34, 43
   emergence of Islamic populism, 33
   social contradictions in the Maghreb, 43
Cold War, 11, 18, 50, 75, 83, 86–87, 90, 95, 188
   context, 81, 87, 94
   destruction of the Left, 87
   international system, 86
   political repression, 77
   social conflicts, 4, 6, 34–35, 43, 75–76, 88, 90, 96
colonial domination
   Western, 3, 8, 50–51, 72, 161, 188
colonial era, 74, 112
colonial state, 51, 88
   repression, 9
communal conflict
   Ambon, Poso, 126
   early post-Soeharto era, 186
   FKAM (Forum Komunikasi Aktivis Masjid) militia group, 132, *See also* Lasykar Jundullah
communism, 24, 53, 58, 61, 89, 103, 107, 117, 118, 122–123
   1965–66 massacre in Indonesia, 75, 90
   bases of support in Indonesia. *See* PKI (Indonesian Communist Party)
   destruction of, 131
community of believers, 2, 5, 157,
   See ummah
Conniff, Michael
   populism as 'eclectic' and 'flexible', 22
consumptive lifestyles, 25
contentious politics, 25
contingency, 159, 162–163, 182, 187
   critical political economy, 4
contradictions of development, 180, 182, 189
   as fertile ground for populist politics, 182
Coptic Christian community in Egypt, 62, 111, 146
corporatist
   organisations, 163
   'representation', 95
corruption, 142, 149
CSIS (Centre for Strategic and International Studies), 105

Dagi, Ihsan, 40, 69
Dahlan, Ahmad, 60
dakwah, 57, 113–114

Darul Islam, 19, 26, 61, 81, 103–104, 108, 116–118, 120–121, 124, 130, 134
   activists, 81, 104, 109, 117, 120–122, 124–126, 129, 130, 135, 174
   against the nationalist state, 129
   alliance with the military, 123
   animosity to the secular nationalist state, 135
   establishment of Islamic state, 107
   former rebels, 76
   geographical spread, 126
   guerrilla warfare, 80, 116, 129
   in Aceh, 119–120
   in Bandung, West Java, 125
   in South Kalimantan, 119
   in West Java, 120
   movement and rebellion, 26, 61–62, 81, 103, 104, 108–109, 116–119, 121–123, 126–127, 130, 132, 135, 153, 187
   networks, 107, 110, 122, 129
   organisational vehicles, 118
   organisationally fragmented, 130
Darusy Syahadah
   pesantren, 125
Daud Bereuh
   Darul Islam leader in Aceh, 119
Davutoğlu, Ahmet
   Foreign Minister, AKP figure, 26
   Prime Minister, 179
debt relief, 164
decentralisation policy, 141, 172
demagoguery, 22
democracy, 11, 15–16, 28, 86, 131, 138, 157, 189
   alien forms of, 1
   and neoliberal globalisation, 160
   as alien to Islam, 185
   illiberal forms of, 149
   in Muslim-majority countries, 14
   money politics-dominated, 19, 138–140, 149, 157–158, 173, 178, 186
   promotion, 160
   rejection of, 13, 143
Democracy Forum in Indonesia, 155
Democratic Party in Turkey, 68, 82, 92
   military coup against. *See* Menderes
   rise of, 82
Democratic Patriots Movement, 161
Democratic People's Party
   student-based movement, 45
democratisation, 85–86, 103, 141–142, 144, 160, 173, 180
   and the growth of capitalism, 160
   early post-Soeharto period, 143
   Indonesian, 187
Densus 88, 127

Index

anti-terrorist unit of Indonesian national police, 112
Destour Party in Tunisia, 10
Dewan Dakwah Islamiyah Indonesia, 81, 127, 128
dialectical materialism, 51
Diamond, Larry
   democratic transitions in the Middle East, 184
Dinçşahin, Şakir, 23
Dompet Dhuafa, 148
Dubai, 162
Dutch, 52, 61, 73. *See also* Dutch East Indies
   administration, 62
   colonialism, 58, 62, 95
   fight against, 26, 92, 118, 174
   financial source for war against, 175
   rebellions against, 53
Dutch East Indies, 8, 49, 51–54, 59–60, 65, 71, *See also* Indonesia
   Islamic reformism and modernism in, 52
dwifungsi
   in the New Order, 186n4

East Java, 52
economic deregulation policies, 84, 94
economic development, 35, 80, 86, 88, 96, 174
economic liberalisation
   in Egypt, 84, 164
   in Indonesia, 164
   in Turkey, 85, 164–165, 177
   'political openness' and, 85
economic protectionist policies, 170
economic reforms, 85
   in Egypt, 164
   in Turkey, 165, 167
Egypt, 2–3, 6, 9–11, 12, 14, 29–30, 34, 38, 42, 44, 47, 50, 54–55, 58, 59–60, 62, 70, 71–72, 76–77, 79, 83–86, 91–92, 95, 97–99, 110–111, 114, 116, 137, 158, 162, 170, 172, 174, 187–188
   destruction of leftist forces, 76
   Islamisation of Egyptian Constitution, 146
   nationalist movement, 57
   trade union movement, 181
Egyptian bourgeoise
   attraction to neoliberalism and democratic politics, 162
Egyptian Business Development Association (EBDA), 169
Egyptian Current Party, 140, 152
Egyptian National Assembly, 83
Egyptian parliamentary elections
   2005, 85, 100
   2011–12, 102

Egyptian presidential elections 2012, 12
Egyptian Revolution
   1952, 57
   2011, 101, 152
El Adl Party in Egypt, 140
electoral politics, 11–12, 98, 100, 130, 160
El Fouly, Ihab, 165, 167, 169
El Khalwatiyah, 100. *See also tariqa*
El-Shater, Khairat, 41–42, 97, 138, 165, 169, *See also* Muslim Brotherhood
El-Zawahiri, Mohamed, 143
Emam, Abdelmonaem. *See* El Adl Party in Egypt
Emmerson, Donald, 14
En Nahda Party in Tunisia, 10, 40, 140, 145, 161, 167
   conflict with trade union, 168
   Islam and human rights, 150
Erbakan, Necmettin, 39–40, 69, 82, 161
   Refah leader, 69
   Turkey's Prime Minister, 69
Erdogan, Recep Tayyip, 37, 39. *See also* AKP
   corruption scandals, 179
   Gezi Park demonstrations, 141
   rift with the Gülen movement, 177
Ergenekon, 176
Esposito and Voll, 185
Estrada, Joseph, 22
ethnic Chinese, 45, 71, 73–74, 94, 111, 171
   big bourgeoisie in Indonesia, 148, 166
   businesses, 72, 109, 121, 166
Europe, 2, 21, 48, 150, 165, 188
   economic crisis, 39
   European Union (EU) economic policies, 169
Ezz, Ahmed, 139

family and gender issues, 5
Farhad, Diaa, 150, *See also* Muslim Brotherhood
Farid, Mohamed M., 1
Far Right in Nordic countries, 21, *See also* Finland; Norway; Sweden
fascism, 28
Fatah, Munir, 61
fatwa, 172
FBR (Forum Betawi Rempug), 112
Feillard and Madinier, 14, 81
felool, 138, 147
Finland, 21
First World War, 65, 174
Five Principles. *See* Pancasila
FJP, 111
   Turkish general elections 2011–2012, 157

Index

FKAM (Forum Komunikasi Aktivis Masjid), 133
FKKD (Forum Komunikasi Keluarga Darul), 128, 129
FLN (National Liberation Front in Algeria), 10
floating mass, 95
   New Order, 154
   policy, 103
   politics, 105, 117, 121–122
food riots of 1977 in Egypt, 164
foreign aid, 94
   and investment, 94
   Indonesia, 94
foreign imperialism, 26
foreign investment, 165
Forkabi (Forum Komunikasi Anak Betawi), 112
Forkami (Forum Komunikasi Muslim), 142
FPIS (Surakarta Islamic Youth Front), 112, 132–133
France, 21
Free Egyptian Party, 1
Free Officers in Egypt, 10, 61, 81. *See also* Nasser
Freedom and Justice Party in Egypt, 37, 111, 152
   AKP as model, 111
   free market capitalism, 41
Freedom Institute, 151. *See also* Bakrie
Fujimori, Alberto, 22

Gabriel, Satya, 78
Gama'a al-Islamiyya, 100
   collaboration with Egyptian Salafists. *See* Luxor massacre
Gambetta and Hertog, 29
Gasbiindo (Conglomeration of Indonesian Islamic Trade Unions), 89
Gerakan Pemuda Ka'bah. *See* PPP
Gerindra, 179, *See also* Subianto
Gezi Park demonstrations, 46, 141, 179
Ghannouchi, Rached, 150
   Islam's compatibility with free market capitalism, 167
   zakat and social justice. *See also* En Nahda Party in Tunisia
Gilsenan, Michael, 29, 168
Gökmen, Özgür, 70
Golkar in Indonesia, 46, 95, 104, 112, 120, 133, 151
good v. bad Muslims, 18. *See also* Mamdani
Grace, Hanna, 83
Gramscian
   'war of position', 114, 131
Great Eastern Islamic Fighters Front, 98
Guided Democracy (1959–1965), 90–91, 93, *See also* Soekarno

Gülen, Fethullah, 3, 24
Gülen movement, 39, 44, 146, 177
Gumilang, Panji, 130
Gumuk community, 132–133

Habibie, B.J.
   and ICMI, 154
   presidency (1998–1999), 102, 153
Hadith, 171
Hadjar, Ibnu, 119
haj, 60
Hakim, Lutfi, 112
Hak-is, 71
Hak-is in Turkey, 71
Halliday, Fred, 7, 31, 32, 77
Hanieh, Adam, 160
Hanson, Pauline, 21. *See also* One Nation Party in Australia
Harmoko, 132
Hasan, Danu Muhammad, 120, 123, 140. *See also* Darul Islam
Hasan, Noorhaidi, 29
Hastings, Justin V., 108
Hefner, Robert, 58
   democratisation within Islam in Indonesia, 16
   rise of 'uncivil Islam' in Indonesia, 16
Hendropriyono, 109
Heryanto, Ariel, 187
Hidayat, Syarif, 130, 156
Hindutva movement in India, 32
Hisbah militia, 112
historical institutionalism, 4
historical materialism, 53
historical sociology, 7, 8, 14, 20
   approach for understanding Islamic politics, 16
hittiste, 43
Hizbullah in Indonesia, 92, 112
   anti-Dutch forces in West Java. *See* Kartosuwiryo
Hizbullah in Turkey, 99
Hizbut Tahrir, 5, 112, 143
   against democracy and system of nation-states, 143
   anti-imperialist position, 168
HMI (Islamic Students Association), 76, 94, 109, 133
Horowitz, David, 1
HTI (Hizbut Tahrir Indonesia), 142, 144. *See also* Hizbut Tahrir
   opposition to Western-style electoral politics, 112
human rights, 16, 150
humanitarian relief organisations, 44

Index

Huntington, Samuel. *See* clash of civilisation thesis
Hussein, Saddam, 164. *See also* Iraq

Ibrahim, Anwar, 156
ICG, 104
ICMI (Association of Indonesian Muslim Intellectuals), 74, 102, 106, 132, 134, 153, 154
  absence of big bourgeoisie, 154
  alliance with the military, 173
  establishment of, 102
  instrument of the New Order, 153
  new apparatchik, 153
Ihya As-Sunnah
  pesantren, 125–126
Imam Buchori *pesantren*
Imam Hatip schools in Turkey, 37
IMF (International Monetary Fund), 69, 163, 164
  Indonesia deal with, 164, *See also* Asian Economic Crisis in 1997–98
  public resentment against, 154
Imran, 129
Imron, Ali
  Bali bomber, 113
Indonesia, 2–3, 6–7, 11, 13–14, 16–17, 24, 29–31, 34–38, 41–42, 46, 49–51, 53, 55, 58–61, 64–65, 70–72, 74–77, 79–80, 83–87, 90, 95, 97, 103, 108, 111, 114, 116, 121, 139, 162, 164, 166, 170, 172, 174–175, 186
  1945–1949 national war of independence, 88
  1955 elections, 56, 91–92
  1959 presidential regulation, 56
  basis for the national solidarity, 26
  Constitution, 147
  constitutional debates about Islam and the state, 147
  democracy, 157, 173
  democracy model for the Muslim world, 185, 189
  destruction of the Left 1960s, 45
  economy, 45
  establishment of the modern national state in, 88
  establishment of the national state in, 56
  fertile ground for new terrorism, 186
  general elections 2014, 157, 178
  growth in inequality between 1990 and 2012, 180
  intelligence apparatus, 120, 122
  Islamic parties, 141, 153, 173
  military, 61, 91, 108, 125–126, 174, 186

nationalisation of foreign companies, 174
  parliamentary system 1950s, 91
  presidential election 2014, 127, 179
  state intelligence agency (BAKIN), 120
Indonesian armed forces, 90, 119
Indonesian Council of Ulama (MUI), 166
Indonesian Democratic Party (PDI), 95. *See also* PDI-P
Indonesian Islamic Army (TII), 118. *See* Darul Islam
Indonesian Islamic State (NII), 81, 118
Indonesian police force, 90. *See also* Densus 88
Indonesian Socialist Party, 89, 93
Inonu, Ismet, 82
international development organisations, 43, 84, 165, *See also* IMF; World Bank
  and global capitalist interests, 160
Ionescu and Gellner, 25, 31
Iran, 5, 26, 44, 54, 79, 150
Iranian Revolution, 1979, 34, 78–79, 163–164
Iraq, 18
Ishak, George. *See* Coptic Christian community
Islam, 32, 33, 35, 59, 61, 64, 67, 74, 78, 93, 99, 109
  and communism, 89–90
  and nationalism, 26
  and Western civilization, 1
  economic system, 163
Islam and capitalism, 33, 51, 159
  convergences between, 159
Islam and democracy, 159, 185
  violation of religious doctrine, 143
Islami Harekat, 98–99
Islamic banking, 166
Islamic Defenders' Front (FPI), 112, 142, 150
  against democratic politics, 186
Islamic Jihad, 98, 101
Islamic Liberal Network (JIL), 151. *See also* Abdalla
Islamic militia groups, 92, 99, 112, 154
Islamic morality, 80, 111, 163
Islamic paramilitary groups, 16, 75, 111, 135
Islamic Republic, 163. *See also* Iran
Islamic Republic of Indonesia, 130. *See also* Darul Islam
Islamic Revolution, 54, 77–79. *See also* Iranian Revolution 1979
Islamic state, 13, 39, 40, 48, 62, 81, 88, 101, 103, 109–111, 113, 116, 118, 157
  and imposition of religious morality, 111
  establishment of, 15, 61, 63, 114, 123, 140
  Islamic parties' 'hidden agenda' for, 139
  morality and good governance, 110
  system of government, 176

Islamic State in Iraq and Syria (ISIS), 5, 18, 184
Islamophobia in the West, 185
Ismailia, 55
Israel, 174
Istanbul bourgeoisie, 39, 111
ITB, *See* Bandung Institute of Technology

Jakarta Charter, 147
Jansen, Robert S., 25
Japanese occupation in Indonesia 1942–1945, 9, 88, 92
JAT (Jemaah Anshorut Tauhid), 49, 112–113, 126, 143
Java, 14–15, 44, 60, 107, 125
Javanese folk religion
   and Left wing political ideologies, 129
   conversion to Islam, 122
   Javanese syncretism, 15, 105, 126–127. *See* kejawen
Jemaah Islamiyah, 49, 100, 108, 111, 113, 119, 132, 185
   and its various splinter groups, 187
   Bali Bombers crackdown, 126
   in Southeast Asia, 5
   Indonesian and Southeast Asian recruits, 108
   intersections between DI and, 124
   terrorist network, 123

KAMMI, 36
Karmon, Ely, 98, 99
Kartosuwiryo, Sarjono, 119. *See also* Kartosuwiryo
Kartosuwiryo, Sekarmaji Marijan, 26, 61, 81, 118, 119, 121, 123, 125, 126, 135
   dispute with the Indonesian military, *See also* Renville Peace Treaty 1948
   establishment of an Islamic state, 123
   guerilla struggle, 127
   Imam and President of the Indonesian Islamic State (NII), 118
   military defeat in 1962, 108. *See also* Darul Islam
KBSI, 89. *See* Kongres Buruh Seluruh Indonesia
Kebumen, 119
Kedourie, Ellie, 185
Kefaya movement, 152
kejawen and
   ex-PKI families, 128
   Javanese syncretism, 126
Kemalist, 38, 40, 82, 97, 99, 110
Kepel, Giles
Kertodikromo, Mas Marco, 61, 118. *See also* Sarekat Islam
Keshavarzian, Arang, 78

Keyder, Çağlar
Khatami, Mohammad, 164. *See also* Iran
Khomeini, Ayatollah, 26, 34, 44, 54, 78–79, 163, *See also* Islamic Revolution
King Faruk of Egypt, 61
KISDI, 155
Koizumi, Junichi, 22
Komando Jihad, 107, 108, 120, 122–124, 126
   origins and invention of, 122. *See also* Moertopo
   relationship with the Darul Islam (DI), 107
Komara, Sensen, 130, *See also* Darul Islam
Kongres Buruh Seluruh Indonesia (All Indonesia Labour Congress), 89
Koran, 32, 51, 61, 118, 171
Korps Hizbullah
Kurdish movement, 3, 76, 86, 99
   involvement in Gezi Park protests, 141
Kuzminski, Adrian, 23

labour-based movements
   Fascist regimes in Europe, 21
   Peronism in Argentina, 21
   Vargas in Brazil, 21
labour protests in Egypt, 181
Laclau, Ernesto, 22, 27–28, 30, 35, 44, 47–48, 75, 96
Lampung, 109, 126
land reform, 89
Lapidus, Ira, 65
Lasykar Jihad, 112, 125. *See also* Thalib
Lasykar Jundullah, 112, 132. *See also* FKAM
Lasykar Mujahidin, 134. *See also* Islamic paramilitary groups
Latin America, 21, 22, 25, 163, 167
Latin American neo-populism
   neoliberal economic policy, 39
Latin American populism, 24–25, 34
League of Young Engineers, 42, 165
Lembaga Mujahid Dakwah, 122
Lewis, Bernard, 1, 185
   electoral democracy in the Arab world, 1
Liem Sioe Liong, 62, 124
Lombok, 129
Long, Huey, 21
Lubeck, Paul M., 43
lumpen-intellegentsia, 120
lumpenproletariat, 28, 44, 103, 107, 117, 135
Luxor massacre 1997, 100. *See also* Gama'a al-Islamiyya

Madiun, 92
Maghreb, 33, 43
Mahendra, Yusril Ihza, 155. *See also* PBB (Crescent and Star Party)

Index

Mahmuddiya, 55
Mahsoub, Mohamed, 152
Majelis Mujahidin Indonesia, 112, 129, 134
Makkaoui, Amine, 42
Malaka, Tan, 53
Malay National Party (MNP), 54
Malayan Communist Party, 54
Malaysia, 108, 122
   British colonial period, 54
Malek, Hassan, 41, 169
Maluku, 125
Mamdani, Mahmood, 18
Marliere, Philippe, 22
Marsudi, Sudirman, 127, 150
Marx, Karl, 51
Marxism, 32
   as 'alien' influence, 106
Marxist theory, 44
Marxist tradition
   of social and historical analysis, 159
Marxists, 50
   in the Middle East, 77
Masyumi, 56, 69, 81, 88–89, 91–93, 95
Matta, Anis, 170
Mawdudi, Abu A'la, 120
Memur-sen, 71
Menderes, Adnan, 68, 70, 82
Menem, Carlos, 22, 163
MHP (Nationalist Movement Party), 141, 179
MI5, 78
   coup against Mossadegh in 1953, 78. *See* Iran
middle classes, 25, 28, 35–38, 42, 45, 97
   anxieties, urban, precarious nature of, 181
Middle East, 5–7, 11, 14, 16–17, 26, 29–30, 35–36, 45, 60, 63–64, 75, 83, 125, 149, 156, 160
   'third wave of democratization', 184
military, 160, 173, 174
   and Golkar, 153
   business protectionism, 177
   businesses in Egypt, 177
   businesses in Indonesia, 175
   businesses in Turkey, 177
   involvement in economy, 173–175
   protect the interests of, 173
Misbach, Haji, 52, 53
modernisation theory, 32, 35
Moeis, Abdoel, 9, 26, 52
Moerdani, Benny
   Soeharto's key aide, 109. *See also* Tanjung Priok massacre
Moertopo, Ali, 105–106, 109, 123
   allegations related to Komando Jihad, 122, 124

associates and protégés in the CSIS, 105
Moghadam, Val, 78
Mohammad, Mahathir, 22
Morcos, Nabil, 83
Morocco, 6, 42, 84, 140
   history of Islamic politics in, 165
Morsi, Mohamed, 41, 46, 100–101, 146, 150, 172
   after the ouster of, 114, 146
   Al-Azhar rejection of, 171
   military led-coup against, 161
   overthrow of, 98, 138, 141
   presidency. *See* Al-Sisi
Mossadegh, Mohammad, 43, 78
   nationalisation of Western oil firms, 78
   overthrow of, 78
Motherland Party, 82. *See also* Özal
Mouzelis, Nicos, 23–25
MTA (Majelis Tafsir Al Quran), 133, *See also* Golkar
Mubarak, Hosni, 2, 11, 38, 45, 58, 60, 83–84, 86, 97–98, 100–101, 116, 140, 152
   and NDP (National Democratic Party), 41
   assistance from the IMF and World Bank, 164
   cronies, 167, 178
   dictatorship, 136
   fall of, 12, 145
   market policies, 41
   political opposition against, 12, 41
Mudde, Cas, 23
Mudo, Asaat Datuk, 56
Mudzakir, Haji, 132
Muhammadiyah, 52, 60, 114, 148, 153, 155, 179. *See also* PAN
Mujahideen Khalq, 54
Mulyadi, Hari, 126
Murdoch School of Political Economy, 8
MUSIAD, 39, 169, 170
   participation in the military-industrial sector, 177
Muslim Brotherhood, 1–3, 5, 9, 12, 36–39, 41, 45, 49–50, 54–58, 70, 83–85, 99–101, 103, 111, 114, 116, 120, 136, 138, 140, 144–145, 146, 151–152, 155–156, 158, 162, 164, 169, 172, 177, 187
   after the fall of Mubarak, 97
   and Salafi against Liberals and Leftists, 146
   and the military, 147
   and Wahhabi influence, 156
   Arab Spring, 10
   banning of, 114
   business groups nurtured by, 161
   clandestine structure, 156

Muslim Brotherhood (cont.)
  competition with Salafi, 162
  economic vision, 41
  Egyptian parliamentary elections 2005, 85
  fragmentation within, 146
  government, 41
  in Syria, 144
  involvement in secular politics, 101
  labour movement presence, 9, 55
  repression against, 57, 85
  Sisters (female activists), 5
  youths, 152
Muslim exceptionalism theory, 142, 185
Musso, 92
Mustaqim, 125
Muzakkar, Abdul Kahar, 119
  Darul Islam in South Sulawesi, 126
  KPPSI influence, 130, See also Darul Islam

Naguib, Ahmed, 140. See Egyptian Current Party
Nahdlatul Ulama, 56, 81
Nahdlatul Ulama Party, 92, 153
Nasakom, 90, See also Soekarno
Nasr, Vali, 35, 51, 162, 166, 186
  benefits of globalisation, 159
Nasser, Gamal Abdel, 11, 36, 57–58, 81, 86, 94, 164
  end of monarchy and British domination, 10
  Third World Movement. See Third Worldism
Nasserism, 45, 76
Nasserists, 46, 57–58, 77
National Awakening Party (PKB), 144, 151, 155, 157, 179. See also Nahdlatul Ulama
National Mandate Party (PAN), 155, 157, See also Muhammadiyah
National Order Party, 176
National Salvation Party, 176
National Workers' Union (SPN), 148
Natsir, Mohammad, 26, 81, 105, 108, 122, 128, 155
  and Kartosuwiryo, 81
  former leader of Masyumi and Prime Minister, 105. See also Dewan Dakwah Islamiyah Indonesia
NDP (National Democratic Party), 41
Nekolim, 90
neoliberal capitalism, 33
new Islamic populism, 3–4, 6, 8, 11, 19–20, 24–25, 28, 31, 35, 38, 42, 43, 46–48, 75, 96–97, 110, 135, 139, 149, 160, 167, 172, 180, 184, 188

a growing social phenomenon, 178
and neoliberal capitalist development, 182
as result of Cold War, 18
conception of *ummah*, 27
contests over economic and political power, 137
encounter with democratic politics, 157
evolution of, 18, 159
in Indonesia, 87, 171, 178–179
in Turkey, 11, 39–40
legacy of the Cold War era, 4
major characteristic of, 34
organisational vehicles, 27, 98
political agenda of, 138
political support for neoliberal reforms, 182
resilience of social conservatism, 152
response to contradictions of development, 178, 182
support for neoliberal globalisation, 170
varied expressions of, 146
New Order in Indonesia, 11, 36, 41, 43, 62–63, 72, 74, 77, 84, 86–87, 90, 93, 95, 102–104, 106–107, 109, 118, 120, 126, 133, 140, 153, 171, 175
  antipathy towards, 104
  apparatchik, 76
  authoritarian rule, 84, 103, 117, 144, 153
  early years, 103, 104, 106, 117, 120, 123, 128, 154, 175
  elites, 102, 130
  establishment of, 88
  generals, 109
  Islamic-based opposition to, 102, 105, 120
  last years of, 102, 154
  movements against, 93, 103, 130
  oligarchic evolvement during, 94
  patronage politics, 153
  repression of Islamic political groups, 117, 124
  secular nationalist-based opposition to, 45
Ngruki, 125. See also Al-Mukmin; Jemaah Islamiyah
NII (Indonesian Islamic State). See Darul Islam
Nizam al-Khass, 100
Noer, Deliar, 26, 52, 60, 62, 72
Nomani and Behdad, 163
North Africa, 6, 14, 17, 29, 35–36, 45, 49, 64, 75, 156
North America, 48
  tradition of populism, 24
Norway, 21
Notodihardjo, 118
Nour, Mohamed, 101, 145, 167. See also Al-Nour Party in Egypt
Nursi, Said, 24, 66

Index

OdaTV,
  persecution of journalists, 141. *See also* Turkey
Old Order in Indonesia. *See* Soekarno
oligarchy, 11, 87
Ottoman Empire, 26
  authority over Egypt, 59
  business and commerce during, 62, 65
  Caliph, 58
  Caliphate, 49, 59
  defeat, 64
  demise of, 174
  Khedive, 79
  See also Turkey
Oxhorn, Philip, 20, 25
Oyak in Turkey, 175
Özal, Turgut, 71, 82, 99
  economic liberalisation policies, 85
  economic reforms, 161, 169
  government, 164. *See also* Turkey

Pahlevi, Shah Reza, 44, 54, 77–80, 163
  inspiration from Kemalist establishment, 63
Palestine, 112
Pam Swakarsa, 154. *See* Islamic militia groups
PAN, *See* National Mandate Party
Pancasila, 95, 106, 109, 128, 174
  as *azas tunggal*, 109
  Jakarta Charter version of, 147
  political system based on, 93
  state ideology, 62
Pan-Islamism, 53, 144
  movement, 59
  outlook of the Hizbut Tahrir, 5
  tendency across the Muslim world, 49
  vision, 49
Panizza, Francisco, 30–31
Parmusi, 105
Partai Daulat Rakyat (People's Sovereignty Party), 154
Party of the Sarekat Islam of Indonesia (PSII), 118. *See also* Sarekat Islam (SI)
PBB (Crescent and Star Party), 92, 132
  establishment, 155
  militia security force, 133
PDI-P (Indonesian Democratic Party for Struggle), 45, 112, 127, 179
  militia and street gangs, 134
Pekalongan, 119
Pemuda Pancasila, 112, *See* Indonesian paramilitary
People's Consultative Assembly (MPR), 147, 155
Peron, Juan, 21
  Peronism, 21, 24
Perot, Ross, 23
Pertamina, 109
Peru, 22
pesantren, 108, 124, 125, 128
  Salafi-oriented, 126, 129
Philippines, 17
PJD (Justice and Development Party) in Morocco, 42
  alliance with Moroccan monarchy, 165
  benefits from political liberalisation, 140
PK (Justice Party), 17, *See* PKS
PKI (Indonesian Communist Party), 9, 52, 54, 56, 70, 89, 90, 91, 92, 106, 118, 127, 128
  agenda of private property expropriation, 81
  demise of, 96
  destruction of, 87
  during Guided Democracy, 91
  strongholds, 106, 128
  subject of colonial repression, 9
PKS (Justice and Prosperity Party), 17, 24, 36, 42, 49, 114, 144, 147–149, 151, 156, 170, 173
  argument on the Sharia, 148
  eradication of *riba* (usury), 42
  figures, corruption scandals, 177
  ideological permutations within, 149
  'opening up' to non-Muslims, 179
  'pure' Islamic parties, 157
  semi-clandestine student organisations, 139, *See also* Tarbiyah
PMKI (Catholic Students Association), 94
PNI (Indonesian Nationalist Party), 10, 45, 56, 89
Populism, 3, 11, 20, 23–25, 27, 30, 37, 180, 188
  and social mobilisation in Latin America, 20
  anti-elitist form of politics, 23
  as elusive concept, 21
  as 'pathology', 30
  characteristics of, 23
  economic policies, 22
  neoliberalism and the merging with, 39
  'neoliberal' form of, 163
  'old rural', 24
  secular nationalist, 178
  Soekarnoist, 45
  'the people' against 'the elite', 110
post-Islamism, 4
PPP (United Development Party), 95, 104, 112, 124, 134, 147, 155
Pranggono, Bambang, 130, 156
Pranoto, Haji Ismail ('Hispran'), 123
Pratama, Rama, 42, 148, 168. *See also* PKS
Prawiranegara, Syafruddin, 95
PRD. *See* Democratic People's Party

Precariousness
  association with neoliberal
    globalisation, 188
  of middle class-ness, 35
predatory elites, 43, 61
predatory forces, 172
Preparatory Committee for the Upholding of
    Islamic Law (KPPSI), 130. *See also*
    Muzzakar
pribumi, 41, 56, 68, 81, 94
  bourgeoisie, 41
  businesses, 92, 161
  enterprises, 94
privatisation, 164
  denunciation of, 168
  encouragement of, 164
  neoliberalism and, 39

Qurdowi, Sigit, 112
Qutb, Sayyid, 36, 39, 55, 57, 81, 120. *See also*
    Al-Banna; Muslim Brotherhood
  anti-Western sentiment, 142
  Qutbist tendencies in Indonesian
    politics, 149

Rachmani, Inaya, 187
racketeering, 112
radical nationalism, 58, 117, 131
  Soekarnoist, 127
Rafsanjani, Akbar Hashemi, 164
Raid, Hasan, 54
Raillon, Francois, 107
Rais, Amien, 153, 155
Rauf, Abdul, 112, 125, 134
religious violence, 14, 138, 187
Renville Peace Treaty 1948, 119
Republican Party in American politics, 23
riba (usury), 42, 51, 165
  religious injunctions against, 171
Ricklefs, Merle C., 14
Ridha, Rashid, 59, 118
Ridwanullah, Qosdi, 125
Rizieq, Habib, 154. *See also* Islamic
    Defenders's Front (FPI)
Robison, Richard, 93
Rodinson, Maxim, 7, 33, 51
routinisation, 150
Roy, Olivier, 14, 35, 120
  'failure of political Islam', 113
  Islam and democratic politics, 185
Rudnyckyj, Daromir, 33
  convergences between Islam and
    capitalism, 159
Russia
  post-Soviet, 172. *See also* Soviet Union

Sadat, Anwar, 86, 94, 164
  assassination of, 76
  credentials as a pious Muslim, 60
  suppression of Nasserism, 76
Said, Edward, 185
Salafis
  alliance with military, 180
  conservatism
  electoral bloc in 2011–2012, 101
  involvement in electoral politics, 102
  movement, 101, 145, 146
  opposition to Muslim Brotherhood,
    101, 158
  political vehicles, 162
  politics, 101, 145, 177
  stronghold in Alexandria, 102
  women's role in politics. *See also* Al-Da'wa
    Al Salafiyaa
Salim, Agus, 51–52. *See also* Sarekat Islam
Salman Mosque, 157. *See also* Bandung
    Institute of Technology
Sangidoe, Moedrick, 134
Sarbumusi (Conglomeration of Indonesian
    Islamic Trade Unions), 89
Sarekat Islam (SI), 26, 49–53, 56, 61, 63,
    88, 161
  and Indonesian working class, 9
  founding of, 121, 131
  in colonial era, 8
  Muslim traders, 127
  'red' wing, 52–53
  'white' wing, 52, 55
  See also Party of the Sarekat Islam of
    Indonesia (PSII)
Saudi Arabia, 121, 125, 156, 167
Scandinavian countries, 168
Secret Apparatus (Nizam al-Khass), 57.
  See also Muslim Brotherhood
sectarianism, 16
security-oriented analysis of Islamic
    politics, 18
Semaoen
  chairman of the PKI, 52
  expelled from Sarekat Islam (SI), 52
Sembiring, Tifatul, 149
Setiono, Joko, 170
Shadid, Anthony, 77
sharia, 4, 40, 46, 52, 57, 60, 113–114, 117, 148
  in Indonesia, 151
  state based on, 40, 113, 127
Shariati, Ali, 120. *See also* Iranian Revolution
    1979
Shia
  clergy in Iran, 78, 166
Shils, Edward, 23

Index

Shinawatra, Thaksin, 22
Sidel, John T., 15, 43, 45, 102
Siliwangi Division, 118, 119. *See also* Indonesian armed forces
Simpson, Bradley R., 90
Sinai, 98
Skocpol, Theda, 78
Sneevliet, Henk, 52
SOBSI, 70, 89
social movement theory, 26
Soeharto, 11, 41, 45, 59, 62, 83–84, 86, 93, 94, 106, 108–109, 117, 121, 134, 151, 153–155, 173, 175
   after the fall of, 3, 16, 92, 106, 132–134, 141, 147, 153, 172
   clan and cronies, 41, 74, 173
   dictatorship, 41
   dissent against, 77
   graft and economic mismanagement, 171
   oligarchic power, 87, 138
   religious and political repression, 68
   rise of state authoritarianism, 87
   See also New Order
Soeharto family, 45
Soeharto, Pitut, 120
Soekarno, 26, 31, 56, 59, 81, 86, 90, 92–94, 118
   anti-imperialist and anti-Western position, 91
   authoritarianism, 87
   concept of 'Nasakom', 90
   first President of Indonesia, 9, 91
   Guided Democracy (1959–1965), 88
   Guided Economy, 94
   shift to authoritarianism, 92
   Third Worldism, 86
Solo, 108, 112, 128, 132, 171
   bastion of Islamic 'radicalism', 131
   significant Christian minority, 106
South Asia, 49, 60
South Sulawesi, 119
Southeast Asia, 7, 15–16, 18, 49, 63, 94, 156
Soviet Union, 78, 86. *See also* Russia
Stewart, Angus, 25
Strarrett, Gregory, 29
structural adjustment policies, 43, 84, 160, 164
Subianto, Prabowo, 186
   leader of party coalition, 179. *See also* Gerindra
   populist political imagery, 179
Suez Canal, 55
Sufi, 68, 82
Sungkar, Abdullah, 108, 123, 128
Supendi, Jusuf, 49, 156
Surabaya, 52
Sutrisno, Try, 109. *See* Tanjung Priok massacre

Sweden, 21
Syaifuddin, Lukman Hakim, 155
Syakur, Sobarin, 134, 150
Syria, 18
   protacted conflict in, 5

Tagammu, 83
Tahrir Square, 46. *See also* Arab Spring
Taksim Solidarity, 141. *See also* Gezi Park demonstrations
Talangsari, 109, 124
   bloody incident 1989, 109
Tanjung Priok massacre, 108, 109, 124, 153
Tarbiyah
   cadres, 156
   movement, 17, 49, 156, 173. *See also* PKS
tariqa, 68, 71, 99
Tasikmalaya, 118
Taşpinar, Omar, 5
Tea Party, 23, 38
Tegal, 119
Temby, Quinton, 100
Teror Warman group, 123
terrorism 12, 16, 18–19, 27, 96–97, 99–100, 104, 106, 114, 123, 127, 132, 186
Thailand, 17, 63, 90
Thalib, Jafar Umar, 126. *See also* Lasykar Jihad
Thawalib community, 53
Tirtoadisoeryo, Raden Mas, 131. *See also* Sarekat Islam
Tjokroaminoto, Raden Mas Haji Omar Said, 118
Today's Zaman, 40
Toer, Pramoedya Ananta, 131
Tripp, Charles, 33, 50, 166
   Muslim thinkers and capitalism, 167
   'social justice' in classical Islamic thought, 7
Tudeh Party in Iran, 78
Tuğal, Cihan, 162
Tunisia, 6, 42
   anti-colonial struggle, 140
   economic inequalities, 168
   electoral competition, 84
   Islamic parties, 140
   nationalist movements, 9
   trade union movement, 77, 168
Turkey, 2–3, 6, 10, 11, 14, 26, 30, 34, 37–39, 44, 46–47, 50, 63–64, 66, 69–73, 76–79, 82–83, 86, 90–91, 95, 97–98, 110–111, 114, 116, 137, 147, 161–162, 167, 169, 170, 172, 175–176, 187–188
   'deep state', 167
   democratisation and economic reform, 169
   economic adjustment policies, 71

Turkey (cont.)
  economic crisis, 165
  economic liberalisation, 164
  geographical area, 67
  gross domestic product, 169
  intelligence agency, 98
  labour movement, 70–71
  Left stream of politics, 71
  military economic interests, 176–177
  municipal elections 2014, 179
  Muslim bourgeoisie, 39
  national-building project, 50
  neoliberal policies, 71, 183
  'post-modern' coup 1997, 69
  radical secularisation, 73
  Republicanism, 64
  secularist principles, 176
  statist model of economic development, 10
  Turkish 'synthesis' 172
Turktelekom, 167
TUSIAD (Turkish Industrialists' and Businessmens' Association), 39
  businesses, 169
  conflict with AKP, 169
TUSKON (Turkish Confederation of Businessmen and Industrialists), 39

Ufen, Andreas, 17
ulama, 29, 54, 59, 61, 150
  and the state, 58
ummah, 2, 5, 6, 13, 19–20, 27–28, 38, 40–41, 43, 47–52, 55–56, 60, 63–64, 68–69, 72–75, 79–81, 87–88, 91–92, 94–100, 102–103, 105–106, 111, 113–114, 117, 149, 170, 179, 189
  absence of big bourgeoisie within, 171
  as proxy for the 'people', 4
  fragmentation within, 55, 157
  homogenous conception of, 149
  internally diverse, 131, 150, 188
  reconceptualisation of, 42
  response to social problems caused by capitalism, 30
underemployment, 35
unemployment, 35, 43
  in Egypt, 180
  in Indonesia, 180
  in Turkey, 181
United States
  assistance to Indonesian police force, 90
  government, 90
usroh, 36
  during New Order period, 36

system of caderisation, 107
utopian socialists, 50

Van Dijk, Cornelis, 120
Vargas, Getúlio, 21
Venezuela, 21
Vertigans, Stephen, 32, 184
Virtue Party in Turkey, 176

Wafd Party in Egypt, 10, 57
  symbol of political liberalism, 83
  sympathisers, 55
Wahhabi influence, 61, 149. *See also* Saudi Arabia
  and Muslim Brotherhood, 156
Wahid, Abdurrahman ('Gus Dur'). *See* NU (Nahdlatul Ulama)
  brief Presidency, 143
  government, 173
  ICMI opponent, 155
Wahyuddin, Ustad, 123. *See also* Terror Warman Group
War on Terror, 1, 7
Ward, Ken, 113
Weber, Max, 31
  analysis of modern capitalism, 150
  concept of charismatic authority, 31
  Islam and capitalism, 159
  religion and economic behaviour, 51
Welfare (Refah) Party, 39–40, 69, 76, 170, 176
West Java, 118–119, 157
West Nusa Tenggara, 126, 129
West Sumatera, 157
Wickham, Carrie Rosefsky, 26, 31, 35
Widodo, Joko, 127. *See also* PDI-P
World Bank, 69, 164
World War I, 9, 59, 65, 67
  post-, 79, 82
World War II, 86, 88, 174
Woyla hijacking, 130. *See also* Imran

xenophobia, 21

Yemen, 126
Yildiz, Osman, 71
  Hak-is and AKP policies, 71
Yogyakarta, 112, 125, 128, 134
Young Ottoman movement, 65
Young Turks, 50, 64
Yudhoyono, Susilo Bambang, 133, 151

zakat, 42, 57, 168
Zizek, Slavoj, 44
Zubaida, 7, 77, 78